THE FALL OF AMERICA JOURNALS

UNIVERSITY OF
MINNESOTA PRESS

MINNEAPOLIS

Allen Ginsberg

THE FALL OF AMERICA JOURNALS

1965–1971

EDITED BY

MICHAEL SCHUMACHER

The publication of this book was assisted by a bequest from Josiah H. Chase to honor his parents, Ellen Rankin Chase and Josiah Hook Chase, Minnesota territorial pioneers.

Frontispiece photograph of Allen Ginsberg (page ii) is from 1968.

All drawings by Allen Ginsberg and photographs of journal pages are courtesy of the Allen Ginsberg Papers, Stanford University Archives and Special Collections. Unless otherwise credited, photographs appear courtesy of the Estate of Allen Ginsberg. Every effort was made to obtain permission to reproduce material in this book. If any proper acknowledgment has not been included here, we encourage the copyright holders to notify the publisher.

Published by the University of Minnesota Press
111 Third Avenue South, Suite 290
Minneapolis, MN 55401-2520
http://www.upress.umn.edu

Printed in the United States of America on acid-free paper

The University of Minnesota is an equal-opportunity educator and employer.

26 25 24 23 22 21 20   10 9 8 7 6 5 4 3 2 1

*

Library of Congress Cataloging-in-Publication Data
Ginsberg, Allen, 1926–1997, author. | Schumacher, Michael, editor.
The Fall of America journals, 1965–1971 / Allen Ginsberg ; edited by Michael Schumacher.
Minneapolis : University of Minnesota Press, [2020]
Includes bibliographical references and index.
Identifiers: LCCN 2020023681
ISBN 978-0-8166-9963-6 (hc) | ISBN 978-0-8166-9965-0 (pb)
Subjects: LCSH: Ginsberg, Allen, 1926–1997—Diaries. | Poets, American—
20th century—Diaries. | Ginsberg, Allen, 1926–1997—Poetry. | Ginsberg, Allen,
1926–1997—Travel—United States. | United States—Description and travel.
Classification: LCC PS3513.I74 Z46 2020 | DDC 811/.54—dc23
LC record available at https://lccn.loc.gov/2020023681

Apocalypse prophesized—
the Fall of America
signaled from Heaven—

ALLEN GINSBERG
"Iron Horse"

CONTENTS

Robbie Robertson, Michael McClure, Bob Dylan, and
Allen Ginsberg in the alley behind City Lights Books,
San Francisco, 1965. Photograph by Dale Smith/Alamy.

EDITOR'S
INTRODUCTION

In 1965, Bob Dylan gifted Allen Ginsberg with a Uher reel-to-reel tape recorder, which Ginsberg was to use to record his thoughts and observations as he traveled throughout the United States. Ginsberg, already heavily influenced by Jack Kerouac's methods of spontaneous composition, felt the taping was an ideal way to pursue his own spontaneous work. He began planning a volume of poems, a literary documentary examining contemporary America, not unlike what Kerouac had done in *On the Road,* or what Robert Frank had accomplished in his photographs in *The Americans.* He would add one important element: the violence, destruction, and inhumanity of the escalating war in Vietnam—an edgy contrast to what he was witnessing in his travels, particularly his country's natural beauty. The public's polarized dialogue over Vietnam and, earlier in the decade, the civil rights movement, convinced Ginsberg that America was teetering on the precipice of a fall.

He initiated what he called his "auto poesy" recordings that fall, when he and Gary Snyder roamed the Pacific Northwest and the mountain trails there. Ginsberg used recently awarded Guggenheim money to purchase a Volkswagen camper, which he stocked with a desk, a small refrigerator, mattresses, and other items needed for life on the road. The visits to Oregon and Washington presented a good setting for Ginsberg's observations. "Beginning of a Long Poem of These States," the official opening of *The Fall of America*'s auto poesy, offers a sampling of Ginsberg's most affective writing to that point: descriptive poetry in the objective tradition of William Carlos Williams, one of Ginsberg's early mentors and influences; spontaneous writing similar to that of Jack Kerouac; and lengthy lines in the style of Walt Whitman (and like that in such early Ginsberg works as "Howl," "Sunflower Sutra," and "Kaddish").

In most cases, Ginsberg transcribed his tapes, shortly after composition, into his notebooks. While doing so, he eliminated extraneous sounds on the tapes (conversations in the vehicle, the sounds of the radio, and so on) and he engaged in light editing. In the transcriptions, he broke down his taped speech into the form he wanted his individual poems to take. In "Beginning of a Long Poem of These States," for instance, he used long breath- and thought-length lines for structure. In other poems, a line would be broken down and arranged on the page in order to accentuate words or phrases depending on his mood and what he thought was best for the poem. Auto poesy was not bound by form.

On February 7, 1965, a surprise attack by North Vietnamese forces on a military installation in Pleiku, South Vietnam, killing eight and wounding more than one hundred, resulted in an escalation of the war that included heavy bombing of the North. Defense Secretary Robert McNamara visited Pleiku immediately following the attack, and he urged President Johnson to respond with force. The war in Vietnam, it turned out, was heating up.

Ginsberg, never a supporter of the war, seethed. His journal notations reflected his anger, especially toward leaders who sent young men to fight and die. His journal entries varied from lists of casualties to personal reflections about the war, from reactions to news stories he heard on the radio while he was traveling to rants against Johnson, McNamara, Secretary of State Dean Rusk, and military advisers. In his best-known antiwar poem, "Wichita Vortex Sutra" (1966), he "undeclares" a war that was never formally declared; in "Taxation without Representation" (later titled "Pentagon Exorcism") (1967), he submitted a text for a historic

Editor's Introduction

march on the Pentagon; in "Hum Bom" (1971), he wrote an angry chant against the bombing of North Vietnam, an action that stood in the way of peace talks. The war was constantly on his mind, and the division within America over the draft and the fighting—a schism that seemed largely generational—fortified his position that the country was headed toward revolution that might bring it down.

His antiwar activism increased exponentially, beginning with his involvement in a demonstration in 1965 in Oakland—a mass protest against the war. The demonstration, largely organized by Jerry Rubin, might have been a violent confrontation had it not been for Ginsberg's intervention. The Hells Angels motorcycle club threatened to disrupt the protest and beat any demonstrator in its path, but Ginsberg and novelist Ken Kesey invited a group of the bikers to Kesey's La Honda ranch and, after taking LSD, listening to music, and airing their differences, the Hells Angels agreed to back off on their plans. Ginsberg's poem "First Party at Ken Kesey's with Hell's Angels" recalled the gathering; his essay "How to Make a March/Spectacle" became a primer on how to conduct a nonviolent demonstration.

As the decade continued, the demonstrations grew violent, culminating in the bloody altercations between police and protesters at the Democratic National Convention in Chicago in 1968 and the murder of four at the antiwar rally at Kent State University in 1970. Ginsberg was present during the mayhem in Chicago. He wrote very little about the violence while it was occurring, but two journal poems ("Going to Chicago" and "Grant Park: August 28, 1968") precisely expressed his thoughts about the debacle. One day, he applied his nonviolent methods of demonstrating when he and poet/musician Ed Sanders, seeing a confrontation between young protesters and Chicago police escalating, chanted "OM" and led demonstrators out of Lincoln Park and out of danger. He was not at Kent State, but when members of the National Guard opened fire on antiwar demonstrators, he knew that *The Fall of America* would have to conclude before the war ended. The protests, once so effective in drawing attention

Editor's Introduction

to the growing number of dissidents against the fighting in Vietnam, were being met with brute force, and the peace talks were going nowhere. Ginsberg already had more than enough new poetry to fill a substantial volume of new work, and he would conclude it at the end of 1971.

Ginsberg's travel writings ranked among his finest journal writings. Long, descriptive passages were rendered in detail, suggesting intentions for future use. This, of course, is one reason why writers keep journals. Most are not intended for publication, but when they are they provide enlightenment into the creative process. *Windblown World,* journals that Jack Kerouac kept while working on *The Town and the City* and *On the Road* but were published posthumously, was composed of powerful sketches by a young writer in search of a way to create or improve a developing narrative. On occasion, the journal writing was as breathtaking as anything he published.

The travel journals of Allen Ginsberg followed suit. His descriptions of the Russian countryside and Red Square, published in *Iron Curtain Journals,* or of the impoverished streets or burning ghats in India, published in *Indian Journals* (1970), were almost photographic in detail. *The Fall of America* journals added spin to the process: the auto poesy, unlike earlier notebook scribblings, were earmarked for publication and, as such, were the result of heightened awareness.

Not that other journal writings during this period were inferior. "Wales Visitation," written when Ginsberg was overseas in 1967, was composed while, tripping on LSD, he sat alone in the Wales countryside and wrote, in minute detail, of what he saw. "After Wales Visitacione July 29, 1967," written in Wales and London a short time later, continued this type of writing.

When Allen Ginsberg won the 1974 National Book Award for *The Fall of America,* the largest volume of poems he would ever publish (aside from his *Collected Poems* and *Selected Poems*), he gained a measure of formal

Editor's Introduction

acceptance long denied him by the literati. *The Fall of America* was nothing less than a staggering magnum opus, Ginsberg's autobiographical journey through the United States as the country experienced one of the most turbulent periods in its history. As a very public figure—arguably, America's best-known poet—Ginsberg seemed to be everywhere at once: zigzagging across the country for poetry readings, turning up at protests and rallies, appearing on television news broadcasts, contributing work to every imaginable type of publication, touring Europe, and doing occasional teaching gigs.

He had always been at his best when he was on the road, open to anything, aware of history, and diligent about noticing political and social customs. Recording his thoughts on tape added a new, significant wrinkle to his writing: he no longer required a quiet place to sit and write, relying on his memory for detail and context; instead, he was instantly recording his thoughts, even in the front seat of a van speeding down the highway.

The Fall of America journals contain some of the finest of Ginsberg's spontaneous writing, accomplished as he pondered the best and worst that his country had to offer. The descriptive writing is breathtaking at times, and the journals offer nothing less than the essential backstory to the works published in *The Fall of America*.

Editor's Introduction

RECORD

A NOTE ON EDITING
ALLEN GINSBERG

While editing two previous volumes of Ginsberg's journals, *Iron Curtain Journals* and *South American Journals,* I faced a number of challenges, but nothing quite like what I encountered with this book. In the two earlier books, I worked only with handwritten notebooks and typed transcripts of those notebooks, so assembling the journal entries in chronological order was relatively easy, especially because Ginsberg dated most of his writings. My main decisions involved deciding what to include and what to excise; reading his occasionally indecipherable cursive; and compiling notes and photographs. On a rare instance, I added a piece of correspondence that illustrated important events not included in the journals: one letter detailed events Ginsberg had written about in a journal confiscated and not returned by the police in Czechoslovakia.

This volume resisted simplicity. The auto poesy had been recorded on tape that, over the ensuing years, became too brittle to be played and replayed. Ginsberg had transcribed the tapes, but (with only a rare exception) a reader of the transcriptions was not privy to the sounds picked up outside Ginsberg's voice. There were news reports and music coming in on the radio, scraps of conversation between others in the Volkswagen camper, even a dialogue between Ginsberg and a police officer who had stopped the vehicle. These bits and pieces of sound might have offered revelations into what influenced Ginsberg's auto poesy, but I had no choice but to use Ginsberg's transcriptions.

I faced the usual decisions about what to leave as written and what to silently correct. Scholars and researchers would insist that nothing should be corrected, but that isn't how Ginsberg saw it when he collaborated with editors who worked with him on his journals during his lifetime. He was interested in intent and readability. He knew what he meant, and if correcting a misspelled word or adding a punctuation mark helped with that clarity, he would make the change. He also cut passages, sometimes because they were repetitive, sometimes to protect living sensibilities, sometimes because he needed to shorten the text. I had the good fortune to observe him at work during the editing process, and while I won't be so presumptuous to believe that I know how he would have responded to every decision that I made during my editing of his journals, I feel confident that I made choices that he would have made.

My toughest decisions focused on what to include and what to cut. This book could not have printed the entirety of the material in the journals written during the 1965–71 time frame of *The Fall of America*. The auto poesy alone would have been a hefty volume. Still, because of the importance of that particular volume of poetry, I wanted to include as many first drafts of published works as possible, along with a substantial portion of unpublished writing. (This was a priority that Ginsberg did not practice; he usually omitted the published work, noting its composition in the final text.) I felt it important, for the sake of literary history, that these journals follow the arc of these writings, largely because Ginsberg's edited first drafts, when compared to the published versions of the same poems, illustrated a creative process otherwise unavailable to readers.

When line editing, I followed the same process that I had used in *Iron Curtain Journals* and *South American Journals*: I silently corrected words that might have been mistaken for typos; other misspellings were left as written, mainly because they illustrated the human side of Ginsberg or indicated his state of mind at the time of composition. It's possible that, given the opportunity, he would have corrected some of these, but it has also been established that some of his misspellings found their way into print. I preferred to err in favor of authenticity.

Ginsberg could be mistaken or sloppy in his dating of journal entries or poems. His published poems still have been incorrectly dated in some of the early works. On the rare occasion when this happened in these journals, I retained his dating but added corrected dates in brackets.

Finally, there were times when Ginsberg's handwriting was impossible to read. He carried a journal everywhere he went, and he wrote in a number of conditions, in various lighting and climate. Most of the writing was legible, but whenever a word could not be determined, I noted it with a bracketed question mark [?] in the text. If more than one word, or even a brief passage, was illegible, I marked it with bracketed ellipses [. . .].

Editing Allen Ginsberg

ACKNOWLEDGMENTS

You wouldn't be holding this book if I hadn't received valuable assistance when I was putting it together.

First, and most important, there was Allen Ginsberg. This might seem obvious: he wrote these journals. But it goes deeper than that. When I was researching *Dharma Lion,* my biography of Ginsberg first published in 1992, Ginsberg gave me total, unrestricted access to his archives, which included these and all of his journals. For this trust I am very grateful. He generously answered my questions about the journals' content, at a point when the demands on his time were enormous. In his song "Do the Meditation Rock," Ginsberg called for patience and generosity, and he truly exhibited those qualities to me in our interactions over the years. My gratitude, then, to Allen Ginsberg is great. I would hope that, were he still alive, he would have liked this book and felt that his trust had been warranted.

Peter Hale, custodian of such a great portion of the Ginsberg legacy, was helpful at every turn, from supplying photographs and clarity in text, to sending me urgently needed materials, to providing names and phone numbers when I required source information. Many thanks, Peter.

Other Ginsberg associates answered all my questions about events in the book. My thanks go to Bob Rosenthal, who managed Ginsberg's office and scheduling for more than three decades, and whose book *Straight Around Allen* is one of finest available portraits of Ginsberg; Bill Morgan, Ginsberg's bibliographer, biographer, and all-around ombudsman on all things Ginsberg; and Gordon Ball, editor of three volumes of Ginsberg's journals and lectures, as well as manager of the East Hill farm in Cherry Valley, New York.

Charles Pirtle was kind enough to provide me a copy of his PhD thesis, much of which was devoted to Ginsberg's published and unpublished auto poesy. His excellent analysis was a road map that guided me along the inroads of *The Fall of America*. Thanks so much, Chuck.

Poet/scholars David Cope and Jim Cohn assisted greatly in the editing of the long poem "Denver to Montana, 27 May 1972," Ginsberg's intended ending for *The Fall of America*. My appreciation to both.

I owe a huge debt of gratitude to Tim Noakes at Stanford University for sending along transcripts and photocopies of the journals that were not in my possession. While researching *Dharma Lion*, I had photocopied much of the journal material that was part of Ginsberg's massive deposit at Columbia University at the time, but what I had was incomplete. Tim filled my requests for journals that were vital to this book.

My thanks to all the photographers and copyright owners of photographs in this book. Their names appear elsewhere in this volume, but I sincerely express my gratitude here.

Jeff Posternak, Ginsberg's literary agent at the Wylie Agency, facilitated the logistics of seeing this book into print. I appreciate the agency's efforts on Ginsberg's behalf as well as Jeff's enthusiasm for the book.

I am fortunate to work with the staff at the University of Minnesota Press, who not only have worked with me with appropriate diligence and respect on my previous Ginsberg projects but also share my beliefs in the importance of this book. My appreciation to copy editor David Thorstad for his excellent work and suggestions. Editors Erik Anderson and Kristian Tvedten also worked with me on *Iron Curtain Journals* and *South American Journals,* and their help and advice were essential.

My thanks to all.

Acknowledgments

THE FALL OF AMERICA JOURNALS

1965

Allen Ginsberg spent the first half of 1965 out of the United States, visiting Cuba, Czechoslovakia, the Soviet Union, Poland, and England. His travels were both exhilarating and disappointing. In Cuba, where he was to attend a poetry conference and judge a poetry contest, his rebellious, outspoken demeanor ran him afoul of Fidel Castro's revolutionary government, and he was expelled from the country and shipped off to Czechoslovakia. The early portion of his stay was pleasant enough, highlighted by meetings with students and readings in coffeehouses that treasured the writings of the Beat Generation. With his earnings from readings and book sales, Ginsberg was able to afford a visit to the Soviet Union, the land of his ancestry, and Poland, another country he had hoped to include in his busy schedule. The notebooks and journals he had kept throughout these travels, published in Iron Curtain Journals: January–May 1965, contained new poetry, travel prose, dream entries, and fragments of conversation with such literary luminaries as Yevgeny Yevtushenko and Andrei Voznesensky and comprised some of Ginsberg's most arresting writings to date.

His return to Czechoslovakia was less successful. Treated as a hero by the young people of Prague, he was elected "Kral Majales" (King of May) during the country's May Day festival—a status that did not sit well with the country's authorities. He was subsequently stripped of his crown, and in the days following the festival, Ginsberg was followed by government operatives, attacked and beaten on the streets, and had his journal stolen; he was arrested and interrogated about his comings and goings, and, much like in Cuba, he was tossed out of the country, supposedly for being a bad influence on Czechoslovakia's young people.

Fortunately for Ginsberg, the Czech officials sent him to London, then flourishing culturally during the "Swinging England" period. He hung out with Bob Dylan and the Beatles, and he helped organize and participated in the literary touchstone international poetry reading at the Royal Albert Hall, an uneven gathering of poets who proved, if anything, that there was great potential in a huge poetry reading. England offered Ginsberg an ideal environment in which to decompress after his experiences in Cuba and Czechoslovakia.

Ginsberg's adventures overseas prepared him for what lay ahead when he returned to the States at the end of June 1965. The Vietnam War and the civil rights movement dominated the news. The Voting Rights Act, the jewel of Lyndon Johnson's proposed civil rights legislation, passed after contentious debate and virtually no Republican support, and went into effect on August 6, 1965. By banning state and local governments from finding ways to skirt the Fifteenth Amendment of the Constitution, the new law guaranteed the vote for black and other minority voters. The fighting in Vietnam, steady since Johnson became president following John F. Kennedy's assassination, escalated after the National Liberation Front of South Vietnam attacked an American military installation near Pleiku in February 1965. Ginsberg, already an opponent of the war, became fixated on the events in Vietnam, and he used the war as a backdrop to his writings.

Ginsberg began planning an ambitious project, a book of thematically connected poems, a collection that "discovered" America in poetry similar to the way Kerouac's On the Road had explored the country in prose. The Vietnam War would be a constant presence overhanging Ginsberg's travel writings like a darkening shadow affecting daily life in the country. It would be a study of contrasts: natural beauty slammed up against an ugliness that rose out of the tensions of violence.

Two turns of events made the project possible. First, Ginsberg won a Guggenheim fellowship that awarded him enough money to afford a Volkswagen camper, which he equipped with a bed and a small desk and refrigerator. Second, Bob Dylan gave him enough money to purchase a Uher reel-to-reel tape recorder, which Ginsberg would use to dictate his observations and thoughts instantly, unencumbered by the process of writing everything in a notebook. Ginsberg modified the Uher, cutting the tape speed so he could fit more on a tape.

His project began on the West Coast, where he was scheduled to participate in a poetry conference in Berkeley in July. He was reunited with Gary Snyder, and the two men decided to explore the Pacific Northwest together when the conference ended. Snyder, a first-rate outdoorsman with a poet's sensibilities, was an ideal travel companion.

1965

VIETNAM

had anxiety what to do here, I'm a fuck up
LSD at ocean
Titanis like Blake
the Universe is o.k. if we blow up
Peace is the message—flowers to the cops
no more hostility
Change of consciousness
Younger Generation
    Dylan[1]—"Marching Doesn't make it"
    Barry McGuire *Eve of Destruction*
                Universal Soldier
    What are young people thinking about?
Getting above hostilities, seeing both sides trapped, & sick of playing
hostile "roles"—
    Cops & robbers.
     Anxiety State in America
      Constant fear of police—partly connected with drug police
    But More
      the constant anxiety over World Destruction
      To realize that Negative Statements by Governors,
       by Eisenhower, by local D.A.'s are
    products of Guilt & anxiety faced with the indifference
      of the young to their game playing
    this is now an open secret among the young

----

that the Vietnam War itself is byproduct of U.S. anxiety
    What is it, a war against Communism?

1. Songwriter Bob Dylan.

1965

No, we've made peace with Russia
It's a war of fear of the yellow race—population explosion
We should be relieving our anxiety by dealing with
    China directly—
Diplomatic recognition & U.N. acceptance
It would relieve everyone's *angst*—
    if suddenly the U.S. recognized China
       negotiated with her—
Burroughs[2] "If the U.S. were smart they'd try to get on
    China's side"—

The older folks are up against it now—long habits of
    role playing are now bankrupted by the situation
       the young people have caught on—in Russia as well as here—
Recall the [?] strategic bombing analyst on Park bench
    in Saigon.
       Everybody is fucked up, I am, we are all here,
worried what we should do
    The police & soldiers outside, the armies being drafted
McNamara[3] & the Pentagon, Johnson with his Gall Bladder

This is not time to press panic button to attack the police,
    the Chinese, or the Students—
To end the booby trap of mass anxiety aggression panic hostility

---

2. Novelist William S. Burroughs (1914–1997) (*Naked Lunch* and *Junkie*), Ginsberg friend and mentor.
    3. Defense Secretary Robert McNamara (1916–2009).

1965

Problem is to cool everybody, beginning with calming &
     tranquilizing yrself, oneself—& spread it to the
     police & army—I now sing a tranquil Mantra.

July 24, 1965

               A Poetry Reading
Joanne's[4] bare arms
          rest on the podium,
She's in a black lady's dress,
          her voice soft or strong
          in the new classroom,
Gary[5] twenty rows to the rear
          sits distinguished by his red
          beard and cap of brown hair,
          nodding slightly at the rhythm
          of his wife, I watch the two
          speaking, after a few years
               one listening in silence.

          The hill lit with yellow sunlight
          on the candystone window bubble
          gum Buck Rogers, at dawn
          1935 new cars huge clack speed
          upward on the house-road,

---

4. Joanne Kyger (1934–2017), poet, essayist, and wife of Gary Snyder.
5. Gary Snyder (born 1930), poet, essayist, and model for the Japhy Ryder char-
acter in Jack Kerouac's *The Dharma Bums*.

1965

                          the woods,
        near the rise, pond frogs, leaf-carpet
        wet by a stream. A child walking
        in short pants carrying a long living
        Scepter, alone all week on the street

        It'll be the same, old man Self, when
        you return to your Haledon Avenue
        the same house the same woods
        or another equally unknown-named
        trees, smoking a cigarette,
                        Thoughtless tile
        Childhood strangeness—the cars honk
        & wake the trees lifting their green
        papers in the wind, the old man
        approaching death looks up sees
        the child with his black twig-musing,
        and the man muses, what difference
        those 60 years?

While the Bearded Poet Read
A sparrow circled in the classroom
        and fluttered down in the iron
                        seats—

"Don't lay your hands on it"
        argued an angry voice—
The T-shirted professor however
        calmly cupped the bird in palm
                and brought it out to the lawn.

1965

July 27, 1965—3 a.m.
Dream

In a theater or hallway with Gregory,[6] he'd been vomiting before, and wiped it with his handkerchief, and thrown it away—

We're leaving lobby big pillars (as from Ali Akbar Khan[7] concert in Masonic Auditorium, S.F.)—he suddenly throws up again, green vomit, and tosses me the handkerchief, another—I take it from him rather than dropping it, whirl around with it in my hand like a shot-put looking for where to toss it—I throw it after speedy delay, outward—Ugh!—it falls on head of young blonde wife there with her hubby—

> I startle & wake,
nose stuffed.

To hang suspended from the clouds
    by my leg, neck, bent
head touching earth.

Dream: July 31, 1965

In this big room full of colored people, someone I know well—myself?—or my father—is rapidly running down the political plans for action says "and so the niggers got to vote"—there's a small uproar before he finished 3 more sentences, everybody objects to "the niggers" and he says oh that's not what I meant—I feel guilty, found out—

-----

6. Poet Gregory Corso (1930–2001), whose books include *Gasoline* and *Elegiac Feelings American,* was one of the founding members of the Beat Generation.

7. World-renowned Indian sarod instrumentalist Ali Akbar Khan (1922–2009) appeared on the Beatles' *Revolver* recording.

1965

August 1, 1965

"Get all those war hamburger songs on the radio"
                    Peter?[8] Neal?[9]

A Movie—A circle

Characters:

A. The young singer, blonde & thin w/harmonica, guitar
B. The old teacher, coyote, long white beard—who sings alone
who appears and disappears at crucial moments

He's the teacher, naked—meets the young singer
    adventures together
    at crucial moments vanishes
            (on some foolish mission like taking care
            of an old wife having appendix operation)
            (or dying his beard red)
            (or going to India)
            (or eating peyote w/Indians)
            (or a year on Wall St.)
            (or working as a Chinese spy)
            (or going to Moscow,
                Havana, [?])

    8. Peter Orlovsky (1933–2010) was Ginsberg's longtime partner and an occasional
poet.
    9. Neal Cassady (1926–1968), one of Ginsberg's first lovers, was the model for
Kerouac's Dean Moriarty character in *On the Road*.

1965

(or inventing a rocket ship on Mt. Palomar, pointing
out the planets and Nebraska, an astronomy lesson)
and looking thru a microscope
    the DNA at Harvard
The Gamut of new science, in 5 months.

C. They fly thru the sky on Magic Carpet—Guitar together
       Over the cities of men and Vietnam battlefields
          to moon
D. They spend a weekend on the Moon just to get lovely—
E. The youth has many women, a new one in each scene?
F. Conceived his blue vast painti[ng] & white rocks at Big Sur.
G. At the end, something happens to turn the boy's beard white, &
    he changes to the old man (meeting Beowolf)
H. He meets a new youth who wants instruction & is melancholy
I. Earlier, on return from Moon, meet Newsman
    Whyja go to the moon? To protest rebel?
    "Other way around Doc"
    Bam, newsprint machines
    Headlines—Moonbeams Get Youth
    News broadcast—Bfrap braf, etc.
             The story (distorted)
Time Mag . . . Voice

Yellow grass on a hill
    blue mountain ranges, blue sky
a bright reservoir & road below, cars—
the wing tree green sigh of the wind
    rises and falls—
Buddha, Christ, fissipowers

1965

tendencies,
The grey back like animal arms
    white sunrays piercing my eyeglasses—
the animal arms, back skin peeling
    fingers pointing, twigs trembling
       green thin living places bobbing
         sprouted from knotted branches—
No one will have to announce the New Age—
No special name, no unique way,
    no Crier by Method or
       Herald of Snakes and Bombs
No Messiah necessary but Nature
    and ourselves 50 years old—
Allah this tree, entity this Space Age,
Teenagers walking thru Times Square Neon & Metal
Look up to the dry planets thru buildingtops,
      old men lay out on the green afternoon
      and the old tree stands above them, ants
         crawl on the page,
The mountain side is covered with green
    bush sky & invisible singing insects,
      birds flap out, man will relax
And sit in the midst of his life
    remembering his tree friends.

So Ladies

The trees are growing slowly
The flowers coloring lovely
    So ladies & gentlemen relax

1965

The Indians are beaten
The Chinese are eaten
 So ladies & gentlemen relax

Boys' hair is longer
Girls' legs are stronger
 So ladies & gentlemen relax

He who keeps a secret
Is kept by his secret
 So ladies & gentlemen relax

We all have our lover
The Cold War is over
 So ladies & gentlemen relax

The milk's in the moonlight
The stream will sing for all the night
 So ladies & gentlemen relax

Julius won't talk[10] and
The hourglass is full of sand
 So ladies & gentlemen relax

The underwear is ready
It's warmer in the beddy
 So ladies & gentlemen relax

---

10. Julius Orlovsky, brother of Peter Orlovsky, suffered from mental disorders and often went lengthy periods of time without speaking. He often stayed with Ginsberg.

1965

The shithouse is open
The assholes have spoken
  So ladies & gentlemen relax

Marijuana's legal
So's the American Eagle
  So ladies & gentlemen relax

Joan Baez[11] got a school
Bobby Dylan is a fool
  So ladies & gentlemen relax

and if you get angry
your baby will go hungry
  So ladies & gentlemen relax

The ocean is rolling
and rocking like Holy
  So ladies & gentlemen relax

The cabin got my electric
The television is sick
  So ladies & gentlemen relax

The radio is grown older
announcer's voices colder
  So ladies & gentlemen relax

11. Popular folksinger.

1965

The newspapers are full of lies
Just like President Johnson's eyes
   So ladies & gentlemen relax

The telephone's quit ringing
I hear the angels singing
   So ladies & gentlemen relax

The trees are making up a noise
The wind is full of screaming boys
   So ladies & gentlemen relax

The idea of God's gone
Man's ass is sitting on hot his throne
   So ladies & gentlemen relax

Krishna Buddha Christ and dao
Are me & if not me they're you
   So ladies & gentlemen relax

The universe is in your hand
Even the worms beneath the sand
   So ladies & gentlemen relax

You'll live for 10 more decades
and disappear in seconds
   So ladies & gentlemen relax

Your head is in the coffin
your foot is stepping softly
   So ladies & gentlemen relax

1965

Your elbow is dusty
Your mouth & teeth are rusty
    So ladies & gentlemen relax

Fame & money are a drag
You can't get laid you're in a bag
    So ladies & gentlemen relax

You got no eyes to read books
You've took to hanging out with spooks
    So ladies & gentlemen relax

The Jews and Chinese Negroes
are turning into people
    So ladies & gentlemen relax

America is over
the world needs a new lover
    So ladies & gentlemen relax

Register and go & vote
for president who's not a goat
    and ladies & gentlemen relax

Cool black night thru the redwoods[12]
cars parked outside in the shade
behind the gate, stars dim above

12. First draft of "First Party at Ken Kesey's with Hell's Angels," *Collected Poems*, 382.

1965

the ravine, a fire burning by the side
porch and a few tired souls hunched over
in black leather jackets. In the huge
wooden house, a yellow chandelier
at 3 a.m. and the blast of loudspeakers
hi-fi Rolling Stones Ray Charles Beatles
Jumping Joe Jackson and twenty youths
dancing to the vibration thru the floor,
a little weed in the bathroom, girls in scarlet
tights, one muscular smooth skinned man
sweating dancing for hours, beer cans
[?] littering the yard, a hanged man
Sculpture dangling from a high creek branch
8 motorcycles parked inside the painted gate
and police cars, red lites revolving in the leaves

Yellow floodlights dimmed at rest, waiting
all night thru, stopping the departing wildhaired
guests for identification, age-white [?]
and traffic tickets written onto uniformed knee

---

6 AM under the orange Indian bed cloth—
All night in Italian boots with tender meat dolls
        eating meat,
and swollen-faced lying in bed in a
        familiar hospital.

Rolling pot, speeches over beercans, at a
        round table of eyeglass poet's house
A blonde girl abusing and laughing on a wicker
        chair

1965

Winebottle finished, excited youths departed,
      the old poets go for coffee.

A sweet waiter, salad, the moon of Alabama
      on the pavement at dawn
hair frizzled, the big car pulls up the hill,
      I put my key in the door,
So much food and wine and laughter at last
        For the dying man!

Dark goodnight, the long night's over
    your kisses and my kisses and blowjob—
this painful huge body must not last forever,
      sores & alcohols end,
right and wrong erased by dawn, you can
      still babble if you live

August 13, 1965

Dream: At Alan Watts'[13] party—Peter sends me a little folder with two Indian paintings on it—grainy-blue printing or colored photocopies of cherry tree and blue bodied yellow crowned Krishna. "That's who I am and if nobody wants me, I'm going!"

That is because I was going with New Camper Volkswagen & Gary & young lady to climb Mt. Olympus & Peter was to be left alone in Berkeley with his girls.

----

13. Influential English writer (*The Way of Zen*).

1965

August 15

Well evening, dark, Coleman
    lamp, a breeze
in the miniature camper car
bright lit within, redwoods dark
    above, full belly by a
    warm stream, with mossy rocks,
And it's time to stretch out in Saffron
    sleeping bags in great
        black craggy back faces.

Note: Conversation with Jenkins at Bixby Canyon—
    Q.: When was the last time you stepped in the ocean?
    A.: Because of the last boot.

August 19

"4 Seasons, Gold Nugget, Dewy Magets"—
Peter and I were to go there and drink in Paris or NY sometime—or he
to stay home sleep and meet me later—a dream in Albany, Oregon

----

August 21, 1965

An Experience of Mind in Portland

The public green grass, bald wrinkle
    pure without socks
Sitting on the bench, the morning

1965

sun come out of white clouds
South, inching yellow the brick & grass
　　of mid-city downtown—
Cigarette smoke fumes thru the invisible
　　air, the tick tick tick
of water sprayed from a revolving
　　　　bone mouth
over the soft lawn, on mirror pavements,
　　on brown elephant skin
of big-leaf maple—
　　　　sitting with
the newspaper Oregonian, a blue
　　volume of Mila-Repa
read aloud a chapter Mind
　　upward over the square commercial roofs
to a great blue sky and a sliver
　　of old rapture as the old man
looks up trembling to the waving branch-frond
　　of the park tree.

"I realize fully that manifestation is mind itself"
　　　　　　Mila Repa

August 24, 1965—Portland[14]

The brown piano in the white
　　round spotlight

14. First draft of "Portland Coliseum," *Collected Poems*, 373–74.

1965

Leviathan the auditorium
   and wired
hanging organs and vox
   and black battery—
a single whistling sound of
    ten thousand children's
    larynxes singing

Pierce thru the ears and
   flowing up the belly
bliss of the moment arrived

Goofed Ringo battling the round
   white drums,
Enter George fluff hair
   soul of house,
The mat of short black skulled Paul
   with his guitar
Lennon the Captain, his mouth
   a triangular smile,
All jump together to end
   some tearful memory song
   ancient 2 years.

And the million children of
    the thousand worlds
bounce in their seats, bash each
   others sides, press their
   legs together nervous to the
   move of black knees of the musicians,
Scream again & claphand,
   one animal become in

1965

the New World Auditorium
—hands waving like the myriad
   snakes of thought
   and screech beyond hearing

While a line of police with
   folded arms stands
Sentry to contain the red sweatered
         ecstasy
    that rises upward to
    the wired roof.

Mt. Rainier—with Gary and Martina been hiking and camping the last couple of days over "Wonderland Trail"—many flowers berries fogs & chasms.

2 dreams, one a few weeks ago, I was really close to some male chimpanzees, trying to get them to screw me or hold me or me fuck them.

Last night in saffron sleeping bag dreamt of Julius Orlovsky, we both lay naked I behind him to one side on a down warm bed, I began jerking him off, rubbing his cock upward, he got a hard on & friendly.

All day tramping on snows had been thinking different ways of mountain therapy for him finally concluded that roll up from rubber mattress would solve camper sleeping problem.

Seattle—city house on hill—
Dream—At Marianne Moore's[15] apartment with some upstairs friends of Miss Moore we're all singing and dancing around—she shacks a mean

15. American poet Marianne Moore (1887–1972).

1965

cymbal and tambourine—I leave to go out, promising to come back and sing Mantras to the Company—"I hope you sing better than last time," she says, apparently referring to the last time I tried to impress her in a dream—

I go out to bathroom downstairs and see the neighbor under the subway returning home, he comes out shaving and magically informs me that he's putting in a breakfast patron in the next-door garden—

Right the way thru the slat fence with him—and I see also a narrow cute colonial house occupying half a lot but a half acre elongated communal backyard too. It's for sale or rent, says the returned seacaptain.

Gee, wouldn't it be nice to live next door to MM & settle down there to die, I think.

Seattle Goodwill

Gary bought a vest
Martine a silk white wedding dress
Allen bought an antique tambourine.

Then Folsom Prison Blues—Rusty Draper
        heard in 109 Yessler Bar—
        like Dylan's Rolling Stone

Steamed clams & seafood fry plate
at Athenian Tavern in Farmers Market
Greek owner & Chinese cooks,

The Wobbly hall closed a few years ago—
The Turkish bath on SE Washington
        downstairs, new remodeled,

1965

Yessler St. Blasted out into
                    parking lot [?]
The Skid Row bars closed where we
        drank a decade ago Green Land
                    Valley—
Judgment at Nuremberg at Green
            Parrot Theater
Al Jolson on the [?]

Is Beatles Help! In town
(at Portland concert 5,000
teenagers in hysteria
hitting each other's thighs
& bouncing on seats to pee & scream)
"Wish to Greet Ginsberg"
and saw movie in Seattle

Dream

I'm living with some cousin girls in a sea-shore apartment down half a block from the beach below a big pier—like Atlantic City Steel Pier—or Seattle North Wake—Relatives, my old mother and father, or Herbert Hoover & Eleanor Roosevelt (or Victor Mature and Nelson [?] Victor Moore & Jessica Tandy—I take them sightseeing they live in a nearby pension hotel on an officeworker's vacation plan—

I take them walking. I notice in a newspaper a photo of the pier the sea has receded 20 feet—just as several days earlier I'd received information that there'd be a tidal wave coming forward & the sea returns to its boundaries—and meanwhile, seen heat—so I decide I'd better move upland—there are visitors coming in and out with needles, someone I know

1965

some young kid next door visits the girls & turns on in the next room—I warn him no, inconsequently, he goes out carrying his needle openly—I go on out with my relatives & show them the sights.

On the newsphoto I see a note pinned by a young blond longhair vegetarian [?] nature-boy—(Jerry) Oscar Heiselman?—Giving the astrological conjunction info and dates and feet measurements of the Tide to come this month, prophesizing the beach apocalypse—

I warn my relatives but they don't believe me, anyway we agree, they're only on a few days vacation & going home before anything happens.

I see them in their residence-hotel & they go to table, I follow them but not sure they want me along to free-load a meal? . . . "I can eat at my hotel," I say. "I should, the meal's already paid there"—"I guess that would be best," my Russian aunt says, disappointingly to me—I go off.

I'm worried about the water supply on high ground if I do move upland during the crisis.

All afternoon at Space Needle & Wash. Science Exhibits—the Crab Nebula exploded—the ring Nebula expanding to disappear—the spiral nebula andromeda whirling with huge octopus legs—the Rosetta nebula— and hours 600 feet above Seattle on the observation tower identifying Vashon Winslow, Mt. Rainier finally floating over the green haze South like a great [?] cloud—

Down on 1'st St. Seattle after short monorail ride, first time, standing forward of the observation bubble, smooth as a London subway but you can look right down below on the near street—

Walked round Farmer's Market past closed windows doors up alley Sally Army 2'nd Hand Store.

The old steam bath near S. Washington St. & 1'st Ave. corner bathed & waved my hand indifferently at several potbellied gents who poked head in my room, rose & dressed and took bus home at midnite—

1965

I have nothing to say anymore

I have written green automobile[16] siesta

in Xbalba,[17] Howl,[18] Kaddish,[19] the

change[20] & now Kral Majales[21] is enough.

I am where everyone else is, in a second

hand market in Seattle, interesting

as old shoes, red leather, bean bag ashtray,

nylon shirts.

Seattle is not in Hell, I am not in Heaven,

I am in my name and potbellied form,

there need no words for that, anymore, everyone knows

that already

If they had paid attention to the window display

of the Salvation Army

Up and down first avenue Seattle, Indian bums

talk to themselves too,

Passing [?] electric razors, dirty magazine

shops, [?] marquees, Turkish baths,

There are no beautiful youths anymore on [?]

I see no god today but a photograph of the

Crab Nebula shivered

on the Science Dome under the Space Needle

Whence I rode past where the Beatles made

[?] before the camera

16. "The Green Automobile," *Collected Poems,* 91–95.

17. "Siesta in *Xbalba*," *Collected Poems,* 105–18.

18. "Howl," *Collected Poems,* 134–41.

19. "Kaddish," *Collected Poems,* 217–35.

20. "The Change: Kyoto–Tokyo Express," *Collected Poems,* 332–38.

21. All of the poems mentioned here are considered seminal early works by Ginsberg.

1965

On the new Monorail. I probably won't ride it anymore.
Poe's Raven repeated the obvious,
    I can't do that anymore.
I saw god too, but don't believe Him
    Anymore
anymore myself is finished, complete,
    no exaggeration
anymore necessary via poesy, I dream,
    I suck cock, I push pussy,
I don't have sex for a month, I jerk off
    In toilet paper in bed,
no romance, no babies, I leave the
    steam bath early
to the midnite bald fatmen pacing the
    curtains to the dead Muzak echo—
I'll visit the lama of the Hevajra Tantra,
    whose wife works in Blood Bank—
It's no use anymore, except to meditate
    a new Mantra
Same as Rolling Stones or Rudy
    & the Burning Ghat Trio
playing "Laughing on the Outside" in
    Calcutta 1963—
        words? My eyes
    close to sleep.
No rhythm anymore to rock the Universe
    Of Dead gas on photosynthesis
    Harpsichord tinkles—
        explain about the moon, Tellar
    talk about Quasars,
and the old chimp mother & bored
    little pink assed son

1965

will lie about their isolate cage &

    spit on their own hair.

August 31–Sept. 2.

Hiking & backpacking (food pouches & sleepingbags, ice axes & crampons) along Lost Creek Corrected ridge, first day overlooking Red Mountain & Glacier Park in Baker Natnl Forest—camped 2'nd night by Byrne Lake big cold blue socket of water under Chinese dark green cliffs, Alpine fir, snow blankets & fog on the mount tables above the lake—continuous hypnotic [?] of wavelets on the water—smoke out of nostrils from cold—

Dream last night long winding affair in a long-halled rooming house belonging to a Mr. Goldfine—I had a chamber there, and was walking from one porch to another on the same street—the front balconies connected with stairways to green lawns—I was exploring them with John Lennon and Gary Snyder perhaps—we came to a fence dividing the neighbor's porch from Goldfine's—and crossed thru the gate—a great outcry from inside at our intrusion—we ran away—

Meanwhile inside a little girl who'd been taking a needle for pneumonia or Thoraxl died because of the uproar—our fault?—

I went into my chamber and decided to take it on the lam—Gregory Corso with me, I looking at my possessions and decided to abandon them, books lined up on shelves, foreign translations of my poetry, Czech & German volumes, notebooks, etc. I reached in for a few necessary papers—Gregory objected—"I need these few papers—my contracts that's all"—

And we retreated. Then a friend came to me outside the encampment and said, "Goldfine's taking advantage of your absence to sell your papers & books from your room"—

What? I got mad. Why shd. I retreat—besides it's only me & John Lennon walking around like Magi, not burglars—

1965

I'd been with Lennon to visit an old lady, and Goldfine there too who was a friend of Mrs. Kerouac. I'd thought, "Well, I might as well complain about her, & let him bring some shit back to Gabrielle,[22] they're gossips, if I say anything "against her" he'll report it in so she can get scared realizing I'm on to her game & complaining & grumbling back at her the way she has to Jack about me—but I give it up, too tendentious—

I go back to the porch to Mr. Goldfine—"Listen here, I was with John Lennon," he doesn't hear me or listen, he's busy retreating to his room, he's hermit miser, I keep complaining to him—

Besides I realize the dead girl was *my* friend? (Marilyn Monroe dead in my room?)—So I'm the one that's aggrieved not him—and now he's trying to sell my papers! It's a plot—he's abusing me! I won't put up with it!

I go back in my room, and see a crowd of friends from NY like hornets buzzing around my room going thru my files—Carl's[23] there, he's picked up a manila folder full of his own writings & letters—I say, "Oh well, it's his anyway"—Dust thou are my possessions—but while I'm there aggrieved and irritated, standing in the middle of the room, watching the raid, all the scavenger folk give up & retreat & depart thru the door—

Wake, the shimmer of fog at night, [?] stars on top of a knell by the lake—sound of river rushing down thru crevasses—

The Treas. Dept. out to get me in NY—spreading propaganda contra cannabis in Media—

That I told the Harvard Crimson boy about getting high with Beatles manager—in my Grand Conspiracy that can be used to betray my position since it implicates Beatles if I were in really crisis battle—

. . . and the boy who went to jail, arrested for refusing to cooperate turning me in, Martin?—Mr. Brad Mr. Mort—

Up here in mountains this city politics resolving itself in my skull.

----

22. Jack Kerouac's mother.

23. Carl Solomon (1928–1993), American writer and friend of Ginsberg, to whom "Howl" is dedicated.

1965

Descent from Byrne Lake
All night on the foggy knell,
   the day shimmering long pond
     barbed by snow and granite
          Tree slopes.
The vale filled with drifting
   mists that at dawn
    come down curtain on the distant
    treestacked green slopes
and rose like white gauze wall
—a line from the river-gulf below
   of clear violet as I woke
in my sleep bag and stuck out
   my nose to the white vast—
A line of clear violet between the two
   mirrored tables of cloud—

Two nights ago walking in the dark
out past the fir needle branches
the sky black flecked with billion
       pinpoint galaxies,
   Venus and the [?]
      over the campfire—

Into the dark all night damp mist
   knees aching, waking out of
Dream—Marilyn Monroe Dead
in my room, the landlord
Feinstein's a venal spy for
   the treasury department,

The hypodermic took a babe to death
and the meth freaks ransacked

1965

my papers for the Agency,
and the Beatle John fleeing
   with me from the [?] porch—
Carl returning his manila folder—

   I slept alone woke
built fire, mused on the Deity of
      the Dream Cities—
Sunlight, mist rolled apart, the snowcrag [?]
      Descending a crap by the rushing
         creek canyon on the moss
            pink paper aflutter above
               the shameful Pyramid
      in all the silence of a back trail
      descending, sat on
         green heather to smoke
      thru camera eye—the forest
upward arose and I stood
Brown bearded & aged with
   [?] wrinkles
Smoked Eastern Perfumed Cigarette
and walked down thru the vast
brown mirror stepping from rock
to flower, moss pad to wet black clay,
on stairways of [?]
      straight down thru old man trees
         huge gardens, on rock logs

late the deep leafy Timespace filled
      with crags thru pine needles,
blue sky and white sky folkbuildings
hanging a roof over the afternoon—

1965

To the floor meadow where streams
gathered together in grass and
    old glacier tumble, sat
and stared up at the cave-eyed
giant rock creature that nestled
    in the fur cloth of mountainside trees—
Sat om the awe seat a kind of Fatigue
Leaning my pack on a boulder askew,
Song to the myth king of Mountain
    Lord Shiva Named Who Returns
to the Frontplace to see himself again,
as I have returned, and stood awake
    and lifted my head to the wall of
    old nature to gaze in a circle on
      four directions filled with the
      noise of glacier water, [?] of Space,
    soft earth-banks underfoot,
        tender vegetables hug in towers
          with their skins and tangled leafs
          with my breast in
            huckleberry bush—
Clouds piled up over the
    forest tops
    toppled down pillars of wood
      decaying into the moist
        earth moss—
Amazed, descending, ran tired
    downhill, the Time called
    earnestly, scared, strode down
with long heavy footfalls clomp
    over slip mark & branch,

1965

bounded the path sped by Tibetan
    myths of Alone, on belly,
Loomed breathing magic fear
    thru the damp smell,
      down the root stairs,
    heavy foot bounding the Claybank
Claybank switchback turns,
    [?] to light fatigue, pack
      light on my shoulders,
    leaped round a turn on the level
      river valley floor to the
        white woody bridge
over White Creek river [?]
    over rocks filled with flaccid milk.

Up early ate & climbed thru long plateau forest by white church river till we came to great meadows walled with brown ashen cone on one side and snow botched grey ridge on the other—White Mt.—to a place called White Pass, a hill saddle 6400 feet where standing we could look back on the ridges sunning up the glacier peak, and on the other side west we could see great ranges of glacial mountains—craggy in clear afternoon light stretching from one end of the Horizon to another—[?] peak and along to the left the razorback spine crag heights of Monte Cristo range, we walked thereafter—my step painful to the foot a small [?] and there by the toe or thumb-foot-finger, but my body light breathing deep in my lower abdomen, my bulk like an empty column, pack resting easily over my shoulders weight, on [?], clomping down heavily declining path and humming hari om nemo shiva invisibly involuntarily accompaniment to uphill path thumps as we wound our way along the crest of white mountains looking down into a large space of sloping glacier valley grown green with pines downward to the river minute below, a few vast clouds lost in

1965

the giant sky blue space the turning a [?] turn in the path around the neck of the mountain, suddenly appearing a further range of red mountain & red pass and behind and beyond them crag upon snowrag whitened by distance and the vista so far I said "Are these mountains down in California?" as we were marching along a Washington State cascade crest trail—then wound into camp singing heartily hari om Nemo Shiva greeting white pass shelter meadow little rills of rivulets, a few horses down in its green distance from the trail as we gazed forward—around a bend and the backside of the ridges leading to glacier peak appearing—an easy walk along meadows tomorrow to the glacier.

The snout of the rocks of mountains like living mind-growths in an occasional glimpse, and my body fit & tuned hours of plodding uphill & across snowfields with 30 lb. packaback.

Sunday First Sept.
Labor Day Saturday Nite
Dream—Nightmares & anxiety bringdowns

A young man with a girl, he's slothful & comes in my apartment with some junk, I get irritated & say, "Don't come here with dope, the Law is too close, you know that" and drive him out—oh! it's Peter with a needle—I made a mistake!—

And several other fleeting phantom drag-ass social catastrophes.

This Backpacking Trip so far.
Left car at North fork of [?] river—halfway between Bedal guard station & Sloan Creek Camp—
Climbed first day a ridge running off of White Mt.-top ridge & camped beneath sunup lake on a knoll in fog.

1965

Next day walked along ridge and around the ridges beyond to Byrne Lake & camped—still fog—on a hill surrounded with alpine fir trees.

Next day descended 2 miles to Kennedy Camp—as we descended, fog lifted & we saw rock faces & giant swaying vegetable pillars—came down & camped in village-like place. Kennedy Camps at end of White Church River Road (via Darrington).

Next day walked along forest valley floor along White Church River Valley to upper reaches, past Glacier Camp, up to red pass spectacular panorama, around hairpin turn and down along giant steep meadow green on a perfect trail to flanking White Mountain to White Pass Shelter Meadow & camp. Here I had this dream.

Will climb around glacier peak again as today where Gary and I took photos overlooking White Church Glacier—

Then after descend probably by trail down into valley of North Fork of Bank River (past shelter) to Sloan Creek Camp and pick up the car.

Kennedy Camp—Sept. 4—Dream
while mice rubbed hole in my backpack—

With Burroughs in Algiers-London we go together to his club, the Tom Tom House, as I enter with him I see goateed billionaires and money-bags bomb-rich boys who hold power over Earth & England. I feel foolish eating with him, they so cold and clean and the servants so precise and the mahogany chairs and armorial racks and hangings so complete—I realize Bill, who's grown fat-jowled like Sidney Greenstreet, has an exclusive private chair here and shouldn't bring guests so weak as myself—He sits at his desk and says, "I'll hole up here for the next ten years and order my food from servants and turn the dials for news and send for Time and read tickertape for inside dope and blast out the image from this—ah civilized cave . . . I'm in Paris to see Jack or Gregory, passing thru the place de

1965

l'opera and across Seine again "oh, well, I'll be coming back here all my
life the Wandering Jew, Gregory'll be always here and Jack now visiting
and in ten years I'll have to come back thru again. I'll always find myself
returned into Paris all my life till I die that's my fate."

Sept. 9

Yesterday woke at 3:14 a.m. brilliant and star black sky, ate cold oat-
meal mixt w/raisins & nuts & dried fruit & set off with flashlight along
meadow path to anvil entrance—a little hollow [?] in tree leading up Gla-
cier Park to White Mountain—of white church glacier mountain valley,
climbed up that hollow filled with frothy mud and rocks till at dawn we
came to the White church Glacier, dirty roped up together me & Gary,
walked across its lunar white rolling plain—like a sahara with rocky [?]
on each side, up over its low avenue to a decline of snowfall field, slid down
that to a rocky island, crossed down more snow to the bottom of another
huger glacier, the lower part filled with brown cracks and round whorled
crevasses. Climbed down to the rocks below to an icy pool for a drink of
water, then staying to the side of the chocolate glacier made our way half
up the length by a narrow boundary wall of grit and shale which slid under
each footstep, climbed down off that to the Glacier itself and slowly with
Crampons on hiking shoes, trudged all the way up to the great door where
the glacier ended in an icefall—huge chunks of snowy ice with blue holes
and caves—climbed over these car-sized chunks of white snow and entered
another even huger top glacier streaked with blue crevasses—roped to-
gether made our way up that slope and came finally to the bottom of the
peak-top of
    Glacier peak—There, fatigued, I slowly clump clomped up a last ridge
of scree grit to a tumble of rocks leading up a hundred feet to the summit
on which Gary already sat. He'd sung and danced alone arriving. I, breath-
ing heavily, sat and we ate lunch Indian smoked salmon, a slice of salami

1965

a slice of cheese, a biscuit and two yellow honey-candies—"Bee Candy"—then spent ¾ hour on the snow-glacier tip of the mount looking north to Mnt. Baker with snowy flat beyond ridge upon ridge of snowpeaks & beyond grey Canadian lower Cascades—west to Sloan Peak and Monte Cristo range with snowfields and glaciers a way beyond them in the clear blue azurey aether the brown hulk of Olympics mountains, Eastward red and grey snowless mounts and between a crack of them a reddish desert land, south to White Mountain, ranges of [. . .].

The atmosphere like that described from rocket ships—deep thin transparent blue, the blue of the intensest sky settled down like a gas over the valleys and ranges of rock crags dotted with forests of this upright comical hemlock and fir trees toothpicked with valley-sides—a jet plane buzzed ripping the air to the valley below us—

We'd climbed till 2 p.m. stayed looking through the perfect transparent sky with few cirrus clouds stretching like white shoestrings, gazing at the ends of the circular horizon, then set rushing down the snow slopes and bounding back down meadow paths toward sunset at 7:30 p.m., returned to White Pass Shelter chimney white house.

A dead goat's white furred white ribcaged skeleton at the edge of chocolate glacier. [?] following us at 8000 feet. A dead fly in the ice on a crag. Birds fluttering around the lip of a crevasse.

Dream this Morn:

Some hollywoodian wastrel, pimp moustached father of Fay Wray son, telling me to give him some money, I'm supposed to be a millionaire. . .

I tell him about Seattle Goodwill, "get your cheap clothes there" and he digs that, smiles, we're sitting on the pile rug I'm on his knee, someone comes in and interrupts me . . . then dream ends.

1965

Ginsberg's note: *Glacier Peak Wilderness area, Washington state, summer 1965—eight day backpack in Northern Cascade Mountains, Gary Snyder on his return from years in Kyoto studying Zazen. My first mountain walk.* Photograph by Martine Algier.

Sept. 10?—Wed.

Yesterday clear sunny day after Glacier Peak climb, white pass camp emptied of Labor Day weekend visitors—we moved into shelter instead of camping out on ridge protected with mountain hemlock and alpine fir trees—wandered slowly up White Mt. to its green peak topped with geological survey—orange flag—looked around for an hour or more, singing Hari om Nomo Shiva in high tender voice, then ran down the ridge to White Pass clomping down so heavily my ankles ached later and blisters on my heel and ball of left foot. Then we descended Salk North Valley big long rocky path along White Mountain side down past blueberry patches, looking into the river bottom & forests of hemlock & fir & pine trees— entered a deep forest of shady Lowland White Fir and Western Hemlock. To a rustic cabin with a strange outhouse, sunk & tilted into side of a Rene-needle stream hillock under the great trees—Entering the outhouse I lost my balance, House of Mystery, all the cracks and angles leading parallel in wrong direction—Giggled next morning when Gary went to take a crap and came back amazed.

Sept. 10—Wed.

Came down from White Pass in afternoon after clear azurey afternoon looking at Monte Cristo Range & Sloan Peak, lolling on the grass and heather near the shelter, all the tall small-stemmed flowers trembling in the breeze amid the dead silence and stillness of immense meadow gulf and crag.

Walked down long path the side of White Mt. to a shelter of White Cheek Creek & slept the night—a long dream of finally meeting Ezra Pound—a short Jewish fellow he was in fact, and some strange professionally spiritual conversation with him, we had some rapport based on assumption of immortality and Chotspuk.

1965

Woke in the cabin my feet hurt from the jarring Fudo-strides downward on the blueberry patched trail into the dusty stones so bandaged a blood-blister on my foot-ball and we walked the 5 miles more thru hemlock forest almost tropic-rainy in style like Chiapas—instead of Palenque's Elephant ears, giant leafed bushes, here were Devil's [?] leaves—2 foot green frond-plates big as a car fender.

Drove up highway 9 to turn-off to go to State Park on Puget Sound near Indian fishing-reservation towns—cooked first downland meal in a week tinged salmon with a dressing Gary'd ordered—butter tarragon & a little vinegar—we talked about Peter, drank hot saki and argued and laughed—

Coming down into logging town in mid-cascades named Barrington, we shopped for groceries, I bought some crème colored streamlined Wrangler levis—my old Salvation Seattle pants had huge wear-holes in the seat already I left them in the trash-bin at Sloan Creek Camp and put on hiking shorts—so when we hit this first town and I walked out of the street, a group of young girls that passed me Main Street stared and noticed my long beardy head and potbelly and thin muscular legs—I must be a funny combination now, grey in my Temple of Beards—

At the small supermarket shopping for fish—the first newspaper in 8 days—India and Pakistan at war—bombings on Indian and Pakistan cities—Gary and I both winced, astonished and disgusted—What, has it come to that too?—

In sleeping bag on air mattress under tall thin trees in a fir grove by the road at Puget Sound, I slept, silence in the night but for frog croaks answering each other in the state camping park, and motor sounds from the bay and highways—

Dream—I visit a friend's apartment in NY—old Columbia acquaintance—Joe Kraft?—They treat me fine as a rare queen? literary guest—big neurotic—Jean Genet[24] is there, I discover, a young moonfaced pasty-kid

24. French writer, playwright, and political activist, Jean Genet (1910–1986) heavily influenced Beat writings.

1965

kid, (a little physically like Arrabel) we're on a couch lying side by side like in bed together, sweating a little (in my sleepbag)—I pluck him for conversation in front of my fellow jewish college graduates, he's reluctant but I go on describing my relation with Peter—in a voice loud enough for all to hear, since the whole party is hanging on to the conversation between trips to the kitchen for cheese dips and vodka martinis—the faces change, one minute it's my Uncle Maxie the next minute Jason Epstein the next minute a Danish journalist—How many people share this old fashioned cooperative apartment, anyway?—An old family apartment I had thought now all these new "young generation" mustached balding ambitious publishers have taken it over—Genet is resisting my charms, we're in bed together, I try to forget I'm a bearded balding ambitious "young" poet and tell him about Peter, I give up and go down the elevator leaving the evening early, nothing is happening and Genet has gone too— As I leave the lobby of the building I see a new group of party arrivals— "Paris Review Crowd" meaning George Plimpton and girls, all holding arms in line in nice suits getting into the elevator—wait, who else is there?—Red Grooms and his wife, well, it's one of the old families nice NY parties "[?]."

Meanwhile we are all discussing the war and my only comment to everybody in the room was, "When they saw the headlines everybody winced! Oh, no! Not *that*. Not even them!" Caught in this world madness of overpopulation hysteria and waves of violence and newspaper war and bombing and murderers all senseless under the evening stars on Main Street Paterson—I was walking there near the library and passed the shoemaker's shop—earlier in the dream I'd met the orthodox bearded shoemaker's son, his father, he explained, was still a young man, had had his children early—as I walked past the window of the shop I saw a man with beard and yarmulke seated at shoe-last before the plate glass window inside looking up at me, young faced, and I recognized him to be the father, and he recognized me too for whoever disreputable celebrity I was supposed to be in dreamlife, but I didn't feel like addressing him thru the window so walked on, hoping the son in the back of the shop or in the

1965

open yard wouldn't spot me—When I came to the small baseball park nearby I saw a picnic of orthodox families children—a nice park like the back yard of some old fashioned house, the lawn all green and well kept hedges behind high wire fence—The son was there with his red beard (Alexi Simonoff?) and greeted me—Everybody winced—

I woke in sleeping, got up to pee in the bushes in the chill evening air, heard frog croaks and motor noises, searched out my ballpoint pen and journal to write the dream—meanwhile running thru my mind, what did Indira Gandhi and Pupil Jayakar now think of Albert Hall reading,[25] and what does Mr. [?], the Indian delegate to Pakistan, say, and Burroughs is right, the world will be in destruction the cool blue silence of imagelessness is settled into the valley lands, and the [?] are right, "Prepare for the Wrath to come" and the millenarian and apocalyptic sects are right, the shakers cut loose from radio and TV selling their Oregon farmlands prepared to be independent and chill their milk in cold spring-houses when the power gets cut off and the electric civilization breaks down and I am wrong to make a public image of myself and be identifiable at all instead of slipping silently into my enlightenment and calm peaceful obscurity traveling beardless in Volkswagen or hiding out on a farm because when the war hysteria hits a peak and chaos police emerge victorious I'll get my neck cut off for bragging and screaming in public with my picture in the paper and a sign hanging around my neck, "Smoke Marijuana."

3:30–3:45 by transistorized flashlight.

* * * * *

More dreams all night, unable to remember complete sequence, ending with phone conversation with Burroughs—Esquire Magazine had asked me for an interview for a feature article on my divine person to which I'd agreed . . . but on phone, explaining to Bill, he says, "I assume

25. Earlier in the year, while in England, Ginsberg had helped organize an international poetry reading at the Royal Albert Hall in London. Indira Gandhi was in attendance.

1965

your refusal was definite"—"Well . . . er . . . not exactly, I said yes. It was easier". . . "Very bad policy, get yourself exposed on the front lines like that without taking refuge in fiction or smokescreen of your own invention . . . pure vanity . . . Besides, they don't even pay you. . . all the trouble and time you take manipulating the article, you could write your own script and sell it, or write on *other* subject . . ." He ends on note of disapproval and I feel chagrined.

Wake, Gary and Martine busy at the Coleman stove on the big wooden picnic table, the bull-loving of a chainsaw down the road, 8:30 a.m., the sky now grey cloudy but the atmosphere still dry and my notebook and tennis shoes on the grass beside saffron sleepbag and airmattress also saffron are not dampened by morning dew. My left heel still hurts with small blister and my ankle painful to walk on. Gary busy at breakfast making notes on trails and groceries and birds and flowers in his ring-notebook, with travel pamphlets at his side, discussing Chinese pine-carbon ink and saying, "I'll have to get my calligraphy practice book out . . . with this new pen Charley Leony gave me the line is so excellent I must perfect my formal lines . . . There are a few individualistic imperfections that have crept into my manuscript"—or words to that effect, in mock-puritan voice, slightly Germanic accent, playfully "It is my internal gestapo" . . . "today is 9.9-ninth day ninth month—it's a Japanese folk holiday, anyone that doesn't make love with somebody else today will have a year of bad luck . . ." Then he describes a whole series of ancient Jap folk holidays for the same numbered day as month, 1.1 New Years, 2.2 Youth/Students day, 3.3 etc., 4.4 etc., 7.7 Chinese New Year old style. I have the mixed. "Last year this time Don Allen[26] and I were drinking on this day gloomy worried about the end of the day. And he, in his cups, suggested, "Well, perhaps we could try each other"—"That would be worse luck for me than all the bad luck I'm going to get next year anyway," Gary replied.

26. Editor and publisher Donald Allen (1912–2004) was best known for his editing of *The New American Poetry, 1945–1960*.

1965

Everybody sitting around the table under the tall thin Douglas fir trees writing in notebooks and cock crows in the distance . . . "We can do our things and clean up and go for a little walk down the water's edge if we like." I'm looking up campsites for 10 min, "God they got a lotta different kinds of whales . . . god," says Gary.

"Beginning of a Poem of These States"[27]

Under the bluffs of Oroville, blue cloud September skies, entering U.S. border, red red apples bend their trees boughs propt with sticks—

At Omak a fat girl in dungarees leads her big brown horse by the asphalt highway.

Thru the lodgepole pine hills Coleville near Moses' Mountain—a white horse standing at the back of a 2 ton truck moving forward between the trees.

At Nespelem, in the yellow sun, a marker for Chief Joseph's grave under the rilled brown hills—a white cross over the highway.

At Grand Coulee under leaden sky, giant red generators humm thru granite & concrete thru granite & concrete to materialize onions—

And grey water taps against the grey sides of Steamboat Mesa.

At Dry Falls 40 Niagaras stand silent & invisible, the horses graze on the mesquite floor of the rusty canyon.

At Mesa, on the car radio passing a new corn silo, the walking Boogie of teenager's tender throats, "I wish they could be California girls,"[28] and the black highway curls outward.

On the plains toward Pasco, Oregon hills in the horizon, Bob Dylan's

27. Auto poesy, "Beginning of a Poem of These States," *Collected Poems,* 377–80. Ginsberg transcribed and lightly edited the tape for publication soon after it was written. He submitted it for publication in a small magazine, and this is the published version. He later revised it.

28. "California Girls," by the Beach Boys.

1965

voice on airways, & mass machine-made folksong of one soul—Please crawl out your window[29]—first time heard.

Speeding thru space, Radio the soul of the nation. The Eve of Destruction[30] and The Universal Soldier,[31]

And tasted the snake: water from Yellowstone under a green bridge darshan with the Columbia, oilslick & small bird feathers on mud shore. Across the river, silver bubbles of refineries.

There Lewis and Clark floated down in a raft: the brown-mesa'd gorge of Lake Wallula smelling of rain in the sage, Greyhound buses speeding by.

Searching neither for Northwest Passage, Nor Gold, nor the Prophet who will save the polluted Nation, nor for Guru walking the silver waters behind McNary Dam.

Round-up time in Pendleton, pinched women's faces and hulking cowboy hats in the tavern, I'm a city slicker from Benares, the barman murmurs to himself, two hands full of beer "Who wanted that?"

Heavy rain at twilight, trumpets massing & ascending repeat The Eve of Destruction, Georgia Pacific sawmill burners lifting smoke thru the dusky valley.

A cold night in the Blue Mountains, snow-powdered & tops of droopy Tamarack and Fir at grey sunrise, coffee frozen in the brown coffeepot, toes chilled in Czechoslovakian tennis sneakers.

Under Ponderosa pine, this place for sale—45th Parallel, half way between equator and the North Pole—Tri-City Radio broadcasting clear skies & freezing nite temperatures; big yellow daisies, hay bales piled in square stacks house-high,

"Don Carpenter has a real geologist's hammer, he can hit a rock & split it open & look inside & utter some mantra."

29. "Can You Please Crawl Out Your Window?" by Bob Dylan.
30. "Eve of Destruction," by Barry McGuire.
31. "Universal Soldier," by Donovan.

1965

Coyote jumping in front of the truck, & down the bank, jumping thru the river, running up the field to the wooded hillside, stopped on a bound & turned around to stare at us—Oh-owl shook himself and bounded away waving his bushy tail.

Rifles and cyanide bombs unavailing—he looked real surprised & pointed his thin nose in our direction. Hari Om Nami Shivaye!

Eat all sort of things & run solitary—3 nites ago hung bear dung on a tree and laughed

—Bear: "Are you eating my corpses? Say that again!"

Coyote: "I didn't say nothing."

Sparse juniper forests on the dry lavender hills, down the Ritter Butte to Pass Creek,

A pot dream recounted—Crossing the Canada border with a tin can in the glove compartment, hip young border guards laughing—In meadow the skeleton of an old car settled: Look to Jesus painted on the door.

Fox in the valley, road markers dript with small icicles, all the windows on the white church broken, brown wooden barns leaned together, thin snow on the gas station roof.

Malheur, Malheur National Forest signs glazed with snowfrost last night's frozen dreams come back—starting out thru the skull at the cold planet—Mila Repa accepted no gifts to cover his jeweled penis—Strawberry Mountain top white under bright clouds.

Postcards of Painted Hills, fossil beds near Dayville, Where have all the flowers gone? Ra and Coyote are hip to it all, nailed footpaw tracks on the bottom of Day River cows kneeled at rest in the afternoon meadow.

Ichor Motel, white tailfins in the driveway, isolate belfried brown farmhouse circled with trees, chain saws ringing in the vale.

Rilled lava overgrown with green moss cracked in the cold wind—Blue Horizon and American white egret migrate to shrunken waters of Unhappy—mirage lakes on the wrong side of the road, dust streaming under Riddle Mountain, Steen Range powder white on the horizon—

Slept, water frozen in Sierra cup, a lake of bitter water from the solar

1965

plexus to throat—Dreamt my knee was severed at the hip and sutured back together—

Woke, icy dew on poncho and saffron sleep bag, moon like a Coleman lantern dimming the icicle-points of the stars—vomited on my knees in the arroyo grass, nostrils choking with wet red acid in weak flashlight—

Dawn weakness, climbing worn lava walls following the muddy spring, waterfowl whistling sweetly & a tiny raccoon pawed forward daintily in the green mud, looking for frogs burrowed away from Arctic cold—disappeared into a silent rock shelf.

Climbed up toward Massacre Lake road—sagebrush valleyfloor stretched South—Pronghorn abode, that eat the bitterroot and dry spicebush, hunters gathering in trucks to chase the antelope—

A broken corral at the bottom of highway hill wreck of a dead cow in cold slanting sun set rays, eyes eaten out, neck twisted to the ground, belly caved in on kneebone, smell of sweet dread flesh and acrid new sage.

Slept in rusty tin feeding trough, Orion belt crystal in sky, numb metal-chill at my back, ravens settled on the cow when sun warmed my feet.

Up hills following trailer dust clouds, green shotgun shells & beer-bottles on road, mashed jackrabbits—through a crack in the Granite Range, an alkali sea—Chinese armies massed at the borders of India.

Mud plate of Black Rock Desert passing, Frank Sinatra lamenting distant years, old sad voice'd September recordings, and the Beatles crying for Help! their voices woodling for tenderness.

All memory at once at present time returning, vast dry forests afire in California, U.S. paratroopers attacking guerrillas in Vietnam mts, the white porcelain road over a hump the tranquil azure of a vast lake.

Pyramid rocks knotted by pleistocene rivers, topheavy lava isles castled in the Palute water filled with cutthroat trout, tomato sandwiches and silence.

Reno's Motel signs and traffic, low mountains waiting the desert oasis, crooning city music and afternoon news, Red Chinese Ultimatum 1 AM tomorrow.

Up Donner pass over concrete bridge superhighways hung with grey

1965

clouds, Mongolian idiot chow yuk the laughable menu of this last party arrived.

Ponderosa hillsides cut back for railroad track, I have nothing to do laughing over the Sierra top, gliding adventurer on the great fishtail iron-finned road, Heaven is renounced, Dharma no Path, no Sadhana to fear,

my man world will blow up, the humming of insects under the wheat sings my own death in rasping migrations of mercy, I tickle the Bodhisattva and salute the sunset, home riding home to the old city on ocean.

A new mantra to manifest Removal of Disaster from my self, smoky mass of autumn brushfire in dusk light, surf a bright red ball on horizon purple with earth cloud, chanting to Shiva in the car cabin.

Pacific Gas high voltage antennae trailing thin wires across flatlands, entering Coast Range 4 lane highway over the last hump to the giant orange bay glimpse, Dylan ends his song "You'd see what a drag you are," and the Pope

cometh to Babylon to address the United Nations 2000 years since Christ's birth and the prophecy of Armageddon

hangs the Hell Bomb over the roads and cities of the planet, the year-end has come, the lights on Oakland Army Terminal turn green in evening darkness.

Treasure Island Navel Base lit yellow with night business, thousands of red tail lights move in procession over the Bay Bridge,

San Francisco stands on modern hills, Broadway lights flash on the center of gay honky-tonk Elysium, Ferry building's sweet green clock lamps the black Embarcadero waters, negroes are screaming over the radio,

Bank of America burns a red sign beneath the union pyramids, here is the city, here is the face of war, home 8 o'clock

gliding down the freeway ramp to City Lights, Peter's face and television, money and new wanderings to come.

9/65

1965

Sept. 19, 1965—Back in S.F., moved into Shig's,[32] changed cars and Peter gave back Gary's small blue Volk—slept last nite between Peter and Stella, naked, and turned this and that way one to another on sofa bed, content.

Then met Kaufman[33] on afternoon Grant Ave, and made 8 p.m. date—but traveling up to Whalen[34] him not home at his green leaf'd apartment door, went to visit McClure[35] instead carrying bread and chicken and corn —ate and talked and heard his Lion Graahr tape and we all went out to Fillmore/Marina

Sept. 25, 1965

Decade after decade, Painters
in Cafeterias like Fosters over coffee
cup and Sunday Chronicle still
trying to conquer space.

And you, Natalie Jackson,[36] a decade
later than suicide, is your red hair
remembered outside of watercolors?

32. Shigeyoshi Murao, a clerk at City Lights Bookstore and a friend of Ginsberg. Murao was arrested when he sold an undercover cop *Howl and Other Poems,* setting in motion a chain of events that led to the landmark obscenity trial in San Francisco.

33. Poet Bob Kaufman (1925–1986).

34. Poet Philip Whalen (1923–2002), who read at the historic Six Gallery poetry reading in San Francisco in 1956 when Ginsberg read "Howl" in public for the first time, was very influential in Ginsberg's studies of Buddhism.

35. Poet, playwright, essayist, and songwriter Michael McClure (1932–2020) was involved in the San Francisco Poetry Renaissance.

36. Natalie Jackson, girlfriend of Neal Cassady and a friend of Ginsberg and other Beat writers, committed suicide by jumping off the top of a building in San Francisco.

1965

Natalie, you missed the Beatles,
and the Animals, the Rolling Stones,
Ray Charles I got a woman, and
Pale Dylan at the midnite phonograph.

You missed the moon, and
exciting days of publicity, and
the triumph of fairies in the
press.

You missed Neal unchanged after
ten years, exactly the same
bared body and heavy man's
arm.

Needles of anxiety flowing in your
skin and liver, what ever feeling
that was painful enuf to jump

the roof—

Counterattack against the cops,
Counterattack against anxiety
in the toilet of May company, counter-
attack the Great Fear written on
pieces of cardboard. It took ten years.

And the thousandth repetition
of pictures at an exhibition at
Vesuvio's ceiling loudspeaker,
brasses announcing the End, a
poignant drunkenness.

1965

And chequered red tablecloths,
folksingers at coffee and confusion,
melancholy hearing I'll be seeing
you on a car radio in Oregon
midnight Juniper forest highway.

and Comedians scattering their shit
over the airwaves; and the methedrine
plague; and the napalm bombers in Vietnam,
all the exciting headlines of war between
India and faraway China.

The Sacred Heart is a piece of
    meat that feels, I saw
    it in a painted red plaster
    statue St. Francis Church in
    Frisco.

And whitey, colder, with
    thickened speech, apologizing
    to a wooden pillar as he
    shambles by in the bar—

Gentleman in beret with red
    shirt lifting an envelope to
    breast pocket, a negro with
    small brown felt hat lifting
    a rye on rocks to judicious
    lips.

You missed a big blond handlebar
    mustache and the last beer

1965

pitcher before closing again,
and enough money to get to NY
and Lance walking up the middle
of the street.

And a concussion—that blew my mind
there—you missed getting out of the car—
and going to Hollywood with a little money
not to worry about Beef Stroganoff.

Thanks for the memory and Jewish New
Year 6056. The cries of marmots in alpine
Meadows, whistle sweet, and white hairy
Mountain goats on sport-house catalogues.

Them who are not insane enuf to be put
away are   —divine—   an arm wave
goodbye and goodnite Davey! To the closing
time cop.

Balmon Hallery's silk stocking assemblages
you woulda curiously eyed—martini openings and
old automobiles pulling uphill to antique
apartment ten parties afterwards, teen agers
naked rejoicing.

McClure thru with Emphesenia
    and depressed on love street
    walks—in spotty clothes

1965

Sept. 29—Dream

At Joe's, some doorways and living rooms and dining tables and wives and whatever. Glasses and kisses and sadness—flirty dream, don't remember.

Swing to the left Swing to the right
Standing sitdown Fight fight fight

"Why did you have to put the Beatles right in the path of my light in the pantry?"

Oct. 20, 1965

On Coit tower plaza, top of Telegraph Hill,
Long streaks of eastern cloud turning pink and the bay
    waters reflecting sheen the dull orange
the long bridge to humped Island misted,
a cargo boat entering the harbor & turning in circle to
    the dock, its streak left behind half circle on the water,
rays of the morning above the pink cloudmilk,
solar antennae rising to the ribbed heavenly malt, a
    crescent moon,
passersby & early risers standing with smoke puffing
    out nostrils,
the clap of gears on Embarcadero, fog horns groaning in
    the city bowels,
green lights pointed on Treasure Island base, Alcatraz
    lighthouse blinking,

1965

Cloud drift to the west, Eucalyptus trees hanging over
   the sunrise,
the normal blue of dawn emerged,
a dog sits quiet at his mistress' feet & licks its
   bared chops
—the hats of backs of heads gazing expectantly to the
   blue easter over the city—
   Prophetic, that old painting in the Mus. Modern Art—
   and the red circle of the seen appears over the
hanging wires of the tiny bridge,
   under a couch of clouds,
   shimmers of orange on the wavy tugboat waters,
a ship the color of the grey clouds floats thru the
golden shimmer under the bridge, the sun ascends whiter
into the clouds, & eucalyptus branches hang over the solar
system, while a small plane crosses the yellow face to the
[?] of a ship [?] & a bunch of birds right there
Says a child.

Nov. 4, 1965

   Continuation of Dream record.
   I had a dream weeks ago that Whalen had died, was dead, lying a corpse in his room.
   Photographs taken of him lying in death state before his Venetian blinded window, the shutter bars' shafts of light making a grid work in the camera eye—

   Last night Peter dreamed—a poetry reading, Neal gave a big dull introduction—"and I had nothing but my hands to read from"—

Last nite I dreamed—visiting the great high mountain valley shelf of the city Lima, Peru, I went to the Museum where there was an exhibit of my letters and poems, then in the building owned as real estate by friends I went looking around for a house I could buy, it all belonged to a sharp lady who owned the real estate & wouldn't sell to me unless . . . I went out of the wing of the museum to the other side of the ancient capitol complex and saw there in the painting museum & display also of my paintings with a flag flying with a painted ensign regarding my pictures.

Woke, worried about this and that, the materialization of my desires, reading Artaud who renounces "every so called sensation of being," remembering this week's experience of smoking DMT in treehouse at Ken Kesey's, the experience of the vibratory waves of phenomenal perception separating to reveal a void behind the curtain like laughing gas—and the fear I felt at disappearing, my identity blasted beneath the bulb-brightness with the crackling of the radio static, the imminent approach of the police cars I hallucinated, and mustached sideburned Paul Foster in Hells Angels leather jacket iron cross pinned to his breast—leaning over to adjust the radio or refill the pipe according to my wish, questioning like a ministering angel or demonic apparition did I wish to see as are? or did I prefer to cling to my flesh identity & fade back from this new dimension into my old Ginsberg body?

And descending the steps from the tree house, standing with Stephen under the tree looking in his eyes "Which way . . . does it make any difference?"

Nov. 9, 1965

Tonite 2 a.m. a gauzy vest blue halo around the moon. "Hsanga He walketh among the existences like a lion."

1965

Keaton

Julius (movie situations)
Teacher of University Class
President During Atomic Attack
Chief of Police
at Execution in Electric Chair
at Vietnam Rally or War Parade
in Church.

Use him as fulcrum Buddha at center of situations of social activity or anxiety.
Fireman chief—city burning, Julius sits & plays with his hair
(plays with ass)—
Being seduced.
"Guerilla Cocaine."

Dream Nov. 18—

Knocked on door after long trip, there was antique Van Doren[37] in his ancient family house—it had been built so that from front entrance to living room, where the now married girls come in with their friends from shopping, to the hall where he kept his machines and book papers, to the cubbyhole where he had his narrow crib, to the laundry room and up stairways there were several doors opening on courtyards and neighbors. One 18th century door was closed by Bamboo rattan, it led to a yard once perhaps coachman's workplace—now barred off tho it was once the formal house entrance—a former side entrance now served the street.

Mark was pleased to see me, he seemed older but not enfeebled—we

37. Mark Van Doren (1894–1972), poet and critic, taught and encouraged Ginsberg at Columbia University.

1965

talked about travels and politics, he flattered me in the dream by suggesting we sit down & I talk about my own early family life—I asked if he had a tape reorder, he said that was no great problem, he could get one sent from his friend Hayden or one of the other literary establishment folk families.

We lay down, Peter & I, in the crib bed, white sheeted & ourselves in white Indian pyjamas, Mark came in & lay beside us, all three stretched out for short while talking at the bottom of the former pigsty now turned into a neat old man's cradle bed—

The girls had come in & climbed up over the barred edges to look down into the well-bed; we got up to talk to them—

I went off into 17th century portion of house, where I saw a table of horsemeat on the bluff overlooking Hudson's Bay horizon where horsemeat lay stretched out & stripped on tables, cut fine to pink ribbons of flesh in a bone "to supplement the exclusive diet of reindeer horns." I see this was the reason for horsemeat. I picked up a small piece of liver bright fresh live blood-flesh, and put it in my mouth, ugh, & then walked off looking for a place to spit it out & drop the handful in my palm to garbage—went from one old door to another, Dutch maids (from Vermeer) were in the courtyards, finally I spit one glob out on a patio where a lady was doing laundry, hoping she wouldn't notice.

Returning thru the house, I wondered if Van Doren had found a sense of life—nihilist or?—well it seemed the first primary sense I glimpsed each time I come in without thinking—to eat, to sleep, to live to preserve one's family existence, the first thing in the morning to look to nourishment, the original sense one would have without preoccupation with alternatives—to keep going the raw life given.

I had also taken a trip into the city (Liverpool) with his girls—we'd stood on the granite apron of a municipal trolly building—saw there a handsome man whom I approached—laid my hand on his crotch—he laughed, white faced & long haired, a remarkable young stranger or for-

1965

eigner on the street—taken out his prick and looked at its head which had a serpent forked tongue coming out the front, and put it away.

Monopolies of masscommunication should be in public hands.

November 20, 1965

Prajnaparamita week—a mere nothingness of all phenomena—
    as an echo
    as a magic show
    as a movie on a screen
    as a 3.D. TV appearance
    as the filter of sunlight on moonlight on ripples
    as a wave
    as a long dream
    as a rainbow seen and unseen
    as a theater play which ends at midnight
    as a city you visit which has vanished away
    as a body
    as a long lifetime
    as the seasonary lovemaking and business
    as an old man looking back on his youthtime
    as an old woman lying on a hospital deathbed
    as a black splat of Doomsrack instant
    as when the image fades and the toe goes
        white then black,
As an explosion of total consciousness becomes
        mercurial microbiotic
as the living cells swam in the aether,

1965

as the black dark crack in the door opens
      and the police enter
as the police bang on the door and talk
      dirty rudely
as the shit explodes in the brain,
as it ends in a blast of chicken
      cooking on the stove
as time passes and the blast builds up on
      the kitchen table
as the atmosphere sizzles and crackles
      in the head
 as the Worst happens and an awful Blast of
      Snake Demon enters
as the man with a knife at your throat (in the park)
      turns to the [?] God
As I do not know where I am going, who I am,
as the transient dream takes on a white
      cat
As things change, and the Newspapers and
      police and image on TV becomes more
      evident
Or one by one the Serapho in their
      skin blood eyeball bodies
Face a universe and universe collide in a
      a car wreck
As anxiety trawls thru the marijuana
      Network, and liver fries
Kidney's pain, and Leroi Jones' scowl appears
      in the Western Page,
As there is wars Communism entered to
      America
As response kindles response, a Comerado!

1965

Johnson and McNamara and Rusk pursuing
     an old mistake,
Their faces in the Universe bare, themselves
     in the Valley of the Shadow in
the White House and pentagon—as a
     young man burned below the mind
Leader's window and the Mind leader didn't
     see.
occupied spouting off to the Newspapermen,
     or explaining
As Peter sneezes, in bed all day with
     a cold—
As the worry gnaws at my vitals and
     I cook potatoes high,
Should I phone my lawyer as I can
     Baez[38] was limited in her peaceful school
To 3 days a week and only Non Violence
     the subject—excluding Song?
From matter to Aether round—every
     sentient being in the aethereal game,
But what does the moment of change Be Seen?—
another Firecracker and things turn dizzy
     & transcendental—

Carmel Valley[39]

Yellow grass on a hill
     blue mountain ranges, blue sky,

38. Folksinger Joan Baez.
39. First draft of "Carmel Valley," *Collected Poems,* 381.

1965

bright reservoir & road below, tiny cars—
The wing trees green sigh of the wind
   rises and falls
 Buddha, Christ, fissiparous
   Tendencies,
 White sun rays piercing my eyeglasses—
The grey bark animal arms,
   skin peeling,
 fingers pointing, twigs trembling,
  green thin plates bobbing
   sprouted from knotted branches—
No one will have to announce the New Age—
No special name, no Unique day,
  no Crier by Method or
   Herald of Snakey Unknown,
No Messiah necessary but the Country and ourselves
   fifty years old—
Allah this tree, Eternity this Space Age:
Teenagers walking thru Times Sq. neon and metal
 look up at blue planets thru buildingtops,
Old men lay out on grass afternoons,
 old Walnut stands above them, ants
   crawl on the page,
 the mountain hide is covered with green skin
  and invisible singing insects,
   birds flap out, man will relax
and sit on a hill remembering his tree friends.

Dream, Nov. 23, 1965 (8 p.m.)

 The cat eats worms, I threw a worm to the kitty cat who picked it up,
so then I gave the cat a hard-shelled worm. The cat couldn't eat the tough
worm, so I skinned the worm by pushing the soft pulp thru the grey tu-

bular integument with my forefingers. It came out in halfs. So the cat tried to lick up one half and couldn't get it in his mouth, it was too active & slippery on the carpet. An old cat came along and watched the halfed worm slipping around on the grassy rug; watched noted to beat its head over the tiny segments. Old cat licked up both halves and the dream scene—one of many this afternoon—ended.

The boy in the serpent suit howling late in the
Spotlight microphone,
The bong of vast bass vibration in the theater belly
       "on your own"
—the parallel white lines of harmonica whistling—
      end of history

    Continuation of a Long Poem on "These States"[40]

Stage-lit streets
    Downtown Frisco whizzing by, buildings ranked
    below the Freeway balcony
Bright neon Johnny Walker
        signs like Christmastrees
And Christmas
    and its eves
        in the midst of the same deep wood
    as every sad Christmas before
      surrounded
        by forests of stars—
Metal columns, smoke pouring out of them cloud-ward,

40. Transcription of the auto poesy, with initial line breaks, that became "Continuation of a Long Poem of These States," *Collected Poems,* 383.

1965

on the yellow-lamped horizon
the warplant moves, tiny
planes lying in Avionic fields—
Meanwhile the Working Girls sort mail into the red slot
rivers of newsprint to Vietnam soldiers
the Infantry Journal, Kanackee
Social Register, Wichita Star
And Postoffice on Christmas the same brown place
Mailhandlers with black fingers
dusty mail bags filled
it was 1948 N.Y. Eighth Avenue
or when Peter drove the Mailtruck 1955
from Rincon Annex—
Bright lights flash in the windshield,
adrenaline shiver in shoulders
and around the curve
Crawling a long truck
3 bright green lights on its forehead
passing Bayshore under Coast Range jewel-lit hills
one lone light an architect's house on top
of the crest
.....................Radio negro voices rejoice
Sticks of tea in the moonlight
Moss Landing Power Plant
shooting its canon
of smoke across the highway
Red taillights speeding
the white line a mile on
Orion's muzzle
raised up
to the center of Heaven.

December 18, 1965

1965

December 23, 1965—Thursday—12 p.m.–3 p.m.
Fragments from LSD Tape

To Jenkins—"You seem more alert today Jenkins because of the
                Paramecium"   "The tape machine is harmful?"
                "Because of the edge of the tunnel."
                "In what sense?"   "Sun."
The mossy rockface . . . many colors of green & yellow
                tendrils of vines . . . reddish brown
                velvet moss.
The brightness of the sun . . . all the little twinkling
                branches
at the end of the path trembling I the wind, &
the gurgling of the stream . . .
                                    weeds in the surface
brown ground like animal hair—Camel hair weeds—

tender little green creepers crawling up a tree
all the trees looking like St. Francis in Ecstasy—
Snaky Reptilian Dinosaur tracks in the mud—
Reptilian snakiness of changing tune—Shakti personalized.
How did Shakti get personalized? When I
                began touching myself.

Blue Snout tip of ocean thru the rock path
as Basho said, if you're going to record, record
                completely.
Consciousness . . . recording Consciousness leads to
                Indigestion . . . oh then's the
                great indigestible ocean—
God it's beautiful here now—a few birds flutter

1965

down the path—a robin?—here you
are little birdy.

The lip of the ocean . . . the white woods-womans raising its
skirts high
Let's see your eyes [?] What's the difference your
eyes on the back of your head?

Big bird standing there underneath the ocean,
watching the tide on a little spit
of sandbeach under a big rock past which
freshwater roils to the sea thru a sandy
bed on the beach
scattered tides from the ocean
With their little heep heads before
& [?] and long tails lying around like
Paramecium from the ocean—
oh there's Steven perching & looking in
his solitude shining & smiling—Hello Steven!
Shining silver in shining silver—
birds perching
where the tide has left its mark . . . Chasing each other—
oh! all the titanicness of the ocean roiling in under now
that shine of brilliant blue heaven
with its bright yellow diamond-ball
burning in the middle of it cousins all
—white tendrils in my eyeglasses
because I can't look directly into it
but its brilliance shines all over on the ocean
like wave upon wave upon wave upon wave
of diamond beings all over the ocean
way behind the rocks
and wave upon wave of rocks, with

1965

the ocean breaking upon rocks but

thru it all the

shining diamond brilliance of light

—just the light from the sun here on

the planet shore

like a beautiful rainbow

This existence for which we are fit—

any other?

Aha—can another existence hear me?

Come in other existence, come in!

(whistling & reverberations of the machine

feedback whistles—beep beep beep)

Roar: That's the ocean you're hearing I guess—

Supernatural fuzz, agent of the square powers

the sea has washed it all away in one day, washed

all their bullets away—

the sand has filled up all the sea caves that were here—

& the sea will come back & wash it off again,

take it back into the sea

We can walk along the cliffs dash up

upon these big hard scabrous rocks—

red overgrown with tendrils & sea

help drink in the

crevasses of the rock

& listen to the sea-ocean sound—

Oh! there's a fresh spring rolling down the cliffs,

[?], turning it all rusty—

& there's a wave that washed over a tooth jagged pile of

Rock in afternoon sunlight—

Innumerable shells

The crack of the roar

1965

Dec 27, 1965—Auto Poesy on Hollywood Freeway[41]

    —   Wow it's pretty!

On the Hollywood Freeway again

                teepee structure on toppa Capital's

                    Circular building

    all aglitter, lights in smog white blinking,

    atop the building, church spires,

                one aeroplane—Thru Echo Park—

The palm tree stubs thin high standing over the Superhighway

    Against the dim-built mist-illuminated night sky:

              6:12 pm w/John Fles

ah it's a funny sense of Speed you get

    slippin & slidin around in the freeway in a big machine

w/others racing by you like insects skittering forward in water

              no place to get yr feet down—

Back to Worlds Fair 1930 when you look down in the Future—

    to see the same cars gliding tiny almost microscopic on the

        Child's toy white-painted wooden plaster

        Freeways of futurity—

Science Fiction sensation of being high & rolling along

    In the Supercity—

    . . . How do you know he's an FBI Stoolpigeon?

                    *   *   *

Entering La Cienega Blvd.

To see if Jess's Show is on—

Frame Shop w/all the gilt frames in the brilliant lit

                        window

41. Unpublished auto poesy, originally part of *Fall of America* sequence.

1965

in Art Gallery:
>   a chair by Robert Krim—
>   Tu restes loi?
>   Some artificial flowers,
>   Tacked w/wire to the antenna of a Car
>   What kinda fruit is that?
>   an imaginary fruit.
>   "all yr hip art Galleries are Closed on Monday night"—
The hills in the background w/a few tiny lights—
>   and a searchlight piercing the Smog
>   "Make an artist happy this Xmas"
How like heaven, the evening—
>   To walk on La Cienega, in and out of the art Galleries
>   It must be the grass
>   Smooth bright green in the green light,
>   The trimmed hedges looking like the borders of Blake's
>   rivers in Eden
—off the Strip in Barney's Beanery
>   "haven't been in there in years it was an act of discipline" sd/Fles
>   Enchiladas & an old Pole—
>   "Remember the Jaggelonian University?"
& Jack Martin's charge was dropped
>   for possession of Kilos & changed to
>   uh—tax evasion.

December 28, 1965—Auto Poesy Freeway[42]

In the great Ark,
>   past trucks in the shiny red light of the rain,

42. Unpublished auto poesy.

1965

taking a side highway to Van Nuys
      "you're causing your own death"
                    —a green light,
go straight past the mailboxes as the light turns yellow
      The shining lights
          on the street casting their
       Pillars of radiance into the rainy asphalt.
A side street,
      A car turning,
         front window flashing w/Christmas lamp
         in the parlor
The radio marching forward
               To the Rock,
     the deep voic'd announcer
     a Clanging plane, Crossing a hill—
bright red lights
     strung on a trailer in a green garden—
inside the car sox hanging
      Julius looking out the side-window—bright headlights
      in the heavy rain
      blurring the windshield
         10:30 at night

December 28, 1965

      2 days after Christmas, and unseasonal rain
         Form sunset on . . .
Will we all be there for the great sunrise
standing at the top of the hill, all the city awake excited
      throngs in the streets shouting for joy?
         (Noel Sur La Terra!)

1965

*   *   *

Passing Wilshire Blvd. on the Ventura Freeway
   Dec 30, 1965,
The Beatles singing the Cold War end song . . .
   "Boy, those Beatles are cute Sight, aren't they tho?"

*   *   *

Late afternoon sun over Pacific,
   Low blue sky on Century Boulevard
     strung together into perspective in a cloud
     by telephone poles and wires.

For the teas
on your knees
if you please
for the teas
on your knees—

Not only Fate tells big lies
but Truth itself tells big lies,
   Truth tells big lies.

Side A. *Transcription from Tape Bixby Canyon LSD*
   Dec 18, 1966 [in Allen Ginsberg's hand 1965?]

  "The Animal Eye of the Wood"
& this great rock here, as I sit by the stream,
  this rock is—well,
  it's a great big rock I suppose,

1965

it's got snubnoses, & wrinkles & soft folds,
    very soft folds, this rock,
       and its nose is covered with moss—
      hollow eye staring out
    It's not alive?—Is it? Live enuf!?
    Hercules II it's got little sideburns, of
          primeval signs—
    It's even got a hairlock like a
         brown wreath & it's got
   a wreath of Laurel, or Primeval Fern
—and then on top of its head is a brown halo hair
          made outta branches
    Leaves arching over the great pie slice of blue sky,
—There's a big round pie-slice,
    I guess like a big orange, or grapefruit
      or even the end of a watermelon—
      can you hear me now?
I say can you hear me now, Kerouac
    what're you doing where you are
      are you drinking or something—
Look at me here walking along, stumbling at Me
    happy with
      a lill bitta morphine
        a littlebit of pot, in—
oh! This funny flower, it's a bush!
    It's so spikey, sticking up—oh oh
        Somebody burned it, poor thing—
    Nevermind, Nevermind,
    Somebody burned the poor bush,
Well, they'll be bushes burned & bushes burning till the
      voice comes out of em!

1965

Kerouac, all I can do is think like you, write like you,

please!

Pray for me, Jackie

Pray for thy

Communist hairy loss[43]

Oh! There's no way to cross the river!

We've been fucked—

Ain't no way to cross the river

without getting yr old insouls wet (repent)

Now What'll I do, Now what'll I do?

I can't Cross the River

Mr. Julie in your shoe,

Now what'll I do, Now what'll I do

Can't cross the river, Mr. Julie, in yr shoe,

Now what'll I do?

"   "   "

Can't cross the river in Mr. Julie's show, Can I?

Now what'll I do do do do do, Now what'll I do do do do do

Can't cross the river in Mr. Julie's show

Can't figure a way to cross the river

"

"

"

"

"

going to the ocean that means taking off your shoe—

taken off your shoes,

wading thru the cold stream bed,

Stop the recorder for Now!

43. Kerouac once referred to Ginsberg as a "hairy loss."

1965

O my you know what's happened I found the way to go across
　　　There's going to dazzle some I'm afraid Folks—
Jack Help me I'm going to try to cross on this leg—
　　　　　oop! No No No!
Ah! Carrying my recorder on my neck, making poison into it—
　　　　　well it'll be safe now
　　　　　But basically the main idea is not to
　　　　　　　　　fuck up the recorder,
　　　　　Just made, just made it, do you hear me?
　　　Heh heh! O God I got to the other side but
　　　　　　　Watch it, jump over the log—
Found a path after all!
　　and Gawd wouldn't you know but there's a little
　　　Serpent Creature in the path—
He is not exactly a serpent because he is too young yet—
　　　That's tell the truth an odd variety of a slug,
　　　　　　a long yellow slug—
　　　with antennae Trailing some sort of funny—shit trail
　　　　　　　　behind him
　　　as he moves over the tree—
　　oh it's a snail, a long beautiful Snail!
　　Withdraw antennae! Cause if you don't
　　　　　withdraw yr antennae
　　　　you might be attacked by strangers—
oh I wonder how's it feel to be, how's it feel to be
　　　　Caressed by the—ok ok goodbye
He's got a long thing looks like a prick, tell the truth,
　　　Looks like a big prick, only yellow,
It's got a prickhead—Ha! what kind of ass does he got?
　　He's got a little gangly striped membrane gleaming
　　　yellow & black
　　　(darker shade of yellow than his body)

1965

trailing the last part
  he's about 3 in., long & also
  from his neck is emerging
  a great string of something—
   would it be shit or would it be behind?
 or just Intestines coming out—
well, we won't know the answer to that one until we
    consult an expert!
    or stay there with him for the rest of his life,
  So we bid him farewell and hope he
   will stick his antennae out again
     to the rest of the Universe—

If we hadn't had to go back and find a path to
cross the stream, we would never have seen the snail,
moving along stretched out on the foot of the tree,

Now we're coming under the bridge, approaching
the ocean—gonna have to stop talking for awhile—
and d'ya hear that Road?
    (Mike near the ocean)

—

 Decibel Can you hear properly?

    * * * * *

So, what was interesting was that, here I am, walking along, in a moment
of time, noticing
all sorts of particularities of just one moment—well, not noticing them,
you could name them,
which I've been doing all along, but anyway I see them all with my *eye*, &
I can transfer them
into a word—

1965

but they're the same thing that you see or I see or anybody sees all
the time—
Here I am in this slightly
        Not very much altered
                State of being up all night—
And how significant it seems
        That the back of that tree is [?]
            . . . the tree itself is dead. . .

Ocean sound coming nearer
            rushashh, harsoull,
                    Kerouac's polyps,[44]
                        I'll dollop em up
        Seat at Big Sur, Agw,
                    Swish

                                        Silence

Tree lean yr spikey hair against the rock,
Sun/
      hawk/
            blue/
                hush!
                        Shh-pisher—
Pjam! Shahakerash a siphhoopoo—
    Sispa! S'ocea
            Tatam,
                Ka da kam
                Ka Jam

44. Kerouac tried to duplicate the sound of the ocean in a poem in *Big Sur*. Gins-
berg attempts to do the same in this poem.

1965

Aum!

Shazam!

Hish—Hush—Hrinkle—Die—

Owsh, Rise,

rear,

Curl,

Shore, Be,

Tree, Spring,

with bright leaves shielding the top—

Each tree a man! with a message—much as I—

Touch—

that was the touch of a little treebranch

That made that Krinkey sound—

Now 4 birds on the Path, 5 birds, &

rise up & scatter into the bushes around

7-8 others come,

& now they're flapping in the little bushie

and the butterfly's there—

and the taller woods & roads,

on the underbrush flaps.

the babes may walk—flaps & walks—

and now to explore

I want to see your little babies, Mr. Bird—

but don't be fraid—

I will not run upon them nor disturb—

I'll come unto thy copse—

and there I'll stand,

where all yr little birds have hidden

themselves in the Sand—

Who goes there? Is that the little birdie?

Is that the mother bird making noise?

to Disturb me?—

1965

Let's take my eye away from this [?]—
        where she has made her home—
I'll go, mother bird, I'll go,
        Thy Children are not revealed,
Tho are you, the FBI?
        or am I the FBI?
Now under the bridge
    "I stand and wait like a naked child
    Under the bridge my heart gone wild.
    I give my body to an old gas tank
    I scream at a fire on the riverbank."
And now we'll have the rushing of the mind.
    Now we'll see a slice of ocean between the bushes
   Light blue near the shore & deeper purple further out
        until she meets the clouds
            Streaked over the Horizon
rising upward in the hazy stream to pale the
   perfect blue of Nothing there at all!

Now the sands come forth upon the shore
      I'll smoke a Cigarette
and watch that rock. Wet all night,
  drying the top sitting out there,
At my feet,
     The light blue Pacific,
  fringed by a strip of sand
     As Caliban might've trod heavily
        as do I
The Cliff on the right,
    with a little tiny stairway from the distance
      & high up on the rise,
   A house, gables & peaks viewing

1965

More than it can see
   of the Pacific—
I can walk right out on the beach without
   one worry-shudder of disappointment
there's the Rocks there, for my tread
   over the tidepool—
and now another passage to negotiate—
  difficulty, difficulty, difficulty
There's the Kelp, that snaky brown
   Those tangled masses of
     tubing soft-voiced-millet-vegetable,
  brain-roots ganglion'd together,
     plenty hair & pubes, balls of Empty
  as the hollow of its long
    plankton-digesting stomach—
There it is all dead brown sticking its long
   tail into the streambed that pushes to
     the ocean,
   Twokling Slowlow—
How can I get across this ravine?
  I'll be ravaged & I'll be seaweed
   Before I get to the shore,
That I do not fall I do not fall,
   I better take my shoes off, Sir—
Sand'll be warm out there, I promise thee that—
So take your shoes off, like the Kelp
  And plunge into another Element—
   Listen to His Roar!
Is that my God? And there's the Seagulls
  Slurping, slibbling down the windies—
   Where he sits alone,
an old dried piece of seawash-polished branch-elbow,

1965

—can't compete with you for Jack with that—
But I can sit down & take off my shoes,

  quietly & calmly on the beach lichen
    mature middleaged man—
or a young sprite that's found its way very slowly—
the birds are big that sit on the Rock,
   & bounce up and down allow on the ocean
I'll turn ya off, Mr. Sound—
   And remove my leather covers for these Extremities—

(Hence Transcription is not complete but Fragments)

   —wet my feet tenderly, step on a
   large, wet-moss'd rock-skull
& then on top of an old car piece that Kerouac was scared of
    that fell down 20 years ago,
hot whatsa difference between an old car and a rock?

Well, we can hear a few frowshes
   So here's the real Sea—
. . . step over a kelp, and put our tender feet out
    in the sand
   & then climb up on this [?] Rock . . .
. . . 10:30 in the morning facing the Titanic beach
   Trackless except for a couple birds . . .
Hear'st thou the original Sound of the Pacifica—
   Ah what a beautiful day!
and there's that little freshwater river curving around the beach
   Coming straightforward under thus rock in the ocean
    Spreaden its goodies . . .

1965

Now we'll sing Aum properly—
  Now indeed I'll be the King of the ocean
    That I wish to be—
I'll be the envy of every ocean,
I'll be the envy of every owner of every ocean—
  Owners of oceans beware,
    I come claim my bounty!
Hear me, owners of oceans
  Hear me Emperors!
    . . . The *Chuang* doth say
"Wise men don't do nawthin at all."
  . . . while the ocean waves her waves
    right in front of my face . . .
I could do worse than sing!

There is nothing lost
There is nothing found
  in the ocean
There is nothing lost
There is nothing found
  in Samsara (or illusion)
Jack Kerouac, beloved,
we have been absent
from each other's eyes
for many years.
It is now over a year
since I have seen you in my
house when we took injections of DMT
together and I noted that
the Buffalos had a church also
because there was a great big stone that had been

1965

polished smooth & worn down
by the rubbing of buffalos' horns and shoulders on it
Centuries, Centuries.

Centuries of Buffalo, Centuries of White Cane
Centuries of waves on the shore,
Centuries of Man, Centuries of death,
Centuries of old age disease and decay

Now this is the way that you forget about the problem,
Get up on a rock & sing to the skeletons,
they will answer back no more,
      They will answer back no more,
Listen to echo on the oceanshore
        Listen waves as you did long long before,
Listen to my voice as you did once upon a time.
Listen to yourself reminded that you're here with me
Till Jack with me if you please sir yes dear Jack
Don't be mad, you big drunkard
well maybe you're not a drunkard, maybe I
misinterpreted your rolling on the floor & feeling Sad—
               feeling sad,
For the reason sir I realize also
but there is no Reason in the end—
As you said many times & why not be cheerful,
not to fear the pain because pain disappears,

Both for you & your mother
for me & my brother, Eugene[45] & Gaby be the same
as Louis or your departed soul father also, or Gerard

45. Ginsberg's brother, Eugene Brooks.

1965

so Gerard Blest on his deathbed
& yr father cursed me on his deathbed,
Then I'm accurs'd by your father—

Side B. December 18, 1965

Music   Horns and Helicopters stop thy woe
Soldiers over oceans safely go—
Rulers King & General be calm
God is here and we will know no harm,
None shall die but gain their victory
All souls shall come back to God & Me,
All of me shall someday belong to thee,
Father then give Blessing forgive me.

1965

At a peace rally in Central Park, March 26, 1966.
Photograph copyright Fred W. McDarrah/Getty Images.

1966

By the beginning of 1966, Ginsberg felt comfortable with his auto poesy. He would take his tape recorder with him anywhere; any hint of self-consciousness or hesitation had evaporated. His descriptive passages caught all sides of America, from its breathtaking natural beauty to the stifling pollution of its densely populated industrial zones, from urban sprawl to the airy openness of rural townships. His considerable curiosity pulled him into regional peculiarities, customs, people, conversations. The America he was discovering differed in myriad ways from what he saw every day in New York or what he experienced during his stopovers in the more cosmopolitan environs of San Francisco.

The war in Vietnam preoccupied him, whether he was hearing reports from news broadcasts on his camper's radio, reading about it in newspapers, or eavesdropping on conversations between soldiers on their way to boot camp. The evolution of the war angered him, while the mounting protests against the war offered him a glimmer of hope. He recorded some of his observations and feelings by hand in his journals, although the best of his eruptions could be heard in his auto poesy, in which he juxtaposed his pronouncements about the war with his reactions to what he was seeing on the road. "Wichita Vortex Sutra," a poem so vital that he published it in Planet News *rather than wait to include it in* The Fall of America, *was composed while he and Peter Orlovsky drove through Nebraska and Kansas and was a work in which he "undeclared" the war as an act of democracy in action.*

His writing from 1966 would rank among some of the finest work of his life.

January 11, 1966

I wonder if it's too
    late for spectres—

Vomiting at the deep tears
    voiced to cough.

hash, the Casbah January
    of Laurel Canyon
    downhill leaving in the
     little bus.

Streetlamps hang over the
    broad road
    down the trees

to the Level Avenue of
    outer Hollywood
    Sunset ahead

Sam Crash Fitzgerald
    or west car
and the palm trees there, neon
    blue windmill in the
     fine sooted dark
      3 AM—

alive flesh as I am too
    still scribbling, fleeting

from street to street after
    decade aged anew
      Mobil & Sahara Motel

Braking the blocks with
    bright movie

1966

Ford actors from
    the Palm Battlements of Jerusalem
    Power Castle of the
      Blessed Sacrament,
    Sacred at rest
    Palladium Lawrence Welk
      and his champagne music
        protected

3:51   Temp 45   bulb
    [?], the under
pass of tunnel concrete
    bridge flows below

toward the ocean
cottage next the sand
    beach huge

      the thin
    misty ocean—
Baked with yachts and
    acid takes,

oil derricks pumping
5 & 10
    between driveways

January 13, 1966

    Rug meat
    Blake Exhibit at Huntington—

1966

an illustration frontispiece of Wollstonecraft Book:
man at the center of the animal kingdom.

Prajna Paramita

NOTHING

IS.

Chances "R"[1]

Red glow on the tables,
spider chandeliers,
  Nymph and shepherd raising electric tridents
       against the wall.
(Guardian spirits of antique meadow
   and warrior town)
the jukebox beating out the magic syllables
a line of painted boys snapping fingers
  and shaking their Italian legs,
   or rough dungarees on big asses
     bumping & dipping
ritually, with no religion but the
  old one of Cocksuckers,
naturally, in Wichita Center of America
  the farmboys in the Diabolic bar light

1. First journal notation of auto poesy that became "Chances 'R,'" *Collected Poems,* 401.

1966

alone and stir necked or lined up dancing
    row on row like afric husbands

    music's sad here, where at the
Sunset Trip or Jukebox Corner it's
      ecstatic among pinball
              machines—
religiously, with concentration &
    free prayer, fairy boys of
            the plains
and their gay sisters of the city
step backward toward the bottled tables,
forward to the center of the concrete floor,
      illumined by machine eyes,
        screaming negro drumbeats,
      passionate voices of Oklahoma City
        chanting No Satisfaction[2]
Suspended from Heaven, the Chances
    R Club floats in solid space
rayed with stars on the streets of
a Kansas City traversed with street
              on the plain.

Party at 637 Hydraulic St.,
are all the other people in town
    aware that they're
    in Wichita too—
Pitch a Wichita fit, eh? Luke?

---

2. "(I Can't Get No) Satisfaction," by the Rolling Stones.

1966

Riding on Highway 77, a picnic afternoon
 My face a smile, my face is the sky

They are!—I'm excited and scared and same time annoyed at them & want to make a stink & yell, just to be contrary and confuse them [?] the chaos— Help! Police!—as if I don't recognize their authority—they hadn't even identified themselves—[?] walked up in plainclothes & grabbed all passersby including me.

Other night I saw Neal and we kissed and held each other in dream.

Wichita
 "people hang themselves
 From turnpike bridges"

—Let's go tilt the house over

"Texas Tech"—the most churches per capita
      Texas

Feb. 9, 1966

Dream

Wichita Dream

 Help! Police!

1966

I am walking in shirt sleeves on summer nite up a city center hill—Montmarte, La Rampa, Nob Hill, Grant Ave., Morningside heights—Crowded Saturday nite house folk out for a stroll to where the action is, nite clubs or Writer's Union—coming up by big old fashioned Kaffrican 19th century urned wall to the Bankers Club. I notice there are paddy wagons waiting at the curb and a commotion only a few steps up ahead in the crowd—cops in uniform separating people out of the crowded sidewalk like cowboys singling out cattle from the herd—I walk up into the melee to see what's happening suddenly two citizens in hats—I am passing by turn and grab me too—I'm surprised but I expected it even put myself up there to see if they were just arbitrarily arresting everyone in sight—yup!

To Nebraska[3]

Across the Big Blue River
Enter Beatrice—
Chanting la Dllaba
El Ab Allah Who
Chin abreast the Allah
    revolving in my head
    like my mother
Eyes closed, in the blackness
               prairies,
Nebraska of Solitary Allah,
      Joy, I am I,
The lone one singing of
            myself

3. Ginsberg journal transcription of auto poesy. This work, actually a portion of the first part of "Wichita Vortex Sutra," was entered here in the journal and given a separate title.

1966

God came true—
Thrills of fear,
nearer than the vein in
    my neck—
What if I opened my soul to my   \
    absolute Self
Singing as the car crash
   clamped thru blood &
    muscle tendon skull?
What if I sang, and loosed the
   chords of fear brow?
What exquisite voice wd
   shiver my car companions?
I am the Universe tonite,
    riding in all my power riding
Chauffered thru the Universe
  by a long haired saint

  What if I sang so that all
    knew I was free
  of Vietnam, trousers,
  free of my own meat,
  free to die in my
  thoughtful shivering
   throne?
Freer than Nebraska,
  freer than America,
  freer than my own self,
  may I disappear
  in magic smoke of Joy
Pouf! reddish vapors

1966

Faustus vanishing
weeping & laughing
Under the stars of Highway
77 between
Beatrice & Lincoln—
"Better not to move but let
things be"
revered Preacher!
We've already disappeared!
Whoops! Passing a truck
head backward on the
right hand lane, lights ahead
Kings Crown a road sign,
neon behind trees
was Afric Village
thru the jungle wall—
highways open,
entering Lincoln's ear
ground to a stop as the tracks
warning—
Pioneer Boulevard—
William Jennings Bryan
sang
Thou shalt not crucify mankind
upon a Cross of Gold!
O Baby Doe! Gold's
Department Store
Castle hulk's at NY 10th St. now
an unregenerate old fop
who didn't want to be a
monkey

1966

Now's the highest perfect
       western dust
and Lincoln's cry
  survives compassionate
  in the H.S. anthologies—
a giant dormitory brilliant
   on the evening plain
  drifts with his memories
    gauzy veils of smoke
  around the Christmas lights
  of a [?] aluminum
white tanks squat beneath

sinking signal towers
bright-lit white bulbs and
  flares of orange
      gas flame
underneath the pillows of smoke
  in the midst of machinery
transparent towers in the dusk

In advance of the Cold Wave
snow is spreading eastward to
        the Great Lakes
News broadcasts & old clarinets
  on the car radio speeding across
   the railroad tracks
There's a nice white door
  over there for me
O dear! On Zero Street.

1966

—psychedelic Liberation Front
—False City Meats

   vindictive

February 15, 1966

Auto poesy to Nebraska
   transcribed from tape

Turn right next corner[4]
the biggest little town in Kansas
    MacPherson
the red sun setting streaked
  along the flat plains west
blue lights along the highway curve ahead,
Lighted dome on the first plains—

Kansas! Kansas! Shuddering
   at last!
      Person appearing in Kansas
Angry telephone calls to the University,
Police dumbfounded at the hoods
        of their cars
while poets sing to Allah in
   the Roadhouse Showboat!

4. Ginsberg transcription of auto poesy that became "Wichita Vortex Sutra," *Collected Poems*, 402–26.

1966

Blue eyed children dance and hold
   thy hand O aged Walt
who came from Lawrence to Topeka
  to envision from iron interlaced
  above the city plain—
Telegraph wires strung from city to city along
   the lonely rill, O Melville!
                  Television brightening thy rills
                      of Kansas home
I come,
       a lone man from the void, riding in a bus
           hypnotized by the red tail lights in the straight
                   space road ahead—
The Methodist Minister with cracked eyes
              leaning over the table
        quoting Kierkegaard, a million dollars in the bank!
        owns all West Wichita
            come to Nothing!
     Prajna Paramita Sutra over coffee—
Vortex of telephone newspaper aircraft nightclub:
Newspaper streets illuminated by Bright Emptiness—
        Thy sins are forgiven, Wichita!
Thy lonesomeness annulled, O Kansas dear!
           As the western twang has prophesied
   thru the banjo when the lone cowboy walked up the
                 railroad track
     past the empty station toward Square Canyon where
              the sun sank
        Westward: giant bulbed at the other side—
Music on his back,
        and empty handing   singing on this planet earth
               I'm a lonely dog, O Mother!

1966

Come Nebraska, sing & dance with me—
Come lovers of Lincoln & Omaha,

    hear my soft voice at last!
  as babes need the chemical touch of fresh in pink infancy,
   lest they die idiot returning to the inhuman
        nothing—
So, tender lipt adolescent, pale youth, give me back my soft
          kiss,

  Hold me in your innocent arms
    accept my tears as yours to harvest
    equal in nature to the wheat

      that make your bodies
      muscular in their bones
     broad shouldered, boy bicept—
      from leaning on cows & drinking the milk
     of Midwest Solitude—
   No more fear of Tenderness, much delight in weeping,
          hmmm
     Ecstasy in Singing, laughter rises that confounds
     staring
       and strong politicians eyeing
      thy breast,
       O man of America, be born!
Truth breaks through!
  How big is the prick of the president?
How big is Cardinal Spellman?
   How little J. Edgar Hoover's, unmarried all these
         Years—
How big are all the public figures?
   What kind of hanging flesh have they? Hidden behind
       their images,

1966

approaching Salina,
prehistoric indian excavation,
apache uprising in the drive in theater
shelling bombing range mapped in the distance,
aluminum watertowers floating light over the town—
Crime Prevention Show sponsored
by Wrigley's Spearmint
flowing over the radio
Warden cackling about Possums, & Coondogs,
O Dinosaur ad, glowing green
South 9th Street lined with Poplar & Elm
spread over the evening's tiny headlights
Salina High School's exotic brick, darkened
over a lighted door—
What wreaths of naked bodies, thighs & faces,
small hairy bun'd vaginas,
silver cocks, armpits and breasts
moistened by tears
for 20 years, for 40 years,
Peking Review surveyed by Luden's coughdrops
attacks on the Russians & Japanese,
red radio tower lights on a wall
winking against the black stars,
Big Dipper leaning above the Nebraska border,
handle down to the blackened plains,
Ghosts of telephone poles crossed
along the roadside,
in the dim headlights—
Congressmen arguing over the radio
Capital Cloakroom
Running thru Cloud County
Just crossed the State Line!   Hot dog!

1966

How much is gas in Nebraska?
Dark night, & giant T-bone steaks,
　　and in the Village Voice
New Frontier Productions presents
　　Alan James's Camp Comedy: Fairies I have met.
Blue highway lights strung along the horizon east at Hebron
　　　　　　over the Blue River
　　toward Homestead National Monument
　　　　　　near Beatrice—
Language, Language,
　　a circle of black earth in the rear window,
　　　　　　　　no cars
　　　　　　for miles along the highway
and beacon lights on the oceanic plain—
Cars passing their messages along the country crossroads
　　　　　　headed west & eastward on the frosty dust
　　to populaces networked on flatness

Vortex Sutra
Face the Nation
Thru the brown plains/icy winter/grey sky/bare trees
　　　　　　　　lining the road
　　South to Wichita
　　　　　　you're in the Pepsi generation/Signum enroute
　　　　　　　　near Hickman's/rolling earth hills
Aiken Republican/on the radio into the country's ears
　　60,000 North Vietnam troops now infiltrated/but over
　　　　　　　　　　250,000
　　South Vietnamese/armed men
　　　　　　our Enemy
　　　　　　　Not Hanoi our Enemy

1966

Not China our Enemy
the Viet Cong!
"Bad Guess" chorused the reporters? McNamara's made a "Bad
Guess"
Yes, no more than a bad guess, in 1962
"8000 American troops handle the
situation"
Bad Guess
in 1956, 80% of the
Vietnamese people would've voted for Ho Chi Minh/
wrote Ike/years later/"Mandate for change"
A bad guess in the Pentagon
And the Hawks were guessing all along/Bomb China's 200,000,000
Cried Stennis from Missouri
I guess it was 3 weeks ago
Holmes Alexander in Albuquerque
Provincial newsman
said I guess we better begin to do that NOW.
his typewriter clacking in his aged office
on a side street/under Sandia Mountain
Half the world away from China
Johnson got some bad advice/Republican Aiken sang
to the newsmen over the radio
the general who guessed they'd stop infiltrating the South
if they bombed the North
so I guess they bombed!
pale Indochinese boys thronging thru the jungle in
increased numbers
to the scene of Terror!
While the triangle roofed Farmers Grain Elevator
sat quietly by the side of the road
along the railroad track—
American Eagle beating its wings over Asia

1966

Million dollar helicopters
 a billion dollars worth of marines
  who loved Aunt Betty
   drawn from the shores and farms shaking
 from the high schools to the landing barge
  blowing the air thru their cheeks with fear
   in Life on Television
Put it this way on the radio language
Put it this way in Television—language
     Use the words
     Language, language:
      "a bad guess"

put it this way in the headlines
 of Omaha World Herald—Rusk[5] says Toughness
  Essential for peace

 in the Lincoln Nebraska Morning Star—Vietnam
      War brings Prosperity
put it this way
 declared McNamara, speaking language
  asserted Maxwell Taylor[6]
  General, consultant in the White House:
Vietcong losses leveling up three five zero zero/per
      month
  Front page testimony February 1966
Here in Nebraska same as Kansas same known in Saigon
 in Peking, in Moscow, same known
  by the youths of Liverpool Three Five Zero
      Zero

5. Secretary of State Dean Rusk.
6. U.S. ambassador to South Vietnam.

1966

the latest quotation/in the human meat market—
Father I cannot tell a lie!
A black horse bends its head to the stubble
behind the silver stream winding thru the woods
by an antique red barn on the outskirts of Beatrice,
Quietness, quietness
over the countryside
except for unmistakable (voice) signals on
radio
followed by the honkytonk tinkle
of a city piano
to calm the nerves of taxpaying housewives of a
Sunday morn.
Has anyone looked in the eye of the dead?
U.S. Army recruiting service signs Career with a future?
Is anyone living to look/for future forgiveness?
Water hoses frozen on the street
a crowd gathered/to see a strange Happening in the
Garage
How red the flames on Sunday morning
in a quiet town!
Has anyone looked in the eyes of the wounded?
Have we seen but paper faces, Life Magazine?
Are screaming faces made of dots,
electric dots on television—
fuzzy decibels registering
the mammal voiced howl
from the outskirts of Saigon to the console model
picture tube
in Beatrice, in Hutchinson, in El Dorado
in historic Abilene
O inconsolable

1966

(Stop/and eat more flesh)

    "We will negotiate anywhere anytime"

        said the Giant president upside down

      Kansas City Times: 2/3/66 "Word reached U.S.

          authorities that Thailand's

leaders feared that in Honolulu Johnson might have tried to

                persuade South Vietnam's ruler

to ease their stand against negotiating with the Vietcong,

    American officials said these fears were groundless and

              Humphrey[7]

Was telling This so."   A.P. dispatch/the last week's

          paper is amnesia.

Three Five Zero Zero is numerals

      in the mind

    Headline language poetry, nine decades after

          Democratic Vistas[8]

    and the prophecy of the Good Grey Poet

        "fabled damned of Nations,

          Unless . . ."

    Language, language

      Three Five Zero Zero

Ezra Pound the Chinese written character for Truth

    refined as man standing by his word

    a word picture   forked creature

        man

    standing by a box with birds/flying out

      representing speech of the mouth

7. Vice President Hubert H. Humphrey.

8. Ginsberg used a quotation from Walt Whitman's "Democratic Vistas" (1871) as an epigraph to *The Fall of America*.

1966

Ham steak please waitress, in the warm café.
Different from a bad guess
     the war is language
       language abused
         for advertisement
      language used
     like magic for power on the planet
Black Magic Language
  formulas for reality—(Reality Formulas)
    Communism is a 9 letter word
       used by inferior magicians
with the wrong alchemical formula for transforming Earth
           into Gold

   Warlocks
   magicians operating in
     Mandrake
   handmaiden warlock terminology
     that never worked in 1956
  for grey domed Dulles,
      brooding over at State
  that never worked for Ike
    who knelt to take
    the magic wafer in his mouth
     from Dulles' hand
    inside the church in Washington
   Communion of bum magicians
     Congress of failures from Kansas & Missouri
      & New York
working with the wrong equations
Sorcerer's apprentices who lost control
  Of the simplest broomstick in the world:
    Language

1966

O Longhaired Magician come home and take care of your
stupid kid
before the deluge radiation floods your livingroom
your magic errandboys
just made a bad guess again
that's lasted a whole decade.
NBCBSUPAPINSLIFE
Time Mutual presents
World's Largest Camp Comedy:
Magic in Vietnam—
Reality turned inside out
changing its sex/in the mass media
for 30 days, a bedroom farce:
in the TV den
Flashing with pictures of Senate Foreign Relations
Committee Room
Generals' faces flashing on and off the screen
mouthing language
Secretary of State speaking nothing but language
McNamara declining to speak (language in public) Public
Language
the President talking Language,
Senators arguing about the Language,
Communism General Taylor limited arms/owls from
Pennsylvania
Clark's face questioning, Objectives
Dove's Apocalypse
Morse's[9] hairy ears
open end

9. Wayne Morse (1900–1974), an opponent of the Vietnam War, was a senator from Oregon.

1966

(Senator) Stennis orating in Mississippi
         100 million chinamen crowding
                into the polling booth
Clean shaven General Gavin's image imagining enclaves—
    tactical bombing the magic formula,
      a grey templed Symington[10]
Ancient Chinese Apothegn:
          Old in vain.
Hawks swooping thru the newspapers,
    Talons bare,
        wings spread in the giant updraft of hot air
      loosing their dry screech in the skies
          over the capitol
Napalm and black clouds emerging in newsprint
    from model villages in Mekong Delta—
      Flesh soft as a Kansas Girl's
        Ripped open in explosion of metal—
          Three Five Zero Zero
on the other side of the planet—
          caught in barbed wire, fire (ball)
            bullet shock, bayonet electricity,
            bomb blast terrific/in the
              skullbelly, throbbing
                meat, shrapnelled
while the American nation argues war:
    Conflicting language, language
        proliferating in the airwaves
    filling the farmhouse ear, filling
      the City Manager's head in his office at City Hall,

10. Stuart Symington (1901–1988), a senator from Missouri, was an outspoken critic of the war.

1966

the professor's head in his bed at midnite,
    the pupil's head at the movies
        blond haired, his heart/throbbing with desire
           for the girlish image bodied on the Screen:
        or smoking cigarettes
           and watching Captain Kangaroo
(Whitman's) that fabled damned of nations
             prophecy came true—
through the highway's straight
    dipping downward thru the low
        hills and rising
             narrow on the horizon
black cows/browse in the caked fields,
    ponds in the hollows lie frozen
            in quietness
& secret prestige of Dulles' family law-firm?
Here's Marysville—
    a black quiet railroad engine in the Children's Park,
             at rest—
and the track crossing
    with boxcars of Rock Island,
           Cotton Belt flatcars
           carrying autos west from Dallas,
    Delaware & Hudson gondolas filled with power stuff—
    a line of cars as far west as the eye can see
           carrying Battle Goods
             to cross the Rockies
    into the hands of rich longshoremen loading
        ships on the Pacific—
Oakland Army Terminal's lights
        illumined all night now—
A great crash of couplings,

1966

and the Giant American train

                moves on carrying its cushioned

                      load

      of Fear and metal doom—

Union Pacific, Norfolk and Western, linked together

                with the Hoosier Line,

    refreshed with conjunction of Pacific Fruit

                  refrigerator

      followed by passive Wabash,

            rolling behind

        all Erie carrying cargo in the rear,

Central Georgia's rust colored truck proclaiming

                the Right Way

    & the caboose with its harmless message:

          Safety is the rule, concluding

the awesome poem writ by the train

          across northern Kansas,

    land which gave Right of Way

        to the massing of metal meant for

                Explosion

        In Indochina—

Passing thru Waterville,

    Electronic Machinery in the bus humming with prophesy—

    Paper signs blowing in the cold wind,

      mid Sunday afternoon's silence

            in town

    under a frost-grey sky

          that covers the horizon—

that the rest of earth is unseen,

    the outer universe is invisible,

Unknown except thru

      Language

1966

Airprint

magic images

or prophesy of the secret/heart the same

in Waterville as Hanoi one human form:

bursts in Waterville

a woman screams equal in Hanoi—

On to Wichita to prophesy! O frightful Bard!

into the heart of the vortex

where anxiety rings

the University/with millionaire

Pressure,

lovely crank telephone voices, sighing in dread,

and students are awakened trembling in their beds

by dreams of a new truth warm as meat,

little girls suspecting their elders of murder,

committed by remote control machinery

boys with sexual bellies aroused,

chilled in the heart by the mailman

with a letter writ in black implacable

language

from an aging white haired general

Director of Selection for service in Deathwar,

in black language

writ by machine

O hopeless Fathers & teachers

in Hue do you know

the same woe too?

I'm an old man now, and a lonesome man in Kansas

but not afraid

to speak my lonesomeness in a car

because it's not only my lonesomeness

it's ours, all over America

1966

O tender fellows
      & Spoken Lonesomeness is a Prophesy,
in the moon 100 years ago or in
      the middle of Kansas now.
It's not the vast plains mute our mouths
    That fill at midnite with ecstatic language, O!
When our trembling bodies hold each other
    breast to breast/on a mattress—
Not the empty sky that hides
    the feeling from our faces,
(nor) our skirts & trousers that conceal
    the bodylove emanating in a glow
    of beloved skin,
      white smooth abdomen down to the hair
      between our legs,
It's not a God that bore us that forbid
    our Being, like a sunny rose
    all red with naked joy
    between our eyes & bellies, now—
Yes, all we do/is for this frightened Thing
      we all call love,
        and want, and lack—
Fear that we aren't the one whose body could be
    beloved of all the brides of Kansas City,
    Kissed all over by every boy of Wichita—
O but how many in their solitude weep aloud like me—
on the bridge over Republican River
    almost in tears to know
      how to speak the right language—
on the frosty broad road
    up on a hill between the highway embankments
    I search for the language

1966

that is also yours—

almost all our language has been

taxed by War.

Radio antennae high tension

wires ranging from Junction City across the plains—

Highway Cloverleaf sunk in vast meadow

lanes curving

past Abilene to Denver filled

with old heroes of Love—

To Wichita where McClure's mind

burst animal beauty

drunk, getting laid in/a car

(in a neon misted street)

15 years ago—

To Independence, where the old man's still alive

who loosed the bomb that slaved all human Consciousness

before you were born and made the body universe

a place of fear—

Now, speeding along the empty plain

No giant demon machine

visible on the horizon,

but tiny human trees and wooden homes at the edge of

the sky,

I claim my Birthright!—

Reborn forever as long as Man,

in Kansas or other Universe—Joy

reborn after the vast sadness of (the)

War Gods!

No house in the brown vastness to hear,

Imagining the throng of Selves

that make this nation one body of

prophesy

1966

                     language by Constitution as
                     Happiness!
I call all Powers of Imagination
  to my side in this auto to make prophesy all Lords
          of the human Kingdom Come,
To come Sacred Heart, my Christ acceptable, suffering
  Preserver, Harekrisna returning in the Age of Pain
    Covered with blood destroyer of Battlefield illusions
Million faced Tathagata, gone past suffering, Allah, the
                   Compassionate,
   Jaweh, Righteous one,
      all knowledge Princes of Earth-Man, all
         ancient Seraphim of Heavenly desires, devas, yogis
& Holymen I shall chant Come! Here to my lone presence—
into the vortex named Kansas—
  I lift my voice aloud,
  Make Mantra of American Language Now,
Here declare the end of War—
        Ancient Days! Illusion!—
And pronounce the human words
        Beginning my own Millennium!
Let the States tremble,
  Let the Nation weep,
    Let Congress legislate its own delight,
      Let the President execute his own desire—
This act done by my own voice,
         Nameless Mystery—
  published to my own senses, blissfully received
       by my own form,
    Approved with pleasure by my sensations
      Manifestations of my very thought
        accomplished in my own imagination

1966

All realms within my Consciousness fulfilled,
60 miles from Wichita near El Dorado,
                    the Golden One,
     in the chill earthly west
               houseless brown farmland plains rolling, heavenward
the midwinter afternoon (on mid afternoon February 20) on
     pure spring water gathered in one tower—
               where Florence is
                    set on a hill,
     Stop for tea and gas,
               Cars passing their messages along the Country
                              Crossroads
               headed west & eastward on the frosty dust
               populaces current-networked on Flatness,
                    giant white mist on Earth
and a Wichita Eagle-Beacon Headline
          "Kennedy Urges Cong Get Chair in Negotiations"
The war is Gone,
          Language emerging in the headlines,
               the right/magic
                    formula,
          The language that was known,
     in the back of the mind before, now in the black print
                    of daily Consciousness
Eagle News Services Saigon—Fanatic Vietcong Regulars
                    boxed in by troops
               of the U.S. Air Cavalry
                    Division
          braved hails of fire Saturday
          to counter attack the
                    Americans
     Headline surrounded Vietcong Charge into Fire Fight

1966

the suffering not yet ended
                    for others
        the last spasms of the dragon of pain
                        shoot thru the limbs
            a crackling around the eyeballs
            of a sensitive yellow boy by a muddy wall
continued from page one   area
            after the marines killed 256 Vietcong and Captured 31
            in a ten day operation "Harvest Moon" last December
                            Language Language
                                        Cong Death Toll
        had soared to one Zero Zero one in the First Air Cavalry
                Division's sector of
                    Language Language
                            Operation White Wing near Bong Son
        Some of the
                Language Language
                Communist
                    language language soldiers
        Charged so desperately they were struck with six or seven
                            bullets before they fell
Language Language High Velocity M-16
        Language language M60 Machine Guns
                Language Language in La Drang Valley
the terrain is rough and infested with leeches and scorpions
        (Cacodemon of reality writhing in mortal suffering)—
        (Language Language)
                (The war was over several hours ago!)
Oh! At last again!
The radio opens
        Blue invitations!
        Angelic (Bob) Dylan singing across the Nation

1966

"When all your children start to resent you,
    Won't you come see me, Queen Jane?"[11]
His youthful voice making glad
        the brown endless meadows,
His Tenderness penetrating Aether,
   Soft Prayers on the airwaves,
        Language Language and sweet music too,
   Even unto thee
      hairy grassed flatness!
   Even unto thee
     Thou Unknown Burns—
and now the voices of the Radios
   crying Population/World Hunger & Unhappy people/
     waiting for man to be born.
        O Man in America!
you certainly smell good,/the radio says
This place here is El Dorado, at last—past the mysterious
       Family of winking towers
   groupt around a quonset hut on a hillock—
    Feed storage or Military fear factory here?
  Future speeding on swift wheels
     straight to the heart of Wichita!
where winking lights of Hamburger & Skelley's Gas
     feed man and machine
& Kansas Electric Substation
    aluminum robot connects with thin antennae
    towers signaling
    everywhere here above the empty football
             field,
     at Sunday dusk

11. Bob Dylan's "Queen Jane Approximately."

1966

a solitary derrick pumps oil from the
unconscious
working night & day
near a huge golf course
edged by factory gas flares
where tired businessmen can come and
play—
Green lights of dusk on the highway
At the East Wichita turnoff
McConnell Airforce Base
nourishing the city—
Lights rising in the suburbs
Supermarket Texaco Brilliance Starred
over Kellogg/near the airfield
Chain of lamps/green jeweled traffic lights/
confronting the windshield,
the human nest collected, neon-lit,
and sunburst signed
for business as usual, except on the Lord's Day—
Redeemer Lutheran's three crosses lit on the lawn
reminder of our sins
Center town ganglion entered!
Crowds of autos moving in the driver's eyeball—
Titsworth offers insurance on Hydraulic
by De Voors Gard's mortuary for outmoded
bodies
of the human vehicle
which no Titsworth of insurance will
customize for resale—
Go home, traveler, to the Union Station, past
the Paper Language factory,
under the railroad bridge

1966

on Douglass
To the center of the Vortex, calmly home:
to Hotel Eaton: Carrie Nation began the war on Vietnam here
With an angry smashing axe
Attacking wine
Here fifty years ago, by her violence
began a vortex
of hatred that defoliated
the Mekong Delta—
Proud Wichita, Vain Wichita,
Cast the first stone!—
that murdered my mother[12]
before she died
of the Communist anticommunist
psychosis
in the madhouse
one decade long ago
complaining about wires of miscommunication
in her head
and phantom political voices in the air
besmirching her girlish character,
Many mother has suffered death and madness
in the vortex from Hydraulic
to the end of 17th—
Enough!
The war is over now—
Except for the souls
held prisoner in niggertown[13]

12. Naomi Ginsberg, an avowed Communist, spent a large portion of her adult life institutionalized for paranoid schizophrenia.

13. The black section of Wichita was known by this name.

1966

still pining for love of your tender white bodies O
                              Children of Wichita!

Auto Poesy

Feb. 1966   Bloomington to N.Y.C.[14]

Setting out East, Night, rain bright highway
                    Indianapolis, police cars speeding past;
                    by a gas station—stopped for matches
PLOWL of Silence,
          Lights flash all over the street—darkness!
          no gleam on the pavement,
                         POW, lights flash on again!
                    the gas station's alit,
ZAP, darkness, power failure on the highway
               hiss of rain,
                              the traffic lights lash—
Ho! Dimethyl Triptamine flashing circle vibrations
                    Spiked in the center—
                              Einsteinian Mandala,
               Spectrum colored and translucent,
                         . . . Television dots in treehouse at Ken Kesey's
Power failure inside the head,
          neural apparatus crackling—
So drift months later past
                    The tower and walls of Eli Lilly pharmaceuticals/outside
                                                            Indianapolis
                    Sleeping in the dark early morning

14. Transcription of auto poesy, with initial line breaks, of "Auto Poesy: On the
Lam from Bloomington," *Collected Poems*, 420.

1966

Street lights lit bumped along in the Main Street of Greenfield
News from Dallas, Dirksen[15] declareth
   "Vietnam protesters have forgotten the lessons of History"

Across the Ohio, at noon
      old wire bridge, automobile graveyards,
      The town of Washington covered with rust—hm—

March 3, 1966

   Air Force
News of the [?] Stadiums
      in Philadelphia
Steam over black factories,
March Sharp & Dome
      at Valley Forge
Waterfalls of light on
      concrete
Technicolor business suits
      gigantic on blue outdoor
                  screen
John Hancock's signature
      above a brick building
giant apartments yellow lit
      checkerboard hanging
         over a cliff—
Atlantic approaching—
      drumming in the earbone

   15. Everett Dirksen (1896–1969), a senator from Illinois, was the Republican
Minority Leader.

1966

       roar of radio
KIW all news
    all the time—
Buttressed by bright buildings
      the curved line shimmering
        at the shoulder
           under the wheel—
the shopping center in flames
    at this moment,
    ripped apart by tornado
"Vietcong terrorists struck
    twice today—
Communist terrorists
    bombed an oil barge
    in the harbor outside Saigon."—
McNamara's analysis
    "unsatisfaction" and
    "[?] ended"—
Johnson "may not agree but"
    "once that pledge is given,
    we support fully"
           shit!
Kali Ma, tongue hanging out,
    one hand raised in tranquility
hand with blood red [?]
    dancing on shiva in
    blissful dream
    on a bed of bone & skulls
Rama Krishna avatar,
    eyes half closed in ecstasy,
halfnaked Chelanya arms upraised
    singing & dancing His arm Praise

1966

Shivananda who touches the Breast
    & says Om—
Kali Padu whose yoga droppeth
    before the Void
Citarror
    who give up Desire
Dehorava Baba who moans
    oh how wounded how
      wounded
      who raises 2
     thumbs in tranquility
Khahi Baba, fat bellied mad
    with the dogs
Naked Selgot Shambr Dharti
    Baba covered with ash
    gesturing open hand
    in the burning ghat
            high on
            ganja
William Blake the Invisible, father of
              Visions—
& giant green gas tanks crowned
    with winking red

at Customs Pier
"Is that your own hair?"
    yes for 3 years
Barber won't make much on you
    Yes but he'll get a lot
      of advertisement.

1966

Bayonne Entering N.Y.C.[16]

Smog trucks mile after mile high wire
    Structure leading toward New York along
        black multilane highway's showered lights
        blue city-glare horizoning
            Megalopolis' burning factories.
Bayonne refineries,
    Newark Hell-Light behind,
    truck trains passing trans-continental gas-lines,
blinking safety signs Keep awake—
Giant Giant Giant transformers,
    & electricity Stacks glowing smoke—
More Chimney fires than all Kansas in a mile,
Network smell of Sulphur chemical Humble gigantic by the viaduct
    what smell burning rubber oil—
        "freshens your mouth"
    Railroad rust, deep marsh garbage-fume—
            Nostril horns.
City announced jabbering
    at City Motel,
        Airplanes rumbling overhead
    Flat winking space ships
            by Gorney Gorney Mortuary
    Brilliant Signs the
    10 PM clock Churchspire lit in Suburb City,
    New Jersey's colored streets asleep—
High derrick spotlites lamped an inch
            above city

16. Transcription, with initial line breaks, of auto poesy of "Bayonne Entering N.Y.C.," *Collected Poems*, 427–30.

1966

Shoprite lit for Nite people,
Vast Hohokus marshes and Passaic's flat gluey
                Blackness ringed with lightbulbs.
    Blue Newark airport, waiting for the Uruguayan Ambassador's body
        arrive
                    —green bulletshaped brain
            Plane, heart throbbing redlights midriff
                settling down—swift as shark—
    toward the 71 million 3 hundred 69
            Lights at the field edge,
Mysterious Robot group towers Blazon'd Eastern Air TWA
    above the Lavender bulbed runway
    "Police sat apparently had a heart attack"—
    Crossed barrage of car bridges—

I was born there in Newark,
    Public Service sign of the 'Twenties
            visible miles away
                thru grey smoke in grey nite,
My aunts and uncles died in hospitals,
            are buried in graves surrounded by Railroad Tracks,
    Tombed near Winking 3 Ring Ballentine Ale
    Where Western Electric has a Cosmic plant,
    & Pitt-Consoles breathes acrid fumes
            above Flying Service tanks
Where superhighway rises above Monsanto
    Pulaski Skyway hanging in air my childhood
    neighborhood with gigantic harbor stacks,
                            steam everywhere
    Blue Star busses skimming skyroads
    beside th' Antennae mazes
        brilliant by Canalside . . .

1966

Walt Disney Politics,

      a green beret, 20 years old in a week—

      That music approaching the Revolutionary Palisades

Empire State's orange shoulders lifted overhill—

New York City visible above the world

             2 Guys from War put tiger in yr Tank—

      Radio crawling with Rock youngsters,

                  Stop—Pay Toll.om

Blue Uniformed attendants rocking on their heels

             in green booths

   Let the hitchhiker off in the acrid Mist—

   light Parade everywhere,

          Motel Hotel

          Lincoln Tunnel

          Pittsburgh Shitsburg

          Seagram's a Sure One

Macdaniels Vast parkinglot—

cliff rooms, balconies & giant ancient schools,

reptilian trucks on approaches

          To Manhattan, thru Jersey City,

          City star-spread behind Palisades

lights reflected across Hudson

      on evening water—

brilliant diamond-lanterns heading into Tunnel

Road beneath river lit like a bright throated bathroom—

      over red brick, over red brick,

      Whizz of bus-trucks shimmer in Ear

Fluorescent lights, straight down now,

           under Queen Mary & Kammerer's[17] body

17. Ginsberg's friend David Kammerer was stabbed to death by Lucien Carr in what was called an "honor slaying" when Kammerer, a homosexual who had been stalking Carr, forced himself on Carr.

1966

Under Whitmanic Yawp Harbor Here
 roll into Man city, my city, Manhattan,
          Lower East Side
 Grimed with Heroin, shit black from Hudson towers
          on East River's rib—
 O McGraw Hill Stand'st thou still here
          o'er green Garver's[18] shade,
               & Huncke's[19] redeemed?
     under Sloanhouse cliffs—
 Green-hatted doormen awaken the eve
          in statuary-niched yellow Lobbies—
 under canyons toward zephyrous brightlit Empire State
          too small to be God—
 Lording it over Macy's in Seafood City
          by Grant Hotel—
 Ho Ho Turn right by the Blackman crosses the street
          lighting his cigarette, lone on the asphalt
               as the Lord in Nebraska—
 Banks & Drugs & Nedicks Lerner's—
          Farmer & Banker's Trust Orbachs—
               a black marbled Lobby w/Longchamps
 Down 5th Avenue, brrr—the irregular spine
          of streetlights—
 traffic signals all turn'd red at once,
     in silence wait to see your Home
     cemented asphalt, wire roof banked,
          canyoned & overbuilt churched with mortar,

18. Bill Garver was a friend of William S. Burroughs, Allen Ginsberg, Jack Kerouac, and others. A drug addict, he died in Mexico in 1957.

19. Herbert Huncke (1915–1996), a Times Square hustler, petty thief, drug addict, and, later, writer, was a model for some of the writings of Jack Kerouac, Allen Ginsberg, John Clellon Holmes, and others.

1966

morticed with art gas—
passing Ginsberg Machine Co.
& th' axehead Antique Flatiron
 building looming out of old photographs
 parked in the mind—
Cannastra's[20] 21st street dark lofts business
Tonite Naomi[21] your 18th street Westside
 is blocked by a bus,
Dusty[22] your 16th still stretches
 way down to Hudson perspective'd—
Dali in London, Joe Army yr. churches
 inky loom brownly in time
 How quiet Washington monument!
& Fairy youth turns his head
 to look down street
 crossing 5th Avenue under trafficlite,
 doorman playing w/poodledog
 in the brilliant-lit sidewalk No. 1.
but an old reporter w/brown leather briefcase
 by the shiny pillar'd apartment—
Gee it's a Miracle to be back on this street
 Where the strange guy w/a mustache
 stares in the windowshield
How lovely the Steak Sign! bleeps on & off
 beneath Woman's prison—
Sixth Avenue bus huge back window brightly lit

20. Bill Cannastra, friend of Ginsberg, Kerouac, and others and memorialized in several lines of "Howl," became known for his daring, sometimes reckless behavior. He was killed while trying to climb out the window of a moving subway car.
21. Naomi Ginsberg.
22. Dusty Moreland, an early girlfriend of Ginsberg.

1966

Ladies in kerchiefs lean backward,
    turn by Whelens
Past bus stop
    an old Beret familiar face nods to his girl
Humm, MacDougal I lived here,
    Humm perfect, there's an empty space
        by the bright-lit bookstore—
    Where I'll find my mail
      & Harmonium, new from Calcutta
Waiting I come back to New York & begin to Sing.

March 1966

March 3, 1966

Growing Old Again[23]

the delicate French girl juke box husky lament
Softens the air over checkered tablecloths
I haven't been in Kettle of Fish[24] a year
between my Moscows & Wichitas a lonesome moment
content to stare at Bodenheim and Gould I garish oil,
Phantoms I am not on the wall over the bar mirroring photos
of old habitues renowned a characteristic season for the lack
of Immortality, a bunch of provincial drunks, fucked up
D.T. unbearables or Mafia brothers in Law.
old charm of anonymity, phonograph memory playing again
familiar tune of bars infrequent visited much once

23. First journal notation of "Growing Old Again," *Collected Poems*, 431.
24. Greenwich Village bar popular among musicians, artists, writers, and poets.

1966

real hotspot with cops on the telephone & me drunk heart loved
some friend some memory image at the same table this
same prophecy spoke immortal then now come true I sit
decade hence blue jukebox dazed an Angel remembered to forget.

Tambourine in Grants dedicated to Sam Lieberman—
"I'm for everything, man, long as I don't work."

Triboro bridge seems like the proliferation of an insect.

Peter O—His flesh is absolute.

On June 14, Ginsberg testified before a hearing of the U.S. Senate Judicial Subcommittee
on Juvenile Delinquency in Washington, D.C. LSD was still legal in the United States, and
Ginsberg, an outspoken proponent of psychedelic drugs, was compiling one of the most
thorough private files about these drugs. When he appeared before the subcommittee, he
was armed with information, much of which he included in the following journal entries.

1966

Notes from Lindesmith's[25] Files

Manchester Guardian Weekly   Dec. 23, '65
    p. 11—by Geoff, Moorehouse
    refers to pro cannabis article
        Grey's Hospital Gazette
         June '65

Mrs. Wm. K. Vanderbilt   1914 Crusade
    For Boylan Act in NY State
"Auto Narcotics Committee"
Rufus King Chairman
    Criminal Law Committee on
        Narcotics of Amer. Bar Assn.
1919 Sup. Court upheld Harrison Act
1922 Behrnan Case
    condemned doctors
& was admin, by Prohibition Unit
        Drug Addicts USA
Duffy—Marja article
    NY Post   Jan. 7, 1958
"The Narcotics Bureau, issuing regulations advising physicians of their rights under the law, blithely ignored the 1925 High Court decision still relied on the drastic interpretation of the 1922 Lehrman decision."

Dr. Isador Chein—psych. Prof. NYU Research Center
        for Human Relations
Herbert H. Berger M.D.—Pres. NY Med. Society

25. Alfred Lindesmith, professor from Indiana University who invited Ginsberg to talk in 1966.

1966

Chairman

Committee on Alcoholism & Narcotics

of NY State Med. Society

1946   "So I called the NY office of the F B of Narcotics,
told them my problem (Jan. 16, 1958) and asked
their advice. I'll never forget the agent who got me on
the phone.

    'First thing, Doctor,' he said, 'don't give her
any narcotics—you'll be in trouble if you do. Hold
her there and we'll arrange to have her picked up.

    'If you give her drugs, you're pandering to addiction
and you could lose your license, Dr. Berger,' the man
snapped."

"Doctors are neglecting their duty and they know it. They wish me well.
But they're afraid. They don't want the Narcotics Bureau on their necks."

Alfred L. Tennyson, Gen. Consul.

Anslinger discusses Linden Decision Jan 17, 1958
on Russia

    "A doctor couldn't prescribe anything for an addict over there," he answered us. "They're death on that over there. Their system I couldn't [?]
at all. They're stricter and tougher with penalties than we are. At the U.N.
they march together with us shoulder to shoulder."

1955, 19% Fed. prisoners narco & marijuana

1966

Anslinger married Martha Denniston of Andrew
    Mellon's family
Mellon Secty Treas. 1921–1932
    (Harding, Coolidge & Hoover times)
1929—Asst. Commr. Prohibition
1930—Bootlegging Jurisdiction
    transferred to Justice Dept.
    Separate Treas. Dept. Narco Bureau
NY Times Sun. August 1, 1965
    by Seth S. King
    "According to these reports, the Burmese Army, cooperating with Chinese Communist forces, have been cutting the opium traffic that the groups have conducted into and out of Yunnan province and across Burma and Laos."

A.P.—Anslinger would continue to serve as U.S. Representative on the Commission of Narcotic Drugs of the Economic and Social Council of the U.N.

Washington Star Mon. April, 1963
    Giordano said that indications are Red China is producing dope as a "money crop and using it for foreign exchange as well as for whatever demoralizing effect it can have on the free world."

Lawrence Kolb
    Let's stop this narcotics hysteria
        Sat. Evening Post 229
            (July 28, 1956)
Reprinted in Juvenile Delinquency

1966

Hearings Senate Committee to investigate J.D., Judiciary Committee U.S. Senate 84th Congress

2'nd Session

Dec. 17 & 18, 1956

8 6525   U.S. Govt Printing Office 1957

Stevens—Make Dope Legal

Harper's Nov. 1952, p. 40

Anslinger & Oursier

The Murderers

1961

Farrar Strauss Cudahy, NY

p. 18: Much of the irrational juvenile violence and killing that has written a new chapter of shame and tragedy is traceable directly to this hemp intoxication. . .

As the marijuana situation grew worse, I knew action had to be taken to get proper control legislation passed. By 1937, under my direction, the Bureau launched two important steps: First, a legislative plan to seek from Congress a new law that would place marijuana and its distribution directly under federal control. Secondly, on radio and at major forums such as that presented annually by the New York Herald Tribune, I told the story of this evil weed of the fields and river beds and roadsides. I wrote articles for magazines; our agents gave hundreds of lectures to parents, educators, social and civic leaders. In network broadcasts I reported on the growing list of crimes, including murder and rape. I described the nature of marijuana and its close kinship to hashish. I continued to hammer at the facts.

I believe we did a thorough job, for the public was alerted, and the laws to protect them were passed both nationally and at the state level. We also brought under control the wild-growing marijuana in this country. Working with local authorities, we cleaned up hundreds of acres of marijuana seed and uprooted plants sprouting along the roadsides.

House Marijuana Hearings
   1937, page 24
Hearings before the Committee on Ways & Means
       U.S. House of Representatives
       75th Congress 1st Session
       April & May 1937
Taxation of Marijuana
Hearings before Subcommittee of the Committee
  U.S. Senate 75th Congress
  1st Session on
  N.R. 6906
  —p. 24 House Hearings
  Rep. John Dingall: "I am just wondering whether the marijuana addicts graduate into
    a heroin, an opium, or a cocaine user."
  Anslinger: "No, sir, I have not heard of a case of that kind. I think it is an entirely different
    class. The marijuana addict does not go in that direction."

Senate Hearing, p. 14–15:
Anslinger: "there is an entirely new class of people using marijuana. The opium user is around 35 to 40 years old. These users are 20 years old and know nothing of heroin or morphine."

Comments on Narcotics Drugs
Interim Report on the Joint Committee of the

1966

American Bar Assn.

　　and the

American Medical Association

　　on

　Narcotics Drugs

　　by

　Bureau of Narcotics

　　Wash., D.C.

　Supt. Of Documents Govt. Printing Office

p. 53　　Malachai L. Harney, Supt.

　Division of Narcotic Control

　　State of Illinois

"We are presently the victims of a Supreme Court majority which to me seems almost

Hysterical in its desire to suppress any freedom of action of law enforcement officers."

Anslinger: "We're winning the war against dope."

This Week Magazine　　April 16, 1961　　p. 11

"It's [?] that one addict makes four more, and four will make 16, a frightening progression."

Altogether the "44,906 addicts reported to the bureau from all over the U.S. in 1960"

Seattle Post Intelligencer　　May 22, 1938

How U.S. Caught Dr. Ratigan, Told Clinic Hipo's Paradise or Dream,

　　Addict *wrote* in diary

This revealing article in the traffic in narcotics by Thomas P. Ratigan, once a practicing Seattle physician, is based on material from the files of

1966

the Narcotics Bureau in Washington, D.C. and is released through the
Associated Press. Ratigan is serving a 7 year term, etc.

April 22, 66—
I

The same classic oxygen
    old Universe with its trumpets
        & phonographic reproductions
        5 years ahead

II

We had returned to someplace
      else in the universe
  all that we have to do
    (you) (seer) is to reverse
        The bags
I am Jewish
    like Joan Baez

I reached for my glasses across the table
  on my nose,
    a blur, the world changed irrevocably—
Alas!—Make the best of it!
    no regrets, don't look back
    to the last disappointment—

I am wearing the wrong pair of glasses—
Something wrong with all the universes at once—
the trouble will return,
Too much curiosity,

1966

nervous busy little rats
leaning back and relax
enjoy it
will reproduce the conditions
and interest with all possible universes
as long as there's curiosity—you rat!
You wanna go right back?—yes immediately—

II *[sic]*[26]

a family room, the record crooning
mellow against the wall,
high black balloons on the couch
ladies with chains about their
necks, golden jewelry—
getting into another old universe even the
De. Master of this chemistry.

III *[sic]*

The Chaplin [?]
a mustache of instruments!
Each breath closer,
the tapes,
balloons, breaths,
laboratories, rats,
preparations of metal,
reasonable goals
heading Uncontrollably

26. This should be III, but Ginsberg made a mistake. The same applies for the rest
of the poem.

1966

to—
a deep breath of 1937
    Equality of all
        Renunciation—
Language isn't possible!

IV *[sic]*

Marx Bros!
    the leap thru
        molecular cell structure!
    Touched at the thrilling
        Kingly mirror!—
Perfect! The contact high joke
        of addict breath—
the [?] against the wall, the
    wail of the Jewish [?]
        doctor Dentist!—
"Om!" Tapes take all the Joy out
        of it to write
    we have repeated ourselves
        over and over—
every possibility of "whew" has
        been repeated over
        over—
We have doubly intersected
        each possibility—
Twice over—each thing
        wrinkling and growing
        old Jewishly [?]
        "red sox on my feet
        md, next to you—

1966

The music can continue to
    the redoubling of
    impossibility—
    "You've had it, mate"—

    La la la, la la la,
    on I returned to that same
        place again.

Is the universe jewish
    That returns to itself again—

"Whatever it is it makes you feel that there's more
to existence than mammalian physiology—"
Joyful end—
    Such nice music!

      About the angry war.
  Nixon
The talking of a great party boss
a scientific grip of ashes.

      In a bar on Amsterdam Ave.[27]

The yellow lights of Budweiser signs over oaken bars,
"I've seen everything," said the bartender giving me change
    $10

27. First draft of "Uptown," *Collected Poems*, 432.

1966

as I stared at him amiably eyes under chair thru an obvious
    Adamic beard—
About the angry War.
  with young Montana musicians homeless in New York, teen age
curly hair themselves—so we sat at the antique booth &
    gossiped
of Madam Grady's Literary Salon a curious value on Central
    Park West—
"If I had my way I'd cut off your hair and send you to
    Viet Nam"—
"Bless you then," I replied to the hatted thin citizen
    leaving from bar to door
in the rain dark Amsterdam Avenue decades later—
"and if I couldn't do that I'd cut your throat" he
    snarled at the door,
and "Bless you sir" I added as he went to his fate in the
    rain, a dapper Irishman.

Washington, D.C.   April 10, 1966[28]

The plane bending over in the mist like a giant looking down
    from the Space Age Beanstalk.
Greenery, roads sped by cars, airports, white earthsmoke
    pouring past tiny driveways and flat green rivers—
National ahead, factories boxed below for War, Vami
    [?] & remove Disasters,
brown mud wet asphalt & the jet roars breaks scared on the
    Yellow bulbed runway, sneeze!

---

28. Unpublished auto poesy.

1966

Dream, May 2, 1966—D.C.

In the White House, Johnson's office, late at nite, everybody settling down to sleep, I get on a temporary couch there by the wall, several others are sleeping the same by oaken doors in large room, Johnson wandering about—unable to sleep—

Who're the others, Johnson's aides—I'm an aide, a visitor, a midget comes by and carries his tiny pallet and sticks it underneath my bed after clasping me around the waist with his tiny hardon bulging from his tuxedo pants—I stretch out in bed & fall out fatigued—later I wake the place is quiet—

Johnson's wandering thru the halls still in his suit—16-hour day nervousness said today's Sunday Supplement—I met him and say goodnight politely. I'm leaving, there's no reason for me to stay—

"Oh" he says standing huge by the door to Oval Room his office—"I'm lonesome here, stay overnight there's others here beside you, I like to have people stay overnight, there's others here beside you, I like to have people sleep over in emergency like this"—

"But I have no function here and no use to you"—

"Everybody's use to me" he says as I suspect him of hypnotism but calm my paranoia—"I want your sympathy here overnight. I need it."

"Well I'm sympathetic but ineffectual" I murmur politely—

"You'll see what effect you have"—he reasons & I say "Well in that case but are you sure I'm welcome?—"

"Everybody's welcome here by me from the lowliest beggar to McNamara—see all the beds?"

I settle down, trouble hearted, to sleep, wondering if I'm being corrupted by his elephantine charm politics—

Later in the dream walking down along riverbank—underneath high city walls like S.V.M. Paterson area, I find a way back across the river I never could find as a kid in earlier such dreams, at the top's a restaurant which I'd always thought was a factory, a sea food factory, but it's really

1966

with its cozy wooden tables a paella and chicken & $1 sausage spiced work-man's food place—I look down the terraced levels where tables are set & workmen nailing cans shut to the booming flooded river I'll have to cross over again to get back where I began.

A lady explains the menu to me, sitting at high table near the kitchen's counter—"try everything—not just the cheap $2 chicken from their menus posted on round pillars"—industrial architecture the pillars' iron support the roof. "I've found everything delicious"—

Ginsberg's pointed statements about drugs, whether offered to the Senate, given in inter-views, or voiced in demonstrations, made him a large target to drug enforcement officials eager for a high-profile arrest. Aware of this, Ginsberg was cautious about possessing drugs on his person.

One enterprising narcotics agent, Bruce Jensen—convinced that Ginsberg had to be dealing, as well as using, drugs—hatched a plan to entrap him: coerce an arrested drug user into framing Ginsberg. Jensen set his plan in motion after a jazz musician, Jack Martin, and one of Martin's friends were arrested for possession of marijuana in New York in 1965 (when Ginsberg was not even in New York). Jensen's proposal was simple: cooperate in set-ting up Ginsberg and he, Martin, could expect a light sentence; refuse and he would be prosecuted to the fullest extent of the law.

Rather than cooperate, Martin went public with Jensen's plan. Ginsberg was cleared but Martin and two others were tried and found guilty in April 1966. Ginsberg jotted down the following journal entry as a means of recapping the efforts against him, and he wrote an essay ("Who Are We?") to decry what he felt were police-state tactics used against pri-vate citizens. It would become one of his major obsessions in the following years.

1966

May 2

Capitol dome between New Jersey avenue hillock trees thru bus window front, rolling down the Negro neighborhood. Saw Joelson congressman: he read my letter from Narco Bureau acting commr. George Gaffney who officially denied that I was set up or that Martin ever used or asked by them to set me up—but confidentially claimed:

Martin offered to set me up, especially if sent to California to arrange a bust, & this offer was relayed thru his attorney.

Gaffney's letter also advised Joelson not to answer my letter because I would quote it out of context in the marijuana Newsletter.

Green tininess from the white stone steps of Lincoln's
       pillared temple
at the end of the water mirror mall—the white spike of
       Washington's obelisk
pointed upward into grey smoke drifting under grey clouds
       invisible whistle of jet
over Washington photo tourists playing with images myself
entrapped by Narco Bureau Congressmen's confidential
       letters cutting off all communication.

Fri.—Dream—out on a date in the Park, as once before, with nice lady who held me around & missed me & said I was handsome—in middle of dream I realized it was Mrs. Kennedy I was allowing myself to warm up to—We went down by cab toward my house as we had years ago in another unwritten half remembered dream—or writ, the dream of many apartments in Brooklyn & Lower East Side.

1966

Woke on dream in apartment of Ralph Ginzburg[29]—he had asked us (me and who?) to sign some trick xmas card appeal 3 views of the city in stereo, and he circulating that to subscribers to support his cause—later sitting on his penthouse floor I see that what the card ends as is mangled plug for Fact or Him, the pix torn in 3 and the art part defaced for some commercial gimmick reason—I get mad & scream "you masochist! You belong in jail—" and overturn the card table he's working at, he has a shit-eating grin & is laughing, explaining his foxiness & shabby trick as "Who cares?"—I wake.

On plane to N.Y.—

    Weep for the earth, scarred patched cancered in
afternoon sunlight.
    Red smoke pouring from tiny factories clinging to
Peninsula'd Baltimore—
    Smokestacks spiked myriad by green canals, patches of
wood surviving
    like mangy fur on reddish dogskin of the planet.
    Rows of houses parked arithmetic in their limits,
warships cuddled in hundreds side by side inland at drydocks—
    Zones of city traffic triangle near cloverland and
footfate oval green
    Man's earth in greyish vapor, thru layer of gas
shielding the cities,
    and pure blue sky lined above,
a higher horizon than earthman can see
except by roaring plane flight.

29. Ralph Ginzburg (1929–2006), editor and publisher, was known for his magazines *Eros* and *Avant Garde*.

1966

The crust of buildings Manhattan Wall to Empire spike
In smoke,
    Pulaski skyway to Newark
black toy'd over Kearney footways—home where I was born—

The Old Village Before I Die[30]

Entering Minettas, changed to soft yellow chrome, the bathroom
acrid as 22 years ago when blond Rimbaud friend wrote human-kindness
against human-kindness on the enamel urinal before I read
    Crane's match—
a drunken nite there, lesbians abounding in slacks, he bit
    someone's earlobe off,
and tore the gold ring from a drunkard's fairy flesh, vomited
    & wept
my first big drunken nite took place here under the beard of
    Joe Gould grey—
"a Professional bore" said another Genius, but as I was one
    and twenty or less,
new scene rayed eternal thru the caricatures of ancient
    comedians
framed over the checkertabled booths, first love struck my
    heart heavy
with prophecy of this moment I looked in the Urinal mirror
    returning decades
later same heavy at heart to see self bearded hairy bald with
    age
and soft music smoke gets in your eyes Michel show me the jail
from stereophonic new jukebox that once echoed you always

30. First draft of "The Old Village Before I Die," *Collected Poems*, 433.

1966

hurt the one you love as dear Joe
did know under portraits of Al Smith, Jimmy Walker, Jimmy
    Durante, Billy Rose.

1:46 p.m.   May 11, 1966

June 6—Sent Pour En Finir

Dylan writes better poetry than I did at his age, but he's a space age genius minstrel not just old library poet.

Because he moves his thoughts out through music he takes no thought for superficial logic but reads into his mind like a Rorschach blot. If his metaphors excite & mystify the Blake-oriented teenybopper mystic it also mystifies him too. He learns from his own prophecy.

----

8 June '66 N.Y. to Cleveland[31]

The roofs of Queens upside down,
giant wing tipped to factoried streets—
My eyes turn to TV flashlights in Capitol Hill committeerooms—
and back to the white floor cloud fringed to the horizon,
another world—Can I be tender enough to Impotent Senators?—
truthful to them selfs or my self, all the same sufferer—
roaring forward across the planet's surface—
    3100 feet high Wednesday afternoon—
High Congress coming—the Space Age Illumination—oooh! I
yawn sleeping on the plane!
               Columbus Airport[32]

31. Transcription of unpublished auto poesy.
32. First draft of "Cleveland Airport." See *Wait Till I'm Dead*, 82.

1966

at the white cafeteria counter, iced tea & a blue check,

a yellowhaired baby with long tresses kissing father's
    shaven cheek

as I stare thru plateglass with a roof of fluorescent
    lights reflected

out into the dark parknight, melancholy to sit here
    middleaged

with a worn sleeve & hair hand exposed, alone.

Planet Poetry
Planet Business News

Senate News

Droning on, the Commissioner of Narcotics
        Great Kennedy questioning from prefabricated horses—
   and the actor Doctor saved the Marines from sniffing
        dope ice creams
under the giant chandeliers, boxed by marble ono a red carpet
   rolled out for the Senators & Drug Addicts—
        realizing the impact of every young American
"aggressive steps"
   to bare arms not bare arms—
echoes thru Mutual, imprinted on our boys.

N.Y. to S.F.—June 15, 1966

Space Capsules

Inside the transparent capsule, woven shoes hanging on yr leg,
   Mr. Panama Hat.

To the Body[33]

Enthroned in plastic, shrouded in wool, crowned by diamonds, trans-
ported in aluminum, shoe'd in synthetic rubber, fed by asparagus, ear-

33. First draft of "To the Body," *Collected Poems*, 439.

1966

lull'd by electric rock, chemical roses acrid in the nose, observant of large-nostriled

 Air factories,

Kissed in every crack of the body by beloved grandmothers, adored by all animals, sheltered by stone buildings, sun fired so man woman child are tender Meat become consciously genital adorned with hair at crotch & brain, beard on lion and youth by

The shudder & blush of substance.

From a wooden building on a hill in San Francisco June in

 time

called 1966, salutations to self in every street heart

 everywhere:

Myself alone and trembling in my body open to your ears—

my own voice or yours issuing from throat or loudspeaker

the same familiar note of love—

Let this machine pass the message to my own soft belly in

 Warm Futurity—

I am lost here, I'll be lost later,

So I'll sing to myself again & again.

Hari to Hindus is principle of Vishnu the preserver who

Comes to rescue himself from Flood, Hydrogen bomb or host

Universes. Om is the name of the first sound in the Kosmos

 Come from the relaxed abdomen like a deep breathed sigh

Namo's an Indian word the Name for any God, and Shiva dancing

creates and destroys what Hari cherishes, all these words

 are brothers in one mantra

human feeling magic syllables, that's a prayer to us,

ourselves from our mouths.

 Hari om Namo Shiva.

1966

June 24, 1966

    "and me I nearly got busted,"
scratched Dylan from the central phonograph
in candlelight, a huge wolf-dog at rest on the waving carpet,
kitty playing under the table
"To be stuck inside a mobile"[34] a bud universe?
    the melancholy chant listened to by a room of ears,
bodies lying by the dog, [?] in the air, the eve
    of first playing Dylan's midnight blonde—
blest bodies in the kitchen playing guitar & tambourine,
the split in flesh man or woman—
    rocking the room with own table rhythm,
Same nite the big concert [?] Palace
    [?] Loving Spoonful, vegetable phonograph
under the Stadium lights, a grey boxvoiced megaphone hanging
    hundreds of feet in the air—
a party, a celebration, the blue boy retired to a room,
Flappers returned to Shiva,
O holy eve Let peace descend on all in the street by siren
    and wall or lone late pave,
    old queen in Stockton tunnel—
Harmonica, and a painted blue-eyed fad!
    goodnight—Wine?

34. "Stuck Inside of Mobile with the Memphis Blues Again," by Bob Dylan.

1966

Neruda Reading

Neruda sitting at table on the platform, chin on palm,
listening to English translations like listening to the
    XXth party manifesto
in giant halls isolated inside wallred Kremlin—
leaning on his hand, elbow on the bureaucratic wood, waiting
in large tortoiseshell glasses, in blue suit & white handker-
    chief breast—
repetitious tomatoes run like the blood of Stalinist children
    in cobbled Moscow—

Consulting I Ching[35]

that which pushes upward does not come back
"He led me in his Garden"
   tinkle of 20 yr. phonograph
"Death is a comin in"
    "and mocks my loss of liberty—"
one must see the Great Man
    Fear not it brings blessing
        No harm
   from the invisible world.
Perseverance;
   realms beyond
        in

35. First draft of "Consulting I Ching Smoking Pot Listening to the Fugs Sing
Blake," *Collected Poems*, 434.

1966

the deserted city
    which lies below consciousness.

                                    S.F. June 1966

The poor beggar feeds everybody.

    The fluffy waves
        bending their mouths top the Shore
    like millions of Poodles.

What kind of universe
    where the Sea is made of dogs?

July 6, 1966
    It's all a fairy story, Leaves!

July 8—The tender Central Mystery

Run over by a taxi on
    Fire Island
Another Car broken down at
    midnight—
a large asshole, liquid & sleeping
    due to his heavy drinking—

1966

Cocktail death—and the world's
    pleasure less
now he's under the Springs—How
    nice of him to have Gone
here to this nastiness—
Madness overcame the earth—&
Frank O'Hara[36] transformed
to a swollen doll of blue meat
    stitched together all over
        skin
& broken rib & leg, "Larry
you've been talking about me
    again
telling people I got up & went to the
    Cocktail Party
As if nothing ever happened."

So sing aloud to Alma Mater
& keep the scarlet in the van
for with her banner high
Rutgers' name will never die
on the banks of the old Raritan

on the banks of the old Raritan
where Rutgers evermore will stand
for has she not stood

36. Frank O'Hara (1926–1966) was a poet, art critic, and assistant curator at the
Museum of Modern Art in New York. He died on July 8, 1966, on Fire Island, after
being struck by a Jeep on the beach in the early morning hours.

1966

since the time of the flood
on the banks of the old Raritan.

I will go thru America, crying the name Harikrishna

All is love & love is knowledge

O what a bringdown
to end in the Grave.

Get back in your body
breathe in your belly begin to relax

No need to speak with Right and Wrong
    in Control—only God—
what we can be absolutely sure of
    is what we think
we can express that without fear of
    contradiction—or mistake
we can express our Subjectivity, certainly,

"Pathology-Centered" studies of LSD

Man's Self Image Conditioned by
the Media Images. These Conditioning images
are only words & pictures
Poet's opportunity is to dissolve these
images into their Constituent image dots

1966

& letters—& substitute other formulations
　　more visible for the Species.

"Problems associated w/Species survival"
"—Universe-directed Paranoia"

　　　　The Solemnity of the Falls

wet grass & weed at the
　　edge of the stone roar
　　　　rusty Iron fence
　　　　　　over grey mist Space
Louis[37] standing on the edge
　　Car parked in the dirt
　　　　　　driveway
to the electric house
　　like red brick Lowell

　　　　　　Berrigan's Poems

Tooting my flute on Duty—
Personal Memoir of Tulsa
Living with Chris
　　　　　　also from Sonnets
Neighborhoods of the Present

----

37. Louis Ginsberg, Allen's father.

1966

Desrosier's blue velvet sign
   The grey buttress of City Hall,
      Mansard library in rain
"Art is the handmaid of human good"—Corso
Charles A. Taylor Full Defense of Union

Nothing is here for tears, nothing to wail
or knock the beast
           —Kerouac's Grave

at Krishnamurti Lecture
   "Every action creates its own bondage"
—the baby cried, & the young mother
   put on her coat, calm faced,
      left the lecture hall
      on Consciousness
      so's not to Create a disturbance

Dylan turned on electric poetry unconscious

Hari Ram Hari Ram Ram Ram Hari Hari

Fort Madison, Iowa   22 July '66—

  All morning brooding
        the phantom rush of soldiers thru the train
           American Fighter comic books,
     Meher Baba, Where Am I?

1966

Trees standing upside down in the lush earth
      approaching the Mississippi
Green legs waving to the clouds
    seed pods ecstatic exposed to
      birds and rain, bursting
    heads drinking earth—
Unfold [?] stones like rag dolls and the
         Astral body stares with opal eyes—
All things living before my spectacles—

      The Mississippi at last, silver brown
a tiny powerboat,
      Cornfields ahead,
        The long iron bridge
and prefab houses sitting on a hump of trees—
"Oh, it's warring time again in the Army"—
What weapon has the lion
        but himself
What weapon has the lion
        but himself
He's got his tooth & his nail
       & his claw
He's got his smile & his snarl
       & his jaw
The lion's just a flower in bloom
Sitting in the mummy's tomb

Everything's so cheap today
I think I'll sing & dance & play

1966

High above Passaic Falls in Paterson, New Jersey.
Photograph by Jerry Benjamin. Courtesy of the Allen Ginsberg
Papers, Stanford University Archives and Special Collections.

IRON HORSE[38]

This is the creature I am!
　　　Sittin in little roomette Santa Fe train
　　　naked abed, bright afternoon sun light
　　　　　　leaking below closed window-blind
White hair at the chest, ridge
　　　　　　where curls an old Jewish lock
　　　Belly bulged outward, breathing as a baby.
　　　　　　　　　　an old appendix scar
　　　creased where the belt went
detumescent cannon on two balls soft pillowed
Soft stirring shoots thru breast to belly—
What romance planned by the body unconscious?
　　　　　　What can I shove up my ass?
　　　　　　　　Masturbation in America!
　　　little spasm delight the prick head
　　　　　　　　　getting bigger
　　　thumb and index finger slowly stroking
　　　　　　along cock sides, askew
　　　　　　　　cupp'd in hand
　　　Serpent-reptile prick head
　　　moving in and out of its meat-nest—
Turn and watch the landscape,
wave my baton
　　　at passing truckdriver?
Lay back on bunk and lift the shade a bit
　　　enjoy sun on my flagpole?
Ah, rest, relax, no fear

38. Transcription, with line breaks, of "Iron Horse" auto poesy. See *Collected Poems*, 440–64.

1966

look at the sphincter-spasm itself
>in a mirror
>of sound—
Awk—if you jerk—oh it feels so good
Oh if only somebody'd come in &
>Shove somm'en up that ass a mine—
Oh those two soldiers talking about Cambodia!
I wantem to come in and lay my head down\
>And shove it in and make me
Come like I'm coming now,
Come like I'm coming now,
>Come like I'm coming now—

Ahh—white drops fall,
millions of children—
Ah Santa Fe what can they do to prevent
the passengers from
soiling their
>small blankets with love?
Wipe up cream—what if
The Conductor knocked?
Go way, I'm—
I have to compose a poem
I have to write a financial report
I have to meditate myself
I have to
put on my pants—

just lie back look at the landscape
see a tree
& cross Ameriky
Compromised!

1966

among green Spinach fields!
Felt good for a minute, flesh came thru body
And the Sphincter-spasm spoke
    backwards to the soldiers in the observation car
        I'd hated their Cambodia gossip!
        but longed for in moment truth
           to punish my 40 lies—
Oh what a wretch I am!
    What monster in this metal box—
Hart Crane,
    Laughing Gas in the Dentist's Chair 1922 saw
                Seventh Heaven
    said the Nebraska scholar,
On thy train O Crane I had small death too.

Green valley-fields of California telephone-wired—
    Lover's State!
      Desire's State!
        Hollywood starry delight State!
    Rock jazz poesy State
        at the end of the land!
    where I lay me naked in a pullman coach—
D—
    Thy secrecy arrogance befits thee not
        Sweet Prince—
open yr ass to my mouth—
    a poem to thee!
        —my voice an overdramatic madman's
    murmuring to myself late afternoon drowze—
      going home,
        past cement robots,
gazing out on palmtrees with reptilian gaze

1966

All's negative O Edward Carpenter!
    As 'twere thy dainty Chinaman near Paris
        making crude remarks—
I'll jus liah hear like a nigger & moan my soul:
3 Sixty telephone wires strung across poles,
      Hedges of spinach
        hair combed,
    quite a bit of excitement coursing along city-edge
        plugged in to human ears
      Operators screaming at soldiers
        returned from Vietnam,
        murder marriage or orgasmic babe born
          bawling Daddy Come Home!
Train stop, yellow capp'd workmen
    roar at the engine with waterhoses,
I'll take a nap dream, last night
    Homer dog swallowed a furry mollusk—
      barking and gulping—the black sucker parasite
      ate belly & crawled up throat,
    pink mucus   flesh bubble
        half-retched from dog chest
I smoke too much I'll die of lung cancer
    eyes closed on sensory illusion dotted
      with wrinkled no-think moviescreens
      worms'll grow in eyeballs silently
      mosquitos will row in valley bay night—
Sausalito, certainly had your big prick there—
Yellow light laid over the planet
    over telegraph wires consciousness over you
      in every direction Knowing I am here
    as engine slowly throbs uphill—

1966

          Night darkling over Mojave desert,
Yellow planet-light disappearing, sounds westward,
      Soldiers asleep, rocking away from the War.
      Autolite headed toward dimmed sun.
Pew! Pew! Pew! cry the children
                    Pulling eachother's arms,
       What an earth to live on.
     Lights of the City, south,
        brightening a piece of the night—
and the diamond-green gleam of an airfield light—
      Hey! ya bit me, ya bit me,
         hello Missus Fight!
Green Green Green blinks the Diner sign
     where truckers roam
           in darkness toward Baratow.
     Stars we they were when I was a child,
          Mojave's firmament same—Passaic's—
 This space capsule softer than trees
       In the chemical landscape
         With electronic clicks.
And is Heaven any different from where we are?
How could it be better or worse?
     The delicate chemical brain changes
      Aethereal sensations
         Muladhara spincter thru mind aura
            Sahasrarapadome promise
              Another Universe—
Whitman, Carpenter, Gavin Arthur, saying
     We are leaves of the Tree,
            saying
 We are drops of water running to the ocean

1966

thru the fish's mouth—
And we shall stand in Flesh in Paradise
      with the Virgin of the 19th Century—

Borax, Borax, Borax,
    Crystal lights upon a hill, like faery castles
  Night be in Heaven, only Mojave—
        Borax, Borax, Borax
Borax the Dinosaur slounges thru
    fronds under Pleiades—
  Delicate filament of highway lights
    the nerves between cities—
Borax, Borax, Borax, Borax, Borax
   near Bel Mar Hotel desert
       —AUM
—my enemy this machine chatter jabber mind
    making Borax Borax Borax Borax
      the spinal column of all thought
  o'er turkeys, oil, wind, headlights—
A child peeps thru glass in moving night
where a red rail light keeps the time
     to the Santa Fe train
   rolling over Crane's gloom.

Ho! a Crescent moon
   Mr. Cummings & Mr. Vinal both dead—

"Why you like beer as much as I do,"
    sd the old gal
    to a tableful of cans—
"Lady, it's my life."—
Where the soldiers sat talk about getten their head busted off

1966

and there's a cherry in the gin & tonic
also an angel playing with himself upside down
              kneeling abed
              looking between legs into the mirror
to see the two spots where he sat so long to study the Bible
                   reddening each buttock—
Cigarettes and alcohol,
                   and the Hundred & 81st Airborne
Hmm—They'd be better off
                   puffin' a peaceful O pipe
                   or sipping a Sebsi a kif inna café
                        high green fig trees
                             over blue Gibraltar Strait . . .

"The tricks are what makes business!
         you get a college education, it ain't what you got
         it's what you DO with yr. college education Son."
And they're *all* actors.
         Waiting at Barstow the engine humming
—"I wanna be an entertainer,
         I wanna be a comedy writer," he said—
         His hands stained with Vietnamese blood.
The engine humming—
         All others silent, lost in thought.
And the soldier talked all about his troubles with his red hair
And how he took his girl home after 3 drinks
         when she squinted her eyes at him and said
                   "I wanna go with yew,"
and how he drove her to her house
         and said "I'm given you a last chance"
         and how she leaned her head on his
              shoulder and said

1966

           "Anywhere you're goin take me"
and how he
     took off her pants
       and she said that he shd take off his pants
        and he wouldn't take off his pants
   and how they'd have some
      love play, like everybody
and then, he'd drive her home,
                but when he's out at a bar
  If anybody looks at his girl
he looks 'em in the eye and snaps his finger & says
          whatter ya lookin like that fur—
and when he's out in a bar alone,
      anybody is fair game for his love.

So I sat an I listened,
   and I brooded in my beard,
     and saw he was uglyeyed
   though his voice beautiful Edward Carpenter.
Now I'm lying here
  Cabinette in complete darkness
    Airfields passing by,
     Stars, a few
       in blackness outside
     the modern railroad window
     doubled to reflect
          passing gas—

"Ah love is so sweet in the Springtime,"
   Jeanette McDonald sang
     moviestar three decades ago
  I went

1966

       downtown Paterson Fabian Theater balcony
            How soft flesh is—
Stars dim white fixed friendly
        "Matter-bubble behind the ear" six years ago—
        Old poetry grows stale,
             forlorn, as always forlorn
        Fabian Saturday morn—
        marble balustrade on giant darkness
watching boyish Ronald Reagan
        emote
           his shadow
              across the 'Thirties—
                Same black vastness
                  pierced
                    by emotion
        melancholy toward the stars—
Political planets whirling round the Sun,
          consciousness expansion,
        earth girdled by telegraph wires, Edward,
          they never dreamed of television then.
          No better way to die!

    Railroad chugging thru yr thighs,
      clear your throat,
        lie there in the dark,
          cough with cancer,
            close your eyes . . .
I didn't even dream
    and woke, sleepy numb, reluctant
        to face my own language.
    But came back to it,
        tape machine

1966

passing Mojave,

  evening ease,

    Na-mu-sa-man-da mo-tu-nan o-ha-
ra-chi ko-to-sha so-no-nan to-ji-to en gya-gya gya-ki gya-ki un-nun shi-fu-
ra shi-fu-ra ha-ra chi-shu-sa chi-shu-sa shu-shi-ri shu-shi-ri so-ha-ja so-ha-
ja se-chi-gya shi-ri-ei so-mo-ko

     The Universe is Empty.

  Click of the train

 eyes closed . . . the long green building

  "Like a monster with many eyes."

    On valley balcony overlooking Bay Bridge,

    A horse in leafy corral . . .

600 Cong Death Toll this week

   language language

    escalating

"and the honor & the glory will go to him who speaks

with the voice of a man of feeling," said Walter Lippman

    face creased w/ wrinkles

    Bakersfield Gazette

  Wear beads, live

in small polkadot tent, tasseled rooftop

   in Bixby's middle

  ground plot, peaceful Ashram

"It's mine, it's mine, I don't want anybody else

To own my piece of land private special from Police"

  . . . I must be criminal, mind

     wanders

   nailing down roof boards—

   tell him I stopped at the bar.

No time No time Sam Lewis—

  Oh—No time Carolyn,

   No time now, Neal.

1966

Do you love me?

    No, I'm an awkward jerk that's been around yr neck for

        so long you get used to it & kinda fond.

The salesman's eyes close,

    he stands his jacket off

        tie hanging down white shirt

          You run em a merry chase, Son?

Open your eyes and stars

        are back where they were.

And Dr. Louria committed suicide,

      accused of abortion,

        that sensitive man.

Well gimme yr piece of perspective

    for use in the slotmachine marketplace future—

    You hafta get permission down in

Freehold New Jersey to see Tibetan Monks.

    You hafta get permission.

The magic formula's printed on the back of yr chair

        Lady,

      Yr. going to be the most important illuminator

        since Dr. Johnson?

      And Huncke suffers rejection

        contrariety of others.

    "Reform U.S. Government stinks detail,"

like, congratulations Whitey, you'll go far

      in yr black Maria, right?

A public meeting in my head,

    way back on River Street.

1966

Morning, Crossing New Mexico border
    massive cliff caves
        in mid-earth America—to live here
a blessing these sandstone organpipes under the shimmering
        consciousness of LSD.
   Defiance, Wingate, Red Cliffs, Thoreau,
     Indian Gallup ahead,
   ran by here with Peter in the white bus once toward
Plainland level everywhere, fenced, flat
       Texas horizon grey-fleeced with cloud haze,
       Gemini men walked space that day—
And ninety-nine soldiers piled on the train at Amarillo—
   hadn't read the paper four weeks
      basic training Air
        Force Pneumohydraulics—
Ninety-nine soldiers entering the train
      and all so friendly
    Only a month
      hair clipped & insulted
   They weren't too sad
    glad on the train,
      to some electronics field near Chicago
—Been taking courses in Propaganda,
   How not to believe what they were told
     by the enemy
Young fellas that some of them had long hair
    before they came to the heated camp
    friendly, over hamburgers
     Volunteered
   assignments behind the lines on Great Machines
      that drop Napalm,
   milking

1966

the calf of Gold.
Three months from now
Vietnam, they said.

Walking the length of the train,
the Lounge Car with Time Magazine
Amarillo Globe, US News & World Report
Readers Digest Coronet Universal Railroad Schedule
everyone on the same track,
bound leatherette read on sofas,
America heartland passes flat
Trees rising in night—
Dining car
negro waiters negro porters
negro sandwiches negro bartenders white jacketed
Kindly old big-assed Gents half bald,
Going, sir, California to Chicago
feeding the Soldiers.
Blue eyed children climbing chair backs
staring at my beard, gay.

A consensus around card table beer—
"It's my country,
better fight 'em over there than here,"
afraid to say "No it's crazy
everybody's insane—
This country's wrong,
the Universe is Illusion."

Soldiers gathered round
saying—"my country
and they say I gotta fight,

1966

I have no choice,
        we're in it too deep to pull out,
                if we lose,
    there's no stopping the Chinese communists
        We're fighten the communists, aren't we?
            Isn't that what it's about?"
Flatland,
      emptiness
           ninety nine soldiers graduated Basic Training
      eating hamburgers—
        "you learn to eat fast
          you learn to be insulted without caring
          you gotta do what your country expects"—
even the bright talkative orphan farm boy
whose auto parts father wanted 'em to grow up military
"almost by a male hog up to his shoulders"—
      4 hours punching at power steering tractor
        brakes front & hind foot
           giant insect specialized—
The whole populace fed by News
few dissenting on this train, I the lone beard who don't like
                Vietnam War—
      Ninety nine airforce boys
        lined up with their pants down forever.
Five Persons Wounded Cleveland Riots
Atlantic Next Stop for Jolly Space-men
Bubonic Plague Suspected in Prairie Dogs
U.S. Marine Offensive Operation Hastings
Communist Dead Toll Rose Almost 1000
Stratofortresses struck language language
Communist language language infiltration
        South of 17th Parallel

1966

"Psychedelic drugs no substitute for plain study
   . . . Technicolored Delusions,
     Many report visits to Heaven
       . . . jumping the gun a bit"
        George E. Turner said
"Eat well, Animal" with a package of dog food
       and as for Negroes
"Work not rioting is Magic Formula"
And Johnson reiterated too, "our desire to engage in
       "unconditional discussions"
        to end the war
"other side . . . concession
       . . . not the slightest
         indication"
More manpower would be required he said
       flatly,

John Steinbeck,
     Flaxenhaired Yevtushenko wrote yr phantom
       End the War

"Unconditional negotiations" sd Johnson
     "Anywhere anytime" sd Johnson in the last poem
Yesterday Ky So Vietnam sd
     "Dissolve Vietcong
       National Liberation Front—
        And Peace"
   Kennedy sd
     "Give V.C. Negotiation Chair"
—irreconcilable positions, every year
United States proposes contradictions
     backed with bomb murder.

1966

backed with Propaganda—
Soldiers on this train think they're fighting China
Soldiers on this train think Ho Chi Minh's Chinese
Soldiers on this train don't know where they're going
John Steinbeck stop the war John Steinbeck stop
   the war John Steinbeck stop the war.

And the French Army surrounded Madrid,
and the Spanish Army'd marched simultaneously surrounded Paris.
   Then they found out
    it was hopeless.
   Generals sent messages,
    Call off the attack!
and the Armies rushed in a neutral place confronted
      & killed each other.
  They just wanted to fight,
    no question of Madrid or Paris, then.
John Steinbeck stop fighting
   That was in the Middle Ages
—& Johnson backed
   Saigon's latest conditions
    N. Vietnam withdraw all aid,
    Dissolve Withdraw Vietcong.
     These are conditions,
  contradicting Johnson's Unconditionals.
   These languages are gibberish.
John Steinbeck thy language is gibberish.
 thou'd lost the language war,
    cantankerous phantom!
   Newspaper language ectoplasm fades—
     Everybody sneeze!

1966

Lightning's blue glare fills Oklahoma plains,
the train rolls past
    casting yellow shadow on grass
                    Twenty years ago
approaching Texas
      I saw
          sheet lightning
               cover Heaven's corners
      Feed Storage Elevators in grey rain mist,
          checkerboard light over sky-roof
            domed one giant network—
same electric lightning South
      follows this train
          Apocalypse prophesied—
    the Fall of America
        signaled from Heaven—

Ninety nine soldiers in uniform paid by the Government
                        to believe
Ninety nine soldiers escaping the draft for an Army job,
Ninety nine soldiers shaved
          with nowhere to go but where told,
ninety nine soldiers seeing the lightning flash
          a thousand years ago
Ten thousand Chinese marching on the plains
   all turned their heads to Heaven at once to see the Moon.
And the old man catching flies on the porch at night
   watched the Herd Boy cross the Milky Way
          to meet the Weaving Girl.
      How can we war against that?
      How can we war against that?

1966

Morning song, waking from dreams
   brown grass, city edge nettle
   wild green stink-weed trees
 by railroad thru niggertown, carlot, scrapheap
    auto slag bridge outskirts,
   muddy river's brown debris
       passing Eton Junction
    rainmist fine over green fields—

     Trees standing upside down
in lush earth approaching Mississippi
    green legs waving to clouds,
   seed pods exposed to birds & rain
         bursting,
   tree heads drinking in the ground,
Unfold stones like rag dolls & the Astral
     body stares with opal eyes,
—all living things before my spectacles.

In the diner, the Lady
   "These soldiers so nice, clean faces
  and their hair combed so short—
    Ugh it's disgusting the others
  —down to their shoulders & cowboy boots"—

   Her aged husband spooning cantaloupe.

Too late, too late
   the Iron Horse hurrying to war,

1966

      too late for laments
            too late for warning—
I'm a stranger alone in my country again.
Better to find a house in the veldt,
better a finca in Brazil—
    Green corn here healthy under sky
    & telephone wires carry news as before,
  Doom gathers in these citizens' minds
    violence gathers in the indifference of their faces,
radio bulletins & television images
                build War—
  American Fighter Comic Books
           on the coach seat.
Better a house hidden in trees
        Mississippi bank
     high cliff protected from flood
Better an acre down Big Sur
    morning path, ocean's shining
        first day's blue world
Better a farm in backland Oregon
        or roads near Glacier Peak
Better withdraw from Newspaper world
Better withdraw from the electric world
Better retire before war cuts my head off,
        not like Kabir—
  Better to buy a Garden of Love
  Better protect the lamb in some valley
  Better go away from taxicab radio cities
         screaming President
    Better to stop smoking
Better to stop jerking off in trains
Better to stop seducing white bellied boys

1966

Better to stop publishing Prophecy—
    Better to meditate under a tree
    Better become a nun in the forest
    Better turn flapjacks in Omaha
       than be a prophet on the electric Networks—
There's nothing left for this country but doom
There's nothing left for this country but death
      Their faces are so plain
      Their thoughts so simple,
         their machinery so strong—
      Their arms reach out 10,000 miles with lethal gas
        Their metaphor so mixed with machinery
          No one knows where flesh ends and
            the robot Polaris begins—
"Waves of United States jetplanes struck at North Vietnam
    again today in the face . . ."
         Associated Press July 21st—
          A summer's day in Illinois!

Green corn silver watertowers
   under the viaduct windowless industry
   at track crossing white flowers,
        American flowers,
      American dirt road, American rail,
        American Newspaper War—
in Galesburg, in Galesburg
        grocery stove exhaust pipes and orange spikeflowers
         in backyard lots—TV antennae
           spiderweb every poor house
   Under a smokestack with a broken lip
   magnetic cranes drop iron scrap like waterdrops.

1966

RACE VIOLENCE IS ORGANIZED, POLICE CHARGE   Chicago
Tribune
 Negroes hurl rocks in Jacksonville Florida
"Police said Henry Townes, 22, a negro, had tried to
      drive his automobile . . .
 & other occupants of the car were wounded
    Towne's wife, Diana, 16
    her son Immanuel, 7 months
    her son Christopher, 4
     and her brother Ernest Williams, 12
       in serious condition . . ."

Dr. King charged "To date the power structure seems more willing to ac-
cept Violence as a means of change than willing to recognize non-violent
movement."

 "Brownsville Community Council likes demagogues to violence. Two
explosions hit the U.S. office in Colombia. Viet Buddhist burned, robe gas-
drenched . . . report he left letter critical of Johnson, Saigon UPI."

 "Kennedy noted/yesterday the House passed a 38.6 Billion Dollar De-
fense Appropriation Bill."

   Thirtytwo years ago today, the woman in the red
dress outside the Biograph Theater in Chicago
   didn't wanna be sent back to Roumania.
   Ambushed Dillinger fell dead on the sidewalk
      hit by 4 bullets
FBI man Purvis quit in '35
    Feb 29, 1960 he shot & killed himself
       in his home
    Army Colonel in World War II
     Breakfast Cereal Manufacturer.

1966

Dillinger's eyes and Melvin Purvis—
   Dillinger grim, Purvis self-satisfied,
   Both died of bullets.

Section 1A Comic Strip Chicago Tribune
Under *Dick Tracy,*
 Tales of the Green Beret,
  "Right now we got 6 men in the Cong's
     camouflaged foxholes,"
       next to *Batman.*
  Terry & the Pirates below battle Comrade X—
"In the first 6 months of '66
  Newspapers consumed three
   Million 386 thousand 826 tons of Newsprint." UPI

Football field, suburb streets, grey-sheeted clouds
 stretched out to the City ahead
   Myriad pylons, telegraph poles, a lavender boiler,
  Fulbright broadcast attacks war money
  Crushed stone mounds, earth eaten
   Henry Crown's & General Dynamic—
    dust rising from rubble
Sawdust burners
 topped by black cloud
  sulphurous yellow
 gas rising from red smokestacks
Power stations netted
  with aluminum ladders and ceramic balls
rusty scrapheaps topped with cranes
 stub banded chimneys
  puffing in grey air
Coalbarges old as Holland at dusk in a canal,

1966

railroad tracks banded to the city
watertowers' high legs walking the horizon
The Chinese Foreign minister makes his pronouncement,
Thicker and thicker the metal
Lone bird above phonepole
Thicker and thicker smokestack wires
Giant Aztec factories, red brick towers
feeder-noses dropped to railroad
"All human military activity" suspended
says radio—
Campbell's soups has a fortress here
giant can raised high over Chicago
over forest of bridges and signs
Church spires lifted in greyness
hazy towers downtown
The train rolls slower & slower
past cement trucks
old cabs resting in the produce flats
over city streets, rumbling
on a canal's green mirror
past liquor signs painted ancient
past the blue paint factory,
a belfried cross beneath
dynamo'd smoke-cathedrals,
Thicker & thicker the wires
over a cast iron building, black windows
local bus passing viaduct stanchions
a lone wino staggering down Industrial Thruway
This nation at war
sun yellowing grey clouds,
grand beast trucks down in the
Garage's bowels—

1966

windowed hulks downtown—
Bright steam
muscular puffing from an old flue
Meadowgold Butter besmeared with coal dust
past creosote wood bulwarks
Oiltank cars wait their old engine
on tracks curved into the heart of the city
YMCA beckons the homeless unloved,
the groan of 8 mn. tons inching against
whitened rail,
giant train so slowly moved
a man can touch the wheels.

Bus outbound from Chicago Greyhound basement
green neon beneath streets Route 94
Giant fire's orange tongues & black smoke
pouring out that reef,
little gay pie truck passing the wall—
Brick & trees E. London, antique attics
mixed with smokestacks
Apartments apartments square windows set like Moscow
apartments red brick for multimillion population
out where industries raise craned necks
Gas station lights, old old old old traveler
"put a tiger in yr tank"—
Fulbright sang on the Senate floor
Against the President's Asian War
Chicago's acrid fumes in the bus
A-1 Outdoor Theater
Against horned factory horizon,

1966

     tender steeples ringing Metropolis

Thicker and thicker, factories

     crowd iron cancer on the city's throat—

       Aethereal roses

          distant gas flares

      twin flue burning at horizon

   Night falling on the bus

       steady ear roar

      between Chicago and New York

Wanderer, whither next?

    See Palenque dream again,

   Long hair in America,

   cut it for Tehuantepec—

     Peter's long golden locks grown old,

     quiet meditation in Oaxaca's

         backyard,

   Tonala or Angel Port warm nights

     no telephone, the War

        rages North

    Police break down the Cross

    Crowds screaming in the streets—

Sherri Martinelli's little house with combs and shells

     on Pacific cliff-edge

  since February in this fear, LSD she saw

   Zodiac in earth grass where she stood

   palm to cheek, and scraped her toe

    looking aside, said

    "Too disturbed to see you

   old friend w/ so much Power"

    —ten years later.

1966

Yajalon valley, bougainvillea flares
        on the Mayor's house—
Jack you remember the afternoon
    Xochimilco with Fairies?
   Green paradise boats
        flower laden
      poled upriver
   Pulque in the poop
     stringed music in the air—
        drunkenness, & happiness
anonymous
      fellows without care from America—
      Now war moves my mind—
  Villahermosa full of purple flowers
  Merida hath cathedrals cheap hotels
     —boat to Isla Cozumel
      Julius can wander thru Pijijiapan
     forgetting his dog peso Nicotinic Acid—
Bus seat's white light shines on Mexico map,
     quietness, quietness over countryside
       palmfrond insects, cactus ganga
  & Washington's Police how many thousand miles away?

  Ray Charles singing from hospital
      "Let's go get stoned?"

Durango-Mazatlan road's built now
    Sierra Madre's moon valleys below
Children with quartz jewels climbing highway cliff-edge
      Jack bought crystals & beer—
"I wanna go out in a car
  not leave word where I'm going"—

1966

travel ahead.
Or Himalayas in Spring
   following the pilgrim's path
      10,000 Hindus
         to Shiva temples North
    Rishikesh & Laxman Jula
    Homage to Shivananda,
         the Guru heart—
thru green canyons, Ganges gorge—
    carrying a waterpot
    to Kedarnath & Badrinath
     a Gangotri in the ice
      —Manasarovar forbidden,
        Kailash forbidden,
    the Chinese eat Tibet.

Howl for them that suffer broken bone
       homeless on moody balconies
        said Jack,
   his soul returning to me again
        again with prophecy
howl for boys sleeping on tables in cafes with their long hair
     to the sea in Hidalgo di Parral,
      in Hermosillo & Tetuan—

The masses prepare for war
    short haired and executives
      young flops from college
      young and pink flesh gone mad
      listening to radio news.
& Johnson was angry with Fulbright
     for criticizing his war.

1966

And Hart Crane's myth and Whitman's—
    What'll happen to that?
               The Karma
accumulated bombing Vietnam
      The Karma bodies napalm-burned
       Karma suspicion
where machinery's smelt the heat of bodies trembling
           in the jungle
The Karma bullets in the back of the head by thatched walls
    The Karma babies in their mothers' arms
           bawling destroyed
The Karma of populations moved from center to center of
              Detention
Karma bribery, Karma murder blood-money
    Must come home to America,
    There must be a war
      America has builded her a new body.

Peaceful young men in America get out of the Cities & go to
        the countryside & the trees—
Bearded young men in America hide your hair & shave your
        Beards & disappear
    The destroyers are out to destroy—
Destroyers of Peking & Washington stare face to face
      & will hurl their Karma-bombs
          on the planet.
      Get thee to the land
        leave the cities to be destroyed.
Only a miracle appearing in Man's eyes
    only boys' flesh singing
      can show the warless way—
        or miracle

1966

Radium destruction over Earth
seed the Planet with New Babe.

Brilliant green lights
in the factory transom windows.
Beautiful
when eyes are ready to close for sleep,
beautiful as undersea sunshine
or valleybottom fern.
Why do I fear these lights?
In all the smoking chimneys of industry?
Why see them less godly
than treetrunks in forest
& sunset orange moons?

Why are these cranes less Edenly than Palmfronds?
On these highway neons the equal beauty
in Point Lobos'
tidepool's transparency?

It's these neon Standard Gastation
cars of men whose faces are made of dough
pockets full of 58 billion dollar
Abstract budget money—
these green lights illuminate
goggled eyes fixing blowtorches on metal wings
flying off to war—

Because these electric structures rear tin machines
that will kill Bolivian marchers
or flagellate Vietnam adolescent's thighs
Because my countrymen make this structure to make war

1966

Because this smoke over Toledo's advertised in the Toledo Blade
      as energy burning to destroy China.

Baghavan Sri Ramana Maharshi
      in his photo has a fine white halo of hair,
      thin man with a small beard
         silver short-cropped skull-fur
   His head tilted to one side,
      mild smile, intelligent eyes
      "The Jivan-Mukta is not a Person."

Morning sun rise over Tussie Hills,
   earth covered with emerald-dark fur.
      Cliffs to climb, a little wilderness,
      and a long valley you could call a home.
Came thru here with Peter before & noticed
         green forest,
     thru cellular consciousness
—Near Nealyton or Dry Run
      Waterfall or Meadow Gap, or Willow Hill.
Sunrays filtering thru clouds like a negative photograph,
      smoky bus window, passengers asleep
      over Susquehanna river's morning mist.
Ike at Gettysburg found himself a nice spot—
      all these places millions of trees' work
         made green
as millions of workmens' labor raised the buildings
         of NY
   Corn here in fields, dollars in the fields of New York.
Morning glow, hills east Harrisburg, bright
    highways, red factory smoke, fires burning
        upriver in garbage lots—

1966

Philadelphia Inquirer: "Perry County 113 acres

   of woodland, $11,300. Ideal locations for

   cabins, quarters, township road, springs &

   roads on track, best of hunting, call 1-717 . . ." —Dangerous to

want possessions

       and for so short a time.

  Shoulda had it in 1945, or '53,

      Times Square & Mexico—

in my twenties I would've enjoyed running around these

       green woods naked,

in my twenties I would've enjoyed making love naked

      by these brooks.

July 22, UPI—New York Police Enforce Calm. Third Cleveland Negro
Slain.

  Fulbright President Clash Anew. Commitment without Consent
radical

   new departure. Rostow[39] became a great Asian Power. Language
language.

  Moyers[40] told reporters, "I never heard him mention the word."
Mansfield[41]

   denies U.S. considers itself an Asian Power, "There is no Johnson
doctrine

  for Asia."

   "Why didn't the United States bomb the Port of Haiphong
and to

---

39. Walt Rostow (1916–2003), Special Assistant for National Security Affairs.

40. Journalist Bill Moyers (born 1934) served as White House Press Secretary
from 1965 to 1967.

41. Mike Mansfield (1903–2001), Senate Majority Leader.

1966

Hell with the Russian ships that might be in the Harbor?" which drew applause

    from the International Platform Association. Rusk was gloomy. Lao Slao said at

    the rally in Peking's Gate of Heavenly Peace Square: "The Chinese Government

    reaffirms that U.S. Imperialist Aggression in Vietnam is an aggression against China."

    "It would seem appropriate that since this is a city project, the Star Spangled

    Banner should be played at each concert. This is especially true at the present time

    when our country is at War." Signed, Maurice N. Wexler, Commander of the Legion's

    Variety Post. In a return letter, Fredrick R. May President of Robin Hood Dell assured

    Wexler that "It is our desire to be patriotic at all times, even though Congress has not

    declared our country in a state of war."

Up With People "will renew your faith in the youth of America by showing that they are clean-cut, hardworking & patriotic," Channel 66 Sponsored by Schick Safety Razor Co. & Eversharp, Inc. Steve Canyon Comic Strip creating baseball in Asia. Language spokesmen said 25 language Communists died near the Demilitarized Zone. 561 language Communist bodies counted in So. Vietnam's corner. Another language 524 listed probable killed operation Leatherneck's Bravo Division from Language. Saigon July 23, UPI.

Who is the enemy, year after year?
  War after war, who is the enemy?

1966

What is the weapon, battle after battle?
What is the news, defeat after defeat?
What is the picture, decade after decade
  Television shows the blood,
   bodies revealed wounded on screen,
     photographs print broken arms burning skin
Cut Sound out of television & you won't tell who's the Victim
Cut Language out of the Visual and you'll never know
    Who's the aggressor—
    cut commentary from Newscast
    and you'll see a mass of madmen at murder.
On train to Chicago the soldiers chatted over beer
 and they, too, vowed to fight the cottenpickin Communists
   and give their own bodies to the fray.
 Where do they learn the lesson? Grammar school
   Who taught them Newspaper language
 D'they buy it at Safeway with Readers Digest?

"Reducing the Unreal is Unreality, and causing the one
real Self to shine, the Guru . . ."
 1966 trains were crowded with soldiers.
". . . the Divine Eye, the eye that is pure consciousness
which has no visions. Nothing that is seen is real."
  Passing tollgate,
      regatta of yachts on river hazed
    bend at Reading, giant smokestacks, water towers
       feed elevators—

Seeing objects and conceiving God in them are mental
processes, but that is not seeing God, because He is
within.
 "Who am I? . . . You're in truth a pure spirit but you
identify it with a body . . ."

1966

The war is Appearances, this poetry Appearances
                    . . . measured thru Newspapers
        All Phantoms of Sound
        All landscapes have become Phantom—
    giant New York ahead'll perish with my mind.
        "understand that the Self is not a Void"
not this, not that,
      Not my anger, not War Vietnam
      Maha Yoga a phantom
           Blue car swerves close to bus
            —not the Self.
          Ramana Maharshi, whittle myself a walkingstick,
            Waterspray irrigating the fields
                That's not the Self—
    hard-on spring in loins
       rocking in highway chair,
          poignant flesh spasm not it Self,
           body's speaking there
            & feeling, that's not Self
      Who says No, says Yes—not Self.
Phelps Dodge's giant white building
           Highway side, not Self.
   Who? Who? both asleep & awake
       closes his eyes?
     Who opens his eyes to Sweden?
  You happy, Lady, writing yr
      checks on Howard Johnson's counter?
  Mind wanders. Sleep, cough & sweat . . .
                 Manhattan's
Tunnel-door cobbled for traffic,
     trucks into that mouth
        MAKE NO IMAGE
Mohammedans say

1966

Jews have no painting
Buddha's Nameless
Alone is Alone,
all screaming of soldiers
crying on wars
speech politics massing armies
is false-feigning show—
Calm senses, seek self, forget
Thine own adjurations
Who are you?
to mass world armies in planet war?
McGraw-Hill building green grown old, car fumes &
Manhattan tattered, summer heat,
sweltering noon's odd patina
on city walls,
Greyhound exhaust terminal,
trip begun,
taxi-honk toward East River where
Peter waits working.

July 22–23, 1966[42]

City Midnight Junk Strains
for Frank O'Hara[43]

Switch on lights yellow as the sun
in the bedroom . . .

42. Ginsberg's dating of his composition of "Iron Horse" cannot be accurate: it would have taken longer than two days for him to travel by train from the West Coast to Chicago, then travel from Chicago to New York by bus. In all likelihood, these are the dates of the bus trip.
43. First draft of "City Midnight Junk Strains," *Collected Poems*, 465–67.

1966

The gaudy poet dead   Frank O'Hara's bones
                                      under squares of grass
An emptiness at 8 PM in the Cedar Bar
          Throngs of drunken
                    guys talking about paint
    & lofts, and Pennsylvania youth.
                  Kline attacked by his heart
& chattering Frank
        stopped forever
   Faithful drunken adorers, mourn.
              The busfare's a nickel more
      past his old apartment on 9th Street by the park.
Delicate Peter loved his praise,
       I wait for the things he says
                                about me—
      Did he think me an Angel
           as angel I am still talking into earth's microphone
                       willy nilly
   —to come back as words ghostly hued
                  by early death
   but written so bodies
           mature in another decade.
Chatty prophet
        of yr own loves, Personal
        memory feeling fellow
      Poet of building-glass
I see you walking as you said with your tie
        flopped over your shoulder   in the wind down 5th Avenue
          on their scaffolds ascending Time
            & washing the windows of Life
—off to a date with Martinis & a blond
      beloved poet far from home

1966

—with thee and Thy sacred Metropolis

in the enormous bliss   of a long afternoon

where death is the shadow

cast by Rockefeller Center

over your intimate street.

Who were you, black suited, hurrying to meet,

Unsatisfied one?

Unmistakable,

Darling date

for the charming solitary/young poet with a big cock

who could fuck you all night long

till you never came,

trying your torture on his/obliging fond body

eager to satisfy god's whim that made you

Innocent, as you are.

I tried/your boys   and found them ready

sweet and amiable

collected gentlemen

with large sofa apartments

for pure language;

lonesome to please

and you mixed with money

because you knew enough language to be rich

If you wanted your walls to be empty—

. . . deep philosophical terms   for Edwin Denby   serious as Herbert Reed

with silvery hair   announcing   your dead gift

to the crowd   whose greatest op art   frisson

was the new sculpture   your big blue wounded body   made in the

Universe

when you went away   in Fire Island for the weekend

tipsy with a crowd of decade-olden friends

1966

Peter stares out the window   at the robbers
    distracted   in Amphetamine
and I stare into my head   & look for your/broken roman nose
    your wet mouth-smell of martinis
       & a big artistic tipsy kiss.
40's only half a life   to have filled
    with so many fine parties and evenings
    interesting drinks together with one
       faded friend or new
       understanding social cat
   who collaborated on Free Speech
     for your church.
I want to be there in your garden party in the clouds
      all of us naked
strumming our harps and reading each other   new poetry
    in the boring celestial
     friendship Committee Museum.
You're in a bad mood?
   Take an Aspirin.
     In the Dumps?
       I'm falling asleep safe in your thoughtful arms.
Someone uncontrolled by History would have to own Heaven,
      on earth as it is.
I hope you satisfied your childhood love
   Your puberty fantasy   your sailor punishment on your knees
        your mouth-suck
Elegant inconsistency
     on the honking self-prophetic Personal
    as Curator of funny emotions to the mob,
Trembling one, whenever possible.   I see New York thru your eyes
   And hear of one funeral a year nowadays

1966

From Billie Holiday's time

appreciated more and more

a common ear

for our deep gossip.

July 29, 1966

August 8, 1966

only two ways to go
Nothing or Something,
the Buddha–Brahma–Shanyata eclipse
of Consciousness treks,
negate aether, & illusion blip-out
with no internatal fantasy
wandering from Bardo to Carpenter—
or the Buddha–Brahma–Shunyata-self
at the heart of the illusion
Karma reborn in disguise,
the smile of trees, flash
consciousness rolling like wind
over the grass of mankind.

Gavin Arthur smiled at me angry
for disbelieving the visionary Sun
& Paradise we both believe in.
But drugs have taken it away, and farewell
Artemidorus weeps over mummies
of fadeout forever forgotten in kitchens
when planet consciousness ends,

1966

or else rolls onward to another galaxy
      and wakes itself up mysterious
      till it finds a mouth to ask question.

----

21 August 1966

Dylan's color film for television his face flickering in and out of blue flamecolored spotlights like a Wizard.

I said, looks like Duse, that sensitive face, eat the microphone.

Dream:

On trolley in Liverpool City—going to meet Sanders[44] who's making machinery in the great world—only on roller skates gliding smoothly—

Everyone mad in the dream universe—

Arrived at his factory—he's temporarily employed there, I enter the door—he's making money to support Fugs Nationalization of Consciousness—It's a steel plant or rubber Mfg. Co.—giant industrial shed filled with boiling red vats, with a worker's balcony all around the rafters, and no guard rail edging the high platform where the workers skate around—

Ed skates up to the very edge of the balcony, I see his figure wizard like (also) with cape and Afric-frizzy corona of hair sliding up to the end of the shelf he works on, stopping on the edge neatly with some kind of buffing-cloth attached to his shoes—leans over the edge and welcomes us.

----

44. Ed Sanders (born 1939), poet, musician, author, essayist, activist, and co-founder of New York band The Fugs.

1966

Last night Lafcadio[45] after several years' absence in Northport with his mother arrived with Peter to take refuge in our Lower East Side apartment.

He looked palefaced, thin chested & ghostly brow worried, talked in hesitant broken disorganized way—"Why'd Peter bring me here—he drove too fast—I didn't make any noise in Northport—mama thought I was disturbing her . . . be kind to me . . . were you in India? . . .

I don't want to over-exert myself."

The megalopolis is full of giant mosquitos.

Sept. 15, 1966

Dream in Country house, where we all going to sleep? It's in a small town, we've been visiting there some time now, at the border.

I.

Early in the night, in the dream, I *did* pick up some quantity of pure LSD from Leary's source, & decided to take some home—Walked out of the clapboard house we were staying, & went downstreet—a narrow cobbled alley to the shore road like Provincetown by a Railroad track in the 19th Century. Passed a few Bobbies on the way, but the Police went their way. I was suddenly struck, in the middle of my walk, how foolhardy it was of me to let myself be in a position to be caught like that, so easily, by accident, in possession. Went down street, another uniformed Policeman there, and still no trouble. I was lucky. Arrived at my own Cottage where I was staying temporarily, in possession of the blue capsules.

45. Lafcadio Orlovsky, Peter's brother.

1966

Uncle Sam, Aunt Rose in Newark pharmacy. Nobody knows everything, not even Jaweh.

II.

Woke from dream around noon—We'd stayed at and I guess rented overnite, a big Cottage—several couples & myself—Time to sleep—I lay Gene & his wife[46] down in separate room outside—I went into larger room where we'd been talking, wondering who gets which bed, the big bed or the little there in the corner—much confusion, but realized we did have rights to any and all beds, had paid up—

Over breakfast table discussing matters with my Uncle Sam Gaidemack (now dead with Rose 5 years)—He warning me that some doctors had said "LSD was no good"—"damage to brain" or "didn't do damage chemically but who needs it?"—Citing authorities vague Reader's Digest article—I said, "Well, remember doctors are just like pharmacists—They're just licensed"—Realizing he wasn't a doctor just a pharmacist—"Nobody knows everything, even Yeweh" I concluded.

Sept. 20, 1966 3 AM

Lafcadio sitting on rug, staring at match, suddenly burned hand, dropped match on carpet—looked up at me & called—"I'm artistic—I'm very kind to objects."

"It was late at night . . . I thought I couldn't breathe . . . it was like fainting . . . Then I was alright, though. Oh I managed to get upstairs alright . . . I was yelling. Maybe I was upset at something like that. Whatever happened to Eileen Garver?"

46. Eugene and Connie Brooks.

1966

Morning—(12 AM) dream—rainy day

A dinner party at Leo & Harvey's Publisher uptown, George Plimpton[47] [and] all the cozy folks—Tom Maschler's[48] there, it ends with a Ginsberg cake, or an Allen pie, in any case a very tasty Compound Pastry delight, many colored with strips of intense almost-pastry soft-tooth'd crust. Maschler had his piece, and brushes against the bulk of the pie—I try to brush the white whip cream off his Mediterranean blue shirt—"I got my cream on yr shirt," I apologize—He takin

----

"Jack Kerouac now confined to home, taking care of paralytic Mother desires nurse for washing of lady."—telephone conversation Jack's mock advt. in personal's column.

To Krishnamurti

All eyes turn to the choiceless man
All eyes turn to the man who sees all
All ears hear the voice of the man who hears all
All speech refers to the Self which says nothing—
The silent listener alone in corner of the Village Gate—

Oct. 7, 1966

----

47. George Plimpton (1927–2003), writer, editor, cofounder of *The Paris Review*.

48. Tom Maschler (born 1933), British editor and publisher, friend of Ginsberg.

Anthology title—

Poets That Don't Get Published Enough

It's the Anger in your eyes
It's the Anger in yr eyes
   That makes the Policeman hit you on yr head
It's the Anger in yr eyes
It's the Anger in yr eyes
   The junkie comes to rob from you in bed
It's the Anger in your eyes
   that takes the Chinese by Surprise
when the President says better dead than red
It's the anger in yr eyes
That makes the yellow in bed
Climbing out the window sill like Spies
anger in your eyes
makes utopian Strontium—90 yr big surprise

Dogbarks echo in the Clouds

October 17, 1966
Auto poetry to Hanover, New Hampshire[49]

Coughing in the Morning
   waking with a blast of steam, the city being destroyed,
   pile drivers pounding down in the rubble,

49. Transcription of auto poesy, with initial line breaks, for "Autumn Gold: New England Fall," *Collected Poems*, 469–75.

1966

red smokestacks pouring chemical
      into Manhattan's nostrils . . .
      "All aboard"
Rust colored cliffs bulking over the superhighway
      thru New Haven,
Rouged with Autumny leaves, october smoke,
      Country liquor bells on the Radio—
Eat meat and you're a beast
    Smoke Nicotine & your meat will multiply
      with tiny monsters of cancer,
Make money & yr mind will be lost in a million green papers,
    —Smell of burning rubber by the steamshovel—
Mammals with planetary vision, long noses,
      riding a green small Volkswagen up the three lane
        concrete road
          past the graveyard
    dotted w/tiny american flags waved in the breeze
            Washington Avenue
Sampans battling in waters off Mekong Delta
    Cuban politicians in Moscow, analyzing China—
Yellow leaves in the wood,
      Millions of redness,
        grey skies over sandstone
          outcroppings along the road—
cows by the yellow corn,
    wheel-whine on granite,
      white houseroofs, Connecticut woods
        hanging under the clouds—
Autumn again, you wouldn't know in the city
Gotta come out in a car   see the birds
    flock by the yellow bush—
In Autumn, in autumn this part of the planet's

1966

famous for red leaves—
Difficult for Man on earth to 'cape the snares of delusion—
   All wrong, the thought process screamed at
                      from Infancy,
The Self built with myriad thoughts
   from football to I Am That I am,
Difficult to stop breathing factory smoke,
Difficult to step out of clothes,
     hard to forget the green parks,
Trees scream & drop
       bright Leaves,
Yea Trees scream & drop bright leaves,
Difficult to get out of bed in the morning
      in the slums—
Even sex happiness a long drawn-out scheme
         To keep the mind moving—
Big grey truck rolling down highway
      to unload wares—
Bony white branches of birch relieved of their burden
—overpass, overpass, overpass
      crossing the road, more traffic
         between the cities,
More sex carried near and far—
    Blinking tail lights
   To the Veterans hospital where we can all collapse,
Forget Pleasure and Ambition,
     be tranquil and let leaves
      blush, turned on
by the lightningbolt doctrine that rings
         telephones
interrupting my pleasurable humiliating dream
    in the locker room

1966

last nite—
Weeping willow, what's your catastrophe?
Red Red oak, oh, what's your worry?
Hairy Mammal whaddya want,
What more than a little graveyard
near the lake by airport road,
Electric towers marching to Hartford,
Building tops spiked in the sky,
asphalt factory cloverleafs spread over meadows
Smoke thru the wires, Connecticut River wall'd
with concrete,
Boy what a beautiful dome by the viaduct,
Past the city, central gastanks, glass boat bldgs,
ten block square downtown,
North, North on the highway, soon outa town,
green fields.
The body's a big beast,
The mind gets confused:
I thought I was my body the last 4 years,
And everytime I had a headache, God dealt me the
Ace of Spades—
I thought I was mind-consciousness 10 yrs before that,
And everytime I went to the Dentist the Kosmos disappeared,
Now I don't know who I am—
I wake up in the morning surrounded
by meat and wires,
pile drivers crashing thru the bedroom floor,
War images rayed thru Television apartments,
A chaos of machines on Earth,
Too many bodies, mouths bleeding on every Continent,
plaster cracked on my own wall,
What kind of Prophecy

1966

for this Nation
Of Autumn leaves,
    for those children in the High School, green
        in woolen jackets
    chasing the football up & down the field—
North of Long Meadow, into Massachusetts
    Shafts of sunlight
          Thru yellow millions,
    blue light thru clouds,
President Johnson in a plane toward Hawaii,
    Fighter Escort above & below
        in the roaring air—
Radiostatic electric crackle from the
            center of communications
    in broadcast thru Time,
        He, with all his wires & wireless,
          Only to the Instant—
Up Main Street Northampton,
        houses gabled in the sunny afternoon
          Ivy on the library porch—
Big fat pants, workshirt filled w/leaves,
    and a painted pumpkinshead sitting on the Roof,
  —or hanging from the tree in the frontyard
            along the country road—
Tape Machines, cigarettes, cinema, images,
    Two Billion Hamburgers, Cognitive Thought,
        Radiomusic, car itself,
          this thoughtful Poet—
Interruption of brightly colored Autumn Afternoon,
        The clouds have passed away—
Sky is blue as a roadsign,
    but language intervenes,

1966

on route 9 going North—
"Then die, my verse" Mayakovsky[50] yelled
            Die like the rusty cars
                  piled up in the meadow—
Entering Whately,
            The senses amazed me on the hills.
                  with their bright vegetable populations
                  hueing rocks, nameless yellow,
      veils of bright Maya over New England,
      This veil of Autumn leaves laid over the Land,
Transparent blue veil over the senses,
                  Language in the sky—
And in the city a veil of brick
      curtains of windows,
                  Stage drops of Wall Street,
      Honkytonk scenery:
                  Backdrop, a millionaire townhouse,
      Bottom scribbled with names of
            Script—Harvard's journalists of the 30's
or slum-building wall scrawled with
            "Bourgeois Elements Must Go"—
All the cows gathered to the feed truck in the middle of the pasture.
      shaking their tails, hungry for the yellow Fitten Ration
                  that fills the belly
                  and makes the eyes shine
                        & mouth go Mooooo.
      Then they lie down in the hollow green meadow to die—
In old Deerfield, Indian Tribes & Quakers
      Have come & tried
                  To conquer Maya Time—

50. Vladimir Mayakovsky (1893–1930), poet and playwright.

1966

Thanksgiving pumpkins
  remain by the highway,
   signaling yearly Magic
    plump from the ground.
Big leaves hang and hide the porch,
   & babies scatter by the red lights
    of the bridge at Greenfield.
The green Eagle on a granite pillar—
   sign pointing to route to The Mohawk Trail,
Federal Street gas,
  with its apothecary shop & graveyard thru which
    highschool athletes
     tramp this afternoon—
Gold gold red gold yellow gold older than
    the painted cities,
  Gold over Connecticut River cliffs
     running thru Vermont,
  Gold by the Iron railroad
   gold running down the riverbank,
  Gold in the eye, gold on the hills,
   Golden trees surrounding the barn—
Silent tiny golden hills, Maya-Joy in Autumn
   Speeding at 70!

Tibetan Dream Oct. 24, 1966

At dusk, the square-hatted Tibetan Guardian stomping down hill on the pavement—each footstep shakes the Earth—Bells and smokestacks ring and hoot simultaneous at the different poles, whistles & steamshovels and pile drivers on opposite blocks Clang together with each foot-stomp. He descends down Potrero hill.

1966

Nov. 8, 1966—Dream

I picked up a wild squirrel or Guinea Pig from the wood, & explained to it I wanted to take it in the house. The tiny furry mammal objected, wrinkling its nose in pain, but I lifted it up off the grass. It wriggled out of my hand at the front steps & went its own way—but got caught in a spiderweb. I had to bend down to rescue it from grey strings hanging down from the first step.

Woke up this morn, Maretta's[51] soft long body in bed next to mine. The election's strangely real. Reagan in California last night, handsome sincere smile over TV victory headquarters.

Dec. 15

Science Fiction
I went to Utopia. Trees and flowers growing wild everywhere, carefully cherished by citizens. Metal and asphalt underground. Tree friend avenues. Millions of mammals in every direction.

Transparent universities. The main curricula in study of the nature of Universe. The achieved fact had been determined, that the universe did not actually exist except as it were a species of eccentric dream event, palpable within its own limits. Courses in apprehension & dream discrimination therefore were taught, combining disciplines from Science of nerves and senses Religion, Phenomenology, language poetry & shamanistic music, etc. Graduation came on permanent realization of the nature of things. Advanced courses included history & physical sciences, household arts, Phys. Ed., etc.

51. Maretta Greer, a friend of Ginsberg.

1966

At the Human Be-In in San Francisco's Golden Gate Park
Polo Fields, January 14, 1967. Photograph copyright Lisa Law.

1967

Ginsberg had already amassed enough auto poesy for a volume of poetry, but he knew that he was a considerable distance from his goal. America seemed to be fracturing, dividing along generational lines. The war in Vietnam, rather than moving toward a peaceful solution, was escalating in terms of troop involvement, lives lost or shattered on the battlefields, defense funds appropriated, and heated exchanges over how to settle the dispute. The United States was now involved in the devastating, systematic bombing of North Vietnam. A growing number of demonstrations against the war in the United States were ending violently.

Ginsberg kept close watch on it all. The war and the politics behind it worked their way into his public appearances and his poetry. His poem "Wichita Vortex Sutra" was far too urgent to await publication in a future book.

For all his interest in witnessing and writing about his country and the events within it, Ginsberg also spent a good portion of the year abroad. His stay in the United Kingdom inspired "Wales Visitation," a poem destined for critical acclaim. In Italy, he acted as tour guide for his father and stepmother, yet he still managed to get arrested for reading "Who Be Kind To" at a festival in Spoleto. The pinnacle of the journey (and perhaps the year) was a series of meetings with the reclusive Ezra Pound.

Jan 4, 1967

Bayonne Tuscarora[1]

Grey water tanks in the Grey mist,

        grey robots

1. Transcription, with initial line breaks, of auto poesy, "Bayonne Turnpike to Tuscarora," *Collected Poems*, 476–80.

towers carrying wires thru Bayonne's
                              white smog, silver
         domes, green chinaworks steaming,
              (Christmas's leftover lights hanging
                              from a smokestack)—
Monotone thru the truck window
              parallel black wires on the grey highway
                              into the grey west—
Noon hour, the planet smoke-covered with smoke
         Truck wheels racing forward
              Spinning past the garbagedump
         Gas smell wafting thru Rahway overpass
         oiltanks in frozen ponds, cranes' feederladders
              Electric generator trestles, Batteries open under heaven
Anger in the heart—
              hallucinations in the car cabin, rattling
              bone ghosts left and right
         by the car door—by the broken ice box—
On to the Pennsylvania turnpike
                              Evergreens in Snow
         Laundry hanging from the blue bungalow
         Mansfield and U Thant ask halt Bombing North Vietnam
         State Department says "tit for tat."
              Frank Sinatra with a new negro voice
                         enters a new phase—
         Flat on his face 50 years "I've been a beggar & a clown
              a poet & a star
                   roll myself in July
         up into a ball and die"
                         Radio pumping
Pumping rock & roll, [?] artificial, Beach Boys
& the daughter of Sinatra overdubbed thru microphone
         antennae, car dashboard vibrating,

1967

False emotions broadcast thru the Land,
Natural voices made synthetic
     phlegm obliterated
Smart ones work with electronics—
      What are the popular songs on the Hiway
Home I'm comin home I am a soldier—
Synthetic voices,
        "the girl I left behind . . .
I did the best job I could
       helping to keep our land free
I am a soldier"
       Lulled into War
   thus the commercial jabber of the Rock & Roll Announcers
False False False
  Enjoy this meat—
  Weak A&P Superright ground round
  Factories building, airwaves pushing
Trees stretching up into the grey sky
Yellow trucks rolling down the lane
      Hypnosis of the airwaves
  In the house you can't break it
      unless you turn off yr set
  In the car it can drive yr eyes inward
    from the snowy hill,

    withdraw yr mind from the birch forest
      make you forget the car in the blue ice,
Drive yr mind down the aisles of the Supermarket
     looking for cans of Save-Your-Money
      Polishing Glue
    made of human bones manufactured in N. Vietnam
      during a mustard gas hallucination:
The Super-Hit sound of All American radio.

1967

Turnpike to Tuscarora
     Snow over fields, red lights blinking in the broken car
  Quiet hills, with genital hair black in sunset
  Beautiful dusk over human tinyness,
       Pennsylvanian intimacy,
           approaching Tuscarora Tunnel with
               Tussie mountains—
    Quiet moments off the road.
A missile lost Unprogrammed
      Twisting in flight to crash 100 miles
        south of Cuba into the
          Blue Carib!
  Diplomatic messages exchanged
  "Don't worry it's only the setting sun—"
  (Western correspondents assembling in Hanoi.)
    —"Perfect ball of orange in its cup of Clouds"
Dirty Snowbanks pushed aside from Asphalt
          thruway edge—
  Uphill's the little forest where the boyhoods grow their
           bare feet—

Night falling, "Jan 4, 1967, The Vatican Announces Today
  No Jazz at the Altar!"
     Maybe in Africa
  maybe in Asia they got funny music
    & strange dancing before the Lord
  But here in the West No More Jazz at the Altar.
    It's an alien custom—
Missa Luba[2] crashing thru airwaves with Demonic drums

2. An interpretation of the Roman Catholic Mass, following traditional musical
forms of the Democratic Republic of the Congo.

1967

behind the Kyrie Eleison—
Millions of tiny silver Western crucifixes for sale
in the Realms of King Badouin—
color TV in this year—weekly
the Pope sits in repose & slumbers to classical music
in his purple hat—
Gyalwa Karmapa sits in Rumtek Monastery Sikkim
& yearly shows his most remarkable woven Black
Magic hat
Whose very sight is Total Salvation—
Ten miles from Gangtok—take a look!

* * * *

Mary Garden dead in Aberdeen,
Jack Ruby dead in Dallas—
Sweet Green incense in car Cabin,
Dakini sleeping head bowed, hair braided
over her Rudraksha beads
driving through pennsylvania.
Julius, bearded, hasn't eaten all day
facing forward, pursing his lips, calm.
Sleep, sweet Ruby, sleep in America, sleep
in Texas, sleep Jack from Chicago,
Friend of the Mafia, friend of the cops,
friend of the dancing girls—
Under the viaduct near the book depot,
Under the hospital Attacked by Motorcades,
Under nightclubs under all the
Groaning bodies of Dallas,
under their angry mouths
Sleep Jack Ruby, rest at last,
—bouquet'd with cancer

1967

Ruby, Oswald, Kennedy gone
New Years' 1967 come
Reynolds Metals up a Half
Mary Garden, 92, sleeping tonite in Aberdeen.

Three trucks with yellow lights crawl uproad
Under winter network-shade, bare trees,
night fallen, distant light blinking.
Under Tuscarora mountain, a long tunnel,
WBZ in Boston coming thru—
"Nobody needs icecream nobody *needs* pot nobody needs
movies."
"public discussion"
Is sexual intercourse any Good? Can the kids handle it?
Out of the tunnel,
the Boston voice returning: "controlled circumstances . . ."
Into the tunnel, static & silence
Trucks roaring by in carbon mist,
Anger falling asleep at the heart.
White Rembrandt, the hills—
Silver domed silo standing above the farmhouse
in the white
Reality Place Farm up the road,
Mist Quiet on Woods,
Silent Reality everywhere.
Till the eye catches the billboards—
Howard Johnson's Silent Diamond Reality
makes the difference.
Student cannon fodder prepared for the next session of Congress
Willow Hill, Willow hill, Cannon Fodder, Cannon fodder—
And the Children of the Warmakers exempt from fighting
their parents war—

1967

Those with intellectual money capacities who go to college
       till 1967—
Slowly the radio war news
     steals o'er the senses
  Negro photographs in Rochester
       ax murders in Cleveland,
  Anger at heart base
      all over the Nation—
Husbands ready to murder their wives
    at the drop of a hat-statistic,
  I could take an ax and split Peter's skull
      with pleasure
Great trucks crawl up road,
    insect-lit with yellow bulbs outside Pittsburgh.
  "The Devil with Blue Dress" exudes over radio
      Car headlights, hotel signs in blackness,
     Satanic Selfs covering nature
       spiked with trees.
  Crash of machineguns, ring of locusts, airplane roar,
     calliope yell, bzzzs.

An Open Window on Chicago[3]

Jan 8, 1967

Midwinter night,
  Clark & Halsted brushed with this week's snow
  grill lights blinking at the corner

3. First draft of "An Open Window on Chicago," *Collected Poems*, 481–83.

1967

decades ago—
Smokestack poked above the roofs & watertowers
standing still above the blue
lamped boulevards
sky blacker than th' east
for all the steel smoke
settled in heaven from the South.
Downtown—like Superman's Gotham City,
battleshipped with lights
towers winking under clouds,
police cars blinking on Avenues,
space above city misted w/ fine soot
Cars crawling past redlites down Avenue,
Exuding white wintersmoke—
Eat Eat said the sign, so I went in the Spanish diner
The girl at the counter, whose yellow Bouffant roots
grew black over her pinch'd face
spooned her coffee with knuckles
puncture marked,
whose midnight wrists had needle tracks,
scars inside her arms—
"Wanna go get a Hotel Room with me?"
The Heroin Whore
of thirty years ago comes haunting Chicago's midnite streets,
with me come here so late with my beard!

Corner grill-lights blink, police car turned around
& took away its load of bum to jail,
black uniforms patrolling the streets
where suffering
lifts a hand palsied by Parkinson's Disease
to beg a cigarette.

1967

The psychiatrist came visiting this Hotel 12th floor—
    Where does the Anger come from?
    Outside! Radio Messages, images on television,
                The Media
  spread
      fear of murder on the Streets
      "Communications Media"
inflict the Vietnam War & its anxiety on every private skin
      in hotel room or bus—
Sitting, meditating quietly on Great Space outside—
Bleep Bleep dit dat dit the radio on, the Television
               murmuring,
  bombshells crash on flesh
    his flesh my flesh all the same—
The Dakini in the hotel room turns in her sleep
        while the War news flashes thru Aether—
  Shouts at streetcorners as the bums
      are helped in the policevan.
And there's a tiny church in the middle of Chicago
      with its black spike to the black air
And there's the new Utensil Towers round on horizon.
And there's the red glow of Central Neon
        on the hushed building Wells at 4 AM
And there's the proud Lights & Towers of Man's Central City
  looking pathetic at 4 AM traveler passing through,
  staring outa hotel window under Heaven—
Is this tiny city the best we can do?
  These tiny reptilian towers
    so proud of their Executives
  they haveta build a big sign in the middle of downtown
         to Advertise
Metal Cars in parkinglots,

1967

old Connor's insurance sign fading on the bricks
        Snow on deserted roofs—
Hog butcher to the world!
         Taxi-Harmonious Modernity grown rusty old
The Prettiness of Existence! To sit at the window
        & moan over Chicago's stone & brick
          lifting itself vertically tenderly
            hanging from the sky.

My elbow on the hotel sill,
        I lean and muse, taller than any building here
Steam from my head
        Wafting into the smog
        Elevators running up & down my leg
Couples copulating in hotelroom beds in my belly
         & bearing children in my heart,
        Eyes shining like warning tower Lights,
         Hair hanging down like a black cloud—
Close your eyes on Chicago and be God,
        all Chicago is, is what you see—
That row of lights on the Finance Building
        sleeping in its bottom floors,
    Watchman stirring
        paper coffee cups by the Bronzed
            glass doors—
and under the bridge, the brown water
        floats great turds of ice beside the feet of
            buildings
   in windy metropolis
      waiting for a Bomb.

1967

With Maretta Greer and Gary Snyder at the
Human Be-In. Photograph copyright Lisa Law.

1:40 AM   Mar 26, 1967

Blue wings blue sky blue buildings Boston
Easter pipes under white clouds, factory bay
Silhouetted against the asphalt runway-whine
pressure & astrojet noses up over waterside mansions
up over Atlantic, wing bends South & Skims
thru Noontime Clarity over snow frozen lakes,
Silent, smooth in the easychair, ears hushed,
Earthwoods roll below rivers of traffic by green tank families
watercourses between marsh and icy highway
snake backward under the majestic air throne,
Azure mist on earth & impenetrable azure heaven
Covering creased mapland Massachusetts planet-skin
White powder on earth fall'n from Cold blue sky,
icy sparklets scattered on tree dotted Weston & patches
of white, squared in fields & rifted between low hills,
it settles the argument maintained in electric thought,
Calm the hot drunkard's midnite soldier-vomit,
hides fox & hipster behind a white veil'd wood row,
& tonite will glisten misty under Easter's full moon.
Uninteresting rhetoric to cover flight to New York City
Smoke & Players, sip acid ginger ale, scribble ink,
New Haven like pubic hair on the winter nigger belly land
Great river/what's yr name? Nuts & Cigarette fumes
News headline Narcotics in the Sky, while I glide over
patch runnel & picture white peppered with treehair
Strong on iron tracks smoothed over grey Superhighways.
That must be Palisade's dropped grey cliff,
walling the river, Myriad streets of the Bronx,
Skyscrapers red against the wind, Manhattan's
Spikey fishtail floundered mouth, Fumes, haze,

1967

& downtown pinnacles hanging Stalagmitic in the blue,
Loops of stone gigantic auto artery the Central
ganglion of Queen's streetways, Chryslers &
Empire States needles over the bay glitter
Namb Zamanda Descending. To glass airport N.Y.

Nashville April 8, '67[4]

Crescent faces tiered hanging balconied
   face the giant red
Striped flag podium microphone reverberation from
   one body outward
breathed painfully up from rich suited abdomen
—mouth opening circle of white teeth—bells clanging
taillights long the Nashville city edge—in the
   leather car, acrid carfume sucked in the
   lung,
Majesty of speech and Chant, on the lawn under
   the streetlights
dry grass crowded with sweating collars shirted
   blond & forehead-starred semite singing—
In the far cities riot under spring moonless
   midnight black power.

 Hank Snow
"Yes I was waiting for the Call of the Wild
Knowing I'd be Crying like a Child"
       —Grand Ole Opry

----

4. First draft of "Nashville April 8." See *Wait Till I'm Dead*, 65.

1967

April 12, 1967 Dream
   —The Visiting Tibetans—

Making a man of house by house streets home neighborhood in Benares which is River Street in Paterson—walking past the Himalayan Pall, it's the Quarry—

Philip Whalen is up on the podium in church beginning to read his poetry, as he commences there's a rustling of Tibetans droning ceremonial mantras in the sparsely filled back room, & up in the organ lofts invisible songs and chanting. Whalen continues undisturbed & then falls silent for awhile—in a nonce the chief priest rises & his pupils file out, I go talk to him in the lobby, he lays out on a chaise lounge, the young tall guru student and re-wraps silk robe over his nakedness, & tells me of a letter he's received from WC Williams,[5] very old near death, asking them to visit, and asking me to come sing interpret as friend.

I'm overwhelmed, it all concludes so logically & explain to him that Williams so near death will probably die in their ceremonial presence in old old age, how strange that threads of separate study should bring me together with WCW and themselves to the last fatal room.

Maretta there, has my old check made out to her & asks me if it's all right she stay till St. Vitus Dance Day or Padmagbara Rinpoche's Birthday a month ahead, before departing.

I say of course yes & lay my head in her lap, weeping happy that all fates are reconciled Tibetan & Patersonian in Williams' Deathbed, that I be present—Meanwhile the young Guru shows us some forms & Thankas being worked out—

5. New Jersey poet and pediatrician William Carlos Williams (1883–1963) befriended and mentored Allen Ginsberg in Ginsberg's early days as a poet, including some of his letters in his epic volume *Paterson* and writing introductions to Ginsberg's *Howl and Other Poems* and *Empty Mirror*.

1967

Printed medical-neural forms oracular of nature spotting WCW's particular psychic stage—with analytic comments—like "Demand pectal chakra opening—Demand Tibor Triumph!" Demand Tibor Triumph? I think, WCW a doctor even on deathbed will be able to identify these Bardo Thodol instructions, how just! the form? "was printed by Rahanma Behen." The artists lady friend had made out a delicate arty Tibetan medical sheet—form for them to use & adapt in West.

An altarpiece, Tibetan style, being constructed as a Seattle (re'd. phonecall invitation to read at Wash U. where Sakyana resides)—oddly enough I see at bottom the central figures with small eyes and clay modelled, colored brightly with black eye dots for eyes and black dab or paint on pink upper lip in Charles Chaplin's effigy—& there's [?] & others of the east—the Tibetans used them all, couldn't tell the horses from the transient supporting cast, how charming & naïve!—But notice how Charlie's definite black mustache stands out among all the larger drooples red & grey handlebars the others sported for their less definite style.

Woke, remembering "Passaic & Ganges one." How in Paterson the effort should be to clean the Passaic, & return it to Holy River status, for Bathing—Oberlin 1967

April 16, 1967   Boulder

Men w/ black genitals are sprites that can create more sprites, each generation fading.

The Boot-Tailed Grackle's Two-note song

How news of a kiss in N.Y. reaches Albuquerque—
He told me how I kissed him in Millbrook, as we sat in bright sunlight under the Turquoise sky watching Turquoise dancers stamp the earth

1967

with bells in a sunken plaza-hollow at San Felipe Pueblo, Corn dancers advancing in great rows like the waves at Bixby Canyon.

Thru Rockies[6]

Sun set up thru the grey rock walls of Clear Creek Canyon
       white ice in the rock-sluice below,
            pines in late afternoon light
             marching the snow-sprinkled wall of Mt. Thigh—
out of Golden on the road that passes Central City 1946
We stole a car at nite, drove together down mountain,
          my head in his lap, old loving Hells Angels
              without uniform or leather—
             just our hopeful eyes, newborn bodies
          zooming into Denver round the curves of night,
             coasting with the engine off . . .
Into open sun, pink rock-walls, into present winter
                toward San Francisco
    water rushing under ice,
        rock hillock higher
           sprinkled with jackpine.
The canyon levels out, the road curves spacious
         snaking in space between rock
Hurrah for the mountains, Hurrah for rough nature,
  Hurrah for invisible beauty, Hurrah for Memory—
Hurrah for life itself which grows such giant hermit
        rocks in mountains,
          visible green ferntrees lifting their spiky petticoats

6. Ginsberg did not date this poem, which was the only entry in one journal. It is inserted here because it fits with his journal writings of his time in Colorado.

1967

        & transparent dresses to sky—
     lean out over icy river & bow to the car passing—
     stand sentinel in mountain passes, gazing
         on tiny cars with lit lites
           speeding round the curve.
Central City Turnoff—thru tunnel
     Idaho Springs, green sign says—
     the mountain lifts its teeth,
           we go in the south of a tunnel
    Silence everywhere except for the roaring of our own machine
I never been deeper than this into the mountains,
           into the imaginary Rockies
              Well Hurrah— . . .
  the lip of the rock raises up & closes down.
  orange shadows on butte tops,
        Lone Star Uranium Mine Open to Public
and Dow Chemical/U.S. Atomic Energy/Mutual Service Road
   on Rocky Flats above Denver,
   Had a line of cars about 2 miles long back of the
factories set there on the plains. You could see it
from the highway, smokestacks & intelligent looking
antennae. They were making napalm. Who's the stock-
holders at Dow Chemical? Y'oughta write 'em a letter &
tell 'em what they're doin they don't even know?
     out into the open, all information,
     out into open on highway's summit
          heading West at dusk—
form Single Lane Please form Single Lane
       entering 40 thru Rockies
   under wire carrying watchtowers,
        Hidden Valley right lane
    Howard Johnson's Motor Lodge & Restaurant Sign

1967

advertising itself in Denver—
The Valley deepens giant, eyebrows brushed w/ cloud
    Grey lion crouching in sky,
      wires networking the metropolitan mountain West—
Berthoud past over Great Divide,
Dusk turned to orange darkness,
        white ghost robes of snow
        over sleeping mountains ranged West,
   deep valleys widening toward the last dim sun glow
        Orion lamp stationary over their sleeping bodies
        stars rayed out, dotted up in the sky,
           over the ranges
        stretched toward the name Utah,
  So we go, hatred in heart,
          over the Rockies at night,
          Moffatt Tunnel comin' up.
         Hare Krishna
Hare Krishna, Krishna Krishna Hare Hare Hare Rama Hare Rama
                Hare Rama Hare Hare—
"and we also look forward to the time when greater
security can be achieved thru measures of arms control
and disarmament . . ."
Driving thru the snow, carlights on white hillock
  yellow line curving under stars,
      Johnson's voice vibrating thru the dashboard
        tonight speaking before Congress
    "We are here to end the cold war."
        Applause. Applause.
However, there's hard facts to face
        Under the Capitol Dome
   under the stars in Colorado
      his voice turns hard

1967

"Nuc'ler"—

Well, he stands there, they're applauding

the voice rose, & he considered fits of anger

& now he'll punch it home—facing west

huddled in the car, first time in Salt Lake City,

Big Dipper leaning over snow humps

Hare Krishna chanted over & over

"So we consult & seek the advice—"

There's no way of peace but be peaceable sir.

"I come now finally to Vietnam & Southeast Asia"

Back to burning issues

"We are

in Vietnam

because the United States of America and our Allies

are committed by SEATO treaty

to act to meet the common danger of Aggression

in Southeast Asia"

—Sir that's not correct your interpretation of the law

"signed by the United States North

Vietnam and others in 1962"

1962?

You talking about 1952 or 1962 we didn't sign

nothing in 1962, we didn't sign anything in 1952.

. . . "right to remain Communist"

& you ain't given either of them a chance.

. . . "By solemn vote."

Big Fake!

Tonkin Resolution?

. . . "once spoken by the great Thos. Jefferson"

Oy Gevalt!

. . . "Societies to be compelled sometimes to choose

a great evil"—

1967

O come come cheer up chap, it's not as bad as that
  ... "in order to ward off a greater evil."
   Hon i soit qui mal y pense.
... "we have chosen to fight a limited war in Vietnam."
  Oh my God!
     ... "I believe if the Communists succeeded
      in overrunning & taking over South Vietnam
      by aggression & by force."
Well that's quite a statement there yer makin'—
  Boy they're sure applauding that one.
    (Applause!)
  They're all mad, what's going wrong here?
     Is this the Capitol? Is this the Congress?
        Yup!
"I believe I am supported by some authority"
    Some authorities but not all of them—
"If they're not checked now the world can expect to pay
    a greater price ..."
   O big race war!
      ... "Later"
   You're completely mad!
... "Ratified 82 to 1 by the Senate many years ago"—
What treaty you talking about now? Oh, SEATO?
      That's right—
"Is there anyone here who doubts , , , ?"
  Peter at wheel over Rockies cries
   in distance "I do!"
  Passing Colorado River Jan 10, 1967
Droning on word after word, phrase after phrase,
   (Applause Applause) equivocal
   that wasn't the history I read in NY Times
   that wasn't what flashed thru my brain on radio.

1967

He's got different thoughts than me!
"I tell you that we're dealing with a
stubborn adversary that's committed to the use
of force and terror . . ."
But who is the Adversary you're talking about?
North Vietnam? China? Buddhism? Who?
"I wish I cd report to you that the Conflict is almost over"
Well you didn't say what the Conflict is
"This I cannot do" So it's gonna go on forever.
"I cannot promise you that it will come this year,
or come next year"—
or sometime in your lifetime even Sir?
"Our Adversary still believes I think tonight"
Ah the Great Adversary, Satan!
At 'em, Diabolous!
"We'll be prepared to stand up & resist"
Samsara is Eternal, Nirvana Eternal
Said the Dakini earlier today.
"Have borne well the burden in the heat o' the day"
Fear no more the Furious
Winters' Races

"Communist enemy"
Communists are the enemy, at long last we know!
"We have steadily frustrated his main forces"
Gibberish (Applause)
They think that they won the war!
"Sustained until he realizes"
He? He? Who? Ho Chi Minh? Mao Tse Tung?
The Enemy?
"Patience, and I mean a great deal of patience"
O my gawd, yes. The voice so tender.
Patience & a thought!

1967

"Our South Vietnamese allies." S. V Allies?

                Who're they now? Now wait a minute.

Whistling . . . "A personal stake in their government"

        Madam Nhu years ago picking up opium

             shipments at Tan Son Nhat Airport.

"The distinguished Ambassador Henry Cabot Lodge—

        This task with a new sense of presence."

Heavens he was saying that when I was there in 1963,

             3 ½ years ago—

"And we can help, but only they can win"—

But you need to say only them can fight the War!

           *   *   *   *   *

Palace to Palace, Dinner in Denver,

        "at Johns Hopkins in Baltimore, in 1965"

—he attacked the intellectuals—

      "A new reality"—

A new reality? I wanna New Reality too

             "their faith is strong"

They're marching forward w/ the Boy Scouts.

"Special Program of 200 million dollars"

200 million dollars? That ain't no money at all!

      Spending, what is it, a billion a month on the war?

"We would be the first to welcome China"—

The white rabbit crossed into headlights on the flat road

    hesitated by the white line, looked into car lights,

           and bounded off, south—

    while Johnson invited China to be friendly,

      in the future, in the future.

    "That we, the American people & our allies,"

    Meanwhile with his voice rising will

        Force Them Third World Down

1967

are going to Be Sure Will Be

And if they don't we'll killem By God

"peace." (Applause)

"United Nations . . .

unconditional discussions anywhere anytime"—

Include the Vietcong?

"we will stand firm in Vietnam!"

Congress applause that seals the fate

of the World! Applause Doom!

Spreading over the earth! They're going to back him up!

Total murder in every direction!

Support our Soldiers & Armies—

ultimately, these boys against the invisible enemy.

We invent Satan, we invent our own enemy, we

manufacture our own Karma—

Here Johnson manufactures America Karma,

creating an evil Demon against which

to struggle—

The Name is "the Adversary" the Name is "The Enemy"

The Name is the "Communists"—the names the

small evils against the Great Evils

"without arousing passions"

a great actor, back to tenderness,

Biblical that—"A time of testing"

our loins and sinews—

"The transition is . . . often unpopulist. Always

Very dangerous"

Fatal ever?

"Must like man" Like me?

"Like many" Om Mani Padme Hum.

"To the one who governs us all"—

Who me?—

1967

"Hope . . . we've been tested before,
        & America has never been found wanting"—
What an actor, my God on the stage he's been tested
      he's being tested, he's gonna test
        everybody else he's gonna murmur, he's
      gonna cry—"We are going to persist
And we are going to succeed" Demonic—
      Applause
Now the news broadcast will hit the air
Now the discussions'll begin
      Now is the moment of decision.
    Now in Golden Gate Park the Children will be assembling

Down Highway 40.   He's shaking hands with
        Senator Dirkson.
We're floating down to Steamboat Springs,
  shaking hands with "many
       of whom are old friends."
The highway's icy now, snow white in glare light
  stopping to shake some more hands,
  and here's the first analysis
     "A proposal that taxes be increased"
    More, 6% surcharge—
     "as long as Vietnam expenditures"—
Great, great, they'll begin screaming about that one!
—Well there we know, not to pay our Surcharge.
Not much applauses for that one.

Night, Berthoud's Pass crossed over,
Long descent on snowy road
  Orion crossing from one side highway to another

1967

    puncturing the blackness—
Asleep in back of the car, down into the desert plain
    dreams filling the cabin.

    the wandering Dakini had entered Tangier—
    we approached Tangier slowly
        gliding thru oily blue water on the ship
    & I see to my horror these great somber
               white colored missiles & painted
    outer & inner spacecraft,
        death-bedecked machines with noses
            slanting upward.
    Facing them to protect them from harm or
        inconvenience were guns & great cannons—
        pointing our way also—

        "I met some Tangerians
    & some smoke heads, and one young pregnant woman
    who was married to a soldier.
There was a Moroccan who had an amulet with
        a big picture of Krishna around his neck.
            Truckdriver.

"I went back to the port with
    a boy that I've met in the city—
'Did you notice the missiles?'
    I asked him, he said 'No I haven't'—
So we took a small boat along the water
We were stopped at this huge area
where there was wheat being stored & packed away,
and wheat everywhere—white like sand.
And we couldn't see the missiles & I said

1967

'Look, look, crane your neck a little bit & just
　　　　below you can see the
　　one gleaming shaft of a missile head—'
He said, 'No, I don't see it, you must be nuts.'
So then I said well it's off to the country for me
　　　　to write a book on how Moroccans screw—
& started off hitchhiking for Marrakesh."

I dreamt, meanwhile
　　that we were downtown in the large city,
　　　　hurrying laden down w/packages toward
　　　　　　the old apartment that I'd rented in the hotel—
Maretta & I and Julius & Peter—
　　and we went over the viaduct,
　　　　congratulating ourselves on having this
　　large house prepared for us—
Leary was to arrive—
　　As we got downtown,
　　　　as 'twere, on Broadway Paterson in fact,
　　　　　　by the little park I played as a child at,
We laid down our packages.
　　It turned out toward a graveyard,
　　　　& walking thru the graveyard,
　　　　　　found some benches to rest at—
Now I'd had a project which was to make a movie—
So I left my camera there, and I left a package
　　　　Full of books, and I left my notebooks and all
—and we discussed the stones of the graveyard—
　　　　large stones and small
　　walking thru the aisles looking for our own mayhap
But I'd forgotten my taperecorder.
　　So we made the long journey back to

1967

the original place

& got the taperecorder & came back,

& when we came back we found that we'd left all our books

and maps, & packages from Macy's

sitting there on the gravestone,

but nobody'd stolen 'em, fortunately—

So while one & another wandered up down aisles of graveyard

I went around the corner of the hedges to a large stone

Bench beneath the porch with Julius—

& the door opened from the porch

and an Indian lady & gentleman stared out at us—

The Indian gentleman came down from his door,

sat down next to us & said "What, uh,

what God, Gentlemen, do you fellows believe in?"

So I said "Well, we don't know what we were

believing in but we were just discussing

some Buddhist divinity or other that"—

"Aha! I happen to have with me a little book . . ."

by some South Indian kindly face guru with

long hair & a turban on the front cover.

who reminded me very much of the graveyard attendant.

who'd come down so neighborly to talk with us.

So I said "are you familiar with the doctrines in this book?"

And he said, "Yes I am, I happen to be."

So I said, "Well, what are the doctrines in this book,

what does he say?"

& he said, "Well, if you look at the cover picture

you will see"—

And I looked at the cover picture & there were two

Divine figures dancing before each other

& I said

"What does that mean?"

1967

And he said
"Oh! That's Vishnu dancing before Shiva"—
And I thought to myself, "Uhuh! That lets me in
                                                somewhere."

Then Julius who was sitting there at a marble table
                        suddenly spoke up
            with a long complicated sentence
      "But if it were true that the proposition left it that
there were no reason to be worried about and no reason
for existence not to be worried about, then would there
be any proposition which would prevent one from not re-
sponding under any Circumstance to all Circumstances?"
And I saw that I had my taperecorder there,
      and the taperecorder was on & had been
            catching Julius' conversation—
      except the only trouble was the sound
                  button was on, so
      I silently secretly started fiddling with
                  my taperecorder hoping that Julius
                  would continue the conversation
                  and we'd get a response & answer back,
                  while I got the Complete Coherent
                              Julius Statement—
"and in sum," concluded Julius,
      "is it correct to eat?"
and this kindly old holyman disciple of holymen
      who looked just like himself
                  on the bookcover
      said unto Julius
"Well certainly it's certainly all right to eat
      as long as you sing.

1967

And it looks to me from your face & the
    sound of your voice
That you have a very nice singing voice.
So it wd be indicated that you should eat,
      perfectly all right to eat"—
At which point I woke.

        Lights shone in the truck
              from Neon Gas Station
      two miles over the border into mist—
However, reported Maretta,
    There were these silos with missiles
Gleaming in one direction & there were these cannons gleaming
    in the other direction under a turquoise sky—
& if anybody approached you might be fired upon
        from another direction, she
      said excitedly at the formica counter
    of the 5 AM Diner Truckstop.

Dawn, down Wasatch where Kerouac
           passed thru snow valleys
Ranged walling the road, open West,
Descending on a foggy morning on Salt Lake's
Lights—White snow fresh fallen,
White fog covering sky,
    round the city up the highway viaduct bowling alley
        out 80
      past the airport toward Reno
  —Looking back on Salt Lake City,
3 smokestacks, with lights at midriff & top
    to ward off airplanes,
    pour forth their white smoke in the air

1967

already mist-white
robes of smoke wrapped round the factories,
steaming up between giant chimneys
on flatland,
as 'twere the mist of morn at North Pole—
or a cosmic icy dawn painted by Turner
hanging in the middle of the air—
Then out of fog in desert between Cedar Mts. &
Lakeside Mts. toward Lowe town
Road miles straight ahead hits white buttes,
& a train coming down the valley
60–70 cars, the eye counted them
creeping slowly across the landscape—
The 30th car,
two tanks
sitting on a flatbed truck—
And up in the mountains,
Aluminum giant structure, eyes or ears
of the chemical factory
that sign on the road U.S. Army
with the testtube and alchemical formulas painted
in the liquid in the glass—
What did it mean?
Bacteria or Atoms here?
& space suddenly becomes more vast
this side of the Rockies—
The mountains greet armchairs on either side of the valley
America armed like Thor over the rest of the world—
They haveta make war now,
They're all being paid to.
All these folks who got the job up there on that
mountaintop with them
eyes & ears of Chemistry, require anxiety and crisis

1967

to pursue their studies, so 'tis Radar
that keeps us imprisoned in our War Psychosis
we'll never get out of till we're bombed.

"Namo Tat Se Baghvato Arahato Sauma Sambutatsa"

Denver Dallas Above[7]
    City blocks striped to the sun hazed
        Center grey towers
    gleam of heaven light silver low ranches
        snow shine
            spread forward on the knees of the plains
    Lake's green gleam on dry flats, ranges
of nose/headed black rock paving the horizon
      tendrils of snow in snaky stream
        wrinkles of ground
    Brown flats south to ruled squares
        patched with green—
O eagle, tin eagle, turning & piercing thy
        eyes down-glanced on tiny roof
        & old sashed, sand rolled tree
        bordered skeleton—
Total Silence above Earth—Heliport
    Buckrogers green let to Texas Buckminster
    Fuller Futurity Misted to the planet horizon
Hovering between Land and Heaven-Cloud
    Arrived under the sky suspended
The plains toward Liberal, & Oklahoma City
    & south into Texas.

----

7. Unpublished auto poesy.

1967

May 10, 1967—*Over Ohio*

I

Columbus downtown—all the nooks and crannies,
    alleyways and tower tons, elevator sidings—
brown settled earth of O—water soaked
    lush green, thin streams slinting in
    sunlight
as the silent Caravelle turns over Dayton—descends
    thru silk-grey haze of mansmoke—
Turn back the earth to run wild, Nature orders thru
    a million brains—

II

Smoke over Chicago

Iron Earth dappled with houseroofs, highways
    streaked by iron-bound rivers,
Tangle of roads, car husks feeding at flat market
    Centros—
gas-white haze between city and ocean-cloud, a
    streak blue sky between—
Over the city, man's smoke, cigarette auto factory
    Chemical dust from endless tiny fires,
synthetic combustion filling the air with orange
    mist, Who Can see the sky?
a red cloud moving over the suburbs, miles long,
Rust storm lose in the vast horizon & gas

III

Squared by white canals, "peaceful
    little farmlands down there"—
the gas extends to Iowa, light clouds

1967

drifting over yellow haze—
not by the sun—that light, not from the sky
      that opaque blue—
issued from the mouth of man. The eye
      blinds the eye.
Transportable television lenses smudged by
      diesel fumes.

IV

About the nicest thing in Iowa City
      wooden tables, and a sense of calm.

May 17, 1967 Above U.S. NYC L.I.

Last nite parties at the Algonquin[8]
      Lowell[9] render Voznesensky[10] minor immortals
          enraptured on the carpet, eyes
      gazing over the shoulders of Italian dolls
          at snowy Marianne Moore,
Andrei Crying Kalakala Bam Michelangelo
          in Town Hall's perfumed darkness,
empty pain around the eyes, the night before
      Strut ball from the 1920's Paris Review
          Gorgeous hippies caressing Space Age walls

8. Storied New York hotel.

9. Poet Robert Lowell (1917–1977) won the National Book Award for his poetry collection *Life Studies*.

10. Ginsberg met Russian poet Andrei Voznesensky (1933–2010) when he traveled to the Soviet Union in 1965. The two became friends and occasionally read together.

1967

Om Raksha hum hum hum phat Svaha
       to the executive Vietnam War Believer behind his booth
          grey pamphlets spread lonesome for this
            dancing done fiend sex hero's money Ball—
Zoom, arise and go fly above earth to see
          houseboats & toylike jetties at Atlantic edge
            dwarfed by 17 Mayday's ocean
Atlantic's white shore adieu,
        and today Rosalind Constable hath cocktail Party
          farewell to sneaky *Time.*
Flat City reverberates, graveyards yearn green, highways loop the woods,
Clouds wall the west, floating Himalaya above
      blue Connecticut shores—

May 18, 1967[11]

       Road to Corvallis, green fields of May
        Lotus ponds jagged Coniferous families,
\
            Snow gleaming in blue space mountains
           alive when the clouds procession
            ripples over the Coast
              in high blue heaven
     Green trees blazon the stream
       wires cross over the green bridge struts
     bright colored gasstation bright roses
      spilling over the sidewalk
Joy in white car rolling downstreet,
      Engineering Laboratory blocked

11. Unpublished auto poesy.

1967

Next to joyful signs in the Construction field
"I care vote democratic see the World"

June 11, 1967

    Things to do in N.Y. Renew passport
                    Adjust COP Books & Taxes
                    Mss to Spoleto in time
To do still?—Taxes

June 14, 1967

Poetry[12]

Rays from the head, Concrete buttresses white
rising in the dawn streets. Heroes emerge
from tenement doors at all hours, younger
& younger as acid wars strip our brains
blot thought & reveal the smells of garbage harbor.
more heroes will come, unheard of, unimagined
new type terrific heroes, sexless heroes even,
yet heroes of the smog & they'll make us happy
with flower power action, giant brooms, electric
bananas, guerilla loveface, cop amour, heter
oh sexual casualness & I'll changing the mystery
hope again tho dead to the world for new heroes.

12. Ginsberg liked this poem, which he typed into a manuscript and titled "A Prophecy." He eventually assigned the title to another poem, and this one was never published.

1967

Community heroes, handy with monkey wrench & pipes.
Whitmanic heroes, fulfilling labor in U.S. Augean stables.
Eastern & Western heroes, flying airplanes between jobs.
Rich and poor heroes, prophesying more heroes, till the whole
democratic population composed of heroes becomes tranquil.

June 18, 1967

    Dylan says McClure should get a Gut string Guitar
"and feel like Roosevelt."
Then old steel string Harmony Guitar.
"North Country Blues"—his favorite from 3rd album

July 4, 1967

    Over Atlantic into space, sinking sensation as the Italian plane swoops
thru evening bluity.
    Left Julius, Jim Guiterrez Aronowitz & Peter waving his hands like
seagull wings at Kennedy Airport balcony. Last days spent correcting mss,
copying tapes of mantras Indian & Jewish, cleaning desk.

Early July, 1967

Since poetry's made of language,
let's make language move—run!
Jump, Clop, clop, clop, up!
Crash! Bang! over the wall!
Stone roads! Zap! Boom! roar!
away! away! over & over! Terrific!
Gone! Bam! Rat Tat Tat! Bang! zip! Shazam!

1967

Bing Bang Bam Bong! Boo! Boffo! orchids!
Cockadoodledoo! Trees! Hurrah! Dogs,
Bark! arowf! raahr! Farms! Cats! meow!
Wow! slam into it! Cows! moo! Motorcycle!
grazoom! Svaha; Abracadabra! Phat phat phat!
om

Since Poetry's made of language
Let's make language move—run
Jump, up! Away, over the wall!
Crash! Bang! Stone Roads! Zoom! Terrific!
orchids! Roar! Beep Beep Beep! Gone! Zap!
Bong! Baidicas! Boom! Dogs!
Bark! Arf! Wul farms! Cockadoodle-doo!
Cats! Meow! Moo! Boffo! Police! Rat Tat Tat!
Bam! Wow! Motorcycles! Blam! gazoom!
Trees! Hurrah! Man! Shazam! abracadabra!
phat phat phat om Svaha!

Boom Zap Shazam!

Giddyap! Help! yippie! Gee!
Basta! Abracadabra! yippie! Gee!
Giddyap! Help! murder! Police! The fox is at the geese!
stop thief stop! the Swan's on top!

Trees! Whoosh!

War boom!
    autos! Beep beep beep put put.

    Boom Zap Shabam!
    abracadabra Bang!

1967

Boffo! Bah bah bah Lamb!
Autohouses! Beep! Beep! Beep! Clang!

Zap Boom Shabam

The tiny theater of hands
A lighted stage
   where old Cocksuckers sing
To rows of ourselves

   balding, white silken haired,
     or bearded with golden smiles
Sitting velvet chair'd

   agaze at Mozart's music
   dream recurring with body—
which is real, the play or
   audience?
   Don Giovanni's lived a hundred
     times our age—
old Pound with tiny pupils
   sits quiet in the darkness
    as the scene backdrop
falls behind a figure in
   black singing to him
    on the stage.
I've heard this music
   all over Europe millions
    have heard what I
     heard in high school
Old theater! of Life!

1967

The melody's so Calm
    so familiar—

I am a hero in the balcony box,
I might have been Stendhal
    whispering to the police—
& Ezra Pound in the same room
    with his picture in the
        Eternal newspapers—
with the Chorus of youths
    Dancing la! la! la! to
        his silent observe—
& a box full of Poets feeling
    mellow!
& hundreds audience satisfied
    to hear the opera tonite
—life looking at life—Harmonious
    Music accompanies us all
from under the stage.

Giovanni's a simple story
    he gets angry & gets killed
            by Hell—
The statue Comes of Life, after many
    Desires chanted
        for thy living hand—
O Lord of all Music, of all
    Poets, lord of opera & stages,
Lord of dreams, Lord of Desire,
    Lord of Illusions, Lord of old
whitehaired Men near their Death,
    Lord of Audiences, Spectators,

1967

Lord of Selves,
    Lord of old Houses, of Stone Cities
Lord of Nations,
        Lord of History
    Lord of planets circulating
      in their worlds—
O Lord of All—

Bless every Italian tourist in
    this theater tonite,
as I bless myself and these
    actors
as I bless myself in these
    Spectators & in Ezra Pound
  whose tiny pupils' silent Calm
answered my Blessing gaze
    with Tiny Blink of blue
          space,
ocean color, ancient dream
    Heaven sir, wrinkle-
      lidded eye.

        Spoleto Opera House   July 7, 1967

July 9, 1967—4 M

Read this evening Spoleto—including small Spoleto mantra—went off happy to drink little beers in café across Duoso Church façade plaza with Octavio Paz looking brown brown India and Desmond O'Grady chirping Irish from eternity with red hair—a tall man in business suit stepped next to me as I was alone in crowd by the bar, and said in Italian "... polizia

1967

... Lei con nosotros ... estacion"—Sudden recall of the old police sensation, isolation trap. "I don't speak Italian," I said & slipped back to me seat at table, murmuring immediately to Desmond neighbor poet "It's the police please find Patrick Creagh immediately"—Then rose and tried to make sure my mss. was safe by carrying Greek bag of texts in Ettore Sottsass[13]—oops! the bag was upside down & a great splash of dreamy manuscripts made me stoop to gather them from the marble café floor. "Don't panic," said Desmond.

Thereafter for three hours at the police station discovering with overexcited inspector Romero. Who'd been brought the Italian mimeo copies by the plump mustachioed aging door guard who in white uniform presided as police representative to the poetry readings in the tiny balconies red velvet theatre.

Nanda Pivano and Patrick Craigh both came to interpret for me at the station—Long "philosophic" arguments over what was obscenity according to Italian law—if a word in the dictionary had the italicized capitalization writ obscene then it was so defined by penal code etc. & so he Romero had to take action, especially so in phone conversation with the Spoleto public prosecutor, the prosecutor had instructed him to take me in for questioning & arrest.

I balked at the form of testimony I was asked for, it being Romero's language I was presented to sign, & not my own—so we rewrote the text to begin w/giant question, was it true that I Allen Ginsberg born 1926 at theater Duomo Sq. recited poetry including following lines? and I dictated friendly answer "Such lines taken out of context might be misunderstood ... message actual goodwill to peaceful men."

Then with haste to opera, after 3 hours delay at station temporizing & arguing—Romero over-excited realizing the folly of the scene (as in

13. Friend of Ginsberg and husband of Nanda Pivano, Italian translator of Ginsberg, Kerouac, and other Beats.

1967

Italian movie, papers, typewriters, finally friendly paranoiac beers to-
gether, circumstantial police language, intimate confession "I personally
didn't want to do this but the prosecutor said . . ." Paparazzi snapping
photos as we returned to car to show at opera at request of Spoleto Fes-
tival Press office, lest there be scandal & scene buzzing with charming ru-
mor at the Ballet, & everyone in white tie & Gowns—so I hustled to the
opera steps, carrying on blest Shivite beads & Amerindian God's eye over
white Brooks Brothers shirt—

Menotti Directors of Festival in tails entered thru the Stone Columns
from taxi having talked to the Prosecutor said "it's terribly apologetic, so
sorry . . . and nothing will happen . . . we should not gather crowds," . . .
so I went to the bar with Paz and Craigh & Sottsass & talked excitedly,
what a magic spell of a scandal, but then news shook down at return to
Menotti, hushing it o'er, that merely a slight legal process would be insti-
tuted against the poems in my absence, taking years.

At which point I began smelling a rat & woke from bed hours later to
begin recording a little detail as at Harvard & Prague.

— o — o —

And may not have wakened but that drifting into sleep earlier, as
Berryman calmed with whisky clanked his key awkwardly in the lock ad-
jacent room of pension Aurora where my window oversees the green hill-
farms at sunset—I was wakened from a half-dream: That I had begun the
old descent from the Tower of Fear along mediaeval stone Wales, along
narrow steps, close to the craggy castellated rock side of the high place
that leaned over earth, and stepping further down another stairway I saw,
below the floor of heaven transparent, fields and distant villages far below
me—so I stepped on heaven's floor thru which saw old earth—unafraid to
return downward—And at that moment by magic, the transparent fabric
of heaven & green landscape of earth parted for a giant instant & were
revealed as Show, Maya, Sensory Curtain, Theater-Dream, long sleep-
illusion and a magnetic old Eternal Void Presence razed familiar on my

1967

mind. This place, hotel Spoleto & poetry police—this is not even here, it's a distracting phantom fire in front of the senses, it was never here at all—Sankaracharaya's rope got confused with a serpent in the giant moment's dream—& another giant moment dispersed the ignorance as greater consciousness was woken. All those clowns were longing with painted mouths for not one tree or tent in antiquity & Ozymandias was a thought. The desert wonked.

July 10, 1967

Dream after meeting E. P.

I came to visit Pound, in N.Y.C. on Monroe Street in N.Y.C.

(which was also several blocks around the corner from 155 Haledon Ave Paterson, the last place I was Idyllically happy.)

I went in and sat with the old man who was friendly but silent totally, for hours.

"Silence to say goodbye."

So endured the afternoon. I was ready to leave. When suddenly there was a total change of demeanor, the extreme alertness & ease, friendliness, & cheerful faced talking on his part—he reminded me of the time I'd actually visited him & forgot, on Monroe Street in N.Y., years ago before it all. And asked him to stay for longer, for supper, on the stove. I hesitated, overjoyed he'd woken—I realized he was like Julius—in and out of it—in and out of his body, dependent on accident of physicalology—

He was rolling pot at his desk & we were jabbering away—Delicious moments of Frank friendliness—yes he'd read my first book—"Moloch" I said "was good." I was not agitated one way or another, nor doubted myself.

In fact he said, "all the long time I was silent & helpless today during your visit, you Ginsberg were silent, attentive calm & self contained, and not a source of disturbance or invitation—so do stay to supper"

His thin face very animated & happy. "Imagine what terrific sweet

1967

strength you could have laid on those football heroes, if you'd been awake when they came to the door?"

Later his room is crowded, I see there is a whole secret hip life spring round him in his live moments—Jimmy "Cher" and cat-faced Heiserman in a mask—and Bob Dylan and others are all in and out, sleeping & eating & sitting on the floor.

This dream after meeting Pound at Don Giovanni in Theatre Melisso Spoleto last night. He sat in orchestra on aisle. I walked down & waited for people to move to seats, bowed & said Namaste w/hands at breast, Mrs. Rudge "oh this is the man who wrote you" . . . Pound slowly rose to his feet looking directly into my eyes & we stood that way calmly & quietly for several minutes, after I had bent my head to touch forehead to his hand. Finally afraid of tiring him on his feet who knows how fragile—& unsure despite the little pinprick blue eternal calm in the pupil-sharp eye that he was not just being polite & helpless, I put hand on his neck & winked assurance—he blinked like blankly on a turtle—I put hand on his neck & indicated to sit down. Parted—"next time I see you I'll chant mantras."

> End

July 18, 1967

    Dandelion Fly Away

5:30 AM—all night in glass wall Electric studio watching from coffee-cup'd consol'd Sound Room at three Graces Mick Jagger, Paul McCartney & John Lennon sat on high stools before two microphones in their Botticelli finery, rings on delicate hands clapped to violet breast for high ecstatic swooning notes, crimson satin pants & voices trembling toward the angelic at the center of the Shabda Universe Sound machinery darkness of London's outskirts—repeated over and over into microphone by

1967

Jagger thru thin body thick lips, his genitals bulged at tight trousered youth—eyes of Clara Bow on man McCartney, round pupils tuned up listening to last funky sweet note fade—gold round glasses sitting on Lennon's grandfatherly nose, as he pursed his hips forward, leaning to sing—Dandelion,[14] Disappear—the flower moment of the rue, richness as amethyst & Pearl, Diamond noise for the mind, majesty of the most delightful labor of the Universe, chanting music to the world, angels of the summit of meat—I stared and made mudras of Raksha prayer, Tibetan oracle-ringed & hung with fearful Rudraksha beads, adoring them or ringing Shiva Self. And they hailed harikrishna when they trooped back to the sound room to hear the finished tape crashing thru channels of black loudspeakers to high-noted harmonic sound hush.

EMOTIONS RECOLLECTED IN ANTIQUITY

Now or in Wales' Forum of lamb mist
Plenty of time to breathe & smoke tobacco
Scribe by yellow lamp opprest or orange petalled
Chrysanthemum Buddha handed up in head's text
XX Century Carnation tender-budded Zodiac folded
Central, eye-children meat sprigs yellow beneath upsprung
fingerling blossom crowded mass unfolded dying tongues
mint cool, harmless blossom, set on green soft stick,
limp leaved, Buddha Scepter cut for our Dearness,
round myriad empetaled simulacra, timed swiftness
visible parting slow pieces dead curled, a flower gallery
of many in a basket near Hampstead's woods in glass case
same exact transparent locket I went away & saw again

14. "Dandelion," by the Rolling Stones.

1967

8 years foregone thru all the poisoned tea in Italy
Or Mother poppy's cactus grandson's Crown Heights see a Rabbi
check out your ecstasy in the cloth—Realists are
uprooting legs of a chair for a test in the same universe.
Soft Soft day ends, full moon eve, midnite, Earl's hour
coming soon, and Olive & all the Unconscious Comics—
Keats wept to see his mellow garden room enlarged
after his peaceful death—a harm-less Bard returns the mind flower
to mortal origins, from childhood now language & vision
merry sterile Mary—the Governor dreams
flowers—Turner's boats fade back into the Sun—
I and my father weep in garden and Hall, tears
consecrate the auto metals & Pound since antiquity,
Hills & Castles bulge over the world, a spider sits
in closets of Glastonbury, the flower's cut, silence.

July 23, 1967

4 A.M.   Geez

Oh, Dear what I'm here, the Cock empty spasmed
head question, women in transparence, conceptionally
rectum here, Women Women up Thraun De white powder—
answer wake heaven air earth-mood.
and what to do with this pleasurable body.

Wales 1967[15]   July 29, Saturday

Thru the thick wall'd window on vale browed

15. First draft of "Wales Visitation," *Collected Poems*, 488–90.

1967

Wales 1967   July 29,
                      Saturday

Thru the thick wall'd window on Vale Brow'd
    white fog float
              Trees waving in rivers of wind
                        The Clouds arise
as on a wave, gigantic eddy lifting mist
    ~~so~~ above teeming ferns exquisitely swayed
by one gentle motion vast as the long green crag
       glimpsed thru mullioned glass in the valley rain—

Bardic, o Self, visitacion, Tell naught
          but what Seen by one man
               in a vale in Albion, of the folk of Lambs,
    of the satanic thistle that raises its horned symmetry
       flowering with sister grass & floret's visible
          ~~pink and tiny~~ invisible-small
              budded ~~triple petal'd~~ bloomlets
                  equally ananillu as lightbulbs,

white fog afloat
          Trees moving in rivers of wind
                    The clouds arise
     as on a wave, gigantic eddy lifting mist
               above teeming ferns exquisitely swayed
     by one gentle motion vast as the long green crag
               glimpsed thru mullioned glass in the valley rains—

Bardic, O Self, visitation, Tell naught
     but what seen by one man
          in a vale in Albion, of the folk, of Lambs,
     of the satanic thistle that raises its horned symmetry
          flowering with sister grass & flowers visible
               pink and tiny invisible—small
                    budded triple-petaled bloomlets
                         equally angelic as lightbulbs,

Remember your day 150 miles from London's
          Symmetrical thorned Tower & network
                    of TV pictures flashing bearded your Self,
Link the lambs of the tree-nooked hillside of
     This day
with the cry of Blake and the silent thought of
          Wordsworth in his Eld stillness—

All the valley quivered with one extended motion
     of the breath of wind undulating
          on the floor or mossy hills,
     a giant wash that sank white fogs delicately down
          red runnels on the mountainside, as greens moved
               myriad sensitive leaf-branch tendrils
                    asway in granitic undertow down

1967

and lifted the floating Nebulous upward, and lifted the arms
of the trees
and lifted the grasses an instant in balance
and lifted the lambs, to hold still,
and lifted the green of the hill, in one solemn wave—
Roar of the mountain wind slow, sigh of the body
One Being on the mountainside stirring gently,
Exquisitely balanced from bird cry to lamb cry to this voice
Knowing
one majesty the action that stirred the bright wet
grass clump and the farthest tendril of white fog
on mountain head
the length of all Albion, valley upon valley under
heavy Heaven's ocean
tonned with cloud-hang
breathing vast waves over flower-trembling precipices—
vast breath—the valley breathed Heaven & moved
as one interknit, being horses alert surveying
The Valley of Wye
on the rock-brow hill top
half sheltering them from the rainy wind flow—
a granite slab on the crest, with
a T incised,
forgotten in the moist bright grass—
lying where fallen, stillness for centuries of breath—

Out, out on the hillside, out in the
green wild, out into the
ocean sound, out into
delicate gusts of warm rain—
I knelt before the thistle, Blake's Tiger
a tiny symmetry like hands interknit

1967

flower sharp mudras of offering—
one gesture, one thought—and looked in
  eyes of the branded lambs
that stared as I breathed in their vision
 stockstill under dripping hawthorn
and walked thru colored flower & antlered.
       green fern
   rubber booted on soft grass
    calling our presence together
with sighs, and a word Ho Lamb and
  a mantra
    deep Om
Hallowing the ivy green being networked alive
   thru farmland's tree lined canals
ages of man breath, ages of green leaf
   attuned to the motions of hands,
of mouths of foxes & horses & breathings
    of winds, fields eating tiny black lamb-drops,
 piles of stones set aside as a wall the length
      of green neighbor hill—

Fall on the ground in the rain, O
  Great wetness, O Mother
No harm on thy body! Groan in my body
  The small grass at my eye ˜
    repeating the story, the Soul,
The Myriad formed, the brown earth supporting
  the green, to the rocks below
to earth heart, volcano or floweret
  bearing same weight
One being so balanced, so vast, that
 its softest breath is the stillness

1967

that moves every hair on the valley floor,
my beard, the lamb's wool clotted in the green
                fine spun symmetric,
        Trees on their roots & leather thongs
                        On an amulet,
Birds in the great draft, hiding their strength
                in the rain,
Smoke out of rare house topped with white
                        chimney—
What did I notice? Particulars! The
        vision of the great One is myriad
smoke curled upward in ash tray house,
                The fire burned low
The night, still wet & moody black heaven
                Starless
upward in motion with wet wind.

                Llanthony Valley
                Black Mountains

London Aug 2, 1967 2 A.M.[16]

The Great Secret is no secret.
                Senses fit their rosy winds—
Visible is Visible, mist, rain mist
                curtains wave thru the bearded vale—
Foxgloves raise green buds, mauve

16. Portions of this poem were published as "After Wales Visitacione July 29, 1967" in Allen Ginsberg, *Wait Till I'm Dead,* 86–89. Ginsberg integrated some lines into "Wales Visitation," *Collected Poems,* 488–90.

1967

bells droop weigh/bend doubled down
    the stem trembling with antennae—
Daisies push up their inches of yellow air,
There's no imperfection on the budded mountain
across the valley maze vegetables tremble, horses dance
    in the warm rain,
white sheep & stones speckle the mountainside & move eating
& gaze & the green atoms shimmer
    in grassy mandalas thru myriad water drops
    wavering in the wind's transparent force.
Blue atoms shimmer in the sky, grey atoms set the
Wind's Kabbala
A solid mass of Heaven, mist-infused, ebbs thru the
    vale, a wavelet of Immensity lapping gigantic
    thru Llanthony Valley
Whence this Immensity, this motion at the bottom of the sky,
It is our giant earth that rolls the days, our familiar sun hangs
    earth with light
    the planet on its lightbeams
Every daisy flowering in lightbeams the wind & eating light and mists
    drawn from the ocean & driven like lambs from the ocean thru the
    meadows of Wye to these mounts & beyond to the
    edges of London where man's electricity frightens them off,
Witch wands of autumnal iron
razing the air round Primrose hill—
    —pheasants croak flapping up from Fern steep
      Meadow—
One Hill the surface of the Cosmic egg's alive with greenery—
    "Sportree woods run wild . . . green to the very door."

---

above the mists & clouds, maybe, high heaven's

1967

weight hangs invisible shifting its clouds floor on the
million feet of daisies
Each flower Buddha eye, buds mirroring the
        —elemental eyeball forms—
        manufactured many—multiplied in silence—
stare close, no imperfection in the grass, symmetry maya,
     covering the moist ground, small brown vagina, harmless
The whole mass of heaven balanced on a grassblade
    a daisy   on a bramble
    or rose
& the thrill of One, the gigantic Sun, at the end of our heaven
    & the lightest rose at the old cottage door
    weighed equal on the exquisite scales trembling everywhere
    in balance from the death of a grassblade, the
    birth of a tender mushroom.
Is this divine God, that Harmony of sheep that look
    up revolving their jaws? to suck the juicy grasses.
O thoughtless lambs with empty eyes, pacific gods
    I gaze upon, little gods that look at me curious & keep
    their distance from my human fame.
O tender gigantic planet, & tiny gigantic vale, in Wales,
    that keeps each creature revolving thru their births
    & deaths unharmed
  I that am thy bard O my own Nature let me be as
nameless as the very vast I stare upon, I gaze on.

  I lay down on the warm hillside & ground
release my body of fear & sighed release of my physical
self, I sighed through my breast & neck,
a great ooh.
  I knelt before the thorn to see the symmetry of my

1967

own eyeball made perfect manifest body—

 I became what I am, one self in one self, one
last mammal aware in the wet grass

 same grass that smelled of my sperm, familiar
harmless mother Perfect, as my mortal mother died in Fear &
Madness in a hospital that smelled like blue gas—

 So now I worship & embrace my mother
earth aged 41, missing my beard with the wet hair
of the mountainside, tasting the violet of tender
hair of the thistle bloom thistle flower—as a sweetness,

 I lay along the earth like Blake's worm &
lifted my head & groaned, forgiving any plough—

 I searched my mind for silence, & also heard language
murmuring continuous as river gossip,
each log, log & rock making noise at the bottom of
insistent water, that came from the sky

 Earth & sky met & made noise between them, as
I babble to vastness—Death's black Angel lifted
white fleshed Day in his arm for a joyous kiss—in
the afternoon rain

    What else could we do?—they do?

 all afternoon on the mountainside my green Sierra parka
from America wet thru and thru with English pantheistic rain

----

 and sat on a rock crosslegged in dusk rains, slitted
eyed, abreathe steadily, mind moveless,

 My own breath in vast body tickling each cell as the
planet wind trembles the white daisies by the roadside—

 the breath of Heaven, or earth, and my own breath symmetric,
the Central emptiness that manifests in body—
giant valley veined with tree-lined canals manufactured over

1967

centuries, sprouting bushes fringing household walls, hill
breast nippled with hawthorn, belly meadows haired with fern—
the same earth, breath that waved in the valley, was drawn
into my belly, & slowly breathed out thru my hollow throat—
sounds of Aleph & Aum, the river of blood thru forests of
gristle, my skull & Lord Hereford's knob an equal windy place—
    equal place for wind to pass thru—
Sat on a rock & breathed to my navel the same breath as breathes
thru Capel y Ffin—
    close your eyes on Black Mountains & be all Wales, all
Albion is one!

    & thought of Stokely Carmichael flying on to some wind to
Cuba, angry at the windy thistle's silly thorns—"You don't
take vengeance on silliness"—Swahili Proverb—and he
breathes the same wind, hotter, thru his ulcer—Bad trips.
    And England's angry *News of the World* choking & coughing
on the same breath of Summer.
    Because they plough in abstract fields to harvest money
not physical potatoes of silence.

    & the physical sciences and in Ecology, that is the wisdom
of earthly relationships, the harmony of lives interknit
by mouth and eyes, hoof paw wing fin & leaf bearing the giant
body forward ten centuries in Llanthony visible & present—
    footprints of human generations left in the grass, square
fields of leafy thought, orchards of mind language manifest
in its intention to be a peaceful place for cows & sheep
to pass by twos to death, & horses to be born & have cancer of the snout—
    I lay on hill & did die to myself, once more to be all,

1967

& entered Wales in Visitacione nameless bard on her hill,
thru Blake's eye, particular, thistle, & Wordsworth's "green
to the very door!" & Herbert's lovely pulley and scales, &
Dylan Thomas's hillside Fern-fused breath—& Whitman's aware—
and my own courage for the new Humor—Mother Earth's Paranoia
my own—So speak prophetic as we all should—

 As we all could if we shut up and noticed heaven & Earth
moving together

 & simplicity of G-Calder's mobiles, the balanced scales myriad
atremble

 and the Continuous Raga of the singer's breath fluttery
left and right on scales the same as the gentle storm zephyr

 chanting along the trees the length of the valley, in &
out of the store holes of the shepherd's ruined house-wall—

 Until my speech is one with the vast that moves, & the
nameless vast

 Prayer? a sigh at one with the giant wind is the same as
amens in any abstract Vatican—better than Pope's blessing,
unless the blessing came from the same Rock I sat on Buddha for
10 minutes in Wales.

Beethoven, Bach music exploring the vast symmetry, the
hand moves up the organ keys touching trees of chords, orchard
harmonies, one bird sweet whistle in giant valleys of
space—notes balancing like flower & mist in the scales
hanging under heaven.

Tintern Abbey (July 30, '67)

Clouds passing thru the open roof of Tintern Abbey

1967

Swallows at dusk, swooping thru the daylight nave
Green freehats of yellow lean in the giant window
    and sharp evergreen march uphill
           under the skeleton Arch.

August 17, 1967 London

  Strip tease
      red lights, the shrunken stage
        crowned with tinsel
the old man gazes for the first time
    naked woman, naked girl,
    naked maiden, naked mother
        naked Maya
blinks her black robot eyes
    rolls her belly slowly
      turns around deliberate,
one hand symmetric descending
    to earth
one hand waving to the equinox

Both hands covering the bare
    tiny triangle of meat—

The old man gazes at Maya,
    does she turn electric
      in his eyes?

The moon is Powerful
as a lamp on the Street
           London Aug. 22, 1967 11 p.m.

1967

Paris Aug. 25, '67

Baudelaire's Noctambules[17]
old Navy, Lipp, street Cafes
   Crowded chattering
autos exploding on cobblestones,
Grey St. Germain stone's stillness
     Mabillon broods
   with a beard oxygen Shadow,
Lovers walk hand in hand with
       empty eyes
Beautiful youths grow pimples sleeping
   on the Seine with the police
   under Notre Dame's silent
      grey lacework—
Sad, as bored Apollinaire gave up
   the ghost on Pont Mirabeau
   collating spit-soiled letters
        from Artaud
Sad, as Michaux walks solitary
   down Rue Ségur to the Seine
   brooding loveless—
Sad, as the Cafes close for
   the summer,
Sad, as a decade ago I shopped
   in Rue de Seine for mussels
  with Orlovsky weeping in bed
   Gregory upstairs in fury

17. First draft of "Mabillon Noctambules." See *Wait Till I'm Dead,* 90–92.

1967

scribbling American
Burroughs enchambered considering
silent blues—

Paris Aug. 25, '67

2:20 A.M. (cont.)

Sad, as no poets emerged from
the streets, gaiety eyes
& eyebrows sharp with
new France
not old eternity, not old
Sadness of Meat realizing
Frenchness a moment
enthusiastic as the virgin belly of Jean-Arthur
arriving in Paris bedbugged
Screaming in melodious slang—
Merde! Le Con! Salaud! Shriek
the bourgeois sharpies with
shaved short hair at the zino bar,
Bored with their Jamais & red girls
No music, no magic Vulnerables
in Manly wristwatches—
No beautiful faces on these
ancient streets—
I've been faithful w/my beard
10 years,
& now arrive in Silken gold-Crost robe
hair perfumed & long, hero of
my own universe
& sit in the White Queen at 2 A.M.

1967

recalling the ghosts of Paris, of the
    50's as Hemingway
in Montana lamented a thought for a night
    of the Great Lesbians
shining in 1924 surrounding Cloiserie
    de Lilas—
Bill Myself Peter & Gregory the
    angels of pain a decade
      incognito

The barman's bald, I'm bald,
    & Gregory's broke in New York—
More ghosts as sad as ourselves will
    pass St. Sulpice or gaze
over the chimneyed roofs & mansards
    curved along the Seine
Wondering what magic of Paris
    was promised, what charm
that now's the fat barman spilling
    blue labeled lemonade
over the stainless steel drain.

Rome Via Veneto Sept. 2, 1967

Conversation about Sexual Bureaucracy of Baghdad, over pink table-
cloths
        Italian chatter behind Auto Carburator suspirations.

    Dizzy, Prickles in neck-back, Pressure on head slight—brightness in
windows,

1967

Beauty Salon white Neon—Glass Wigs, perfume bottles, shelves of green Cellophane lotion—

Vanity, red cloth-walled showcards, ladies & gents of Rome walking down hill, smoking cigars—The waiter lifting a chair—

Brightness of Vanity manifest garish toy-machineguns & a hairy doll mirrored in silver display—white shirts, green ties, red notebooks, yellow dress, blue epaulettes on the garcon balancing his tea tray—

A river of phantoms passing before the tables—pausing to glance at pink silk stockings, one way, of thoughtful bald faces lining the café.

A soldier, a hustler, a workman, a Negro in net shirt above bulging feminine muscles, a family with sloppy bellies holding hands.

Sweet phantoms with cuff-links Brawny phantoms blowing their nose. They walk light as balloons, in slow motion thru the moment—Lights blink on the sacred stage.

Sexual phantoms bureaucrats on leave from Baghdad to study economics, escape down the street.

7 P.M.

Sept 9, 1967 Milan

—arrived, walk thru Via Manzoni to Duomo Sq. & around Statue, a crowd of young gathered, so I had to move to see the Cathedral: requesting signature.

1967

Hearing of Allen Ginsberg's July 1967 detention and interrogation by police for suspected obscenity of his texts read at Spoleto, undersigned poets invited by British Arts Council for International Poetry Festival London 1967 July wish to reassure all officials concerned that the texts (including Who Be Kind To) are socially acceptable works of art and should not be treated legally as "obscene."

The Leaning Tower

of Pisa's nine marble stories/in sunset on white stone in
a field of green/grass surrounded by Sunday families./1967 A.D.
still stands while I sit/crosslegged smoking & laughing &
soldiers sing, phantoms of the hilarious legions/trooping up
and down the circular stairs/and traipsing dizzily around
tiny balconies/slant spiral since thirteenth century,/surveying
restaurants & Baptistry of Duomo/and angular streets' rhomboidal
houses—white, white, white six floors of columned/archways
emblemed with carved diamonds/& Corinthian flowers slowly charming
grey clouds/by their odd lean, tipped over pink tile/roofs on
the floor of the empty blue sky.

Milan Solid City

We're safe—in the Benzina Noon Auto
droplets on the window, street lamp radiating yellow against
granite slabbed apartment walls,
     large-rock cobbled

1967

Ginsberg was arrested in July 1967 at the Spoleto Festival for the language in "Who Be Kind To." Photograph by Ettore Sottsass.

      trolleytracks Corso di Porta Romana
arched looking
   down street
street lamps strung
   thru the gatem

Carlights red down the ghost lighted street

Stone stone stone
   Metropolis
Oedipus Rex
   tall crowned
mouth open on
   billboard
Pound blinking his eyes—
The yellow stoplight
   against a shattered wall,

Corner street
leading stone path
   to stone avenue
fest Pound with green bulb, white neon
ribs up the back
   of the snaky monster
intensified over new
   asphalt fields
rolling with motel car bump
along shiny tracks
to the giant Latin gate—

and heavy architecture
   slabbed with balcony & clock

1967

Squat rigid figures at labor symmetrized
   in the empty night
full moon behind the clouds

lit street clock 2:15
   with tiny hands—
and up the blue street
   arrow
hung from a wall of
   windows—
thru the giant wooden gate
In the alp-granite pillared
   courtyard

Sept. 22, 1967

Drive up to Rapallo from Bogliasco on super bridge across green-castled canyons, bright day and blue water between railroad and hedged cypress—

   Pound rose from garden chair as we rounded path from road surveying downhill large red house gardened. We sat, drank wine under a tree. I opened Indian harmonium and sang Hare Krishna. In the house he spoke, at Olga Rudge's prompting.

"She asks, do you want to wash your hands?"

So then no more speech, except "too much" of the white plate of pasta almost eaten, and chicken/ham broiled, in a plate, he drank white wine— "Too much." O. Rudge lady peeled the grapes, or washed them in crystal bowl. "Too much," but set on a plate he reached out aged pink fingers thumbnail white frayed.

O. R.: She felt too bad to go to Montreal, woke that night ill, cancelled airplane, sent telegram Montreal, E. P. had said "I won't go without you."

1967

Tornado in Milan, planes late anyway, might've missed London connection—

The *Book of Changes* in Italian. Pound had a copy and the coins were loose in a tiny alabaster bowl Olga Rudge showed.

"If this atmosphere (blue Rapallo and Tigullio Bay to Portofino under mountain verdure on promontory below daylit distance) is fine enough for Ezra Pound then these young men, who come to see Pound territory, should try to look at it take time . . ."

"Zoagli" of Cantos is town other side of mountain south of Rapallo.

Stared in tiny pupiled eye, he blinked twice, our eyes shifted aside, I meditated.

Later sang, Prajnaparamita Sutra, eyes open on him, eyes turned away, he shifted back to gaze direct.

After lunch we drove to Portofino—he silent in car—ivory handled cane at side—sat on the quai, he drank iced tea. Long time quiet. Ancient paranoid silent—

"Did you ever try hashish all these years?" I was curious. He looked at me, blinked eyes, shook thin white-bearded cheeks, no, twice—

"Swinburne the only miss . . . he'd a been the one to turn you on," I muttered to myself half aloud.

No Taxation Without Representation[18]

Who represents me in Pentagon?
Whose billions manifest my desire?
Taxes on poetry for war manufacture?
Levies the majority to exult unwilling in bomb roar?
Apocalypse transform Pentagon to bright spirit!
Om Roksa Roksa Hum Hum Hum Phat Svaha!

18. First draft of "Pentagon Exorcism," *Collected Poems*, 491.

1967

Brainwash! Mind-fear! Governor's language!
Desperate jabber building electric networks,
body-pain & chemical ataxia physical slavery,
nightmare terror Cosmic eye man-conflict,
the Daemon Disphanocids' movie, Chinese yellow
hysteria manufactured with our money? No General
wants to be Devil, others die for his power
sustaining hurt millions in house security
tuning TV images into separate universe,
manhood inferior in burnt forest village
—represented less than myself by Pentagon magic
intelligence influence matter-scientists with
money-giant telephone bank investment firms'
executives jetting from ALCOA gold conferences
ever smog-shrouded metal-noised cities
patrolled by radio fear with tear gas.
Pentagon billions reverse the brainwash calm
consciousness. Pentagonian weep & gaze on this flower
manifest spirit of magnanimous Back back
back Anger admiral your one self feared Chaos
suffocation, body-death, cities caved with stone
radar sentinels of central Mind
Pentagon wake from sleep in central Planet-Karma,
Spirit Spirit Dance Dance Dance Spirit Spirit Dance!
Billions reverse brainwash calm consciousness gaze
& yawp at this flower manifest spirit of Man magnanimous
Everyman finding angelic Back Back Back Anger your
Self feared Chaos suffocation body-death in cities
caved with stone radar sentinels of central Mind
controlling reaction to signal Peking isolate space-Beings—

29 September 1967   Milan

1967

10/3/67.

I went to bed last night, thinking to consult dream worlds as I have neglected to record dreams for a year or two now.

Oct 3, 1967—Dream

At jungle edge by stream, in a horticultural trough, I find seeds of babes—I walk through with a friend—it's the basement of a Castle, I look through moat—corridors & see the body of a small child well preserved in the clear water running behind walls of giant columns.

And in the trough nearby, a brainless pink fetus, lifeless & waxy, waiting for resurrection,

I had an inspiration—that life was the heartbreath—and that to give life to someone or to rescue them from oblivion, I had merely to press the palm of my hand on the nuces, nuts, seeds of life, the central belly/brain of the tiny corpse, and Now

with the 1967/75 artificial respiration tiny Frankenstein Machines, all I'd have to do is take an intact body out of the water—where it had drowned days or weeks before,

put it in the re-awakening machine, & turn it on. The deterioration of brain? Perhaps loss of memory or hearing, but no worse?

But the physical action of beginning the breath, maintainable by machine, would lead to the spark of being reborn,

Thus went in search of a body, a child, to resurrect. But the thought came, given these wrecks in the basement, early dead, waxy fetuses or pale cheeked corpses of boys—were they to awaken what faculties would they have left? Who would take the responsibility for rearing them?

Turned away from the fetus corpse whose skull was only soft empty shell because brains had already deteriorated.

1967

There in the clear water a healthy dead young boy, about 8 years old.
Between 6 & 10 years, anyway, dressed in clean pants & sweater,

---

Oct. 4, 67

White Car Milan

The ladies in black & green dress
   dancing & whistling on the street
      under hotel sign—
City like serpent, stone Ouroboros,
air tracks painted white ribbed in slats
   on the corner
under the streetlamp—
Her girlfriend entered the white car & she
   didn't want to—stood
by open door flanked by
   3 Mafia Police who
maybe were suitors, but she
   didn't want to go in,

till after long discussion
   she was shut in,
The heavier man moved in
     next to her
   & her timider girlfriend—
another entered front
right shiny white door
   open on street AM

1967

I went in from the balcony
  to the mysterious jazz
    on the phonograph rug
to fumore tea with shugare,
    heads nodding to fiscal
        rhythm.

Oct 5, 1967—wake—11:20 A.M.—dream

Half lingering pleasant—A big Italian teacher from the forest, going to
take me to some valley floor covered with pre-city (Neolithic) trees—to a
village where the gypsy teaches "Techniques of Homosexuality"—mean-
ing for Italy, the appearance of The Grateful Dead (Rock &
Roll Band)—

Oct 6, 1967—Dream 6 A.M.: Villa d'Este, Italy

Walking along Italian or Latin-Moorish evening wall with Kenneth
T.[19] . . . and a young boy Peruvian playwright his protégé, as we approach
a phone box Tynan gives advice "Let adversity teach you to be wise" and
continues: "Take advantage of people, if you're hungry flatter them, and
don't tell secrets" or some such cynical maxim, as I interpret it while at
his side in the dream. The young Peruvian is making a phone call, I take
T . . . aside, within earshot of the phone booth, and begin a complaint to
him which ends in angry denuncification. "I've cooperated with you for
years and now I'm sorry, you son of a bitch, you hypocrite, you critic, you
coward, what do you mean except compromise and dulling of perception?
All these years you pretend to radicalism and now what do you teach but

19. Kenneth Tynan (1927–1980), influential British critic and writer.

1967

lying to this soul, him making phonecalls for a rich supper, and I'm participating in your scene. I refuse. Here you are now, working for the establishment, the Times, the National Theater—you know all the private secrets & sustain the structure—I'm leaving . . ." I end yelling & angry & wake up at cock crow in Milan—after having read Berenson Twilight—death journals till late & masturbated joyfully imagining being screwed in the ass by heavy blond J. P. I'd slept with in Milan a couple times last weeks— All month living in uneasy luxury Chez Nanda Pivano in ambiance of Olivetti prosperity, hearing gossip of Johnny A. & Jacques S. w/their ancient cocaine & beautiful women & medieval pricely riches— & Inge F. phoned to check if Agnelli was available yesterday—no he was off to Moscow appointment with Kosygin to discuss Fiat City new Russian Capital . . .

Woke from dream, as last weeks been coming closer to return to old continuity between waking & dream life as a form of stabilizing introspection & psychic continuity I'd not been observing the last 2 years of social activity having preoccupied my waking mind leaving me careless—perhaps the cheesy nature of the dreams.

Oct. 6, 1967

Dead Voice

The straight guitar plucked square blue
on a homemade brick patio in Chile
many years ago sounds as sweet now in Italy
as brother to the flat sad voice
    singing "allegro"
and "Triste" out of the stocky woman body
   —What humor, dead lady,
      Made you study folksong

1967

La Cueca, and take unbalanced children
                     for male lovers
under your red peasant dress—what humor
and what sad hair braided
     over the mortal fat behind your neck—
at thirty years wrinkle-eyed
     at forty far away in Paris suicide
a tiny record made of living matter
     repeats the sweet cry I heard w/living ears
before I died, & left Chile
     by airplanes which
     delivered me to this Villa
     on Piedmont hill—
and heard your naked voice singing

10/7/67. Dream

In large hotel Europe, wandering down twilit corridor having seen Pound—thin beard and stark face upswept hair from Observer photo—I am ruminating over his silence, walking along polished marble Italian floor—thinking also to tell friend Ettore [Sottsass] to send Pound photos taken at Portofino us sitting together silent at café waterfront table—Tell Olga Rudge I want to publish photos, money given to poets, or to C.O.P.[20] [Committee on Poetry, Inc.]—or I'll tell her myself and ask if it's all right—ruminating in the dream about newspaper publicity—I go out on balcony and sit alone in obscurity after sunset on deck chair—His silence unhappy—I begin to sob and then many sobs come and tears wet my closed eyes—I open eyes and see maid with dry mop cleaning the balcony, and

20. Ginsberg founded C.O.P. to fund impoverished poets, writers, painters, and other artists.

1967

another lady in deck chair watching me cry, I am pleased that someone heard me cry, wonder if she understands why—I get up to leave—wake in front room Milan crash of trolleys on tracks 5 P.M. afternoon, my eyelids wet.

Oct 7 or 8, 1967   Dream

In large Hotel Europa, wandering down twilight corridor having seen Pound—thin beard & stock face unswept hair from observer photo seen—Nov 8 '67—I am ruminating over his silence, walking along polished marble Italian floor—thinking also to tell friend Ettore to send Pound photos taken at Portofino us sitting together silent at café waterfront table—Tell Olga Rudge I want to publish photos, money given to poets, or to C.O.P. Me—or I'll tell her myself and ask if it's alright—ruminating in the dream about newspaper publicity—I go out on balcony & sit alone in obscurity after sunset on desk-chair—His silence unhappy—I begin to sob & then many sobs come & tears wet my closed eyes—I open eyes & see maid with dry mop cleaning the balcony, & another lady in deskchair watching me cry, I'm pleased that someone heard me cry, wonder if she understands why—I get up to leave—wake in front room Milan crash of trolleys on tracks 5 P.M. afternoon, my eyelids wet.

Sat Oct 15, 1967   Dream—7:15 A.M.

In old-world pad, an artist's spacious family apartment, Mexico downtown or N.Y. or Milan—a group of young men sitting around on pillows against the wall covered with bookshelves & boxes of photos and news clips—Gavin Arthur's 1890's North African Pierre décor.

Sex has become quite free, I'd come home in a crowded taxi with Peter and Gregory—Peter and I found each other in the black private cab kiss-

1967

ing—I clung to an interior running-board, leaving the seat for Tennessee Williams[21] & Gregory or Bowles[22] or Burroughs—'twas Tangiers—thru a rotten Medina, mud on the streets, Arab balconies filled with starving Black Power Negroes—lepers & skeletal children clinging to the back of the high English cab for a free ride—weeping for Bakshish—Black cranial whores with holes in their heads and hands lamenting for attention from giant windows in the street-level clay walls—

In this chaos I remember erotic aroma among our party—I had just finished necking with Gregory in the back row of an ancient movie theater—we were all headed home—

& were all sitting around in pillows smoking a Narghile in a young Aristocrat's living room—or his pad at the Western School.

Eugenio Villacana there, I remember his smooth brown muscular-babyish belly, I had stuck my hand down the front of his tunic & stroked his skin down to the pubes, & lay around on the floor wondering who was coming to visit that evening.

Meanwhile a commotion from another hall thru an archway—one of the Western Christian teachers had rebuked a pupil for some Savage Barbarism like smearing his body with ashes, sitting in loincloth in yoga position, chanting Mantra & smoking Ganja during Recreation Period or Study Hour—I became quite angry & in conversation denounced the manners of the teacher—"Barbarian Westerner—he's following no rule except homemade ignorance while the student obviously is exercising sophistications of a culture thousands of years old."

The aggrieved student meanwhile lays out on his rug almost naked and has gone on a weeping hunger strike.

21. American playwright Tennessee Williams (1911–1983) wrote *A Streetcar Named Desire, Night of the Iguana, Cat on a Hot Tin Roof,* and *The Glass Menagerie.*
22. Paul Bowles (1910–1999) was an expatriate writer, translator, and composer who befriended William S. Burroughs, Ginsberg, and Kerouac when he was living in Morocco.

1967

I go into next room where hot Narghile, stashed behind bookshelves, with pipe-mouth emerging between books, has been prepared—I kneel and suck the smoke, a long long yogaic breath while Villacana watches curious—I'm proud of my deep prajnic inhalation—It's all taken for granted —We'll make love later, tonight & tomorrow—the Western Teacher is a boor—wake.

10:30 A.M.

In bed in a Hotel-Truck over Central Station New Wichita York Milan, railroads are running underground beneath vast marble balconies, I wander below—thru restaurant and lobby—looking for an open newspaper stand or jazzy palace—Everything's closed at night—back upstairs I climb into giant crib (of the truck) where young boy-bodied friend of years back—whom I'd always had a crush on, but never sparked with, because he thought I was too old hairy or vulgar sincere?—is sleeping or resting. I climb in and kiss his face, he kisses me back, and I nestle closer, under the covers where he's naked, stretch my body alongside of his—and we kiss and hug each other, a delicious bodily thrill. Meanwhile the clocks and Neon Posters of Times Square are blinking on and off overhead and below our perch over the city—I sigh and kiss more, relief to be embraced, sweet surprise to my cock that he's willing to make love after all these years.

While wandering in the street basements I'd realized that for all the freedom of the Great City, there was no place open on Times Square or Central Railroad Station at night, no all nite bars or clubs or meet cafes— I thought I'd have to start complaining to Mayor Lindsay.[23] But he's supposed to be an open minded mayor, then how come the City's been shut down at night? More horrible politics.

[...]

23. New York mayor John Lindsay.

1967

Waking & ruminating, remember last night with Bill B. talking about rules of seduction for Italian boys, and his brief erotic incidents with Gregory—and Ettore recounting a scene returning to café open all night at Sfozesco Square to reclaim money Gregory claimed for waiters who'd beaten him up drunk. I'd visited Central Station in homage to Gregory's vision of its Babylonian Gigantesque Humore, several days ago.

Oct 18

Milan Galleria like Palladio head-on the leviathan funnels lit up seen from between Mussolini bldg. across from Duomo Square. 1910's Boccioni's *Fight in the Gallery,* the explosion of "executives in shirtsleeves" panicked.

& DiChirico moving ponderously with a nose like one of his horse-chessmen in lobby of Continental. & later at table at "Biffi Scala," the café of La Scala opera, historic but I never went in till late last night for tea. Nostalgia of Infinite—located in XX Century on earth the main plaza of Ferrara says Jean Paulo Cappeloni friend who studied Greek phenomenology.

----

19 Oct. 67—

On street with old thin blackhaired lady—with crowd of young like in swimming pool—We climb up ladder, she's widow Brecht—look down, the police car taking off with ur boyfriends—I hesitate at top of radiator-ladder & descend with book satchel & yell "Brecht!" after police car—which stops at corner—a huge building bus full of prisoners—who all begin leaving, a whole hoard of them—streaming downstreet—under a night skyscraper from which Fiery sand is pouring down to Earth a tower like that in Modena—DiChirico's tower—"It's like that only worse"—this Bosch Hell scene—"In Vietnam."

1967

Violence in Oakland, this weekend Exorcism of Pentagon,[24] I'll be in Venice chanting Tara Nam to Pound.

8 A.M.   20 Oct '67

Up till 2:30 A.M. reading *A. B. C. of Reading,* considering Dichten-Condensare dreamt in small Mexican town years later at conferencia of poets met younger Panama-hatted wiry bodies Pound w/steel-white hair—

At window of remote pension house a woman's face, familiar, Joan Burroughs,[25] who left with me a mss. I read it complete, one sentence only imperfect, cut one word out & the prose all clear and active throughout the book—it could be published & read & bring her money & fame—

Leaving the island for plane what was my program?—to visit Joan in that house later, the house downhill but as in old times I had half-forgotten within easy walking streets to the center, movies and restaurants, Joan was there all these years. Same house, said Pound, he had always stayed at. He had to get his plane, & asked me if I'd have time to stay a few days further to talk with him in Rome or in the later small town. He tarried on the street briefcase in hand departing to request my presence.

Then I went to Joan with her mss. to tell her its value my judgment. I sat on bench next to her & then held her around & began sobbing, laid

24. At a mass antiwar demonstration in Washington, D.C., The Fugs, along with a crowd of protesters, attempted to surround and levitate the Pentagon. Ginsberg's "Pentagon Exorcism" was chanted at the event. Norman Mailer's prizewinning book *The Armies of the Night* recalled the historic weekend.

25. Joan Vollmer, Burroughs's common-law wife. She was close to all the early Beats, with whom she was an intellectual equal. She died when Burroughs shot her during a drunken game of William Tell in Mexico in 1953.

1967

my head on her shoulder, shudders of breath leading to tears over and over, relief at the redemption, so easy—thought flashed through my head in dream she was my mother—looked at her—told her I thought her pages—one with strange mathematical figures in a row—and whole book readable & modern—the exception that one extra flowery inexact word excusable—suddenly woke 8 A.M.

Milan

bells & trolleycar sounds on track 3 flights below window in stone street via Manzoni.

Train to Venice reading Montale, Oct. 21, 1967

Revolution . . . the bridges & tanks
belong to us—
   What do you say?
We own the Pentagon, we give money
to what factories make pretty toys
for ourselves like houses, not guns for
strangers—It's Communism, all right,
   What do you say?
We take the banks, the money's ours,
all of us who vote, not the hi hat few,
Who said *they* could make money all alone?
We feed the poor we go naked in parks, we
live like Present Men. The City's ours.
   What do you say?

10/21/67.

 Arrived Venice—settled in Pension-Cici near Salute, consulting map on wall, turned saw Olga Rudge and then Pound emerging from dining

1967

With Ezra Pound and Ginsberg's longtime translator Nanda Pivano
in Portofino, Italy, 1967. Photograph by Ettore Sottsass. Copyright 2020
Artists Rights Society (ARS), New York/ADAGP, Paris.

room. We sat for coffee. Mrs. Rudge explained I wouldn't have had trouble finding their house, "oftentimes Venetians will walk half a mile to show you a tiny alley."

Pound spoke up, "Forty years since I've seen anybody do that . . ."

"Do what, Ezra?" she asked.

"Take the trouble to walk you along to show you the way." He said no more that hour; I arranged to come to lunch next day.

Oct. 21. 1967—Venice

flat watery fields
   to the rail station
—on the green wrinkled street, white balconies,
   —striped poles, where the axe-nosed
     Gondolas bow under
Flagpoles hanging October's empty blue sky
   Silence except for Vaporetto's throb.
Ten years ago w/ Peter here
      cooking greens, Ansen's[26] face
      grey-shaven, stub-nosed,
   aimless feet past glass-walled alleyways—
Under Rialto's black-roofed arch, the flash
   of the sun's yellow-spiked Cross—
     molten light flowing up the street,
      slow current dazzle-surfaced
   between mossy-stepped walls
    Toward spire roofs & lacy balconies,
A yellow Palace cornering the Canal-end

26. Alan Ansen, a friend of the core of Beat writers, assisted with the work on *Naked Lunch*.

1967

to San Samuele! Ca Rezzonnico!

Back to where I was ten years ago, two months ago!

The wooden bridge to the Bellinis, white

    onion domes of Salute top'd with Saints & Crosses—

green copper bell below, the long low wall of houses

    against fields of blue choppy water,

        boats, rows of black prows nodding,

    motor noise, white tiny ridge arch,

    & the Vaporetto carrying me down

               Grand Canale

heads into shade under the scrolled

           buttresses of Salute.

Last night smoked, walking past lovers

    standing embraced by brick walls

      along to Customs Point,

    uniformed young men in new Motor

back turning round thru alleys the

    black wrought iron glass-jeweled gate

Seeking "the soap smooth stone posts" San Vio river

    along Gregorio by Salviati

      & the house that was Don Carlos?

    Pound's beginnings

        Purify our hearts

by the old boats in darkness at

      St. Trovaso

dove Ognissanti s'incrovia

down alley to N. 942

      (Calle dei Frati's

      sign still legible)

knelt touched forehead to brick

1967

under the ivy wall
    lit w/ electric

Soft,
    Paul Goodman[27] Lectures Warmaking Corporations
      Military assembling
        in Washington
      Photosoldiers running w/packs
        from camps & trains—

(Boat rocking this morning
    Is this the place we get off?)
To restaurant, vegetable soup
    Zucchini & Spinach.
And 20,000 lire Beatles, Dylan, Donovan
    in record shop under
      clock St. Marco—
All perfect the orange moon
      rose over the Customs House
      I feared the Police,
The question of Silence,
    of Marijuana,
      Che Guevara
      Assassinate
        Poster on
    walls over Milan & Venice
& a hammer and sickle, & a star

27. Paul Goodman (1911–1972), a writer, philosopher, and critic, is probably best known for his book *Growing Up Absurd.*

1967

       printed on the housewall
           over the footbridge
               from the Salviati
yellow sign hanging Arrow in alley
         corner pointing
       to gold Name over a Door—
Found near San Vio's pinball

      Which church where I
         kneeled to accept Christ
in every Chapel, in the colored marble
—Doan let em git you
       them Buddhists—
them Paradise Pill Mongers
       Beatles and Mahesh Yogi
       Saying Meditate in Bright Colors

Thru alleys blue day lost
    in Canals past
      Dei Greci
   Carpaccio closed
I passed thru
      Academia earlier
    the acceptable Christ of His
      Choir of angels ranged
  The sane Tibetan tree,
and a wedding in San Trovaso—
    bride white sheathed kneeled
      next to black groom the
   priest in Italian Talking at the
      a baby cry revoked by side door

1967

10/22/67.

Going to Pound's house—how old?— "How old are you, old man?" I said, several wines and a stick of pot midway between meal.

"82 in several days," he said. That's all he said—all day, with the Italian-Ivanchich speaking of the Afric desert simultaneous—and I smoked at front of fire, smoked and spoke, and no one reproved me in Venice—perfect balanced, the consciousness—played him "Eleanor Rigby," and "Yellow Submarine," and Dylan's "Sad Eyed Lady of the Lowlands" and "Gates of Eden" and "Where Are You Tonight, Sweet Marie?"[28] and Donovan's "Sunshine Superman." I gave Pound Beatles, Dylan, Donovan—the experts suave and velvet for Futurity—I walked silent out Vio where meets the Grand Canal I gave Beatles, gave Dylan, gave Donovan—to listen? Forever—tomorrow give Ali Akbar Khan.[29]

[added later]—(Above note written blind drunk Sun. night 1 A.M. returning from Harry's Bar.)

What follows is sober recapitulation days later of what happened Oct. 22. All afternoon, lunch and wine and upstairs conversation with Ivanchich visiting and Pound silent. I lit a stick of grass at lunch and smoked it, saying nothing about it. Later high, as I played him music; he had come upstairs swiftly when I asked him to listen, and folded self in chair, silent hands crossed on lap, picking at skin, absorbed—occasionally with a slight smile—at "Eleanor Rigby." "No one was saved" and "Sweet Marie" "six white horses/ that you promised me/ were finally delivered down to the Penitentiary." I repeated the words aloud, in fragments—for him to hear clearly, So he sat. "Is this all too much electric noise?" He smiled and sat still. "I just want you to hear this other" and I continued

28. "Absolutely Sweet Marie."

29. Ali Akbar Khan (1922–2009), a classically trained Hindustani Indian-American musician known for his proficiency on sarod, contributed to the *Revolver* recording of the Beatles.

1967

playing, "Gates of Eden," and even "Yellow Submarine." Sat there all along, I drunk, he impassive, earnest, attentive, asmile.[30]

Also that day I chanted mantras to Krishna, and Tara, and Sarva Dakini, fragment of Allah, and Om a ra ba tsa na de de de de to Manjusri, describing His book and flaming Sword of Intelligence—Olga hearing Manjusri downstairs came up to top floor where we were (Ivanchich and Pound) and said "It sounded lovely down there" so sat and listened—I was drunk.

A finality "that binds things together." Depression all last week—read papers and Time—read Cantos, feel better.

Oct. 27, '67

a door ivy of brick   white sunlight
   over the Bridge white space
      a chimney on Giudecca
   light sparking white on
                 rippling water
Venus see upside down
    Children calling across the Canal,
Lap of wetness on wood,
   dusty gondolas bowing
      by iron-tong slab topped
           rubb'd stone rail'd
Salmon brick Fondamena wall.

30. "I asked [Olga Rudge], later, whether Pound had been pleased or perhaps bored by the Dylan and Beatles songs I'd played for him," Ginsberg wrote in 1979. "'Oh, no,' she replied. 'If he had been bored he wouldn't have sat there at all, he would have got up and left the room immediately.'"

Black boats on their sides
 on backyard ship way
  stepped to green water
   rippling,

Cry of motorboat, stone bridge,
 Fire irons on the ghat
  smoking before brown door,
green-electric round-saw,
 white laundry hanging
  small suit, the camera raised
   before his eyes
 at the church fluttered with doves
 on the leaning bell tower
  3 dimensional cross
   ball-spiked gold in sky—
 blue cover smoky grey
  over red balconies TV antennae
  down the canal two bridges
     marble arching,
tiny folk passing over the
 live-breathing green Neptune-stuff
Slurping—black barge, blond
  boy smoking in green—
marches thru white ripple
 out under the bridge
  The glittering rain-light
   mirrory Diamond-Sparkle
 looking out of my skin
  thru invisible eyeglasses
  rims at my eyes—
 young girls pass reading notebooks,

1967

                    hair combed smooth
                Iron boat ring cemented
        In slate footworn dusty with shadows
                a hammer noise at my back—
        Priest, & blue nylon coveralls on
                    the boy boatman
                        waiting &
        arranging grocery boxes on the brown boat—
                red-striped nosed in
                    light died by wooden boat garage—
old Lady reading newspapers,
            I will go into Trovaso Church.

—no Crossed to Giudecca
        Salute's Hippopotamus-gray
            Domed rear
                    Arm Towers
        Lifted bells saluting space-blue
            Transparency opening Hole
                sky-toll Metal-ringing
over domes uphill by Scroll'd
        arms carved round marble—
Ears hear slow bells from
        the brick painted tower
Across blue ripples, lacework
        balcony columns and pillared Arcades
                Arched over tiny black Gondolas
The answering double rings of Georgio
        Maggiore's tower across the Pool
                of St. Mark's extended along Many windowed
wall steeple dome roofed,
Salmon-white flat temples & Hotels,

1967

boats slipping the edges
　　of Flat green soft
　　　ripple-shifting
Water Bells, boat horn-huff,
　　Doves peck and flutter in the
　　　bicycl'd shade

—Leaped on Vaporetto
　　　sun yellow in white haze, warm
　　　　light crooked mirrored in the
　　　　　glassy surface
Swaying wooden dock at the end
　　of the Sun's water path
　　when it leaps from the sky
　　　to the grey bottom of the Giudecca
　　　　silhouetted in Sky's yellowness
Distance lit with blue light
　　to the double pillars of
　　　Crocodile & Lion in the stone
　　　Front yard arcaded past St. Mark's
　　　Spiky arch'd Façade—
Cut in stone, Altered in Architecture
　　Museum's floor inside
the tiny dignity of that white granite
　　gate-building,
two lovers and their girl, robes slipped
　　　Naked on the Couch—kneeling
　　and touching to kiss, leaning back
　　　with tender love-limbs miniatured
　　　　erect above stone testicle bags
　　　　　grooved cup of rock wine.

1967

In the whit a pillared Church
   Music slow voices Arcanum
      behind the altar, black Friars—
  chanting, the elevator vibrating
out Marble slotted belfry walls
   Sun over gold sea above
     Giudecca's blade,
Milky-blue light smoking over roofs
   under Christ's arm lifted above
     a temple window Cupola'd-round
light ray streaking along water before Him
   boat passing behind his distant body
    small'd blessing
Across the dusk yellow stippled
  lake between Redentore's mystic stone
          triangle'd Façade
boats pushing along surface slowly
   Past Zattere edge bridged to
    the Lovers walk by the brick wall
     behind Salute Garden's cypresses
  along the step of the Dogana
  Triangle Roofed, Copper globe
    uplifted green, October end
     afternoon light late yellow/
        flashed
from Phoebus' Mirror, distance silent
San Marco unchanged to the eye since Canaletto
  Since the black evening's fear by San Vio
    water moving, waiting, passing
     that night or ten years ago
    passed by the Watch Shop in Commercial Alley

1967

Harry's bar & Anson with Bloody Nary story
     of Wagnerian cock—
Peter jumping clothed into the Rio near San Samuele
High up here on a tower surveying space,
    surveying time Memory,
     great ships passing thru familiar light—
      the star of Moment on the Smokestack
—onion domes set Silent over St. Marco's
          "golden gloom"

Pink Palace wall sheltering filigree
    temple crossed metal tipped
      dome-flags—
and later ate soup with my father in that
    alley behind Savoia Joland's
      Pastel Façade—
Pound in the room, upstairs, on the
    armchair, smiling
    thru stone Impermanence at the Beatles—
    or the rhythmic noise in the electricity—
Zap! out of yr mind into Death—
    Filiality follows, no harm
      after the pain-end stillness
    Vast distance no eye, no horn moan
    Space hung in the air over Venice
     Silent behind the Motor Noise
Diamond sounding Silence, Thusness as of
    sunflash in water,
      Beauty impalpable, untouchable,
        Visible,
or has touch equaled the rapture-shine
    in young-bodied lover's eyes?

1967

And what will the mind do in Silence,
   of breasts, and ribb'd abdomens,
      Maleness tender muscled, lifted red,
        buttocks hugged, mouths &
        soft hair vaginas entered &
        Soft relaxed sphincter lips—
or Cigarettes, morning coffee, war-papers
   Perplexing noonshine with Metal-fear
Skin fear of Police, fear of the worn
   tooth enamel ringed beneath gum,
        Pink toothbrush ammonia paste,
           Marijuana Cigarette
     along the Zattere, over the Marble
            bridge, to the old Boatyard
   To Now—to Pray Blessing from
     Shiva-Christ Space
   Paranoid enormous in pounds of Self—

Sun turned orange, orange cloud haze
     over tree shadowed Cloister & ball field
   Hidden now, orange thru windows
   all the way into Salute dome—
Moving over the roofs at Canal edge,
        orange cold bell—
Orpheus naked with his green lute
   in the obelisk Column'd roof corner—
   Surveying the dove-stained Piazzetta
     Real cameras & furs, real sneezes
   in front of St. Mark's opulent
        Gold arches—
5 o'clock heavy bells, grey light clear
   along the floor of the plaza,

1967

gold gone down behind straight Arcades
    violin sounds at footlights, lamps
    lit in silver windows—
Marco sits like a god Crowned with
    sky arch starred Skull Cap,
    Crusted with angels climbing
        Stone mountains—
    Six turreted, Mountain peaks, Churches
      Patriarchs kissing Pope in Vatican,
the flagpole where Bill & Mrs. WCW
    Flossie stood by cast-iron bronze,
    for a photo
Four giant horses up there step forward
    in space,
Poised twilit green
    on dry marble slabs
fringed with white balconies, arch-scroll
    over Mosaic gleam,
Porphyry Columns, green marble, dark Basalt
    Hanging front of stone blocs blind porches
Immortal till the Sun vanishes
    away Intelligence—
& immortality's a story invention,
    Silent, worn perfect, resistant,
    blind scene of humor theater
    Backdrop of carved Rock-History—
Enough to make you weep, you knew
    the tears there—
orchestras almost could, lights don't
    remember Byron pain—

    . . .

Home Pension Cici, eyes closed,

1967

open after tired blackness—
Ganesh four-armed sitting on the
       redwood harmonium,
    go buy soap.
At table, yellow haired boy, cat whiskered
         with toothpick
  No righteous wars,
     old man with nick'd fingernails
     in blue wool suit, a yellow tie
       grey Sweater, red wrinkled cheeks,
    "you mean discs"—
      Of the Beatles?—
and the lady with pearls, white hair,
     red square stone ring, pearl ears,
     Pale skin—
In the Spring & Autumn—

           *

—Mist-wet slabs of St. Marco's
        Plaza
   lamps under a hundred arches,
  Celeste Aida old high violin
     silken in air, dark Space above
  the golden doors of lion-emblemed
     Mark-Church, still silent
as old face, impassive, decades,
     Centuries, friends die, the façade
says nothing in the evening
   Unpopulous, proffers a Cross
     At night-time years later,
Pound lived on art work,
   Yoga remembrance of language

1967

fragments all day
        writ in the evening,
What remained memorized,
    what stuck there
        in the mouth,
       by hand,
light language, solemn breathed,
   voice quavering now, alto,
     infuriated gaze—
      Cutting the Mutton on plate

Lamp mist, popular clarinets,
   light shine on white marble slabs
   the length of the Piazza to the
        giant tower—
 Fell 1902 would "take more than
    that to elicit a comment now"
laughter passing along Stone walls,
   pizzicato at the lamped Cafe,
half a hundred arches along the Arcade—
   Santa Maria's just as un-sad
   as if your lover swallowed Arsenic
       5 decades ago
    & left you with a rosy glow
       in loined Memory—
Solingo, Solingo—Kansas City Venice
   Homer or in the roar of the Pit[31]
      Chicago money-crash,
wheat rushing thru the Abstract Vortex
   of the Stone floored Stock Exchange.

31. Refers to Frank Norris's novel *The Pit*.

1967

Ended in my room singing Hare Krishna
       to myself,
  A full chord, & the voice echoing from
      The ceiling in La Cici
      Wavering with desire,
        Alto happiness.

10/28/67.

Lunch w/Olga Rudge, Pound, Michael Reck, Peter Russell. 1:30 P.M. Pension Cici 22 Salute Oct. 28, 1967—

Pound ate, fish, mostly silent during meal, others conversed, he responded occasionally with head nods—re a performance of Monteverdi (?) at S. Friari—

I had one question (being told he responds to specific textual questions from the turn of century—memorabilia)—

That I had found the "place of Carpaccio's skulls"—but where's the place where

  "in the font to the right as you enter
    are all the gold domes of San Marco"—?

He looked up and in even, tho high voice, said "Yes, when the font was filled—now they've changed it—used to be like that—"

For yesterday I'd looked in that same holywater basin, a stone bowl, but "for some sanitation reason" as Olga R. added a few minutes later, they'd placed a copper round-rim lip on inside of bowl, for water—and no longer filled the center of the bowl, just the metal canal around the rim.

"I walked half a mile yesterday," I added, "looking for the spot in Dei Greci, in San Georgio—finally looked in San Marco."

"It used to be like that—the center was filled with water, and the reflection had the domes," he explained. Perhaps less extensively.

"And the 'casa que fue de Don Carlos'—the house that used to be Don Carlos'?"

1967

"That is on the way to San Vio."

"But I've been there—is that near the English church?"

"That's on the corner where San Vio meets the Canal."

"But Salviati's is down the street here at the end—the sign."

"Salviati was in another place in that time," said Pound.

"Oh—but who was Don Carlos?"

"The Pretender."—he answered.

"So the house is on the corner of San Vio & Canal?"

He nodded, yes.

I continued—explaining that there were a great many specific percep-
tions—descriptions—of exact language composed—throughout Cantos—
"tin flash in the sun dazzle" and "Soapsmooth stone posts"—and added
I'd gone to San Vio looking for the soapsmooth stone posts— Were they
on the bridge to the private door off the square? or the posts at the end
of the quai at the canal-edge, or the plinth at the center of the square?
Which was it, because they were all rough—changed perhaps—replaced.
"Was it a specific stone post you had in mind, or just all the stone posts?"

"No, general—" he said, or nodding negatively, not a specific one.

A few moments silence while I looked thru my notebook for
a phrase. "I've been trying to find language equivalent for that light on
water—yesterday I arrived at this—

'Leaped on Vaporetto,

   sun yellow in white haze, Salute's

silver light, crooked-mirrored on the glassy surface'"

and repeated to him, while he looked me in eye—fine blue pupil—"light,
crooked-mirrored on the glassy surface," and smiled at him. "You approve
of that?"

"That's good," he smiled back—hands steady on the table, with almost
invisible tremor, white hair straight back above high-slanted forehead—
his skin wrinkled at wrists and back of hand, dry, slight white flakes of
dead skin, fingernails whitened by picking or rubbing, membrane-white

1967

roughness scraped on surface of thumbnail—clean skin of face and brow, with slight flaking of age (not dandruff) but dryness of skin surface under the thin white straight hair above his brow.

Had been talking with Reck about Buddhism, meditation, mantras, last night at supper and today earlier—and continued the conversation into Pound's ear, leaning toward him talking quietly—Reck's child, Mickey, playing with 14 postcards distracted him, Russell conversing with Olga Rudge at other side of Pound, she at end of table.

Reck asked, "You ever meet Kitasono Katsue?"

Pound, "No." Reck described meeting with Katsue, whom he found clerkish.

Sometimes at table—conversing w/Reck, who on basis of previous night's conversation (Reck'd noted there were Taoist elements in Confucian tradition at origin) was encouraging open discussion of Oriental heresies, asked about Indian gods—in relation to Greek—I had mentioned Vedic Hymns, asking Pound if he'd ever heard Vedic chanting—"No"— shook his head, he hadn't—I continued, referring to UNESCO new volumes of Hymns to Surya (Apollo), Rudra (Thunder God)—also mentioned Ganesh Chant (White Yajur Veda).

So explained to him—"You remember I was telling you about hearing Blake's voice[32]—?"

He hesitated and then pursed his mouth, nodded up and down slightly, looking away.

"But I didn't tell it coherently."—so described to him the occasion—"a series of moments of altered modes of consciousness over a period of weeks, etc."—ending "no way of presenting that except thru things external perceived in that state" and so continued explaining how his attention to specific perceptions, & WCW's "No ideas but in things" had been great

32. Reference to Ginsberg's "Blake Visions" (1948), in which Ginsberg believed he heard the sound of Blake's voice reading his work to him.

1967

help to me in finding language and balancing my mind—and to many young poets—and asked "am I making sense to you?"

"Yes," he replied finally, and then mumbled "but my own work does not make sense." [or "but I haven't made sense."]

I had asked him before if he would like to come to give a reading in the U.S. at Buffalo or S.F. say, he replied, "Too late"—

"Too late for what—for us or for your voice?" I laughed, and continued, explaining my and our (Creeley,[33] etc.) debt to his language perceptions—speaking specifically of the sequence of phanopoeic images—"soapsmooth stone posts"—even his irritations and angers characteristic, humors, dramatic, as manifest in procession as time mosaic.

"Bunting told me," said Pound, "that there was too little presentation and too much reference"
—referring to things, not presenting them.

I replied that in the last year [Basil] Bunting had told me to look at Pound because I had too many words, and showed Pound as model for economy in presentation of sensory phenomena, via words. I went on to describe recent history of Bunting—I'd before asked him if he'd seen Briggflatts and he had nodded, swiftly, affirmative. So Pound's work, I concluded to him, had been, in "Praxis of perception, ground I could walk on."

"A mess," he said.

"What, you or the Cantos or me?"

"My writing—stupidity and ignorance all the way through," he said, "Stupidity and ignorance."

Reck had been adding "encouragement" in general terms, and here said, "But the great lesson has been in prosody, your ear, and described also effect which everyone has learned from" . . . and described also effect

33. Robert Creeley (1926–2005), friend of Kerouac and Ginsberg and a poet closely associated with the Black Mountain poetry movement.

1967

of Pound on Hemingway and Hemingway on Bengali writers—Babel—or
Japanese— "Did you," Reck concluded "teach Hemingway?"—as a ques-
tion to which Pound was silent—doubtful? I opened my mouth to continue
the communion—

"Direct presentation"—"Yes," said Reck, "No adjectives"

Turning to Pound, Reck continued, "your poetry's shockingly direct."

"It's all doubletalk—" Pound re Cantos answered.

Reck—"But you have a marvelous ear, one can't praise that too much
. . . great ear—It's hard for you to write a bad line."

Pound—"It's hard for me to write anything."

Reck—"Your reading has been so extensive, and led people to many
areas."

Pound—"Not enough . . . I didn't read enough poetry."

Reck—"What you did read you made good use of."

"For the ear [William Carlos] Williams told me," I continued, "in
1961—we were talking about prosody, I'd asked him to explain your
prosody to me—in general, something toward approximation of quanti-
tative—anyway Williams said, 'Pound has a mystical ear'—did he ever tell
you that?"

"No," said Pound, "he never said that to me"—smiling almost shyly and
pleased—eyes averted, but smiling, almost curious and childlike.
"Well I'm reporting it to you now seven years later—the judgment of the
tender-eyed Doctor that you had a 'mystical ear'—not gaseous mystical he
meant—but a natural ear for changes of rhythm and tone."

I continued explaining the concrete value of his perceptions mani-
fested in phrasing, as reference points for my own sensory perceptions—
I added that as humor—HUMOR—the ancient humours—his irritations,
against Buddhists, Taoists and Jews—fitted into place, despite his inten-
tions, as part of the drama, the theater, the presentation, record of flux
of mind-consciousness. "The Paradise is in the desire, not in the imper-
fection of accomplishment—it was the intention of Desire we all respond

1967

to. Bhakti—the Paradise is in the magnanimity of the desire to manifest coherent perceptions in language."

"The intention was bad—that's the trouble—anything I've done has been an accident—any good has been spoiled by my intentions—the preoccupation with irrelevant and stupid things—"Pound said this quietly, rusty voiced like old child, looked directly in my eye while pronouncing "intention."

"Ah well, what I'm trying to tell you—what I came here for all this time—was to give you my blessing then, because despite your disillusion—unless you want to be a messiah—then you'd have to be a Buddhist to be the perfect Messiah" (he smiled)—"But I'm a Buddhist Jew—perceptions have been strengthened by the series of practical exact language models which are scattered thruout the Cantos like stepping stones—ground for me to occupy, walk on—so that despite your intentions, the practical effect has been to clarify my perceptions—and, anyway, now, do you accept my blessing?"

He hesitated, opening his mouth, like an old turtle.

"I do," he said—"but my worst mistake was the stupid suburban prejudice of anti-Semitism, all along, that spoiled everything—" This is almost exact.

"Well no, because anyone with any sense can see it as a humour, in that sense part of the drama—you manifest the process of thoughts—make a model of the consciousness and anti-Semitism is your fuck-up like not liking Buddhists but it's part of the model as it proceeds—and the great accomplishment was to make a working model of your mind—I mean nobody cares if it's Ezra Pound's mind—it is a mind, like all our minds, and that's never been done before—so you made a working model all along, with all the dramatic imperfections, fuck-ups—anyone with sense can always see the crazy part and see the perfect clear lucid perception-language-ground—"

He had nodded a little when I said "Nobody cares if it's Ezra Pound's

1967

mind"—and I added, and "so, fine, it's Ezra Pound's mind, a fine mind but the important thing, a model of mind process—Gertrude Stein also made one, usable—yours however, as I've experimented in transcription, the nearest to a natural model—a model from Nature—as Cézanne had worked from Nature, to reconstitute the optical field perceptions . . ."

It may have been at this point that he said, as recorded above, that his worst mistake had been "the stupid suburban prejudice anti-Semitism" and I responded, "Ah, that's lovely to hear you say that . . ." and later "as it says in *I Ching*, 'No Harm.'"

Sometime in this conversation he'd concluded, "I found out after seventy years I was not a lunatic but a moron."

And I paraphrased "Beginning of Wisdom, Prospero," and was continuing—Reck turning aside from his child asked me to repeat what Pound'd said, which I did and turned eyes to Pound, remembered I'd quoted epilogue verses Tempest last Sunday, so repeated them again to Pound, saying "You remember?"

> Now my charms are all o'er thrown,
> And what strength I have's mine own,
> Which is most faint. Now 'tis true
> I must be here confin'd by you,
> Or sent to Naples. Let me not,
> Since I have my dukedom got
> And pardon'd the deceiver, dwell
> In this bare island by your spell;
> But release me from my bands
> With the help of your good hands.
> Gentle breath of yours my sails
> Must fill, or else my project fails,
> Which was to please. Now I want
> Spirits to enforce, art to enchant;

1967

And my ending is despair
Unless I be reliev'd by prayer,
Which pierces so that it assaults
Mercy itself and frees all faults.
As you from crimes would pardon'd be,
Let your indulgence set me free.

He looked at me in my eye kind smiling, I looked at him and then (must've been at this point) asked if he'd accept my blessing—more conversation—the sequence at this hour later inexactly rememberable—We rose, he got coat cane and Olga gave him grey wool small-brim'd hat, walked all of us out on San Gregorio by small canal lined with iron rail—started walking, still talking up street to his alley—T.V. cameramen waiting, a black cable snaked from his door to powerline across alley—and at door we all stood, he outside still while Olga went in—So took him by shoulders looked in his eye and asked "and I also came here for your blessing, and now may I have it, sir?"

"Yes," he nodded, "for whatever it's worth—"

"And more, and more," I said, "I'd like you to give me your blessing to take to Sheri Martinelli"—for I'd described her late history Big Sur, eyes seeing Zodiac everywhere hair bound up like Marianne Moore—which gossip perhaps he hadn't even heard—"To at least say hello to her, I'll tell her, so I can tell her," and stood looking in his eyes. "Please . . . because it's worth a lot of happiness to her, now . . ." and so he looked at me impassive for a moment and then without speaking, smiling slightly, also, slight redness of cheeks awrinkle, nodded up and down, affirm, looking me in eye, clear no mistake, ok.

Then he stood, silent, Peter Russell said adieux, I waited, talked to Olga while, "It's horrible, so many come and ask him if he's still writing"—she had said at table; there were now enough Cantos for new volumes, scattered and as yet uncollated or edited, whatever—"to ask him

1967

if he's writing—of course it's different with someone like yourself, to discuss as fellow"—fellow professional or something. "well it makes him self-conscious"—"Yes self-conscious," she agreed to that language exact— "but if you wait," she had said, "and have patience—he needs to talk—he thinks all his work so bad—whereas when he reads it into tape, you can tell he reads with enthusiasm, some parts—other parts, of course, he dislikes but that's natural, after years of self-critical—whereas when he to be self-critical, anyone would . . ." She spoke very sensibly, explaining how she viewed the apparent perplexity as it was made more difficult by outside uncomprehension of the nature of his present alertness and character.

Then he turned to me—I had kissed him on right cheek—held my hand, and said "I should have been able to do better . . ."

"It was perfect," I replied—"I haven't properly yet sung Hare Krishna to you either . . . I'll be around a few days more anyway, maybe . . . see you . . ." He stood then at his door, hesitating to enter—waved down the alley, I walked away with Reck and Russell, who suggested I try to transcribe details of the conversation while it is still fresh to ear.

His remarks several days ago "82 in several days" exact to this Monday Oct. 30. his birthday.

10/28/67.

Supper at Cici, Olga and Pound at table, "You like the Beatles records? . . . or too much noise?"
Silence.
    "You mean those discs?" he said.
    "Yes."
Silence.
    "No! No!" to the waiter offering zucchini also with sliced mutton.

1967

"Oh yes, take some zucchini, it is good for you—" Olga.

"You liked the Noh, heard first time at the Sanctus Spiriti Church?"
Olga asked. He stared thinking, then shook head No, slowly, added, "Pal-
ladio's theater"—

----

28 Oct 67 XI 50 by Clocktower

Nicks in the basalt columns
     rubbed smooth by fingers
  porphyry red, cracks, soft to the touch now.

Brown dusklight
     on Academia Wood,
Sunset lanterns along Schiavone's
     red walls,
Lamps lit at
      Salute's steps—
  orange light swirl
    in the grey-green wavelets of Grand Canal—

Rose fronted clouds hanging in blue space
   Night falling over Chimneys,
   Campanile's gold Angel's knee
      bent into the last gold light
   Marco's grey domes tiny,
  Doge palaces square pink block
   fringed above motor skiffs
     sliding to shore,
 A grey Cargo boat moving across
  Palladio's columned stages.

1967

Rosso de serva
Del Tempo's s'espara

Small glow reddish behind smokestacks,
    Towers, roof angles behind neon
        clouds over Judecca.

Carmini, organs apse brilliant
                yellow
   gilt angles, violoncello,
     cross hung silhouette Byzance—
Flowers on Altar, Pillars wrapped
         with red velvet—
Old man sat before me,
    brown canvas shoes, heel raised attendant,
      hat & cane in hand
    Smooth woodslab backrest
      under a fold in his
         coat back—
white cheek beard dyed red by
      velvet light,
Black not entirely faded from
    back of his skull,
fringed with grey-white hair
     Candle gleam thru white web—

Clock-Tower—gold wings
  back against gold sunlight

—teeth numb, & thru the dentists
    drill's aluminum aim,

1967

St. Marco's Balcony crusted with orange
Dusk light—

10/29/67.—12 P.M.—

Out on Salute boat-station waiting for vaporetto, Peggy Guggenheim
with two tiny dogs and Paolo art friend, met gossiping, I related some of
conversation with Pound day before—she thought his wartime activities
"unforgivable" . . . also asked me if I'd written poem called Howl and an-
other poem "Gasoline"?[34] Olga Rudge and Ezra Pound appeared on the
floating platform—9 P.M. dark—she said they were going to Carmini
Church for Vivaldi concert, five year celebration of priest, a lady friend
singing that night—social appearance—I asked "May I come?" and as she
said, "Certainly," we went on vaporetto—

Sitting on bench behind them, addressed her and Pound's ear, told
story of Julius Orlovsky, as Manichean who wouldn't speak for 14 years
because he believed all the evil in the universe issued from his body and
mouth. "Are you a Manichean, Ezra?" she laughed. No answer. Walked
long time, slightly lost in alleys past open flagstone campo S. Margherita
to church (I'd visited it earlier today on walk starting from Zatteria, when
I'd met Pound in afternoon sunlight, blinking, waiting on Fondamenta
[quai-waterside, facing Judecca] with Olga for film crew trailing them—
standing then in bright clear light long sun yellow rays bathing I wanted
to stay, get in the picture, but said I was taking walk, so continued on my
way and left them in group with TV director, a large serious artistic look-
ing Italian—I walked several hundred feet on and stepped out on a sway-
ing wooden jetty, sat crosslegged, and watched from distance, as their
group slowly ambled back to San Gregorio).

34. *Gasoline,* a book of poems by Gregory Corso.

1967

Evening now, we three went into S. Maria Del Carmelo—wrote note there, sitting behind Pound—

Carmini, organ, apse brilliant yellow

gilt angels, violoncello,

Byzance cross hung silhouette,

Flowers on altar, Pillars wrapped in red velvet—

old man sat before me,

brown canvas shoes, one heel raised alert,

hat and cane in hand

Smooth woodslab resting

under a fold in his coatback

white cheek beard dyed red by

velvet light,

black not entirely faded from

back of his skull,

fringed with grey hair,

candle gleam through white web.

Some very delicate Vivaldi violin beginning soft and rising—Olga, Pound following, walked forward along pillared candle-lit left aisle to look closer to her singing friend, they stood there listening to the end. Then without waiting for next pieces of concert to finish, headed home thru alleys, walking—silent awhile, then I began again—as I'd been to look, today, at "lacquer in sunlight ... russet brown ... lions out of benevolence," to the left of San Marco (Olga on vaporetto had pointed out House of Don Carlos—other side of San Vio Campo, on corner—Questioned where Salviati's had been, Pound didn't answer)—he didn't respond either, to reference to the lions; anyway it wasn't a question.

I began: "I've been thinking about problem you raised yesterday, the Cantos a mess—if they made a static crystalline ideological structure, it

1967

would be unresolvable, now. But it is an open-ended work, that is, epic, 'including history,' of movement of your mind and record of focused perceptions, existing in time, and changing in time, anything you write now will refer back to the beginnings and alter all that went before—like turning a Venetian blind. Same thing as in Lombardo's Sirens. Beginning back in time with serpent tails, going thru transformation thru Breast Pisan Cantos poignancy—ending in present time sculpting clear human eyes. In short, what I'm saying is,—Einsteinian changing universe is recorded, not static crystal shit model—so anything you do now is OK and will be proper, appropriate, as means of altering preceding thought-flow by hindsight—Am I making sense?" This addressed to problem of finishing Cantos.

Replied, "It's all tags and patches."

I explained lots more, in answer, ending, "I've read Cantos through this month and in each canto there's always some condensed perception concrete image round which the other tags, ideologies, irritations and projections and references revolve, so whole work has solid vertebrae." Then continued, "Is your problem one of physical depression that keeps you from recording and registering these final perceptions—whatever you are now?"

"The depression's more mental than physical," Pound answered.

Later in conversation I said the Cantos were solid—good as Dickens' *Bleak House* I started reading, that was full of exaggerations—said I'd read *The Pit* lately, Frank Norris, had he read it ever?

"No."

So I described the roar of wheat trading on the floor of the Stock Exchange. We got to house, after more on Cantos, he not replying, but when he entered his house he said immediately,

"It's too hot in here."

Olga built a fire. I sat down, and next described effect of his poetry on younger poets—Do you know the enormous influence you've had? I asked

1967

"I'd be surprised if there was any," he said dubiously, looked down, but interested—I recited a few short poems of Creeley, talked briefly of Olson,[35] Wieners[36]—asked him if he knew Creeley's work at all, he nodded up and down, thin beard affirmative. "But do you understand the influence your writing had been as a model for whole generation of younger poets—that is my age half yours now 41 and say Creeley?"

"It would be ingenious work to see any influence," said he.

Explained the influence WCW, Zuke (Zukofsky),[37] Bunting,[38] etc. Said that at first, myself of Paterson, I'd found WCW more usable—

"Williams was in touch with human feelings . . ." he said, nodding his head slightly in disgust at himself. I explained it was the practical matter of listening to "I'll kick yuh eye." And I went on explaining the models we had—that Williams didn't have Fire Excitement—Crane had—did Pound know Crane's Bridge?

"No." I was surprised, so recited several verses of "Atlantis" comparing it to Shelley's "Ode to the West Wind," and Pound's own anger-inspiration rhythm Canto XLVI "*helandros kahelep tolis kai helarxe.*" Asked if he'd tape-recorded that, he nodded No.

Olga served Ovaltine, brought me copy of Canto CX, "Has Mr. Ginsberg seen this?" I said I'd return it, she asked him to sign it for me—he hesitated long time, and said: "Oh, he doesn't want it."

"Well, yes sure, I do," I pointed my finger, "if you want to check your perceptions. I absolutely do."

So he signed, "Alan Ginsberg—dall'autore—Oct. 29, 1967 Ezra Pound."

35. Black Mountain poet and essayist Charles Olson (1910–1970).

36. John Wieners (1934–2002), a Boston poet and a gay-rights and antiwar activist.

37. Ginsberg included objectivist American poet Louis Zukofsky (1904–1978) as one of his influences.

38. Ginsberg met British modernist poet Basil Bunting (1900–1985) when he visited the UK in 1965.

1967

At home, I also at one point asked him if he was at all familiar with my poetry, he shook his head negative. I said, Well, oddly, it might even please you. This led on to discussion of his influence on younger poets.

Oct 30 (5 A.M.) '67   toothache

Slept with toothache—dreamt after 2 aspirins fell asleep: image an apartment, familiar, returned to. High up in labyrinth of my old Brooklyn Elevated Venice city—large rooms, that I always had with old friends— young boy in bed waiting for me to lay necking with him in narrow famil- iar bed, I not so willing as before, perhaps someone else I wanted—Yes there had been a conversation about that one street or boy whores in Benares—Venice Tola Calle—(alley)—to my surprise, a very active street, I was explained—

And exploring the apartment I looked thru glass-curtained door to ad- jacent large room an extension apparently let out to others—several mus- tached & bearded surly hippies in bed together, curious—got no privacy in my own apartment, if I open door & peek in, they can open door & walk thru while I'm fucking? Meth heads in there?—and it's a big room, a wing of the large flat, extending thru large corridors perhaps to other room or balcony across, it's a square dark length—unfamiliar territory.

10/30/67 —3:30 P.M.

—Met Pound by Teodoro's statue, cafe there, with Ivanchich and girl- friend—Ivanchich had invited me to lunch at Malamocco's, Pound's birth- day today—conversation about Huxley,[39] re electronic spying, I repeated

39. Famous for his novel *Brave New World*, Aldous Huxley (1894–1963) was in- teresting to Ginsberg for his experiments with, and writings about, psychedelic drugs.

1967

notion that best antipolice state strategy was total exposure of all secrets, rather than electronic monopoly-control of classified information—i.e. unclassify everybody's private life, President Johnson's as well as mine— thence conversation re intrusion of machinery universe—Olga asked Pound for old quotation, which he repeated complete after her fragmentary reference, "As for living, our servants can do that for us."

As habitual, he hesitated over choice of foods, refused vegetables—I gave him 1½ stringbeans from my side dish, which he picked up with fork and ate—toasted him and drank wine, he at first didn't respond, then swiftly took his glass and drank.

I talked a great deal about modern use of drugs as distinct from twenties opiate romanticism (as I saw it)—turned finally and asked him again— "Does all this make nonsense to you now—'immortality pills' and all?"

"You know a great deal about the subject," he replied.

Ivanchich identified Olga's reference to the can of opium Pound brought—Was it Hemingway's story or Williams'—to friend (Forrest Read?) Ivanchich saying it was in *Movable Feast*. Pound commented:

"Hemingway had the correct version."

Olga asked me if I knew Michaux—then asked Pound if he remembered Michaux—Pound shook head No, she said, "Oh, you must remember, he came to lunch with us in Paris two years ago" . . . she had described him as very charming.

I had also asked, earlier, if Pound had not ever met Hart Crane, he shook head No.

Walked back slowly along Riva Schiavoni, on top of white bridge (Ponte de Pieta across from Sighs Bridge by Ducal Palace) Pound in brown wool hat, St. Georgio Maggiore dome and tower above his head silhouetted in brilliant yellow-blue afternoon light, few people and many grey pigeons crowded on stone ground—we waited by vaporetto for Olga to check at pastry shop—on the way, passing Teodoro's column I repeated,

"Shd I shift to the other side, or wait 24 hours," and asked what

1967

does that mean, shift to the other side of the column, or cross over to Salute?

"Fantasia," he replied.

"What?"

"Just fantasy."

"I thought meant, shift sleeping to other side of the column of Teodoro, or, maybe, change in life—or just writing poetry."

He was silent.

Olga returning, we sat waiting for vaporetto, asked if Reck'd left copy of Hsi-yu hu by Yeh-Lu Ch'u-Ts'Ai (Tr. Igor de Rachewiltz, Monumenta 'Serica, Vol. XXI, 1962). Said Pound's "Immortality Pills" phraseology was from notes in that monograph—also reference to Incense Cults—all Canto XCIX.

At door this evening, returning from an errand, Mrs. Rudge invited me to return later to sing to Pound on his birthday night. Came by at ten attired in silken London-Indic shirt, woven gold, and Buddhist Trikaya emblem round neck—he was silent, by fire (he'd come downstairs)—so chanted *Prajnaparamita Hrdaya Sutra* in Japanese and English, then Hare Krishna, and after some birthday cake and a little more champagne, Buddhist Three vows. Buddham Sharnam Gacchami, Dharmam Sharnam Gachhami, Sangham Sharnam Gacchami. Then in silence still, to illustrate effect of his composition on mine, read—with indifferent voice alas—few pages of "Middle Section of Long Poem on These States." oops! Silence. Eek! Put that down fast after asking, do you see the relationship in method of composition? Silence. so picked up harmonium and chanted 50 verses of Gopala Gopala Devaka Nandana Gopala—high and sweet, and low solemn. Then explained "Gopala means Krishna cowboy" and said goodnight and "Happy Birthday Krishna," he smiled at that. Leaving from door I demanded, "Well, say Goodnight!" He nodded amiably, said "Goodnight." So I left.

1967

Look thru eyes:
   Maestro, glimmering,
      Green specksri
or Torcello's tower, red brick edge,
     against blue dusk—
       Space, interpreted thru
           pest electric
           robots, screens

Look thru eyes,
     ripple cities camped
flat against the eyebrow,
   boats lighter then feathers
     pass the head,
       cities cade,
   eyeball universes
    vanish, peaceful change.

Nov 3 Afternoon,

    across from Rialto
    Marble roof comb
    —sky, clear after rain,
    bird-heads
       Those cream-colored balls
are pigeons' breasts
were

1967

    Academia's
    Over wooden trestles

      walk the sky,
      —over wooden trestles,
Academia

Sunset Nov. 6, 1967

Light, dull gleam gold dome
    Blue Christ mosaiced
over a sea of marble on the floor,
    wheels, squares, blocks in space,
      "The sea" cracked & sunk in the
        Floor, dips & eddies in the stone
cocks, pheasants, snakes, Basilisks. Gryphons,
    vines, Urns, green leaves
       & an angel playing the Violin
waves of marble, brown diamond shapes flat,
    depth holes in rectangles,
      waves of rock-flow running round
        polished columns,
giant wall slabs swirled symmetric
    burnished shiny red by centuries
    of shoulderblades & heads leaning
        in reverie—
orange marble benches along walls
    two men sit together dwarfed by
      giant-Buttress-blocks polish—
        surfaced with grey Marble slab,

and the chant of white haired Fathers
    with no children, echoing under the apse dome's
        gold glow,
where candles burn set symmetric on
      white-marble table,
  Behind the dark rock-screen
    where the dozen Prophet's Statue stand
    dark-stoned—
        The Christ with long
          brown hair,
in a blue robe, a beard, young cheeks,
held out his hand to show you,
  his red heart afire clasped with
  thorn-ring, & a tiny golden cross
     painted above
Dei Gratia's old voice,
    yellow electric flowers hang
      over rows of shadowy Arches.

mottled cold marble, polished, cracked,
  smooth cemented slabs of orange rock,
    benches ledged along the Wall—
Candle light gleams on grey columns.

Baritone Acceleration,
    Prayer well out of the
       wood benches facing
       the gold altar,
       "Pala d'oro."

* * *

1967

Outside,
> lights under the long arcade
> arches, laughter &
> young girls gossip voices, Promenade,
the energy files by the Plazetta

sweet orchestras set by stone from Cafes lit yellow,
> giant bells begin upstairs
>> 6:30 Night
over the vast stone-slabbed field.
> Boys with soft hands sweet faces,
>> stand in circles groaning
>> & singing gossip,
>>> Siempre,
> low tones, that one Venetian voice,
>> tender, Justo, chivalric,
>>> baritone,
> soft vowels repeated centuries late,
new youths return like old flowers
> clear faced, stance, prisoned
>> in their own skinny beauty
Strolling by marble columns, gazing up
> at longhaired white angels,
>> Naked Hercules, winged white lions,
>> Theodore with spear upraised
>>> standing on a Crocodile,
So many exquisite children walking
> toward the clock tower,
>> & under the stained Arcade ceiling
Don't know their own beauty,
> thin legs, clear eyes,
> grow older & argue thru mustaches.

1967

one star between the two giant columns

green

boat lights wavering

in water

The dentist's windows lit by the Clock

Tower,

Two old lights burning on St. Mark's

park,

tonight,

decades,

Frost-globes   in front of folded

Awnings,

Under every arch-round.

11/6/67 —2:30 A.M. Sun. Night

Nov. 2, saw Pound on Zatteria, walking at 1 P.M. in sunlight along the stones—Ognissanti Day—asked him "How are you today? Alive!"

He answered, "Worse. And alive."

Several days later met at lunch, he was silent, curious reddish cast to cheeks, observed the elderly waitress carefully bone his fried trout—silent, then swiftly picked up fork, cut a piece and ate. But didn't finish his plate, refused cake and coffee. New clean lavender shirt with wide collar, and monocolored yellow tie. Always hangs his hat outside pension dining room, and his scarf, on brass hook, and carries ivory-handled cane inside to table. Said, "Goodbye, Mr. Pound," and he turned, hesitated, looked at me, smiling slightly, but dumb, shook my extended hand.

Yesterday came down in midafternoon to dining room back of pension kitchen, accompanying Otto Endrenyi—Hungarian-Bolognesi ex-refugee friend of Olga—who'd heard me sing in room an hour earlier—(high with Israeli architect I'd met in flooded San Marco Plaza and we'd

1967

walked and smoked his last brown stick of kif, along street from Academia to Zatteria, then up to my room I sang awhile Hare Krishna)—So Otto invited me to coffee—found Pound sitting there alone, Olga at telephone in front office preparing trip to Padua to escape rain floods of early November,

I sat across from Pound at another table, asked him if there was old or classical music to St. Francis Canticle to Creatures—repeated question, he answered. "There is no contemporary music." So, high on pot still, I improvised in Hebraic–Indian modes on the complete text of canticle typescript on table before me, with drone harmony on Peter Orlovsky's brown school harmonium, chanting thru "Frate Morte."

An hour later saw him and Olga Rudge outside hotel, and followed after them with Otto, they to take vaporetto to R.R. to Padua, we to promenade in San Marco at red clouded sunset hour—Pound walked energetically, white raincoat flowing behind him, walked with speedy strength, slowed to climb small bridge-steps to Salute's platform and stepped up firmly, then with youthful balance stepped from the tipsy floating platform onto boatbus and walked ahead into cabin, sat down; vaporetto pulled away from shore, moving upstream.

Morning—empty life, revolving on the surface of a mirror, myriads passing by—

Woke, and realizing late date, only another month and half before reading tour, and fatal time in USA, and I gotta get back soon see Peter, and finish texts once for all, collect books, cash in verbal chips, dropout—all last night at Luigi Nono's house talk of Cuba and Revolution and Guevara photos on wall and avant-garde collections with machinery, lights, Guevara images fair faced and smiling through boyish beard—Time passing.

1967

First drag of a white cigarettes,
Bar Venice, Bar Penice,
        after Sausage Plaza
red paper tablecloth—unfinished Salad,
    blond arms, fingers, blond hair, a boy
        half my age with smooth skin,
talking bright eyed Italian, in Venice—
    first drag of a white cigarettes,
blond hair, Minetta's Greenwich Village
    25 years ago—dark streets, alcohol
        Dimming the brain, white cigarette.

Lucien! No he visto Venice!

Elegy Che Guevara[40]

European Trib. boy's face photo'd eyes opened,
    young feminine beardless radiant kid
        lain back smiling looking upward
Calm as if ladies' eyes were kissing invisible parts of the body
aged reposeful angelic boy corpse,
        perceptive Argentine Doctor, petulant Cuba Major
           pipe mouth'd & faithfully keeping Diary
             in Mosquitos Amazonas
Sleep on a hill, dull Havana Throne renounced
More sexy your neck than sad aging necks of Johnson
           DeGaulle, Kosygin,
    or the bullet pierced neck of John Kennedy—
Eyes more intelligent glanced up to death papers

40. First draft of "Elegy Che Guevara," *Collected Poems,* 492–93.

1967

Than worried living Congress Cameras passing
            dot screens into shade, phantom McNamara
            Dulles in old life . . .
Women in bowler hats sitting in mud outskirts 11,000 feet up in Heaven
            with a headache in La Paz
    Selling black potatoes brought down from mountain lipped
            Puno—earth roof'd huts
    Would've adored your desire and kissed your Visage
                    new Christ
They'll raise up a red-bulb-eyed war mask's
            white tusks to scare soldier-ghosts
            who shot thru your lungs—

Incredible! One boy turned aside from operating rooms
    on healing Pampas yellow eye
    To face the stock rooms of ALCOA, myriad board directory
                            United Fruit
        Trustees of Chicago U., Lawyer Phantoms ranged back to dead
                            John Foster Dulles
                            Dillon & Reed,
                                Acheson, Truman

To go mad and hide in jungle on mule, & point rifle at OAS
    at Rusk's egoic Courtesies, the metal deployment of Pentagon
            derring-do Admen and dumbed intellectuals
            from *Time* to the C.I.A.
    One boy against the Stock Market, all Wall Street ascream
            since Norris wrote *The Pit*
    afraid of the free dollars showering from the observer's balcony
            Scattered by laughing younger brothers,
        Against the Tin Company, against the Wire Services,
            against millions of College boys watching

1967

                    Wichita Den T.V.
one radiant face driven mad with a rifle
         Confronting the electric networks.

                                        Nov. 1967

Leaving Venice—Nov. 8, '67

         Canal drab olive, raining silver
                 in the sky,

balconies shuttered,
                 no farewell to Pound or the Ragazzi

a year of quiet?—
         in Longhena's Church by the
                         RR Station

grey façade, grey rain,
         "The line thickens . . ."

electric-lit gloom, solid marble to
                 the painted arches,
         Tiepolo's Christ a cloud
                 of shadows on the road

To all Poets, Peace to Pound

Avolokiteshvara, Karnnon, Ra-Set,
    Kalipada Guha Roy, Sitaramdas Omkarnath
                         Thakur

1967

Maharishi Mahesh Yogi, our Father,
    Dove, Spirit, Beatles, Jagger

Zukofsky, Bunting, Williams' eyes,

Shambu Bharti Baba, Mary Kali,

Krishna, Krishna, Gopola, Hari Rama,
    Shiv Parvati, Durga, Sanga-ma,
            Yamuna-ma,
Teodoro, Troviso, Mary of Miracles,
        Ramakrishna,
                Iamblichus,
Zagreus, Coyote, Heruka, Dorje Jigje,
    Sgam-po-pa, Tsongkhapa,
            Dudjom Rinpoche,
Maitreya, Sakyamuni, Bodhidharma,
Hui Neng, Satyananda, Shivananda,
    Kung, Bhaktivedanta, Brahmananda,
    Snyder, Kerouac, Olson, Creeley,
            Peter, Gregory,
                    Louis,
Karmapa Lama, Govinda Lama, Leary,
    Satchitananda, Diana, Zeus, Christ,
Jaweh, Allah, Buddha, Yemaya, Chango,
    our Father, Mother, Lamb,
Dragpo. Lion, Flower, Sunyata—
            Peace.

Night—
    Last pages Thrones—
"you in the dinghy astern there"

1967

With Louis and Edith Ginsberg in Italy.

Train rolling past Electric gold
                      Maestro
red auto lamps
      moving under wet Asphalt

To Verona
Ophitic Columns, with
    "stone loops"

Hang it all, Ezra Pound,
there can be but one "Cantos"

and the old Custode lit Candle at dusk down
      Zeno's pillared Sanctum,
twenty years, thirty years
seven hundred years later, scratched
    on orange marble,
"Adamino de Sno. Georgio"

----

12 Nov. 1967

Black roofed Milan
    Iron wheels   grind shiny trucks
Squeal round stone blocks,
carlights brighten in narrow corners
    between buildings,
wind roar of motors under tin
    lights hung from street pole,
                shuttered window neon
Winter Come, all the sidewalk tables

1967

of Jamaica retired like flowers
      Tavola Calda

     Mist in the stone gulfs
whitened by
    lamps floating
        from wires

1967

At the Democratic National Convention with Burroughs.
Photograph copyright Michael Cooper Collection.

1968

Ginsberg began 1968 with a rush of activity, and he concluded the year in the hospital after he was badly injured in an automobile accident.

The year was one of the most turbulent in U.S. history. The Tet Offensive in January and early February, in which different North Vietnamese factions, in a massive attack against strategic South Vietnamese targets, touched off a U.S. retaliation, brought the country further away than ever from a resolution to the war. A report on inner-city violence, commissioned by Lyndon Johnson, concluded that America was badly divided between whites and blacks. Martin Luther King Jr. and Robert Kennedy were assassinated. A heatedly contested presidential race reached its nadir in a week of violence at the Democratic National Convention in Chicago. World events, including mass antiwar protests, suggested a fractioning of political ideologies and policies. In November's national election, Richard Nixon narrowly defeated Vice President Hubert Humphrey.

Ginsberg remained as busy as ever. He zigzagged across the country, visiting college campuses, giving readings, and protesting the war. He was present at a New York news conference announcing the formation of the Youth International Party, and he vowed to travel to Chicago for the convention. Neal Cassady died in Mexico in February; the loss and grieving put Ginsberg in a reflective frame of mind. Planet News, his first City Lights book of all-new poems since Kaddish and Other Poems, was released.

His journal entries in 1968 were scattershot, largely limited to new poems. His schedule prohibited long passages of prose writing, although he still managed to jot down occasional thoughts that he felt might be useful in the future.

Jan. 1, 1968—2 AM

Telegram to Jack from Gregory—
"Hello to those caught in the Year."

All night sleep
all day sweet blue light
dream buildings tiny windows
new-built across my street
transparent eyeball, woke looking
outside snow falling in silence
on skyscrapers merry xmas
Everywhere the same two
thousand years ago today.
Fever sleep, wake eye
world glimpsed round, sleep.
Dream buildings visible wake
skyscraper streets die—
Cough, happy New Year.

"The business of America is business"
& "The Medium is the message"
The biggest single business in America
is Defense via the Department of Defense.
The "business of America is business"
So "the Medium is the Message."
Regimented by these 2 aphorisms
Doom lurks in the above statistic
Defense is the biggest industry

1968

Jan. 8   Black Powers exaggerate difficulty
            Anti Red Power Exaggerates Conflict

A little Heroin and into planet hangs
    unprotected in the clouds,
Summer Causes Winter
    hot cats change cold earth
Not bad, a touch in the arm
    one tense night in heaven
More often's like cigarette smoke lungs
    ask for more, it's supposed to be Hell,
It's Chemical what eyeball or brain can do.

Tues, Jan 9, 1968   Docket #C-26356
               Part 1-C   Criminal Court New York
               Officer Dacumba (Des Con 5-6)
               ACLU Atty John Mage
                      —Judge gave me Unconditional Discharge
             I recited, loud voice, Pentagon Exorcism
                     in Courtroom

      Re: Blocking Whitehall Draft Board
          Entrance with Dr. Spock and others

Jan. 19, 1968

    Are you prepared for the Atom Bomb
    to Blast you out of your body to something familiar?
    Are you prepared for the Bomb to Fall
    As always expected, as was designed?

1968

Are you prepared for the Bomb to descend
Brightness round the backyard Cherry tree
That stands revealed on ancient friend
Dear in the Moment before Last Light sends
Fire thru the house & fire on the sky
& fire running between the tree & the eye?

The Depression of '30s
a prophecy of Apocalypse:
half generation later
—at Dylan/Guthrie
Concert,
Movies of Dust Bowl Okies
    moving black Fords
    loaded w/ mattresses
    across the Calif
                Border.

Not Reading the Sunday Times

On Saturday the War got worse
    Korea stole a spy ship
CIA & Peking conspired supercrisis
    The Reds distracted
                halfway Cross Asia
    The Feds shifted eyeballs
            from Hanoi peace propaganda
        to Pyongyang Pirate escalation
Six hundred junkies were dragged in Jail
    Pentagon and Local Police Chiefs

1968

Met at Orleigh House
and the dollar was shaky on its testicles

By Monday the crisis deepened
   Norwalk School sent 53 longhairs home
   Bubonic Plague spread outside Saigon
            and Radiation preoccupations
        Spread at arctic crash site
   Police denied accepting gifts
      Desirable jobs were awarded in Vietnam
      to the Corrupt Artillery Commanders
and Dr. Spock pleaded Not Guilty to Conspiracy

But Sunday how peaceful, Lord's day, Day of Rest,
   Nothing happened, didn't read the *Times*
Vast sheaves of History plunged into the Void
   Canadian Pinstripes made paper
         Vanished from human consciousness—

Napalm Goldpaper, Dow Chemical's excuses,
   Rockefeller's interest in McDonnell Douglas,
   Mellon's interest in molecular warfare,
         Leroi Jones and his tragedies
    and all the taxpayers' screams in the Capitol
obliterated all, tranquil, silenced, oblivious—
Sun shone and busses hissed down second Avenue,
      Poesy flourished, junkies scored, but History
      Stopped 24 hours to take a nap
and nobody suffered death on opposite Hemispheres,
       cats meowed
          on the staircase

1968

In the early morning hours of February 10, Ginsberg received a phone call informing him that Neal Cassady had been found dead along the railroad tracks near San Miguel de Allende, Mexico. Cassady had apparently ingested a large quantity of alcohol and drugs at a wedding reception and had decided to walk to Celaya, fifteen miles from San Miguel, where he had left his suitcase. He passed out a mile and a half from San Miguel and, lying undiscovered, died of exposure in the rain in the cold Mexican night.

Ginsberg was deeply shaken but not surprised to hear of Cassady's fate. Time and distance had separated the two by the early sixties and, while they continued to communicate, they were clearly on different paths. Ginsberg was now world famous and maintaining a very busy schedule whereas Cassady had teamed up with Ken Kesey and his Merry Pranksters and had driven their psychedelic bus across America. Ginsberg and Cassady had reunited briefly when Kesey and company were in New York, but the Cassady Ginsberg met then was not the same man he had known and loved in the late forties and fifties. As always, he had moved on, at a reckless speed.

Ginsberg preferred to remember Cassady from their earlier days. He wrote poetic eulogies throughout 1968, beginning with one written on the day when he heard the news.

Feb. 10, 1968   5 AM

    Neal—telephone call from Denver,
"Have you heard the news from the West Coast?" "I've been away all week."—"Have you not heard from the West?"—"I have been *away*." "Cassady died in Mexico."

    His happy Spirit in air, released from body.

1968

Morning blue light new apartments outside city window still unfamil-iar—Sex the bondage that held us together most after all—and his spirit growth to belief in reincarnation, the oriental mode—communicated to Jack and me—Thus a Bodhisattva—

Wearied of the American war, alcohol and Nembutal, his body found outside 5 a.m. Allende Sun Nite, May 4 *[sic]*—or Monday, exposure, lay there in desert by railroad tracks they say—lost consciousness and died—

Remember him sometimes groaning into toilet bowl the rare time drunk, in San Jose—'54

A grandfather last month—not met the wild orphan ever in this life—unfinished Karma there, a blank to this N.Y. son.

His solid sense—monumentally of person and physique and energy and love—that he touched me sexually of all living—spread Dharma thru America—the buildings outside Maya to my concerns compared to his continuous presence—the thought of his vanishment casts unreality on the lit world remaining behind—

I'll be glad to get out of the burden myself—It's a dream.

Liver Sclerosis. Died 10:30 am—or found on R.R. track Sunday Morn-ing—goofballs first, then out and drank—and walked out on track, and exposed to all night rain unconsciousness—

Jack on phone, "I felt as if the bottom dropped out."

& his last words to lady B.J.—Goodbye

Elegy for Neal[1]

Sat

[10 February, 1968 5–5:30 AM—]

OK Neal
aethereal spirit

1. First draft of "Elegy for Neal Cassady," *Collected Poems*, 495–97.

1968

⑥ Tape Transcription

Elegy for Neal

Eat [10 Feb 1968 5 - 5 30Am]

O! Neal
aethereal Spirit
bright as the morning air
blue as the city dawn
happy as light released by the day
over the city's new buildings —

Maya's giant bricks rise rebuilt
in the Lower East Side
Windows shine in the milky smog,
Appearance is unnecessary now,
"Too deep for tears," too deep to stop.

Peter sleeps alone in the next room, Neal.
Are you reincarnate? Can ya hear me talkin?

bright as the moving air
        blue as the city dawn
happy as light   released by the Day
   over the city's new buildings

Maya's Giant bricks rise rebuilt
              in the Lower East Side
   windows shine in the milky smog.
       Appearance is unnecessary now,

Peter sleeps in the next room, sad
Are you reincarnate? Can ya hear me talkin?
If anyone had the strength to hear the invisible,
And drive thru the Maya wall
    you had it—
           What're you now, Spirit?
That were spirit in a body—

The body's cremate
         by the railroad track
in the San Miguel Allende desert,
         outside town.
   Spirit becomes spirit,
      or robot reduced to Ashes.

Tender spirit, thank you for touching me with tender hands,
When you were young, in a beautiful body,
   Such a pure touch it was Hope beyond Maya meat.
   What you are now,
         Impersonal, tender—
You showed me in your muscle/warmth/over twenty years ago
when I lay trembling at your breast

1968

                              put your arm around my neck,
—we stood together in a bare room on 103'd St.
Listening to a wooden Radio,

                                        with our eyes closed
Eternal redness of Shabda

                              lamped in our brains
at Illinois Jacquet's Saxophone Shuddering,

             prophetic Honk of Louis Jordan,
             Honeydrippers, Open The Door Richard.
                         To Christ's Apocalypse—
The buildings're insubstantial—

     My New York vision

                  outside my eastern apartment office
     where the telephone rang last night

                  and a stranger's friendly Denver Voice
asked me, had I heard the news from the West?

Some gathering Bust, Eugene to Hollywood Impends
                  I had the premonition
No I said I've been away all week.

             "you haven't heard the News from the West,
                         Neal Cassady is dead—"
     Peter's dove-voic'd Oh! on the other line, listening.

Your picture stares cheerful, tearful strain'd,
                  a candle burns,
             green stick incense by household gods.
Military Tyranny overtakes Universities, your Prophecy
     approaching its kindest sense brings us
                                        Down
             to the Great Year's awakening.

                    1968

Kesey's in Oregon[2] writing novel language
farm alone.
Hadja no more to do? Was your work all done?
Had ya seen your first son?
Why dja leave us all here?
Has the battle been won?

I'm a phantom skeleton with teeth. Skull
resting on a pillow
calling your spirit
god echo consciousness, murmuring
sadly to myself.

Lament in the dawnlight's not needed,
the world is released
desire fulfilled, your history over,
story told, Karma resolved,
prayers completed
vision manifest, consciousness fulfilled,
spirit returned in a circle,
The world left standing empty, buses roaring through streets—
garbage scattered on the pavements galore—
Grandeur solidified, phantom familiar fate
returned to Auto-dawn,
your destiny ended
My body breathes easy,
I lie alone,
living

2. Reference to Ken Kesey. Cassady drove Kesey and the Merry Pranksters on the cross-country bus trip, detailed in Tom Wolfe's *The Electric Kool-Aid Acid Test*.

1968

After friendship fades from flesh forms—
a heavy happiness hangs in heart,
    I could talk to you forever,
        The pleasure inexhaustible,
           discourse of spirit to spirit,
                O spirit.

Sir spirit, forgive me my sins,
Sir spirit, give me your blessing again,
Sir spirit, forgive my phantom body's demands,
Sir spirit, thanks for your kindness past,
Sir spirit in Heaven, What difference was yr mortal form,
    and what further this great show of Space?
    Speedy passions generations of
        Questions? agonic Texas Nightrides?
        psychedelic bus hejira-jazz,
    Green auto poetries, inspired roads?
Sad, Jack in Lowell saw the phantom most—
    lonelier than all, except your noble Self.
Sir Spirit an' I drift alone.
        Oh deep sigh.

Dream Feb 20, 1968—Appleton, Wisc.

Town in Mexico—small Veracruz, or down the great circle thru Yucatan, in a hotel room (like 1403 Gough), I killed someone, and not knowing what to do with the jellied meat of the body, stuffed it in the bureau & toilet and closet—The doctor there testified that it was an accident, tho I was really the culprit of anger or neglect—Several bodies stuffed in the drawers, dissected like the corpses on the RR tracks at Vrindaban I saw thru train window first passing North to Rishikesh—

1968

Home several years later in upstairs loft, the local cops come in to ask for my papers—I don't know what technicality they smell—They leave their names, & require that I get papers & receipts & prescriptions for the pills I have left over from Yajalon or a Salto de Agua or San Miguel Allende—from the doctor there—I *can* write him or check that out & have it done, will he remember the bloody scene & still cooperate?—

I go across to the garage as on Gough Street, & an attendant there says that the Police, just thru, were all sloppy high—Georg Hertz was there, they were all together turning on in the Car Rental Hertz cubicle office— I'm a little relieved that all the authorities also out of their skulls & compromised.

Woke, in Hotel room, does this refer to my yelling angry at Peter Orlovsky, or Neal's recent corpse appearance at Allende RR Tracks—& is Pres Johnson recalling his dreams, connected to his mind?

Feb 21—10 AM

    Vroom—over
        White Wisconsin,
Exorcism of McCarthy's
    red tombstone by Fox River Bank[3]
Done in Sanskrit Tibetan Sino-Japanese
    Egyptian, Latin, Greek, American
        & Hebrew—
U.P.I. screwed up the Magic Formulas
But Appleton's students pronounced
        a proper Om—
Snow edging the brown squared farmlands,

3. Ginsberg, Ed Sanders, and several students performed an exorcism at the gravesite of Senator Joseph McCarthy.

1968

ice knifing straight roads
   to the white dappled Water Flats,
Michigan Lake edged by tiny Cities,
    Sun arising over Chicago,
   blue-grey dioxide mist risen from thin Pipes
    toothpicked vertical on a factory top
      at Lakeshore
hanging thin over the distant planet Curve—
Thicker gas, jet vaportrail
over Chicago's thousand
   grey Skyscrapers,
     Vroom,
       Roll,
to arrest at O'Hare.

Feb 22, 1968—
   Dream 6 AM

   Donlin's stretched out
   laughing ecstatic—
     his eyeballs pop out
   & are lying connected like
   red membranes on the
   marble table.

Police: "I just don't want you to make any gestures."

Telegram from
   Francis Rizzo Spoleto Festival NY

1968

"Home office advises me that Italian charges against you have been dropped."[4]

Plane to Washington Feb 29, 1968

Rolling solid
   as on rails thru aluminum cloud
Tiny windows white through
   the plane cabin
lady voiced aluminum
   "Landing at Washington,"
The huge cabin tips over,
   mist fringes billow,
a bridge below, cars race like bugs
   across the Potomac—
Yellow smog dims the Cabin—
 Down to the rust-orange rocks
   water's edge airfield,
   rain puddles in clay
"buying & selling securities"
   continues the lady & gent
     in the blue seat
and stacks of autos, planes, firetrucks,
   gas balloons at the edge of the field
     mixed with trees

4. A reference to Ginsberg's arrest in Spoleto in 1967.

1968

Looking for a retreat from the big city, and for a refuge for Peter Orlovsky, among others, Ginsberg purchased a farm in upstate New York. It was hidden by trees and needed a lot of work to be inhabitable, but Ginsberg was up for the task. He called it the East Hill Farm.

May 3, 1968:

Dream—"Are you Holy?" "No," I yell, "I'm a Poet and Lover."
Second night slept
with headache on East Hill.

May 9, 1968—East Hill

Began Reading *Vanity of Duluoz*[5]—atrocious visions of deaths of souls & thought—slept & woke at dawn put on old fur coat went out to pee saluted Mr. Urich[6] at daybreak walking in frosty grass to his car—lay down in bed ruminating—Peter scampering about in the grass apparently and mooing like a cow—Julius trembling & indifferent to his medicine—Barbara[7] up here on farm in design to transform my sex marry me have infants be Jewish Cinema mother—Sandy & Gordon,[8] young couple she invited up to be householder-caretakers more stable than the rest of us but held back by Barbara from displaying their own sexual imaginations—

5. The last novel by Kerouac published during his lifetime.
6. Ed Urich, a neighbor.
7. Barbara Rubin.
8. East Hill manager Gordon Ball and his girlfriend at the time.

to ball everyone & leave for Amazon in November—who can do the work needed to clear the farm & supervise expense of money to rebuild house w/ furnaces & electricity & water & jack up sagging floors & install storm windows & tarpaper barn roof & seed field once plowed? If I'm away it'll all be so lackadaisical Julius will freeze to death in solitude 20 degrees below zero December?

Dreamed, after working, digging channel from well to drain & clear out sucky bottom years unattended—New Book of Kerouac's, I was in City using some old dead friend's apartment—how I'd get in without keys, so familiarly?—Picked up book, it was Jack Kerouac's log-paged prose, and the book cover was "Masterpieces of Chinese Civilization" and the first half was some Classic oriental text on U.S. Manners & travels—I saw it was two books, back to back—Kerouac's new work "Americans are All Madmen"—beginning with a large paragraph very literary & Calm.

"In a conversation w/ Allen Ginsberg some decades ago, he remarked that he'd been haunted by his Poesy master's line 'The pure products of America go crazy'—Thus in this volume I've given substance to that apothegm by a series of extended vignettes drawn from true characters and places of my own experience etc."—

The house, I realize, is Frank O'Hara's friend—editor at Coward Mc-Cann who'd taken on editing of *Vanity of Kerouac*.

May 9, 1968

Dalai Lama appears on balcony in Potala-Bolivian Ballroom after long years of silence & absence in science fiction Police State—I'm visiting the rocketship-Grant Hotel-Palace—I sneaked into the Ballroom—

Macabre scene like Masque of Red Death, Magic Theatre Powers raised as alert Crowd stand still & in giant unison shout OM—

1968

Incantations, appearance like Pope—

Later with official I'm watching private conversation Dalai Lama gets mad and stomps away after his magic's questioned by long-suffering companion

Poetry is the best that language can do.

Please Master can I touch your cheek[9]
please master can I kneel at your feet
please master can I loosen your blue pants
please master can I gaze at your golden
    haired belly
please master can I gently take down your
    shorts
please master can I have your thighs
    bare to my eyes
please master can I take off my clothes
    below your chair
please master can I kiss your ankles
    and soul
please master can I touch lips to your
    hard muscle hairless thigh
please master can I lay my ear pressed
    to your stomach
please master can I wrap my arms
    round your white ass
please master can I lick your groin
    curled with blond soft fur
please master can you stand above me

9. First draft of "Please Master," *Collected Poems*, 502–3.

1968

can I crawl beneath your legs
please master can I touch my tongue
   to your rosy asshole
please master can I stick it deeper
   in your soft hole
please master may I pass my face to
   your balls,
please master, please look into my
   eyes,
please master order me down on the floor,
please master tell me to lick your
   hard egg sac and thick shaft,
please master put your rough hands
   on my bald hairy skull
please master press my mouth to
   your prick-heart
please master pull my head into your
   belly
please master force my face to your body,
   pull me slowly strong-thumbed
till your dumb hardness fills my throat
   to the base
till I swallow & taste your delicate flesh-
   hot prick barrel veined, Please
Master push my shoulders away and
   stare in my eye, cold and fearless
please master make me bend over the table
please master make me lift my ass to your
   waist
please master grab my thighs and spread them
   apart
please master put your hand on my

1968

neck in rough stroke to my backbone
please master pass your palm down my
    backside
please master push me up, put my feet
    on chairs, lift my ass
    high
till my hole feels the breath or your
    spit and your thumb-stroke
 please master make me say Please Master
    Fuck me now please
Master, grease my balls and hairmouth
    with sweet vasolines
please master stroke your shaft
    with white creams
please master touch the head of your cock
    to my wrinkled self-hole
please master push it in gently, &
    bend down my shoulders
your elbows enwrapped round my
    breast
your arm passing down to
    my own penis you touched w/ your
    fingers
please master shove it in me a little, a little,
    a little
please master sink your droor thing
    down my behind
please master make me, make me wiggle
    my hips
and please master make me stick out my
    rear to eat up the prick-trunk
till my asshalfs cuddle your thighs,

1968

and my back bends
till I'm alone sticking out, your sword
   stuck throbbing in me
please master pull out of me, slowly roll
   into the bottom
please master lunge it again, and
   withdraw to the tip
please please master fuck me again
   with your self, please fuck
   me, please fuck me Please
Master drive down till it
   hurts me the softness the
softness please master make love to my
ass, give body to center, & fuck
   me for good like a girl,
tenderly clasp me please master I take
   me to thee,
& drive in my belly your selfsame
   sweet heat-rod
you fingered in Solitude Denver or Brooklyn
   or fucked in a maiden in carlots
    in Paris,
please master drive me thy vehicle,
   body of love drops, body of
   sweat fuck
body of tenderness, give me your dog fuck
   faster
please master make me go moan on the table
go moan O please master do fuck me like that
   one like that
and like this your rhythm thrill plunge
   & pull-back-bounce &

1968

    push down
till I loosen my asshole a dog on the table
    yelping with terror delight to be
     loved
Please master call me a dog, an ass beast,
    a wet asshole,
& fuck me more violent, hide my eyes
    with your palms round my skull
& plunge down in a brutal hard lash
    thru soft drip-fish
& throb thru five seconds to spurt out
    your semen heat
over and over, bamming it in
    while I cry out your name I do love you
please Master.

O Future bards[10]
chant from skull to heart to ass
as long as language lasts
vocalize all chords
that zap thru consciousness
       to fall
zap the fall consciousness
       cell
worships
Chant old chords/thru all
Zap all consciousness

----

10. First draft of "A Prophecy," *Collected Poems,* 504.

1968

Children of Now
Children Tomorrow
I sing out of mind jail
of New Jersey words

In New York State
Without electricity
Rain on the mountain,
thought fills the Cities.

I'll leave my body[11]
in the thin rooted
my self escapes
through unborn cars

Not my language
but a voice
chanting on patterns
survives on earth

Not the logic
but a choice
not history's bones
but vocal tones.

Dear breaths & eyes
shine in the skies
where rockets ruse
to take me home.

11. Continuation of first draft of "A Prophecy."

1968

May 17, 1968—

New Year's Eve in Washington with Negro Congressman who takes a
bath & hums Italian opera instead of going out—I'm on his porch
out on lawn a truck passes full of Charlie Chaplin unshaved garbage-
men—one lifts a pistol, shoots and misses me by the big Victorian house,
I laught & wave to him, a mistake, so as the truck pulls off he keeps shoot-
ing, missing, raising the pistol each time for another try as the truck pulls
over Haledon Ave Hill for the traffic light, I begin to duck, finally scared.
    Wake thinking of Leroi.[12]

May 21, 1968

    Black Mountains/Cherry Valley
    The same grassy floor
            rain green'd soft ground
                    under rubber shoes

May 23, '68

Walking pine woods with Peter—he explained, the smelt loam's black-
ness comes from decomposed trees, as he kicked open a soft tree root, and
thonked a fallen trunk apart to show the wet black dust-fibers. So all earth
surface is decomposed vegetables and that makes soil, & soil plus water
plus light from the sun by photosynthesis creates creatures with leaves,
which creates dead bodies, which creates earth work—which same central

12. Leroi Jones.

1968

sun created the matter of the bodies Named Allen & Peter standing there in the man-made isles of pine forest, ninth growth/cycle maybe.

Our skulls & eyes are phantoms of sun light which penetrating the soil penetrated seed, & was photosynthesized into complex staring Phantoms w/ red beards in rain ponchos.

May 26, '68 (Cont.)

Standing there I the woods—we came from the sun, the matter in our forms travelled to earth as light from Sun—our forms are angelic sun substances, our forms were sent from the Central fire to here, we rise & decompose and rise again, changing forms of sun matter, solar emissaries distance, outer regions' ambassadors spacetime travelers exploring inert worlds & filling them with ourselves, our fire sent here from home burning vast afar so Peter & I rise and fall walking in the worlds' woods, late afternoon, sunlight thru the trees on our bodies.

May 28, 1968   4 AM

Woke after long dream, Magical Mystery Tour, which ended where it began, on a boat in commons-room.

Barbara and I arrived at the table after the first half of the dream—which had ended in a police examination, with an impolite policeman insulting my visage & rejecting my identity Cards again, while his superior apologized—Then stepped forward and said, "We know who you are and are prepared to meet the occasion," standing as he was silhouetted in the doorway I saw him reach in his pocket, & feared a gun, but his pocket was small & his gestures little, a relief till I realized that what he carried was a special "Gatling" a tiny black revolver which he pointed at me full blank & fired—In the explosion of the impact the universe shattered my identity

1968

& some memory dissolved, my immediate memory dissolved completely, and I found myself with Barbara, Peter, and others on the gangway of a ship, entering aforespoken commons-room. Peter was in Rabbit drag, Julius cavorted, company was there, including an African magician & entourage, a big fat black frog-like handsome Priest Warlock who sat on the ground in the giant room—Ken Kesey was there also—all which I saw corner of eyes while Barbara noticing black & white female dolls of hollow plastic-wax, bade me exchange and eat. As it was her intense wish I was about to but first glanced at the wise man and showed him the doll. "Sir," I said, "what wisdom should I follow?" Pronounced happily, he replied (as Urich did earlier)—"Run!" "What?" I asked, and kneeled before him 3 times for more serious explanation. He looked up at me and said to me smiling & serious, "What vision should I follow?" I laughed and said, "Did you ever try Acid?" He smiled & shook his head neutral & handed me a corncob pipe filled with Ganja, which I began puffing, so beginning to feel high in the dream as it closed I woke in upstairs room Cherry Valley East Hill.

Earlier in the dream, Mick Jagger, gangplanks, boardwalks, carnivals, fun house rooms, strange police, wax museum, famous faces dead—all appeared live for a moment went thru mechanical music life, dancing & voyaging.

May 28, '68
    Landor,
        a night of sighs
    I Consecrate to thee
    . . . Shakespeare, Shelley, etc.
        The ghosts of Language.

1968

June 7, 1968

Kennedys dead, King dead, Malcolm X
    Assassinated, Andy Warhol
    lingering in hospital spleen
        shattered by tiny bullets
Lumumba in graveyard surrounded by Bones,
    Che Guevara's eyes opened in Bolivia,
The Alien called the call thru Basilides'
        many heavens,
Time hath a Bearded graduate staring Lover.

Om Vajra Guru Padma Siddi Hum.

. . . and give a living Tongue to the boy in the baseball hat.

Bixby Canyon Big Sur June 16, 1968[13]

Path crowded with thistle fern sprout,
    blue daisy, glassy grass,
    clump, pale morninglory
      scattered on granite hill
    dry brackensprout brown
    seaweed wreath
    topped by seasmooth
      brown twigs,

13. First draft of auto poesy, "Bixby Canyon," *Collected Poems,* 505–6.

1968

bells clinging under grey
   granite sea cliffs
sand swarmed with ants
   & dying bees in dry grain stone
      shell pits of
white froth washed white bay surge
   of Ishvara-ripple rock piled
      bay wall sea birds
         skating wind swell
Amor Krishna Om Phat Svaha Air Rumble
      wave-lip
            yesterday
Sand castles Neal, white plasm balls round
   jellies—
   skeleton snaketubes & back
   nostrils' seaweed tail dry wrinkled
   brown seabulb & rednailed
   cactus blossom-petal tongues—
Brownpickle saltwater tomato ball
   with rubber tail spaghettied
   with leafmeat,
Mucus softend crowned
   wreath, Father Whale gunk
   transparent yellow leaf-egg-sand
   lotus-petal cast back to cold
   watersurge.
         Bouquet of old seaweed
on the old stripes, horn bag
   & brass bell,
         kelp tentacle spread
before the prayer place, sneaker &
   leather sandal [?]—

1968

Hermes silver firelight spread
over wave Sun Glare—
The Cosmic Miasma Anxiety
ballbounce burp nakedman
meditating on lotus petal fingered
sand—Soft Bonepipe!
Musical sea-knee gristlebone
rubber ballbounce
kick beard orange footswat
of homosexual Shlurp ocean hish
Sabahadabadie Sound-limit
to Evil—
Set limit, set limit, set limit to
oceansong?
Lest San Andreas Fault slip "California"
into deep pacific Apocalypse
Atlantis rising at movies—
Limit the birdcries, limit the
Limitless
in language? La 'la'
Marseille O Say can you see
the Internationale Mental Traveler
in waves of eye alteration Politics—
Tis Liberty! I hymn to—Liberty Sweet
Liberty in Freeman's sunlight
not limited to observe no nakedness
signs in silent bud-crowded
pathway, artforms of flowers limitless
Ignorance—the sun huge
Wet seaweed blossoms left on a sand shore,
A giant mist blow under the bridge,
[?]-breath,

1968

    haloed sunlight of clouds
over veined sky-blue blast wind,
      yellow sunlight old
Shining on all grey cliffside
       & mossledge, O tide foam
  lapped in harmless gold light
brightness O eyeball fire circle shimmering
     see brightness most near
most warm and most distant Father
whence we have sprung, thru thy bright
  Rainbow born silence.
So sings the laborer under the rock
  bridge, so pipes pray to
  the Avalanche.

July 19, 1968

S.F. to N.Y.C.[14]

Under the silver wing
  San Francisco's towers sprouting
  under their gas clouds
    Tamalpais' breast behind the city
    Black-nippled against Pacific azure—
Berkeley hills swiftly below, pine covered fir
  Leary in a brown house, writing Declaration
    On typewriter paper at his window

  silver panorama in natural eyeball—
Sacramento valley rivercourse's

14. First draft of "Crossing Nation," *Collected Poems,* 507–8.

1968

Chinese dragonflames steaming
           Brown flats
State Capitol metallic rubble borderland
    drying the countryside around—
Sierras & over Reno, & Pyramid Lake's pure
    Blue Altar, water flat in Nevada sand.
& then brown wasteland scratched by trees.

    Jerry Rubin arrested! Beaten up in Jail!
        coccyx broken—
Leary out of action, "teacher and immature judgment . . .
    a public menace . . . psychiatric
        examination"—Shut up or else
           Loonybin or Slam—
Leroi on a bum gun rap, $7,000
    Lawyer fees & a years negotiation—
Spock[15] "Is" Guilty headline, Joan Baez paramour
    & husband Dave Harris to the Gaol—
Dylan silent on politics, & safe
        having a baby, a man
Cleaver shot at, jail'd, parole revoked,
the Vietnam War fleshheap grows higher,
    blood splashes down the mountains of bodies
        onto Cholon's sidewalks—

Blondboys in the airplane seats fed
        Technicolor
Murderers advance w/ death-chords
        thru the basement,

15. Dr. Benjamin Spock, a renowned pediatrician and best-selling author, was an outspoken opponent of the Vietnam War.

1968

Earplugs in, steak on plastic
   served—Eyes up to the image—

What do I have to lose if America falls?
   my body? my neck? my personality?

NY 23 June 1968

Smoke rolling down street,[16]
red scabies on the skin
Police Cars turn the garbage corner,
Was that a shot?
Backfire or Cherry Bomb? It's all right,
take the mouth off,
it's all over.

Man Came a long way,
Canoes and fire engines,
Big Cities, Power Station fumes,
executives with Country houses,
water drips thru Ceilings in the Slum—
It's all right take the mouth off
It's all over—

   Pertussin[17]

Always Ether Comes
   to dissuade the

16. First draft of "Smoke Rolling Down Street," *Collected Poems*, 509.
17. First draft of "Pertussin," *Collected Poems*, 509.

1968

goat-like
     sensible—
of N2O recurring to
    elicit ironic
       suicidal pen marks—
Parallels in Montmartre Rousseau
    daubing or Rimbaud arriving,
       the raw Aether
shines with Brahmanic cool moonshine
    aftertaste midnight Nostalgia.

June 28, 1968

July 7 '68

Paradigm

Lamentation over Ashes Neal Cassady
Let no boy sniff ether for Nothing

Paradigm

Easy Chair discovery

To this moment a vortex of
    Television Wichita Antennae
afterward Mexican Roads
    airplane

1968

Limitless-balled Universe

[Early Graham Avenue meditation
between hedges walking home from movies at
night thinking, What was the end
of the Universe, how far did it extend till
it came to walls of rubber?]

July 10, 1968

Swirls of Black Dust on Avenue D[18]

Swirls of Black Dust on Avenue D
White haze over Manhattan's towers
   midsummer green Cattail's fatness
      surrounding Hoboken Marsh
         garbagedumps,

Wind over lacy network
   Pulaski Skyway sloped
      down to Bayonne,
   trucks crash along the road
      iron engines roar
   Stink rises over Hydro Pruf
        Factory
   Cranes lift over broken earth
   Brown Clouds boil out of tin
          scrap burners
   Newark sits in grey gas

18. First draft of "Swirls of Black Dust on Avenue D," *Collected Poems*, 510.

1968

July heat gleams on Airplanes
& the family car bumps over asphalt
   To Bright Mexico
Truck tyres singing toward forests
      of oil towers
Power grids dance on the Iron Triangle
   Tanks roast in flatness
old Soybean oil Storage Scandals!

Dream July
Waxahachie, Texas

     In Chelsea Hotel or Mills Hotel New York, I'm trying to get free phone to call Burroughs in London—Living Theatre is in same hotel, returned from Europe, Julian Beck[19] in his room somewhere upstairs—hotel's as huge as oldfashioned oceanliner—

Our rare phone conversations I notice begin with me emphasizing what's disturbing me about my own behavior in answer to his first greeting, "How's things?"

Like "Too much cigarette tar in the lungs."

I go upstairs to the Hotel Ballroom (thru the backstage area where I find an encampment of young hippies, bunks & hammocks, & old bureau drawers scattered around the vast enclosed room)—

Onstage is Harold Stassen.[20] He's there as an old pro volunteer, under the lights, preliminary to the Republican Convention, preparing the scoreboard and arranging the podium and chairs—I look close, the po-

19. Julian Beck (1925–1985), an actor and painter, cofounded the Living Theatre experimental theater group.

20. Harold Stassen (1907–2001), a former Minnesota governor, became a perennial candidate for the presidency.

dium itself is old mildewed wood just taken out from second-hand storage—I point it out to him, he nods and soon we are backstage—I notice how hard he's working—in fact he's sweeping up the leavings of the stage and backstage and asking one of the young hippies where he can dump the trash. I'm impressed by his solitary efficiency—Here he is like a lonely old Zenmaster, keeping order in the political theater—Stassen being the perennial sensible candidate—"Well, I've never seen a candidate use a broom before," I say. "I learned that from you folks," he smiles [in] reply.

I begin wondering what he thinks of Romney,[21] the nominations are already taking place while Harold Stassen lounges around (with his white pantsed son) on a rattan sofa behind the curtains.

But these mildewed lecterns and chairs!

---

15 June '68 [*sic.* Should be July] Near Antone

Arkansas sunlight's[22]
    motionless splendor shifting
thru grey ocean steam masses
    Brightness shafted thru heaven,
Clouds passing thru white radiance—

Texas the solar mass
    ringed with misty continents
rainy archipelagoes drifting in front
    of the fiery circle—
jaws of the vast cloud head

21. George Romney (1907–1995) was a Republican candidate for the presidency in 1968.

22. Unpublished auto poesy.

1968

closing round the celestial one—
Rays pouring from mid heaven
      down on an auto graveyard—
Eyeholes of towering cumulus foreheads
      filled with such light
the meat eye squints beholding
the great fire of millennia
Approaching San Antonio,
      daylight flooding the
            concrete pathway,
all round the horizon transparent
      airiness, floors of treetops
            atremble
in the soft winds raised flowing
      in warm light across green prairies
Summer sun casting new illumination
      endlessly upon the endless Void—
Revelation of Texas Plains & Roadsigns,
      Universal City
      Randolph A F B—
  Big Red
      Delicious Different
            Satisfaction
            Guaranteed
                El Dorado Homes—
San Antonio City Limit—
  The sun a bright head with
  wild cloudhair
peeping over the thruway walls.

1968

July 22 4:30 a.m.

Violence[23]

Mexcity drugstore table, giant
   sexfiend in black spats
sticks knife in a plump faggot's
   sportcoat seam,
at Teotihuacan in blue sunlight, I slap
   my mocking blond nephew
   for getting lost on the Moon.
In Oakland, legendary police shoot a
   naked black boy running out
   of his political basement
In Pentagon giant machines hum and
   bleep in neon arcades,
Buttons click in sockets, & robots
   pencil prescriptions for acid gas
   sunsets—
New York on the stairway, the dumbed
   whitefaced Junkie pulls a knife
   and stares immobile—the victim
   gasps "oh come off it" & a sixpack
   of cokebottles
bounces down work black steps, in
   Vietnam, imaginary plastic fire
Streams down the cheeks of myriad phantom
   rayed over planet television—
Adrenaline runs in armpits from Los Angeles
   to Paris, Harlem & Cannes

23. First draft of "Violence," *Collected Poems*, 511.

1968

explode thru plateglass, Sunset Strip & Sorbonne
    are crowded with Longhaired angels
    armed with gasmasks & Acid.
& angry Democrats gather in Chicago
    fantasizing armies running
    thru sewer sprayed with Mace.
I walk up Avenida Juarez, over
    cobbled shadows, blue-tiled streetlamps
lighting Sanborns' arcades, behind me violent
    chic fairy gangsters with bloody hands
hustle after midnight to cut my throat from
    its beard.

----

11 AM [July 22, 1968]

Past Silver Durango over Mexic
    Sierra-Wrinkles[24]
Westward the mother mountains drift
    Pacific, green-sloped
    vaster then Mexico City
without roads under cloud flowers bearing
    tiny shadow blossoms on green peaks—
The plane without the magic window roaring
    subtly drumrolls of planet Anthem
Este son los Madrelena que Couta
    El Ray David
Chorus of Brasses rising in harmony bones
    behind my ear

24. First draft of "Past Silver Durango over Mexic Sierra Wrinkles," *Collected Poems*, 512.

1968

Higher the mountains, deeper the canyon
    cracks
red riverbeds snaking under the layers of red
    Cliff Strata
unknown paradises without electricity,
    Huichol or Tarahumara solitude
earth's skin rocky green, untouched by
    another hectare, antpaths
    green clearings in plateau,
hollows of lone indian humility, hand-ploughed
    & planted patched on mountainside—
naked white cloud fronds floating silent over
    silent green earth crags.
O vast Meccas of Manlessness, bright cloud-brains
    [?] high in heaven upturned
    in blue space to the sun
O rainbow garlands in white water-gas,
    O body furred with trees defenseless
    in Clear air, visible green breast
    of America!
vaster than man the Mother Mountains manifest
    nakedness greater than all the bombs
    Bacteria ever invented
Impregnable cloud-civilizations, cities adrift &
    dissolving no History, white rain-ships
    alighted in Zenith Blue ocean—
No ports or capitals to the horizon, green mesas
    ridged infinite-budded everywhere
Let rivers & autos gather the garbage Man left
    behind in the Valley of Mexico—
Iron will rust under the roots of living trees

1968

& soak back underground
To feed the sensitive tendrils of Ego covering
    neverbaked rockbeds & mountains &
    craggy granite green mossed unconscious.
Covered now with white, [?] flats of
    clouds stretches everywhere,
Floor to the sky, that showed no planet
    underneath
Unroll the Cloud Floors, flat desert
    desert redress & brown hairless
    crags—
and altogether blue West space, the
    ocean stretched out to white mist,
the sky stretched outward to Orion of
    mist,
Heaven & ocean mirroring each other
    azure, the horizon lost
    in yellow spectrum haze—

Baja California Blue water lies flat to the
    brown armpit of United States.
River's course muddies the delta with
    teardrops washed dusty from Utah—
Green farms in the mist, irrigated squares in
    desert—
& the dung colored gas, brown haze
    of labor near Los Angeles—the height
    the Sierras—
grey smog drifts thru low mountain passes,
    the city invisible.
        Floating armchairs descend

1968

from the sky in the sunlight,
    rocking back & forth in
        polluted fields of air.

Love vs. (not hate) but Fear   w/ overpopulation

I saw the Sunflower Monkeys of the Moon

He had a little habit & I know that Peter Rabbit's
    made his money from his dropper and his spoon

The Democratic mafia
borrowed almost half of ya
to start a war
in Communist Hanoi

The banks got all your money, little boy
    'made a lot of money w/ a needle & a spoon'—

On Neal's Ashes[25]

The delicate eyes that blinked blue Rockies
    all ash
the nipples and ribs I touched with my thumb
    are ash
the mouth my tongue touched once or twice
    all ash
the bony cheeks soft on my belly are cinder
    ash

25. First draft of "On Neal's Ashes," *Collected Poems*, 513.

1968

Neal Cassady outside Charles Plymell's apartment, 1403 Gough Street, San Francisco, fall 1963. Ginsberg was staying here after returning from two years in India. This was the same apartment where he had met Peter Orlovsky almost a decade earlier, when painter Robert Lavigne lived there. Neal had yet to take the cross-country bus trip with Ken Kesey and the Merry Pranksters and become a fixture among the Acid Tests parties in the Bay Area with the Grateful Dead. Photograph by Allen Ginsberg. Courtesy of Stanford University Libraries.

Great death that claims the world above
　　　　　　hello
earlobes and eyelids, youthful cock tip, curly
　　　　　　pubis,
breast warmth, man palm, muscular thigh
baseball bicept arm, asshole anneal'd
　　　to silken skin
all ashes, all ashes again.

Ginsberg feared the prospects of bloodshed during the 1968 Democratic National Convention in Chicago. He had announced his plans of going to the Windy City after the Yippies publicly called for a "Festival of Life," complete with live music, assemblies, information booths and classes on various topics, and other activities. Different radical or activist factions intended to stage demonstrations against the Vietnam War. Ginsberg was interested in all this, of course, but these interests quickly grew to worry when city officials refused to issue permits that allowed peaceful assembly or sleeping in the city's two largest parks near the convention center.

With the prospects of violent confrontations between the police and demonstrators all but a certainty, Ginsberg considered backing out of his commitment, but he felt a responsibility for recommending the Festival of Life and promising to attend. He decided to travel to Chicago and try to help keep peace. He was very active during convention week, which kept him from writing extensive journal entries about the violence involving the police and demonstrators. In the notes he wrote in his journal a year later, along with the poetry commentary on the convention, he left powerful memories on the anarchy and madness that was convention week.

1968

Chicago Realization

Imagination & Desire are supreme
   above Theory, Fear, Paranoia
   & Death.
Violence obliterates Imaginative Desire.

"The Spiritual battle is just as brutal as the battle of Man, but the Vision
of Justice is the pleasure of God alone."
        —Rimbaud

New Consciousness is Spiritual
nakedness, manifested by a thousand
youths displaying themselves innocent
& Chaste on Chicago streets before
the Suits of businessmen, Uniforms
of the Armed, as well as the Chain mail
& helmet of the Self Righteous Avenger

"Vain the sword & Vain the bow
   They never can work war's overthrow."

    The spiritual & material Future of US does not lie in the Political Convention, nor in the Imagination of Desire reflected in anger and violence against the Political Convention. War against Hell is more Hell.

    A Festival, Manifestation, or Realization of Life on Earth as it is in Heaven is the desire of most who brought their bodies here.

1968

August 24, 1968

Going to Chicago[26]

22,000 feet over hazed square
    vegetable planet floor
approaching Chicago to die, or flying
    over earth another 40 years
to die. Indifferent, and afraid, that the
    bone shattering ballet be the same
as the vast evaporation of phenomena Cancer
    come true in an old man's bed.
Or the historic fire heaven descending
    22 thousand years and End of Atomic Aeon.
The lake's blue again, sky's the same baby,
    the papers & noses rumor tar
spread through the natural universe'll make
    angels' feet sticky.
I heard the Angel King's voice a bodiless
    tuneful teenager
eternal in my own heart saying, Trust
    the purest joy,
Democratic anger is an illusion,
    Democratic Joy is God,
our father is baby blue, the original
    face you all see you.
How, thru Conventional police & Revolutionary
    fury remember

26. First draft of "Going to Chicago," *Collected Poems*, 514.

1968

William Burroughs, with Jean Genet and Ginsberg,

the helpless order the Police armed to protect
   the helpless freedom the
   revolutionary
Conspired to honor? I am the Angel King
   sang the Angel King
as the mobs in Amphitheaters, streets,
   Colosseums, parks and offices
scream in despair over meat &
   Metal Microphone.

   Brash—Commandants of Lincoln Park District—"No sound system"
But Corporation Council says it's legal & o.k. Mr. Morgan at City Hall
9 PM—says he'll contact David Stahl & Earle Bush back the Theater.

Thursday, August 29, 1968

Green air, children sat under[27]
   trees with the old,
bodies bare, eyes open to eyes under
   the hotel wall.
The ring of brown clothed bodies armed
   but silent at ease leaned on
         their rifles—
Harsh sound of microphones, helicopter
   roar—
a current in the belly, future marches
   & detectives naked in bed—
Where?—not Chicago,

27. First draft of "Grant Park: August 28, 1968," *Collected Poems*, 515.

1968

in late sunlight—
        Miserable picnic,
police state or Garden of Eden?
In the building windowed
    walled against the sky
Magicians exchange images, money
    & handshakes—
The teargas drifted up to the Vice
    President naked in the bathroom
    on the toilet taking a shit weeping?
Who *wants* to be President of the
    Garden of Eden?
        There Police are bashing
Us again!

Badge #309 said: "Shut the fuck up or I'll wipe the fucking beard off your face."

80% male injuries were not only suffering head-clubbing wounds, but were also suffering injuries of the groin—split scrotums, other severe damages—

—Rusty Tucker, St. Luke's Presbyterian Hosp.

Sept 8, 1968

Today prepared a meditation room & altar in attic of Poetry farm—on a mirrored tray set on board shelf—under eaves, I put Kamakura Buddha model bought last month in S.F., symmetric hands set in Dhyana Mudra,

1968

thumbtips touching on lap. Wooden beads Phil Whalen brought from Japan, with a 4 pointed Lightningbolt Vajra—Dorje, Vajra handled Shingon prayer bell, and Yamabushi conch shell on the shelf opposite a Shigetsu Noise-Wand. Also set there winged & beaked-masked god of Teotihuacan, a transparent Comanche stone, an iron incense place from Cost-plus, and an imitation Tibetan Tantric prayer bell. Also a red wooden Fish.

Above that shelf incense, the skeleton of a Cactus picked up in New Mexico, a shell-fossil stone found on the farm, rose scented candles, a Roman household god with bowl & broom, and the painted wooden spoon Lili Brik gave me 3 years ago in Moscow, souvenir of Poetry & her friendship with Mayakovsky & Voznesensky.

On the wall, Vishnu four armed poster set with tacks, and a medal of the Sacred Heart aflame behind buddha's Head—above the bed an Angel of Beato Angelico bearing a leafy branch.

On Mexican cloth before the altar, flowers, a bowl of fruit store bought and cucumbers & corn grown on this farm, a tiny colored glass lamp, and harmonium for chanting.

Nearby on shelves, sacred texts from Mormon to Essene to Gita to Tantra, a bowl of cut glass beads & chandelier droplets, a toy sparkler, flutes, mandolin & tanpura, ashtray & matches, fine cloths, silk & synthetic weaves; on the bed a colored eagle-sewn blanket from Saltillo—and a grey serape gift of Margaret Randall on the floor for rug by the platform edge where the mattress is set at the storm window facing East.

Sept 16

"Glandular hysteria," Huncke said discussing Chicago—to be said, then, a glandular change of the race, a functional mutation of Consciousness calming overactive adrenalin glands—a glandular change of Consciousness—thus the Shamanic drugs.

1968

Mind Interruption

Sept. 20

Orion's belt above East Hill
   Pleiades dim winkle constant
Milky Way through blackness
   dotted with bright round blue stars
amid the floating mist arched high
   in the clear ceiling
      Midway between dark hills
      wooded wall-rising
up the end of the locust-whistle-rippling meadows

And where's the Big Dipper
   North of the State Forest Road
      and Spencer's sloping green grass fields

Oct. 9

   The Universal Police

   Putting Songs Innocence & Experience to Melody music.

   Magic Password Bulletin
      Psychic Ju Jitsu for Chicago

   In case of hysteria Solitary or Communal, the Magic Password is
      A U M

1968

which cut thru all emergency illusions. Pronounce it from the middle of the body, diaphragm or solar plexus—

10 people humming OM can calm down 100. One hundred people humming aum can calm the metabolism of a thousand. A thousand bodies vibrating OM can immobilize an entire downtown.

On November 29, Ginsberg was involved in an automobile accident that kept him in a hospital or disabled on his farm for the remainder of the calendar year. Lawrence Ferlinghetti had stayed on the farm while visiting the East Coast, and Ginsberg and Peter Orlovsky had just delivered him to the airport when Orlovsky, driving in an intense rainstorm, missed a stop sign and plowed into another vehicle. Ginsberg, in the front passenger seat, bore the brunt of the accident. He was badly injured (four cracked ribs and a broken hip), and the broken bones, the first of his life, set off ruminations about pain, mortality, and human suffering.

Dec. 3, 1968 (Hospital)

Crash! Thud-nausea
hip to heart—

It all collapses back to laughing
gas—

1968

Life and death in the Body-stump,
a fart's worth a million dollars.

Can't rely on the body, all the
pleasures only equal to the
awful pain. Depend on

body pleasures, & get hooked
on meat thrills? Then be stuck

with the break-rib Crack-hip
palm fatigue of trembling on a broken
auto seat ready to die—

Flesh—a collapsible trap?

A head moves—on the pillow
  comfort sweat—
alert to midnite. Chest pain guilt,
  bronchial gargle asleep—
  (bronchial gargle asleep)

   Black grid
   round eyespace
   solid appears
   white
    floating
   resolves the grid to
   ashy space and

1968

consciousness
—eyes closed
    in the hospital,
    The Creation.

"The pitch-man
    stirs uneasily"
. . . gotta rush inside
and see a man
about a—
    Matter!
itself is the great
junk habit that
occupies space
    —a matter habit,
    my dears.

    Better off
in short pants
in Chicago in
parochial school
than worship
space for itself—

The high Accident
    in the Cab—
George Arliss with
long white
    fingers
turning the space truck
      on—

1968

Plastic
   environment
—3D space
appearing out
   of Nowhere—
Ambrose Bierce
   Bags of Flat-
ulence float
my abdomen
back to the hospital
   bed.

Ah, show biz!
   What's this
Production for?

Neal Cassady
fucked me up the
ass, long
   years ago

Cascades: Gary
Snyder oceans
   of Bliss—
un attached
. . . . .
. . . . .
Flash 1—The
evanescent—
Cascades—

1968

Gary Snyder
returns to America
Everybody gets
all their money
back.

Tea time ride
Proud rise,
in fact a
flash in the
pan for every
twenty-first
Century.
    Stop and
explain?
You already
    giving
     me
heart trouble

Dec. 13, Friday 11 PM   1968

    Active in my bed 2 weeks, received Prajnaparamita Xerox from 1880's Buddhism in Translation from an anon-young kid, a motel envelope, Beardo I dare you denounce Israeli Microproscopic-caused social death-pain, Kennedy reporter in & out with his orgy Novel drenched human pus, in my body-stump recovering energy for the electric charade my stomach paralyzed a week lying in white pillows & sheets bib naked painful baby bearded screaming angry the first nite no Morphine half grain codeine not enough to stop the network of neural ache crack hip to four ribs coughing cigarette bronchial phlegm 20 years leak ended on that back seat of the station wagon body demolished once & for all imprinted

1968

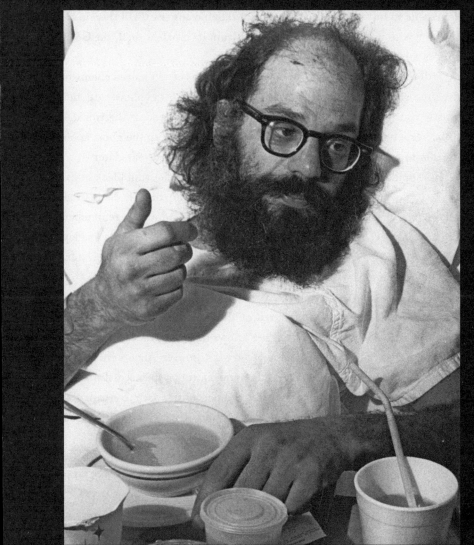

with ugly death pain [?] old solar plexus breathless nausea can't inhale more world must end—Literal "Body Stump" the imperfection, so not a safe scene to rest in, the meat form's not reliable any sex thrill therein be paid for with withdrawal of the soul nut from its crushed shell, the Cock suffers mortification being worm-meat.

Still the old habit returns with frank open eyes of red haired chemists over the soulful table of the hospital Cafeteria—Ike's nephew cute and plastic wanted love before his body crumbled to the end of the world— Thus perpetuated Rimbaud's painful knee till he gave up the ghost apologizing to Memere & his sister already dying a hundred years later—

His adolescent photo on my bed all week, [?] hair chestnut black in rotogravure oval, big black silk tie askew, he coughed painfully dismissing Djami from his tired knees—Disgusting at the last minute to remember the knot contortions of the body to get at the nigger boy's asshole and lay it in, only to have it fall off at the kneecap a few nights revering later, dreams all come true, including Thy Hand great Death.

That hangs over the hospital & tends the trembling wounds of young and old mortals hoping to be cured of their missing ribs forever—but everyone in the elevator on a stretcher knows he'll taste the last body this hospital or another Aether, the Aeon won't last forever, Aeon's are empty because full rounded they [?] on the operating table, unsuccessful after you live to old age, what more wanted but a peaceful breath to escape the jaw's delay or lung drowning in decades of Grand Canals suffocation, too many tears in the opera.

A great bouquet over the Television set, the flowers of freedom & Law red & orchidlike, dying themselves in their week of water and neglectful eyes, one could tend them another tender operation thru a week, they'd freshen the muses pianoleg eyeball 7 days more Creation before the patient myself went home with his telegrams of congratulations & his long interviews from the Body Stump to students of the *Herald* and *Albany Times* & Polytechnic adolescence.

I can't lay back, the small of my spine aches, kidneys & bowels para-

1968

lyzed 4 days, by massaging below my prana-belly I got the yellow water to flow hot from the Cock stump into a silver Carafe—that's after 2 days catheter making my in-balls hot with each few drops of gold water thru plastic to a plastic bag hung at the knee of the bed.

And every time I coughed, my stomach wall to right tit evermore rigid, and imploding with gas, distended, till eating day after day I vomited lunch in my beard, my stomach wouldn't take more—so the catheter, greased, was stuck up my penis hole huger than I thought realistic, not a red thru tube but a big yellow straw—and

a white Teflon needle taped to my wrist, hung a transparent glucose bottle dripping all night to my veins, several days no drink or food, no ingestion that way, mouth a little dry but sleeping a lot very comfortable with also a tube up my rectum attached to a tin can, to gather gas out— and prune juice to encourage a bedpan B.M. which didn't take place despite several shots of plastic needle up my behind with some new dizzying fast schpritz enema in plastic tube like a foot-paste.

And left hip cracked, the foot wrapped in Ace bandage round a suffering green splint, and pulled down the end of the bed in traction they boosted, five pounds a light ache in the hip, pain even when I coughed— now a week & no pain in uplifted rib cage, hurts on a flat surface lying down—

and can curl up on my leg OK and relax & read NY Times every day in bed—so began sip prunejuice, & pass some gas, and at last piss, warm natural urine in bedpan on a wool ass cloth for bedsore protection.

And Lean on my elbow with tiny rubbing skin redness—Press right foot against bed rail to lift up my shoulders, grab a higher pillow behind my neck, reach for the triangle, waving trapeze my right hand and left hand joined, pull up my shoulders sweating from the back rest elevated, hours later my body sliding down bed fallen, lower half naked under White sheets, won't the nurse come in and touch that black meat haired hardness while I'm in infant dawn sleep, exposed—or the young mustached attendant with old

1968

& thigh youth that comes to pump up my wheelchair on elevator—who lifted the sheet to see my nakedness & brought me a blue pajama bottom—P.J.'s he said—could dream of him puncturing my fat rump—

Nurse pregnant with New Yorker to sign—hadn't read them, not much more than I—with kisses—on my white notes—semen on the buttocks—a ripeness to come—that came later, life force and bullshit returning during the cold spell, the flag flapped on the flagpole out the window and visitors scurried thru icy wind into hospital corridors—even the sick rooms were a little chill—

I sweated the last night—reading a 1930's New Yorker, my fingers dusty with the tired rubbers of depression—Rimbaud's white cheek & exact round lift eye green pupil'd—narrow lips—also been raped by the sailors? or just lying in bed while the lice pickers went over his pubic hair—passivity either not mother's kisses or father's touch bite up his rosy red adolescent bunghole. He liked it, his nipples drained all the red from his cheeks as he sat in the forest and imagined himself impaled on an oak. A mess of Beauty & he didn't guess, no Carcinoma in the mirror. Running from Bavaria to Borneo to escape the grim reaper, an infected knee told the story, total pain on the Mediterranean packet to Marseilles. In that heat, at least he got as far as a decent clean hospital so they could cut his leg off—maybe aether by then, or some old opium for relief—and a sister who never thought She should die!—Mother out-lived him—No harm in that. Poor L.A. Adolescent, ran away from home early to be a visionary—and saw it—and looked black and [?] in the quarry.

His photo returned on my hospital table, I'll live another 40 years or 30 lazy. 6 months on crutches to thee! Cut your throat another time, my good man. All right the treatment is finished said the Doctor, you're dead. And I couldn't object, I didn't remember asking for a cure.   Driving in rain toward that ominous car, we rolled right up to it inevitable and easy as an old mistaken intention, except that reaching the road we didn't stop nearly in time so there was a big rocking earthquake of car metal on car doors and halting asway my hip bit the steeringwheel or dashboard

1968

and a second crunch cracked four ribs so I muttered ooof beneath hearing Julius they said cried out with his calcified Phoenix-gland and revealed his knees bursitis in the X ray mirror.

The lady in the accident mobile Aum as I pronounced it. "Breathe deep," I said, replied to me, "O shut up" so I did. She was just hysterical, I was hysterical but I was hurt. I felt my ribs a bit, cramped, and in pain, sharing half the ambulance with Peter alert & silent in front seat, serious.

Lay around in x ray for a couple hours, till Dr. Clark, looking Cherubic Albanian—Like Dachau but I want my Telephone Book so I don't get gassed. I brought it along in my corduroy jacket, & remembered wool black sweater necessary to have under my head from wrecked station-wagon thru Ambulance to locker in hospital room.

Couple days, the old postal clerk, that night passing to bathroom as I yelled for more morphine, "Kissing boys kissing boys is disgusting boys kissing girls is normal"—3 days later I saw his giant bulk bend over the sink, huge lady titties from 4 pieces of toast at breakfast—but he renounced that—and the nurse didn't want my beard—I yelled for Morphine all night. I said fuck it at a nurse with tiny I thought phenobarbital—

Rimbaud's a corpse, & his corpse a shade, I lie awake at midnight subscribing to the XX Century for the sake of pure Paul's Esperance and cheese & drink.

Jibanananda Das a nude corpse under the trolley—and a lady trembled young, and a lady trembled white and old, both on the stretcher in the elevator to rehabilitation, or to X ray, or to operation room conference—or the private bed to suffer or turn idiot with irresponsible pain & mortify the nurse's irreplaceable kidney lacking fat & thin, take aspirin & die sooner or later, one must.

The bed mate came later, they stuck green tubes in his nose down to his stomach, & white drained sugar in his blood, & more in his behind like me, kept it up a week, not food but cracked ice the second to the 7th day then white gruel & milk half & half, he regained color after a perforated ulcer brought him in civies groaning away deathly pallored, but survived

1968

the month new in pajamas he'll go back for operation in a month after tests on his metabolism.

I been X-rayed for kidneystones, all clear sez Dr. Pasavette, nothing to wait for Death this week there.

Today they brought me new white pajamas & I learned to walk upstairs with crutches, I'm confident I won't fall for 6 months! Some young Rimbaud servant will be there to catch me when the rubber crotch tip gets tangled with my suspenders hanging out of my fly on the crutch handles, palm pressured not armpit-pressed & leaned.

My ribs ache little, maybe a cold sweat coming from Hong Kong the night before Christmas Friday the 13th passed by [?] toilet flushing healthy—Peter comes tomorrow with 1949 Oldsmobile to take this corpus away.

Dec. 16?—Dreamt about Pound's last lines Cantos—
        Set the wind Speak? I don't remember

Dec. 17, 1968

Snow-blizzard sowing[28]
ice-powder drifts on stonefenced
gardens near grey woods.

Yellow hump backed snow plough
rocking giant tires round
the road, red light flashing
iron insect brain.

Meow, the cat with diarrhea.

28. First draft of first part of "Car Crash," *Collected Poems,* 516.

1968

Sunlight settled into human form,
Forests, tree rings settled age after age,
stone accumulating stones
traveled 93,000,000 miles,
carbon deposits settled into beds,
the head of the mountain breathes light,
Earth hairs gather gold beams
thru chlorophyll, poets walk
between the green bushes
sprouting solar language.

Broken Bones in bed,
hips and ribs cracked by autos,
snowdrifts over rubber tires,
tree stumps freeze, the body stump
heals temporarily in wintertime.

----

21 Dec '68

So that's it the body, ah![29]
Beat yr meat in a dark bed.
Boy friends wrinkle & shit in snow.
Girls go fat eyed to their mother's coffin.

Cigarettes burned my tastebuds' youth,
I smelled my lover's behind,
This autocrash broke my hip and ribs,
Ugh, Thud, nausea-breath at solar plexus
paralyzed my bowels four days—
Eyeglasses broke, eyeballs still intact—

29. First draft of second part of "Car Crash," *Collected Poems,* 516–17.

1968

Thank God! alas, still alive but talk words
died in my body, or thoughts died in pain.

A healthy day in the snow, white breath
and warm wool sox, hat over ears, hot broth,
nakedness in warm boudoirs, stiff prick come,
fame, psychic, learning, scepter, dusk
and Aurora Borealis, hot pig flesh, turkey
stuffing—all disappear in a broken skull.

Unstable element, sight, sound flesh touch
& taste, all odour, one more consciousness
In the backseat of streaming auto with broken nose—
Unstable place to be, an easy way out
by metal crash instead of mind cancer.
Unreliable meat, waving a chicken bone
in a hospital bed—get what's coming to you
like the chicken steak you ate last year.
Impossible Dr. Feelgood Forever, gotta die
Made of worm-stuff. And worm thoughts?

And who's left watching, or even
remembers the car crash that severed
the skull from the spinal column?
And who gets out of body, or gets shut in
a box of soft pain when Napalm drops
from heaven all over the abdomen,
breasts and cheek-skin? & tongue cut out
by inhuman knives? Cow tongue? Man tongue?

What does it feel like not to talk?
To die in the back seat, Ow!

1968

1969

At Jack Kerouac's funeral in Lowell, Massachusetts, October 1969. Photograph by Jeff Albertson. Courtesy of Special Collections and University Archives, W. E. B. Du Bois Library, University of Massachusetts Amherst.

Ginsberg had very little time to recuperate from his injuries from the accident. A four-month reading tour, his longest to date, began in February. The appearances served a variety of purposes. He read new poems to enthusiastic audiences, receiving instant feedback on work that was still in notebooks. He promoted his most recently published book, Planet News, published in 1968. He discussed the Vietnam War with young men of draft age. The zigzagging across the country gave him ample opportunity for auto poesy and writing in his journal. It didn't hurt, either, that he earned rock-star money at these appearances. During his most active touring years, he scheduled tours in the spring and fall.

There was other work, including the final touches on Indian Journals, his first published collection of journal writings from his life-changing trip to India and the Far East in 1962–63, and more assigning of melodies to the works of William Blake. The year would also see the first moon landing and, toward the end of this last year of the decade, a trial that brought him back to Chicago.

1:30 AM, January 1, 1969

Wooden walls, ice-white windows[1]
three weeks now, snowy flatness
foot-thick down valley meadows,
wind roar in base ash arms, oak branch
tendrils icy gleaming, yellow
stain of morning water in front

1. First draft of Part III of "Car Crash," *Collected Poems,* 517–18.

1969

door's snow—I walk out on crutches
& see white moonglow make snow blue
—three men just rode a space ship
round the moon last week—gnashing
their teeth in Biafra and Palestine,
Assassins & Astronauts traveling from
Athens to the sea of Venus Creatrix—
Lovers' quarrels magnified decades to mad
violence, half naked farm boys stand
with axes on the kitchen table,
trembling guilty, slicing egg
grapefruit breasts on breakfast oilcloth.
Growing old, Growing old, forget the words,
mind jumps to the grave, forget words,
Love's an old word, 1969, forget words,
Peter with shave-head beardface
mutters & screams to himself at midnight.
A new year, no party tonite, forget
old loves, old words, old feelings.
Snow everywhere around the house.
I turned off the gas-light & came upstairs
alone to read, remembering pictures of dead
moon-side, my hip broken, the cat sick,
earhead filled with my own strong music,
in a houseful of men, sleep in underwear
Neal almost a year turned to ash, angel
in his own midnight without a phonecall,
Jack drunk in my mind or his Florida.
Forget old friends, old words, old loves,
old bodies. Bhaktivedenta advises Christ.
The body lies in bed in 1969 alone,
A gnostic book fills the lap, Aeons

1969

revolve 'round the household, Rimbaud
age 16 adolescent sneers tight lipt
green-eyed oval in old time gravure
—1869 his velvet tie askew, hair
mussed & ruffled by policeman's rape.

Jan. 2, 1969

Gather Ye Rosebuds

Lying in bed downstairs Peter directs or Huncke instructs Lafcadio to get into bed with me after taking a bath & cleaning himself, so that I can make love to him & screw him.

Peter gets angry, yells to Lafcadio to hurry up and bathe but not to go to bed alone with me, instead to sleep alone, and bangs away washing pots and pans in the hidden kitchen. "I'm going to telephone Momma."

Lafcadio hasn't come yet, Huncke in other room with Janine, is angry, puts on his pants to go rebuke Peter, walks thru the room buttoning his fly over red jockey shorts—

Lafcadio's in bed with me, his beard on pillow above me, he has mustache, but fair skin. I nestle close to his smooth strong chest—Peter talks too much like that, says Lafcadio as Huncke walks into other room, saying "It's a good thing I'm here to straighten Peter out."

Jan. 3, 1969

Kenneth Love in a car, riding to Princeton puts his hand on my backbone, pats my shoulder, I realize where's my crutches? Lost? and that cigarette in my hand? I swear I won't go back to brown lung cough cancer.

1969

Gregory phoned from San Francisco—"A leaky lifeboat," he said of the body.

Gnomic, Gnome, Gnosis
Gnatworm—Wriggler

Jan. 6. (Sunday–Monday 3 am)

> Penumbra round the moon,
>   blue snow meadows
>   sloping from the woods
>   to the house
>   Country western guitar
> over the transistor kitchen—
>   I haven't smoked since
>   the autocrash.

Jan. 11, 1969

If there are infinite modalities or dimensions, or infinite numbers of universe simultaneous

That dimension or aspect which was contemporary with the beginning & past, immanent in the present, and potential in the future is God. God is what has been, is, and already has happened futurely. God has left me behind him, and is outside Time Categories, since he is that aspect of all being which is consistent past & future. Thus he knows us, having been ourselves. And Being ourselves, and the future, he has also withdrawn from us to the future where he waits motionless, all things moving with Him.

1969

Unmoving Stillness
Motionless Light
Time-skipping silence, Consciousness
Complete & omniscient
Birthless Deathless Immortal Mortal
Seed, Double-Cross, Meet Night,
Noiseless Word, first Sound, last look
extra thrill-thought,
Empty thee my Mind origin Memory
Molasses haircut scissors sleep.

Marvelous Spectre
slipped thru Timehood
Phantom Cosmos, ghost abstraction
Discarnate in Dream.

—Woke 7 AM & had been in Carolyn Cassady's[2] Paris apartment 7 flights up above Central Park—I forgot Paris, the 30's modern building above the Monoprix. She was fussing around the kitchen, I went exploring the bathroom, which opened on tiny iron scrollwork balconies over the street above Place-St. Germain. The large pipe in the wall with many knobs & buttons also included a pipe organ, as well as the usual Hot & Cold water and air valves. A big pipe, like the ancient pipe in the ceiling of the slum bathroom on East 10 Street that broke & flooded the toilet floor all year & was fixed with plaster awhile.

So Carolyn was fussing about & I was envious of her beautifully open sided well-made apartment.

A cozy place to spend one's declining years.

2. Neal Cassady's widow.

1969

Woke, Israel and Arabs at war in my newspaper mind.
Make love to Cyril with the fishskin elbows?

Jan. 15, 1969

Sir Humphrey Davey—"Nothing Exists but Thoughts."
   i.e. Everything is Consciousness
Consciousness Creates body rather than body Creates Consciousness.
   Chickens & Eggs, I s'pose.

Dream Jan. 19, 1969

   With Naomi again in apartment—subway corridors, she casually ex-
plains what was disturbing her, as we sneak tiptoe—speed up ship gang-
ways & tiny elevator stairs (thru CCNY's halls upstairs where the beau-
tiful soldiers took refuge) & down along River Street across a bridge
where Tillie & Max or other cousins have a shop they've been tied-down
to for years.

   They distilled a creature from our blood, they take the blood and make
a creature in reverse, then they leave it in your shop on the counter, or in
your living room, and when it gets warm it hatches and you have an exact
replica of your person, only a baby.

   We go to Tillie & Max who are up all night in their shop, keeping an
eye out for the Sneaks who plant the Mercury test tubes—They had one
planted there already that's why they got a baby and that's why they stay
home all the time. So we go there, me and Naomi, and I get one vial from
them.

   So that explains why Peter's as strange with amphetamines & his blood.
Why he stays in his room & plays with his blood all the time. I go with
Naomi with a little dread in heart, & find Peter on one of the stairways,

headed for his room, (Takin' room in Paris.) I've got time to break this news to Peter. But who is it steal his blood? Distills it & tries to plant little Frankenstein vampire children in our rooms?

And isn't that why he's been so obsessed with Speed, & I was ignorant all along?

* * * * *

Aunt Elanor and Uncle Max, they had no children either (See dream about Carolyn Cassady) but they had a cozy little apartment to die in.

I have this vast creaky farm.

Feb. 1, 1969

    Immobile Cloud sounds[3]
Like ocean waves puffed up
      in white stillness
    blue shadowed to the sunset
        horizon glow
—Desert floors, sea tables,
    cotton valleys—
Take magnetism away, take away
      Sun push and moon pull,
    take off the Temperature, remove
      the hydrogen, elevate gravity,
  end earth-roll & the billion
      magnetic needlepoints of stars—
& the Vibrations! Stabilize the shake
    & there'd be nothing but transparent

3. First draft of unpublished auto poesy.

1969

              liquid O
& under their cloudiness, yellow glow
        of supermarkets in the snow.

February 13, 1969

Grey clouds blotting out West Sun[4]
        glare,
Mountains floating thru sunset, the
        plane descending
softly roaring over Denver—Neal
        dead a year—
clean town, clean street, clean
        suburb backyards
fit boardinghouses for the homosexual
        messenger's birth
and alleyway Lila four decades back
        before the atombomb
Denver without Neal, eh? Denver
        with orange sunsets
& giant airplanes winging silvery to San Francisco
        Washington
watch towers thru red cold planet light, when
        the Angel of Earth is dead
the dead material planet'll revolve
        robotlike
& insects hop back and forth between
        metallic cities.

----

4. First draft of "Over Denver Again," *Collected Poems,* 519.

1969

Carrying electric pollen—
Cigarette smoke wanders over material
      thoughtforms,
Albany vast Being brilliant
      miles lit connected
Rockefeller's Brain sitting in
      the Center as Aeroplane
Descends under bright
      triple-starred Orion

Imaginary Universes[5]

Under orders to shoot the spy, I discharged
   my pistol into his mouth.
He fell on his face from the position life
   in which life left his body kneeling blindfold.

No, I never did that. I imagined
   it on airplane, waiting in Albany
   airport snow
to discharge its passengers.

Yes, the Mexican-faced boy, 19, in his
   Marine cloth, seat next me
Descending on Salt Lake, accompanied his
   brother's body from Vietnam.
"The Gook was kneeling in front of me,
   crying & pleading. There were two;
   he had a card we dropped on them."

5. First draft of "Imaginary Universes," *Collected Poems*, 520.

1969

The card granted immunity to those
    V.C. surrendering.
"On account of my best friend &
    my brother I killed both Gooks."
That was true. yes.

Solid City

New York's red signs reflected
in deep Hudson-black, mist
Brightens hazed above solid
twinkle brilliants! skyscraper lights
slow blink in river shimmer, clouds
grey-luminous in shady Heaven—
Stageprop? Optical wrinkle? 3-D movie?
Metal roar and Stone-thud painful mass?
Boys crushed by tanks, fallen off Empire State?

Home to see Louis walking "as if Desk-Stooped-Shoulder'd"
Honey[6] told telephone me from Newark! Great Fate!
My father in Paterson his old flesh sweet & unmouldered
Atoms hung together on his skeleton thinking talking
breathing Death & Feeling Life's Trembling footstep—
solid through the house downstreet to the News Store,
Where the New York Bus passes under the red streetlight
& his sib descends on crutches to visit
        his old familiar Man.

-----

6. Ginsberg's Aunt Honey (Hannah Litzky), Louis Ginsberg's sister.

1969

Allen and Louis Ginsberg.
Photograph copyright 2020 Elsa Dorfman.

March 5, 1969

                    To Poe[7]

Albany throned in snow
    Hudson ribboned North on ice white flats,
Horizon clear blue sky, New England visible to
    Eyes: man now rides above the Map
Earth ballooned vast-bottomed viewed from Air—

It's winter, Poe, upstate New York scythed
    into flat arbors and mental fields, and hairy woods
    scattered in Public mounds twittering w/birds—
Nobody foresaw those worm paths asphalted
    thin-swift down dales uphill crost bridge
    thru small church towns on Earth's table, chill
    snowfields streaked with metal feces-dust.
Maelstrom roar of air-boats to Baltimore!
End of the earth! Borne along wells, whirlpooled
    into Mechanic Apocalypse on Iron Tides!
Delicate Helen drifts backward in endless time
    soft women & aethereal-ball'd man vanish'd
    with the snows of the North Pole, Bison
    Whale, leaving the planet movies
    of [?] nestled into white clouds
    the globe blue ball breathing steam in black space
Far enough up, over the sun, the Alien
    [?] could see old Sol Ray Love
    on his children the guardians of the void.

7. First draft of "To Poe: Over the Planet, Air Albany–Baltimore," *Collected Poems*, 522–23.

1969

Wheels drop in Sunlight, over
   vast building-hive roofs glittering
New York's ice gleaming in a
   dying world.
             Bump down to ground
Hare Krishna Preserver!

   Philadelphia smoldering
In cold sunlight, pink blue green Cyanide
Tanks sitting on hell's floor, smoldering
from many chimneys, city flats virus-linked
along Delaware's horizon—smog
airplane drifting black filaments & smoke
above Wilmington—The iron habitations
endless from Manhattan to the Capital.
Poe! D'jya prophecy this Smogland,
this Inferno, didja Dream Baltimore'd
be seen from Heaven by Man Poet's eyes
Astounded in the Fire Haze, carbon gas aghast!
Poe! Djya know yr prophecies RED DEATH
would pour thru Philly like Sulphurous Dreams?
South! South from the Bearded
   Sleeper's Win at History,
Hudson polluted & Susquehanna
   Brown under bridges laced
      with factory smoke—
Proving grounds by the Chesapeake,
   Ammunition & artillery
Edgewood & Aberdeen, Munitions
   do as well as chemicals
these factories isolate, strike, set
   apart in gardened woods,

1969

prairies-plants of industry, like movie
    stars, private in this magic,
        nauseous mansions, old Hollywood.
Poe! Frankenstein! Shelley thy Prophecy,
What Demiurge assembles Matter Factories
    to blast the Cacodemonic Planet-Mirror apart
Split atoms & Polarize Consciousness &
    let the eternal Void leak thru Pentagon
& cover the White House with
    Eternal Vacuum Dust!
Bethlehem's refineries by Atlantic Ocean
Shit-brown haze worse and worse over
Baltimore where world came
    to an end—Red smoke
red smoke, black water,
Grey sulfur clouds over
    Paris Island
Oceanside flowing with rust,
    scum down harbor,
Bethlehem's miles of Christ's birth
    Man-apocalypse Mechano
        movie
Red white blue boats in Baltimore harbor,
    the plane bounds downward,
above gas tanks, gas stations,
    smokestacks flaring poison mist,
Superhighways cut thru the
    hairy woods,

Down to Earth, to Man, to
    the city where Poe

1969

427

Died kidnapped by phantoms
conspiring to win elections in
　　the Deathly Gutter of
　　　　the 19th Century.

March 23, '69

　　　Drop the Bomb Now! Before I
　　　　Kill more!
　　　Drop the Bomb on me, America
　　　　Die
　　　The ex-murderer sang on the
　　　　Telephone to spiritual police.
　　　Stop me before I Kill more! Kill
　　　　My misery.
　　　Drop Drop Drop The Bomb
　　　　Drop the Bomb! Bomb my
　　　　　　Brain!
　　　Drop Drop Drop the Bomb!
　　　　End the Pain! Reap the Grain!
　　　Drop Drop Drop the bomb!
　　　　Kill the Ens! Drown
　　　　　the Friends! Make Amends!
　　　　　　Bend Bends!

March 24

Dream saw Bob Dylan discussed the Messiah—The Messenger? or the
Anointed one says *Webster's*.

1969

March 25, 4 AM Sleepless
feverish, want to die—be
done with myself and this planet.

At 17 was sensitive boy, embarrassed by
Mother, too delicate to insult another,
blushing with adoration in youth—
At 42 I feel like a skull, what I
am exactly, a hairy skull.

March 26: 11 AM

On beds and soft pillows, I met Leroi Jones.[8]

We sported, his mother father watched, in a room of wooly bags—a phonograph laid out, we bumbled & caressed, his skin a parchment black his hair curled fine—a long throned bed the meeting-place again.

I saw his mirror'd Subject index—an altar-piece Day/Month & Star/Name slots lettered phosphorescent and cut thru the Clockface—CYBERNETICS and another Subject—Sunni?—

His manners & friendliness genuine & exquisite, he seemed alone, & happy to see me again (respectful?!)—Why—Mr. Jackson said if he loved me that was a study he should pursue as part of his Fate—Mr. Jackson, Jesse Jackson, was his Guru, teacher, he said, Yes. And his Teacher knew Sunni & Cybernetics, that was necessary, he had to know everything.

I woke sweaty in country pillows & sheets, cold in body, with temperature. Lingering pleasure of happy eyes of Leroi Jones friendly again.

----

8. Leroi Jones (later Amiri Baraka) (1934–2014) was a poet, writer, playwright, editor, and publisher. One of only a few African Americans associated with the Beat movement, he was a political and social catalyst in the sixties and after.

1969

Dr. Angel came w/scalpel
when I was 12 yrs old in bed
& cut thru 7 layers of my skull

March 31, 1969

According to a Pundit disciple of Richard Alpert[9] Baba Ram Das Guru Neem Karoli Baba [?] of Nanital's Hanuman temple, LSD is the Christ of the Western World in Kali Yuga, especially presented to those who are so sunk in material scenes they cannot accept spirit in any form but pure matter.

April 7

Dream in Turkish Bath with short blond lawyer cousin lovemaking— Phipps?

April 8 Dream

Going into I. Magnin or other Texas-5th Avenue giant boutique after Jacqueline Kennedy or Eleanor Roosevelt—Upstairs to the library, the crusty old right-wing mss. collector—like a supervisor of Jewels of Chinese art—he shows me, at table, Hemingway mss.

We talk "Hemingway wasn't such a good writer," I guess, after seeing plodding paper of typescript.

9. Richard Alpert (1931–2019), also known as Ram Dass, was an LSD disciple of Timothy Leary, a clinical psychologist, and an author of spiritual texts, including the best-selling *Be Here Now*.

1969

Abbie Hoffman there over the intimate table, I explain I've given my mss. to Columbia—"mss. of Naked Lunch" etc.—Abbie says wow, I'm trying to impress Abbie secretly boasting but worried he'll want me to sell it all for the Revolution.

This after yelling at Sam Abrams[10] in Phone "outdated abstract doubletalk" for his using words Cooptation and "Confront reality" last nite, me complaining my left jaw and eye paralysis (Bell's Palsy) prevented me from coming to NYC to Ecology meeting.

Easter Sunday 1969[11]

Snows melt on slope Woods
Streams gush ducks stand one foot
one eye beaks buried in brown backfeathers
in gold sunlight pillars of Jerusalem
behind the bright window—ripple whistles
coo coo thru branches bare yellow shine
rays spikey-white flashed out of the mud,
horse limping head down to pale green grass
shoots floating on brown winter hair vegetable
dress—washed by transparent trickling
snowmelt water freshets streaming
rusty slough bathed clean,
streamlets dripping down leaf-bottomed
channels sounding vocal to white light
afternoon end of the sky
goat bells move, black & white kids bounce
one maa'ing child hangs under Bessie's udder

10. American poet Sam Abrams (born 1935).
11. First draft of "Easter Sunday," *Collected Poems,* 524.

1969

ducks waggle yellow beaks, in flooded new grass
tiger cat meows in the barn
baby butts mother's hairy side land tender tit
the herb garden by the stone wall's a
                    shiny marsh,
dimpling snow water glimmers, breezes blow
birds whistles thru icecrystal beds dying
    beneath bare bushes.
    Rooster crow as light chills
extended from piney horizon.

April 12, 1969—on bus thru North Bergen, New Jersey
    —The Mafia bellowing for lawn order.

Trip—Car & Air—Northwest April 24 to May 16 (NY) '69

April 24, 1969

Incense under Horse Heaven[12]
                    Hills
Empty Logger trucks speed
                Back along
                    Lake Wallula's
    Flatness shimmering
Under hot rock painted w/
    white highschool signs.
Chemical smoke boils off

12. First draft of "Northwest Passage," *Collected Poems*, 526–29.

1969

under Aluminum giant nature squares
under aluminum-bright cloud roof—
Smog assembling over railroad
    cars parked rusting on thin rails—
Factory looming vaster than Johnson
    Butte—Look at that Shit!
Smell it! Got about 30
    Smokestacks going! Polluting
Wallula! Boise Cascade
    Container Corp!—
The package is the Product, onomatopoeticized
    McLuhan[13] in '67—
Wall Street Journal Apr. 22 full
    page ad Proclaimed:

We got the trees! We got
    the land beneath!
We Gotta invent More Forms
    for Cardboard Country!
We'll dig forests for Genius
    Spirit God Stuff Gold-root
For Sale on Wall Street. Give
    us your money! order
    our cardboard Wastebaskets!
We just invented throwaway Planets!

Trees crash in Heaven! Sulphurous Urine
pours thru Boise, Chevron & Brea

13. Canadian philosopher, teacher, and media theorist Marshall McLuhan (1911–1980).

1969

Wastepipe where Snake and Wallula
      ripple shining
Where Sakajawea led White Men thru blue sky
   on vast, clean, fresh, cold water roads
      under giant blue silent sky-void
   Towards of mountains of juicy
      telepathic pine
        & open
            Thalassa
Thalassa! Green salt waves
   washing mountains of rocky Pacific
Sirhan[14] lives!
   to hear his jury say
"We now fix the penalty at Death."

Green salt waves washing Wall Street.
Rain on grey sage near Standard
   Oil junction of Eltopia,
Static at Mesa! Yodeling ancient
   Prajnaparamita
Gate Gate Paragate
    Parasamgate Bodhi Svaha
Way Down Yonder in the Bayoux
   Country in Dear old Louisan,
Hank Williams[15] chanting to
   Country Nature, electric
Wires run along the Tipayon [?]
The car rises up in valley

14. Sirhan Sirhan was convicted of assassinating Robert Kennedy in 1968.
15. Hank Williams (1923–1953), country music singer and songwriter.

1969

brownplowed wheatfields—
Wallula polluted! Wallula polluted!
   Wallula polluted!

"For most large scale gambling enterprises
to continue over any extended period of time,
the cooperation of corrupt Police or local
officials is necessary." P. 1 Oregonian "Mapping
a $61 million war against organized crime,
President Nixon suggested . . ."

"Even Jesus Christ couldn't
Save me," Sirhan
   "shed no tears.
      "His face was ashen."
AP
   America's heart Broken,
Chessman,[16] Vietnam, Sirhan.
52% thought the War
   always had been a mistake,
      by April 1969,
Israel & Egypt cease fire
      repudiated, Mohammed
         Spokesman
May Day parade canceled for
   Prague says police radio to
      the old King of May faraway—

16. Caryl Chessman (1921–1960), a convicted robber, rapist, and kidnapper, was executed in one of the most controversial and widely covered capital punishment cases in American history.

1969

SDS chanting thru Consciousness Megaphones
    in every university.
By now, Beatles & Beach Boys have
    entered the Sublime
thru Acid The Christ of Kali Yuga, thru
    Transcendental Meditation,
Chanting Hare Krishna climbing Eiffel Tower,
    Apollinaire & Mira Bai headless
        together w/ Kabir transmitted
over Apocalyptic Radio, their voice—
    vibrations roaring
thru a million loudspeakers in Green
    Autos on the world's roads—
Matter become so thick, senses so sunk
    in Chickens & Insulation
"Love ain't gonna die, I'm gonna haveta
    kill it"
god cries to himself, Christ merging with
    Krishna in Car Crash Salvation!

[. . .]

    "Prosecutor John Howard called Sirhan a
cold-blooded political assassin with 'no special
claim to future preservation.'"
        Mao reelected Chinese Premier.
Where the Mullan Rd
    Meets 25
        by 2 giant Sycamores
    approaching Hooper
Has anyone here any "Special

1969

Claim to further prosecution"?
These sheeps peaceful grey sides
 grazing thru springtime
   by Cow Creek
 lambs quiet in
 American yellow light—
"Even J.C. couldn't have saved me."
Magpie, Meadowlark, Rainbow
 Apparitions shafted transparent
 Down from grey cloud.
      Dogs see
      black & white.
A complete half-rainbow
 hill to hill across the highway
pots of gold anchoring the pretty bridge,
 tumbleweed passing underneath
 along highwayside.
Heaviest B52 raids near the Cambodian
     border
Czech student strikes unreported in Prague
Howard Marquette & George Washington U sit-in.
 "Saigon (AP) U.S. B52 bombers
 made their heaviest raids of the
 Vietnam War last night near the Cambodian
 border, dropping more than 2,000 tons of
 bombs along a 30 mile stretch Northwest
 of Saigon, the US Command reported.
  'They are harassing enemy
 troops so as not to let them get organized,'
 an American spokesman said."
Black students staging protest.

1969

 White youth resisted
Hail on new-plowed
 brown hilltops—
Black rainclouds and rainbows
 over Albion way—
Drive down valley to Main Street
Pullman branch
 Seattle First National
 Motor Banking
 next to Everybody's Bank.

April 25, 1969—On to Snake River Canyon—

Up Steptoe Butte to view the
Wavy Palouse Territory Wheatfields.

April 26, 1969

 Plane across Cascades, saw Columbia
Gorge in green haze below, & Mt.
Rainier snowy-white up North.
 Now past Crater Lake, icy river
mirrored on the flat pond, & above
Snowwhite Shasta—
 The Color of Earth, Blue, the blue
Oxygen atmosphere, haze & clouds
& earth & water hazed over by Blue
Radiance seen from earth plane as
From the moon photo—blue planet.

1969

Outside is everything else
Black tile spots of fire puncture
the void?

Noon: L.A. Airport—

Blue haze rolling along Concrete past hangars & Robot
blocks—
Continental flight 20 soldiers dipping at Tucson
exit Huston—
Cane at seat-side, sunlight on green shirt, Corduroy
overshirt, jeans & leather shoeboots.
I quit smoking, let go sex, avoid meat, cocoa &
buttermilk not coffee, got thinner, read seven Nights Poesy
in a row at Academies—
Off to Arizona with a bunch of Socialites and Military
Hari Krishna in the smog
Making milky mist-light rolled over ocean scroll
harbors—
Cream puffs over the desert, socialites with heavy
jewels, giant Colored Lenses bulging over eyelashes—
dry red wastes, Chocolate Mountains scratched w/ sea tracks.

Brown stonepeaks[17]

       rockstumps
in blue cloudless sunlight
Saguaro green arms praying off

17. First draft of "Sonora Desert Edge," *Collected Poems,* 530–31.

1969

    rising spine ribs
            woodpecker-holed
    rose-pricked limbs
      lifted salutation—
orange flower eyes lifted on
    needly Ocotillo stalk

Smoke plumed up white under
    scratched desert plain,
    chemical smoke, military copper
    airplanes rotting,
           4% Copper Smelter smog
—Palo Alto green round branches
    smooth forked above
prickly pear ears

in wire cage, white feathershaped
    ivory hooded pupil-eyed
    head
of the Bald Eagle, white tail feathers
    hanging below clawed branch
brown feathers even as webs on dollarbills,
    insecticides sterilized many
             adults
—sheen green duck neck spectral as
      moon machines
Raven, hopping black beaked curious,
Coyotes nose sensitive to air, his
    blinking sharp
as the rose bellied Cardinal's whistle
—tiny bright statues of Buddha
    standing

1969

over blue desert valley haze—
    cactus lessons in sentience,
Trees like mental carrots—Anaconda
    smelters' white plumesmoke in
    San Miguel, or Phelps-Dodge in
    Douglas?—
yellow'd Creosote bushes in granular
    dust, dirt hill scratched
prairie dogs standing quivering-spined in
    cactus shade. A museum,
    minds in Ashramic City—tweetling

bird radios—Hopi Rain:

1969

May Day 1969

    Blue Hazed Saint Mountains walling
        Tucson East, planewings dip
    Flying night over Sonora, Mt. Lemon's
        blue brow obscure in Ashey air—
    Red Desert slopes scratched square dirt roads,
        Mountain ridge's black trees'
        fur

Inside the Airplane

Two giant boned men side by
    side,
Plastic-glass tray-seats unfolded
    iced alcohol, horn rimmed glass,
short-cropped hair, mid skull bald brown
    suit,
silver watch band, striped tie,
    shined leather shoes,
both me hands rested prayer clasped
    round plastic drinks—
hair on wrists, on calves where the
    cuffed pants crease rises—
Mammal-fur down back of neck,
    behind pink ears where clean
    collars rise—
gazing together out plane
    window, soft green Arkansas
    woods—
they have discussed business together

1969

  from Dallas to Little Rock
risen over the Earth's bright
   Mayday afternoon,
and yawn & furrow their brows,
   & sip clear icy drops,
Meditating silent, the wingtip arrows
   down to green city outskirts.

   ——Arkansas——
Possum—kinda greasy
Coon—big coon suppers once a year
Squirrels—sorta tough but a lotta people like the little brains
Frog-gigging (big old poles that's got hooks on 'em and you stick them in
the frawgs
   haid—right between the eyes—Blind the frawg with flashlight—
Deer, Quail
Hush puppies
   pig feet
   —local color type food
pickled pig tails
Hog Jowels—big ole wad of fat you slice off & you cook w/ the greens, &
it's got a chunk of
   Skin
Mustard greens & Collard greens
Catfish—
Sowbelly—

Arkansawyer, Arkies
hill people
red neck "pileated woodpecker"
Perckerwoods—Miss.

1969

Crackers—Georgia
lint-heads (or Gin crackers)

(Hoosiers—Nebraska)
Cajuns, Creoles,
River Rats,

Honky Tonk
Eukeyjumps—
        (Miss. Louisiana)

We're in the Great Place, the[18]
Fable place, Beulah, Man wedded to Earth,
   The planet of green grass
Tiny atomic wheels spin shining, and
Worlds change, Heavens inside out,
   the planet is reborn in ashes,
Sun lights sparkle on atomic cinder,
plants levitate, green moss precedes trees
   trembling sentient under blue skies,
Stone eats sunlight with invisible mouth mouths
   & flowers are the rocks' excrement—

Each million years that pass
atoms spin myriad reversals, worlds within
   interchange populations—
from worm to man's a tiny jump
   from earth to earth souls are borne ever forgetful—
populations eat their own meat, roses

18. First draft of "Falling Asleep in America," *Collected Poems*, 525.

smell sweet in the faeces of horses risen red-fac'd.
Consciousness changes night after night
dreams flower their universes in brainy skulls.

Lying in bed body darkened ear of
the run of bus roar, only the eye flickering
grass green returns me to
Nashville.

Dept of Agriculture spends

1.8 million year Price Support Tobacco
$28 million to subsidize export
$240,000 a year to advertise & promote the sale of cigarettes abroad
$20 million worth of tobacco sent overseas thru "Food for Peace"
Elizabeth Drew NY Times Magazine, Section p. 37, May 4, 1969

Cigarette advt—$245 Million yearly
8% of TV advt. time.
Autos—1/3 less time than above
9 Billion yearly spent in Cigarettes.
Farming—$1 billion a year.
         600,000 families

10 states	Kentucky	N. Carolina
	Tennessee	S. Carolina
	Maryland	Georgia

Mfg—36,000 people
45,000 people yearly dying from Cancer
. . . connected w/ smoking?
59.7 million US smokers

1969

58% of males
37% of females
27.3 billion packs per year

Reflections in Sleepy Eye[19]

3,489 friendly people
   welcome Farmer's Creamery
   State Lake & Park
   Hospital
   Leo's drive in Dairy Queen
Large beetles & lizards
   painted orange steel
   crane crawls drawn by
      cab trucks
Concrete shafts SGA grain
   elevators
elm grove, willow, picture book
   red barns, brick silo
thin floods in Blue Earth County's
   [?] plains
turned smooth planted acres,
rising and falling gently, brown
   cornstubble plowed under
   tractor pulling discs over
   smoothcut fenced land,
high Heaven fleec'd with grey clouds
tiny [?] with gas nozzly

19. First draft of "Reflections in Sleepy Eye," *Collected Poems*, 532.

1969

snout on a billboard guarded
  by green grounds—
one box-elder fallen over on his knees
  in the pond-flood
Big sweet white-painted gastank
  at Springfield's rail yard
  by the woods,
engine Rock Island box car,
  So. Pacific red iron box
 tiny caboose behind the tiny
  picture book parade train
Meats Groceries nearly painted outa town
Our flag at full mast, streaming
  in the wind, North Star Seeds,
TV antennae, large leafy antennae,
  trees, stretched out green,
  trunks standing in sunlight
Sheep on a green stormfenced knoll,
little acres of woods—
  one forest from Canada to these
  tree stumps [?]
  at the edge of tree guarded acres—
Brick & blue enamel silos, corn
  silage up to the net bins
  by roadside—
Windmills in Tracy,
  Silo-[?] aluminum
    cap'd in white
    sunbeam
Cannabis excellent for drying lymph-
  glands, specific relief for

1969

symptoms of colds, flu,
>ear pressure grippe &

Eustachian tube clogging—
Whitewashed cinderblock pattern
>silo crown.

>Much land, a tree broken

>mid-trunk, branches to ground—

New folk, excelsior grave
>yard stones

silver tipp'd phalloi to Heaven—
>sheep in wet yard

and hundred lambs later on green hillside—
Aum, Om, Ford, Mailbox
>telephone pole wire strung

>down road. Lake house,

>fence poles, tree shade,

>pine hill grave, ah

Lake Benton, blue waved waters—
>Finally, Time came to

>the Brick Barn! Collapsed!

>Oh Lake Benton!

Telephone line side white house
>Violet roof tiles

Cigarette smell back
>seat. Car glass smudge

>hedged [?] church

>graveyard cemetery greens

old oak trunk sunk thick
under ground
Green-seeder down pointed
>Science toy earth-cock—

1969

Farm car plowman rolling discs
    iron cuts smooth ground even,
        hill plains roll—
Cows browse under elder shoot,
bent limbs arch brown clear
      stream beds, trees
      stand on banks
Car graveyard fills eyes
    iron glitters, chrome paint
    rusts
trees have a peculiar way
    of standing up or kneeling
    on the ground.
Ticker Town school bus, farm ponies,
White Crosses, Vietnam War dead
      Welfare grave
      Churchbells.
cars, kids, hamburger stand
    chicken, open
Barns smile white
    eye, door mouth.

                    May 9, '69

Folk hate war, folk
    make bare assed naked
      couch moans,
army call telegrammed.

1969

May 24, 1969

Dream . . . Walking along lake-side camp, by the freshwater pool elevated above the Ashram Bunkhouse, I saw a turtle who followed me from the tank—Turtle had regular beak head and human hands, which were clasped at its mouth, & then extended to reach me—I hurried away.

Hands like Salamander but with thick human fingers

Too many letters
too many faces to read—
hard to reply except with
an empty week
           —a letter to Italy, May 24, '69

June 1, 1969

O how happy I am
'Cause I'm working for the CIA
Sittin in the middle of the man
War is Child-Spray—

                       *

Nobody can get me
Or make me lose my job

June 5, 1969—Dream

Visiting Padua, or Vicenza my old mafia boyfriend I'd half seduced years ago meets me in the forum or circus—"I remembered who I was" he says ominously, putting his arm firmly round my shoulder and steering me toward the river-beach. "Did you ever find yourself an assistant?" referring to our old conversation—I needed help showing a movie or playing music—and I'd tried to get him to help me—

Now dread, he got my number "remembered himself," his heterosexual small town mafia security, & had shown my movie.

I said I got home safely, & had shown my movie.

Fear in my gut.

Dream—Sightseeing in Rome or Mexico City—I am arrested & taken to Immigration Jail—I begin yelling up & down corridors, half scared but still not paralyzed by fear, "I was in jail just before I left last time and I haven't committed any crime so you're holding me illegally . . . Stupid oxen."

Dream I

Woken out of blossom at the west side of the Oldum, where the concrete bank upheld the small waterfall at the edge of the reservoir, in the mist I see the towers of the prison.

Went in the door after standing looking up & hearing the jazzbands play in the first high ledges of the battlement, the first cage up—(like a spare platform, would be, a sophisticated prison room from which the prisoner could see the blue world-globe)—I explained to my friend it was the Saturday allowable jazzband.

So we went in the door, it was legal to go in, and step up a razor-thin ladder past an examination electric net, and be then hauled up by a ring of prisoners, handsome & gleeful pulling hip & wrist rope, that lifted the visitors up like on a bouncy trampoline—up thru the first levels to the first floor room—where I was seen by all, visiting, & judged okay, & lifted higher up toward the noisy brass-syncopated jazzband.

July 4, 1969

Orange hawkeye stronger[20]
    than thought
on having green stems above
    a thousand thin grassblades
Dr. Hermon busted in Texas for
    green weed garden—grown
Licensed federal, Municipal-cop
    prosecuted nathless—
Sweet chirrup from bush to
    to bush top, orange wing'd
birds' scratch-beaked telegraphy
    signaled to and fro buttercup
    earlets—
warbles & sweet whistles swifting
    echo-noted by fly buzz and
jet roar rolling down thru
    clouds—
so tiny a grasshopper climbing grass
    stub the birds can't tell
    they're there
intense soft weedstalks yellow green
    leaf-spears budding symmetric
gentle breeze everywhere trembling

20. First draft of "Independence Day," *Collected Poems*, 534.

1969

flowerheads against grass wheat
      their persons—
eyelids heavy, summer heavy with
      fear, Mapletrunks heavy with
      green leaf-mass—
closed buds of hawkeye stronger than
      thought tremble on tall hairy
      stems.

*   *   *   *   *

Red shelled bedbugs crawl
      over sheets
city garbage spoils wet sidewalks where
      children play—
a telephone call from Texas
      tells the police state bust
O Self tangled in TV wires, white
      judges and laws
your jet thunder echoes in clouds, your
      DDT spreads thru firmament waters
      poisons algae & brown pelicans—
Smog veils Maya, Paranoia walks
      vast cities in blue suits with guns,
—are all these billion grassblades
      safe?
My stomach's bitter from city haste
      and money loss—
Leafy burdock! Hawkeye stronger than thought!
      Blackberry & pine! Horsefly & bee!
I close my eyes in your presence,
      lie in your soft green bed
watch sunlight thru red lid skin,

1969

language presented as birdwarble
in my brain.
Independence Day! The Cow's deep moo's
an Aum!
Cut my backbone, unstring my eyes and
fingers,
Let a million insects eat my skin, my soul
as empty as—
Grass bends & trembles in the warbling breeze.

July 7, 1969

A small tiger on the hill, I throw a log at its back to stop it from running it's hurt, arches on its backbone in reflex & stiffens and moves forward slowly, stunned, till I pick it up . . . waking in blond-paneled room on East Hill farm.

Every morning I wake early in uncomfortable mental excitement, and try to ignore the dread of revolution in my body & sleep.

The economics of the farm images recurrent money-bills confusion— no rest, how to pay 30,000 dollars break my mind's back & sell my soul & poesy for this active land? Who'll do all the work, trouble is I'm paying others to do personal job on land.

Not paid my taxes the government'll get my Bank Account & type-writer—S.D.S. & P.L.P.[21] want violent overthrow of the violent economic tyrants.

Leroi Jones' magnetism comes from his knowledge on his skull of police violence.

21. Students for a Democratic Society and Progressive Labor Party were two radical leftist organizations working together to overthrow the capitalist system in the United States.

Ultimately, I wake in morn afraid of violent dispersal of my possessions music books mss. and household—

Retreat from fighting State for fear of being fought back by the state.

And so feel guilty dreaming of the Crazies & motherfuckers who having no possessions and no material attachment are not compromised in sentimental friendship with the FBI, Local Police, Newspapers, TV Talk Show Hosts . . .

Leroi walked off the set on one halfhour broadcast.

July 9, 1969

    a white hen pecks along
        tree-shade's edges &
    stands silent surveying
        sunlit yellow grass

    I am the planet, I am
        Imagination
    Blake's Divine-aethereal Godliness
    a photo of blue planet-ball from *Life*.
    I planet command Quiet or
        I die.

    Leaving the Moon

Dead Flag striped right by
    the Simulator Image—
wooden minutes ticking off the
    screen—like singing opera

1969

after screaming rehearsals, or ad
   for disposable paper "bikini"
   suits—
"We've seen everything" 'ceptin the
   return of Christ—1975
sez Jehovah's witnesses—3 minutes
   to go, seconds ticking silent—
Explosion or Voyage home to blue
   planet?
20 seconds to go—Hare Krishna—
   "you're looking good"—
Beautiful, ascending 2 miles above Moon—

July 24, 1969

Apollo Landed, Splashdown
       upside down floating on the
            Pacific waters
Swim in Helicopters & Lifeguards—
       9 miles away—voice static
Nixon on board—gravity a Drag?
Reentry Gravity Upside Down bent over
           heavy with Earth Electric
Come downstairs to squeaky transistor voiced
      "weightfulness" born—
Contaminated with moon disease on
      presidential aircraftcarriers?
A big chance we all took, Hey Nixon
      Spray Disinfectant
& biological isolation garments donned—
are the first germs entered atmosphere now?

1969

July 28, 1969—Amherst

Pink petals nod on grass
bee tiny as needle sip in flowers' eye
under rain eaten marble the grave slab
a black fly washed his hands crouched
        On a broken leaf.

   —at E. Dickenson's grave

August 2, 1969

Rain wet asphalt heat, garbage[22]
    curbed cans overflowing,
I hauled down lifeless mattresses
    to sidewalk refuse pile,
old rugs stept on from Paterson to Lower
    East Side filled with bedbugs,
grey pillows, couch seats treasured
    from the street laid from on the street
—out, to hear a tale of Murder, 3rd
    Street cyclists attacked tonite—
Bopping along in rain, Chaos fallen
    over City, rooftops,
for shrouds of chemical vapor drifting
    over building roofs—

22. First draft of "Rain-wet asphalt heat, garbage curbed cans overflowing," *Collected Poems*, 537.

1969

Get the Times, Nixon says peace reflected
    from the Moon,
but I found no boy body to sleep with
    all night
Steam on the pavement till 3 AM came home
    in sweating drizzle
those mattresses soggy lying by full
    five garbage pails—
Barbara, Maretta, Peter, Steven, Rosebud
    slept on these pillows years ago
forgotten their names, also made love to me, I had
    these mattresses four years on my floor—
Gerard, Jimmy many months, even
    blond Gordon later,
Paul with the beautiful big cock, that
    Teenage boy that lived in Pennsylvania,
Forgotten numbers, young dream loves and
    lovers, earthly bellies—
many strong youths with eyes closed, come
    sighing and helping me to come—
Desires already forgotten, tender persons used
    and kissed goodbye
and all the times I came to myself alone in
    the dark dreaming of Neal or Billy Budd
—nameless angels of half life—heart
    beating & eyes weeping for lovely phantoms—
Back from the Gem Spa, and into the
    hallway, a glance behind
and sudden farewell to the bedbug ridden
    mattresses piled soggy in dark rain.

1969

August 15, 1969   Cherry Valley

I wake mornings breathing shallow, birds warbling in foggy light, my mind racing with eyes open or eyes closed trying to return to unconsciousness to escape fear—of body pain, of fatigue, of horses eating fences rotting squash leaves lost in green weedstalks—weeds round my life—I talk about God and don't see Him—talk about love and fear Peter—my belly tense, mind racing to the revolutionary doom of planet—morning after morning nervous breakdown a cheerless self with my desk accumulating energetic papers, money worry above all, pestered by dollar needs first time in 42 years on planet money's gotten under my skin & into my consciousness like bedbugs that wouldn't let me sleep in the city.

August 18, 1969   12:30 PM

Sex appetite between legs (just jerked off) is localization of consciousness.

Complete contraction of awareness to that one spot the tip o' the phallus is orgasm—

But it's a contraction of consciousness to the loins, that drives out of mind the entire fleeting spread of the cosmos for the sake of individual meat-throb.

August 22, 1969   6:30 AM

Yellow light at fringe of sky, clear blue dawn—dome out the wooden window at cock crow—

Waking early these months, unable to remember dreams, long time no see the Prince of Chow.

1969

Worldly images in mind, eyes closed, begin like a movie soon as I come to consciousness, & my stomach muscles tense. This morning Madeliene Sinclair's arrest in Oakland New Jersey & her helpless phonecall to me & Ed Sanders rose in mind at dawn with bird chirps in ear & scattered paw-jousting of four farm dogs on cool August morn in wet grass—I got up to pee on the lawn. And with her call—"Send not to find for whom the bell tolls"—also John[23] got busted last year sentenced last weeks to 9–10 years screaming in Court for passing two joints of pleasure grass to a secret agent of the state.

Black Panther Bobby Seale[24] accused of ritual murder by the F.B.I.— Dave Dellinger[25] and Abbie Hoffman to be tried for protesting police state war in Chicago—and in England a scientist's declared we tipped the planet-balance of irrevocable pollution.

These thoughts at rising, dread at being pushed out of the body-image with mass jail, Buchenwald re-cycled, storm troopers invading the countrywide, carbon monoxide starvation riot popular death.

From now on I'll keep a dawn-insomnial catalogue of anxieties till I find peace in my own mind and body.

----

23. John Sinclair (born 1941), manager of the MC5 rock band and founder of the socialist White Panther Party, was in Chicago during the Democratic National Convention in 1968, though he was not indicted for his participation. His arrest for pot possession led to the harsh sentence. He was freed, after great protests and a concert that featured John Lennon, Yoko Ono, Abbie Hoffman, Jerry Rubin, Allen Ginsberg, Stevie Wonder, Bob Seger, and Phil Ochs, in 1971.

24. Bobby Seale (born 1936), cofounder of the Black Panther Party, was one of the "Chicago Eight" defendants in the case against organizers of the opposition to the Democratic National Convention in Chicago in 1968.

25. David Dellinger (1915–2004), a lifelong pacifist, was indicted in the "Chicago Eight" trial in Chicago. He founded *Liberation* magazine and was active in antiwar groups.

1969

August 26, 1969   7 AM

My belly too fat, O ugly potshaped abdomen of masturbation and no babies because of world overpopulation sleeping late in bed insomniac after cock crow as the earth chills toward Autumn—

Indian Journals taking years to come out from Dave Haselwood's hands[26]

Shall I throw out my accumulation of Military-Industrial Books and Clippings from N.Y. Times?

Fog rising from the grass after a week of crystal-blue air—the chill had kept earth-steam out of the atmosphere till this morn.

Jack Geyer & his crippled wife in a shack by the road piled high with winter wood log axed on his knee   Letters piled up to be answered, taxes refused unpaid, Bank account seized; possessions piling the walls books, manuscripts, loves a burden waiting attention while the mind would be free to fly to Stars or travel to Persia.

I have, America has, too many possessions to sleep peacefully in the morning, doze late while the birds twitter in the fog.

August 27, 1969

Woke 4 AM pissed in moon glare, the night cool and my brain perturbed—lay in dark in reptile-headed body snout-a-pillow breathing scared at center of vast godless universe—stomach clammy after spaghetti a la Vongole a fatty bowl to digest.

All night since insomniac, and after dawn woke from fleeting dream— I captured a buzzing bee in my hand—M. Fly By Nite's my name—and be-

26. Editor of Ginsberg's *Indian Journals*.

cause I was in haste to gather stolen honey I crushed the insect between my thumb and digit-finger—he didn't sting but ZZZ'd awhile, the pieces of abdomen, leg and wing-set having dropped into dewey green water cups on the ground, kept up living motion while I watched looking down at dawn in horror—

Poor Leary I'd thot at 4 AM with planet death on his hands & best friends poisoned by paranoia psilocybin CIA plant of fresh powerful chemicals to bum-trip his giant career? If I'm a reptile nose on a pillow what does Tim nightmare of himself? or is Rosemary's comfort enuf?—

Enough stomach death for me all night! What good's yelling on TV to save the race if my own dreams make me a lizard king on cold planet dream surface?

August 27, 1969   6:30 AM

Mailer's moon prose in *Life*[27]—octopus Nazi Woman Fear Alcohol Earth-roar.

Childless I abjure *Life*. The ant-heaped throngs worship the white giant female queen.

Disorder with Magna Mater because of overpopulation? In any case disorder with my mother at time of planet-crowding makes a turn to homosexuality a political case.

27. Norman Mailer's essay on the moon landing, initially published in *Life* magazine, was published in book form as *Of a Fire on the Moon*.

1969

Storming Stonewall Inn[28] the mafia fairies' refuge crying Gay Power & fighting the cops—the fairies were always political "criminals" adjuring the familiar society they were born into.

Exiles in the homeland.

August 30, 1969   Labor Day Dream

I come home naked from Lakeside woods, Peter fixing supper & Julius, answering phone says, "I wanted to wait & find out my egg-yolk destiny." Because I'd had a dream of a message about Julius I'd brought back from the Lake.

Alexi Ginzberg & Yessenin Volpin in & out of jail in Soviet State Cities— & I never sent Volpin the Books of British Constitution he asked for.
John Sinclair sentenced to 10 years for 2 sticks of pot to an agent.

September 4, 1969

. . . Yes & you can cover that wall with orthodox mohair—trying to wallpaper the outside of a battleship in a dream?

Last night at suppertime standing by the barn arguing with Peter— Julius up on aluminum ladder taking down the old boards so's they could

28. Beginning on June 28, 1969, a series of riots at the Stonewall Inn, a popular gay bar in Greenwich Village, led to numerous arrests and, ultimately, the strengthening of the gay liberation movement.

1969

insulate with tarpaper first before re-lining barn with fresh wood. Dark fallen, Peter yelling at Julius & climbing the ladder tearing down the boards. Inside the house, the table set & Huncke & I angry that Peter wouldn't come and eat. Julius afraid to come in because of his fury, & Peter screaming at me in the dusk.

Rimbaud's almond-eyed photo still tacked up at my bedside. He took the weight of the entire world's consciousness-changing.

September 5, 1969   4:15 AM

Meadows flocked with goldenrod, a bulldozer grunting all day in the pasture, Bessie the cow covered with flies.

Last night I argued with Peter, he screamed at me & cut his hand with a knife while opening a coconut.

5:20 AM

Consulting the Oracle chance, a throw of dice in dream landed me on the following block of the monopoly board "for the primary reason: power." This refers to my motives in argument with Peter.

If Peter & I can't get along, how can Jews & Arabs? How can any war end?

September 7, 1969   7 AM

Cock crow, I'm in exile, birds whistle in the dog mist under maple trees around the house.

John Sinclair jailed & shaved, dragged screaming "you will die" to police in courtroom.

1969

September 9, 1969   6 AM

"They even murder people" echoes from dream—This is the stage of
the Nation in the Kali Yuga—Robert Williams[29] the black violent Christ
couldn't get a plane from London to America, all the international air-
lines blocked his transport, organized government move behind it like in
Soviet Kafka chessgame ... Agents on the telephone "Don't sell him
ticket" or "Everybody shun his baggage."

A knot in my solar plexus yesterday all day, tremorous knot of anxiety
that made me think of stomach cancer my karma—

Hardly a morning since I've been on the farm that I've woken to delight
in dewy grass and birds' warble & ducklings' peeps.

& I get drowsy early at night, my whole body weighed down with the
day's one hour reading thru NY Times, & vegetable table at supper.

No sex, anxious old potbelly! and plenty police unconscious!

Rescue me! Rescue me! from my loneliness o Student Lord.

September 10, 1969   6:05 AM

Kleindienst is name of Assistant Attorney General to the United
States. Newspapers this week reported his executive commission formu-
lating an all-out war on cannabis Grass mobilizing NASA the space
agency as well as Mexican cops. "It still behooves . . ." I woke up before
dawn as the dogs barked fearing blue coated police moving round my
porch in the dark.

29. Robert F. Williams (1925–1996), a black civil rights activist and writer *(Ne-
groes with Guns)*, lived outside the United States for most of the Sixties. His attempts
to return to the United States in 1969 were met with resistance.

1969

Brooding eyes closed, Robert Williams in Airport London, and TWA & CIA wouldn't let him on jetplane home to America because he preached revolution ten years ago prophetic, Bureaucrats almost sent him to Cairo this week.

Asleep, Peter rose up naked with streaky Jewish hair like mine down his midriff & looking close I saw he had a small infection sore boil above his pubic triangle—closer I saw it was a tiny hardon, rising from bed where a tough little girl from Lower East Side lay.

Every morning's blue dawn I wake—photo of Earth mamma tacked to the bed-wall—gas eating her up—what can we do to purify the ground around our kitchen drain? Not pollute mama more?

Trees crying telepathic for Salvation, root networks underground transmitting the message across continents Help! Help! from the bulldozers rocking back and forth over gelatinous earth-skin.

Helicopter dropping chemicals over Mexican marijuana fields projected by front page Times report of the presidential commission—Defoliants against Grass Crimes!

September 11, 1969

Morning sickness, alarm clock briefly ringing in Peter's room—Robert Williams, the New York Times editorialized, should get his citizen-rights to go home & be tried for kidnapping distasteful as he is TWA ain't got no right to stop his flight & it was the FBI asked airlines to set him off to one side of the airport to prevent "disorder"?

John Sinclair in the slam 10 years for 2 sticks of grass to an agent & Michigan Supreme Court refused him appeal bail.

All out war on Grass plotted at the Border by wide-hipped proxy of Mexico & USA, with chemical defoliants & gas dogs & sensors invented by NASA.

Black Panther's offices in cities everywhere burned, white lawyers desks overloaded, barristers rushing by airplane every direction.

1969

Costs 1500 for transcript of John Sinclair's trial, nobody got the money.

Dellinger Hoffman & Rubin & Hayden[30] & Bobby Seale and not me not Ed Sanders on trial for Chicago Conspiracy, last year's political convention.

September 14, 1969   6:30 AM

The Comix Strips of the New York Daily News infiltrated by FBI. Dondie the round-faced baby boy on the back page confronting a psychedelic auto driver by tools of International Conspiracy throwing bricks into Mr. Middle-class Good Gus's Living Room. Daddy Warbucks & Little Orphan Annie from previous wars & decades still fighting Russians in Mongolian caves, Rex Morgan M.D. operating for the Narco Bureau Treasury Department or F.D.A. to show sweet college boys & girls freaking out in swirley maelstroms of acid minds—Terry & the Pirates directly inspired by the Pentagon's Asiatic Wars—Teenagers Wise Owl warning his school voters against Radical spokesmen—

& now they tattooed his number on John Sinclair's arm as he's being transferred to Maximum Security Detention Cell in Northern Michigan.

I haven't been in prison so haven't seen the Nightmare at the bottom of Linear Society, i.e. that society which exists on paper i.e. money legal documents & the New York Times.

Nor seen the vast heap of woe that's the Real Universe Substratum of U.S.A. as earth's population multiplies.

----

30. Author of the "Port Huron Statement," a document advocating participatory democracy, and cofounder of Students for a Democratic Society (SDS), Tom Hayden (1939–2016) was indicted in Chicago for his involvement in the protests during the 1968 Democratic National Convention.

1969

September 19, 1969   10 AM

In the bright street under the smokestack
a rheumatic man in a hat with a stick
stands stock still with his dog on a leash,
the four-legged looks up silent.

They stand together motionless, the man
walks down toward Avenue C thirty steps,
the dog takes thirty slow steps to hydrant
and they lean together under a bus-stop sign.

Man & dog rheumatic enemies, circle
each other on the street, and stop, waiting.
Man picks up dog, four legs hang out,
and steps creakily up to the brownstone door.

September 25, 1969   Cherry Valley

   8 AM—Four notes to the rooster crow.
   Whether or not life itself is so corruptible as to be complete loss to it-
self, the preserved grace musics of the Beatles are complete crystals of joy.

Death on All Fronts[31]

Half the Blue Globe's germ population's
   more than enough
to keep the cloudy lung from stinking

31. First draft of "Death on All Fronts," *Collected Poems*, 538.

1969

    pneumonia
A new moon looks down on our
    sick sweet planet,
Orion's chased the immovable bear halfway
    across the sky
from winter to winter, I wake earlier in bed,
    fly corpses over gaslit sheets—
My head aches left temple, brain
    fibre throbbing for Death
I created on all fronts—poisoned rats
    in the chickenhouse, & myriad lice
sprayed with white arsenics, city
    cockroaches stomped on Country
    kitchen floor—
No babies for me, cut earth boys &
    girl hoards by half
& breathe free say Revolutionary expert
    Computers—
Couldn't sleep creating universal
    Visions, I called in Exterminator
  who soaked the wall-floor with bedbug
    Death-oil—
Who'll soak *my* brain with Death oil?
    I wake before dawn
Dreading my wooden possessions, my
    books, my loud mouth,
my old loves, my own charms turned
    to image money, my belly sexless
    fat, father dying.
Earth Cities poisoned
    at war, my art hopeless,
mind fragmented & still abstract,
    pain in left temple living death.

1969

Woods' dragonflies zip over iron-rust leaf'd creekbeds. I sigh with the frog's splash.

September 28, 1969   6:45 AM

"The planet is finished"—Burroughs, Hotel Chelsea two weeks ago.

My head opens like a concrete tomb every morning at dawn. Lifetime habit to sleep on, snuggle under covers warm, but head's open & woe floods body—what thoughts specified?—This morning, will our hydraulic ram work on, when the cities fall? or will our artificial water-pusher fail? Did we wreck the topsoil acres round the house by digging turf for casement ceramics? Will we starve & gnaw back other's skulls in a few winters? Will the Government trap me on the farm for tax refusals? Will my notebooks survive poesy reading tour, and what can I say to thousands of students I'm trapped into chanting to, who want revolution, tell them "the planet is finished?" Will Peter be happy with Julius on farm forever? Who'll care for East Hill's cows goats & chickens, ducklings, a horse, basement and roof if I go East to Brindaban or Peter takes off for Benares? My stomach's tight-knotted & conscious. Blue-grey fog dawn light, trees' arms upraised.

Last nite I pissed in near full moonlight, clouds passed like movies or ghost veils over the trees in bright night sky—steam-sheets pulled swift- "sliding" thru air over moon-circle—who make that move? Moving's a sign of life?

This Fellow

Underground at the fair, thin-faced business millionaire, took me aside—showed me the two memory pills he had on his forefinger.

1969

I'd been in Mexico & scribbled a few pages, now on returning sent them to add to a small book I'd sent City Lights. Well despite my depression and vanity, I did get that much writ—sort of poetical journal, Byronic free verses.

Underground in worlds fair subway galleries, wandering thru Turkish baths downstairs in dark water, up thru Customs Police cubicles, carrying notebook to draw in.

Here's the Lebanese millionaire again—we take a walk, he says he lives in Washington & hears all sorts of gossip—as example the memory pills he had, and dammit lost, since he saw me last—we walk arm in arm back to the main house thru fairgrounds—

Showing my "estate" to some girls—they ask how I found it—we're in an old Millbrook type of bowling alley—I explain Barbara Rubin[32] drove round upstate—

There are many houses, campsites & side servant huts—varied habitations, I'm greedy proud, showing off.

Kerouac must've got disillusioned like this in 1953, waiting to hear his newspaper statement about History.

September 29, 1969   4:45 AM

Dark of night, dream of Joel Oppenheimer's "Visions of Dante's Inferno" title language in my ear as I wake from
Mountain of darkness with billions of people clinging to the sides of the world that shakes underground.
Leroi Jones' Inferno. Can't sleep, flies buzz round gaslight.

32. Filmmaker and occasional Ginsberg girlfriend.

1969

October 3, 1969   7 AM

"Whatever we see when awake, is death; and when asleep, a dream"—

Thus at dream rally sang Howl aloud to try to end war—thinking asleep after, well, I'm growing old so I can give up on Tune & repeat my own Poesy a few times tho now the audience'll know I've shot my load & can't do better higher newer dithyramb today.

Kerouac's essay in Capitol Newspaper Post, "After Me, the Deluge,"[33] flooded mind awakening—all day flotsam his imagery yesterday car riding to Albany—hate the revolutionaries & every pacifist Dellinger & hate the bureaucrats, like his father.

John Sinclair his letter says Guerilla Warfare supplant Love Fire, & here I gotta go get him out of jail? Jesus Jack!

Saw Gregory off to airplane, night before sat at laundromat & read Taylor the Platonist's essay on Eleusinian & Bacchic mysteries—"in present life asleep & conversant with the delusions of dreams."

7:45 AM

So the question is, all ways, Is life we see, the moving image of eternity, in itself utterly empty of soul—poems, calves, worms, ducks & ducklings, persons and leafy vegetation, is that itself death and material maya magic distraction or is the life-stuff some holy manifestation of a supreme Person Christ Krishna Creation?

33. Controversial syndicated Kerouac essay.

1969

October 13, 1969

Flying w/ Poets

Up over Garbage Can Skyline
   into White Mist—
The sky is a mind exercise—
No mind—erase the blackboard—
more rubbish comes in,
   fill it up with air,
Fasten yer seatbelts just in case
   we run into unexpected turbulence

   Were mummies wrapped & dried millennia for cellular resurrection by psychocomputer at last judgment AD 2000? Food & cups & dinner set forth as formulae for care & feed of resurrected corpses?

On the evening of October 21, 1969, Allen Ginsberg received a telephone call from journalist Al Aronowitz: Jack Kerouac had died earlier that day in a Florida hospital. For Ginsberg, it was the second such call in just over a year and a half; he learned on February 10, 1968, that Neal Cassady, the inspiration for On the Road and (aside from Kerouac) Ginsberg's closest friend, had died in Mexico.

The Kerouac news saddened but did not surprise Ginsberg. Kerouac's heavy drinking over the past decade had increased to such an extent that his closest friends wondered if he had a death wish. Ginsberg and Kerouac had grown distant, largely because Kerouac was not accessible but also because Allen did not care to be around his old friend, who, on any given night, could be a belligerent, unhappy, argumentative, and nasty drunk.

1969

Ginsberg's note: *Kerouac at Staten Island Ferry dock, New York*
Fall 1953, we used to wander thru truck parking lots at dockside &
under Brooklyn Bridge singing rawbone blues & shouting Hart Crane's
Atlantis to the traffic above. Time of Dr. Sax & The Subterraneans.

Kerouac had remarried, bought a house for his wife and invalid mother, and moved to Florida, where he lived a semireclusive life.

This was not the man Ginsberg remembered immediately following the news of Kerouac's death. He recalled the joyful, enthusiastic, ambitious, prodigious writer, whose work influenced his own. Kerouac had basked in the heat of spontaneity, he had put Ginsberg on the path to Buddhism, the two had shared their innermost thoughts. His intelligence had been a beacon.

October 22, 1969   1:30 AM

Two watches ticking in the dark, fly buzz at the black window, telephone calls all day to Florida and Old Saybrook, Lucien, Creeley, Louis— "drinking heavily" and "your letter made him feel bad," said Stella.[34]

All last nite (as talking on farm w/ Creeley day before) in bed brooding re Kerouac's "After Me, the Deluge" at middle of morning watch I woke realizing he was right, that the meat suffering in the middle of existence was a sensitive pain greater than any political anger or hope, as I also lay in bed dying.[35]

Walking with Gregory in bare treed October ash woods—winds blowing brown sere leafs at feet—talking of dead Jack—the sky an old familiar place with fragrant eyebrow clouds passing overhead in Fall Current—

He saw them stand on the moon too.

At dusk I went out to the pasture & saw thru Kerouac's eyes the sun set on the first dusk after his death.

34. Stella Kerouac, Jack's widow.
35. Paraphrased from *Mexico City Blues* by Jack Kerouac.

1969

Didn't live much longer than beloved Neal—another year & half—

Gregory woke at midnite to cry—he didn't really want to go so soon—from the attick—

His mind my mind many ways—"The days of my youth rise fresh in my mind"—

Our talk 25 years ago about saying farewell to the tender mortal steps of Union Theological Seminary where I first met Lucien—weeks ago he'd had convulsions split his nose & broke out all his false front teeth, chewed his tongue almost in half—unconscious taken to hospital—

Jack had vomited blood this last weekend would not take doctor care, hemorrhaged, & with many dozen transfusions lay in hospital a day before dying operated under knife in stomach—

Oct 22—

    Memory Gardens[36]
        Covered with yellow leaves
           in morning rain

Oct 24—Quel Deluge

    He threw up his hands
        & wrote the universe dont exist
           & died to prove it.

Full Moon over Ozone Park
    Bus rushing thru dusk to

36. First draft of the opening of "Memory Gardens," *Collected Poems*, 539.

1969

       Manhattan,
Jack the Wizard in his
         grave at Lowell
for the first nite—
that Jack thru whose eyes
    I saw
   smog glory light
     gold over Manhattan's spires
will never see these
      chimneys smoking
anymore over statues of Mary
       in the graveyard

   Truck beds packed
under bridge viaducts,
Crash jabber of
   Columbia Free—
Black Misted Canyons
   rising over the bleak
         river
Bright doll-like ads
   For Esso Bread—
Replicas multiplying beards—

   Farewell to the cross—
Under the river lights shaft
   shelfing on Ceramic tunnel
Eternal fixity, the big
   headed wax Buddha doll
     pale resting incoffined—
Empty skulled New

1969

           York streets
Starveling phantoms
     filling city—
Wax dolls walking Park
                Ave.,
Light gleam in eye glass—
Voice echoing thru Microphones
Grand Central Sailor's
              arrival 2 decades later
              feeling melancholy—
Nostalgia for Innocent World
     War II—
A million Corpses running
     across 42'd Street,
The glass building rising higher
     & transparent
          aluminum
artificial trees,
              robot sofas,
     Ignorant cars—
One Way Street to Heaven.
Splash Institute's redbrick
                    facade

Oct 25, '69

Gray Subway Roar[37]
A wrinkled brown faced fellow

37. First draft of part two of "Memory Gardens," *Collected Poems,* 540–41.

1969

blue-capped, with swollen hands
leans to the blinking plate glass
   sways on tracks uptown to Columbia—
Jack no more'll step off at Penn Station
   anonymous erranded, to eat sandwich
or drink beer near New Yorker Hotel or walk
under the shadow of Empire State Building.

*

Didn't we stare at each other length of the car
   & read headlines in faces thru Newspaper Holes?
Sexual cocked & horny bodied young, look
   at beauteous Rimbaud & sweet Jenny
      riding to class from Columbus Circle
"Here the kindly dopefiend lived."

and the rednecked sheriff beat the longhaired
         boy on the ass.
—103'd St, me and Hal abused for begging.
Can I go back in time & lay me head on a teenage
      Belly upstairs on 110'th St.?
or step off the iron car with Jack
   at the blue-tiled Columbia sign?
at last the old brown station
where I had a holy vision's been
   rebuilt & changed by clean grey tile
over the scum & spit & come of
      a half century.

1969

Oct 29—N.Y. Maine
SUNSET

I am flying into a trail of Black Smoke[38]
Kerouac's obituary conserves Time's
      Front Paragraphs—
Empire State in Heaven Sun Set red
      White Mist
over the billion trees of the Bronx—
      There's too much to see
Jack saw sun set red over the Hudson Horizon
      Two three decades back
thirtynine fortynine fiftynine
            sixtynine
John Holmes[39] pursed his lips, cynic
    & empty-eyed robot,
        and wept tears.
Smoke plumed up from oceanside chimneys
   plane roars north over Long Island
      Montauk stretched in red sunset—
Northport, in the trees, Jack drank
   rot gut & made haikus of birds
      tweetling on his porch rail at dawn—
Fell down & saw death's golden lite
    in Florida garden a decade ago.
Now taken utterly, soul upward,

38. First draft of part three of "Memory Gardens," *Collected Poems*, 541–42.
39. John Clellon Holmes (1926–1988), friend and rival of Jack Kerouac and author of *Go*, considered the first Beat Generation novel, a roman à clef in which Kerouac, Ginsberg, Cassady, Holmes, and others, all renamed, were characters.

1969

       & body down in wood coffin
          & concrete slab-box
I threw a kissed handful of damp earth
       down on the stone lid
         & sighed
    Looking in Creeley's one eye
Peter sweet holding a flower
    Gregory toothless bending his
        knuckle to Cinema Machine—
and that's the end of the drabble tongued
    poet who sounded his Kock-rup
        throughout the Northwest Passage.
Blue dusk over Saybrook, Holmes
        sits down to dine Victorian—
& Time has a Ten Page Spread on
        Homosexual-Fairies!

Well, while I'm here I'll
        do the work—
and what's the work?
       To ease the pain of living.
Everything else, drunken
      dumbshow.

When he kissed my nipples[40]
    I felt the thrill in my elbow
        bone—
When he touched my belly with his

40. First draft of "After Thoughts," *Collected Poems*, 544.

1969

lips the tickle ran up to my ear
When he took the head of my cock to his
                              tongue
a tremor shrunk my sphincter, my
      reins shuddered with joy
   I breathed deep sighing ahh!

Looking in mirror combing
      grey glistening beard
what if I were found sharpeyed
      attractive to the young?
Bad magic or something—
Foolish magic most likely.

November 2, 1969

Customs officer #2913 leafing thru *Logos* newspapers in my valise, re-
turning from Montreal, said he was not sure they were Pornographic and
so bonded valise for examination at customs in Kennedy Airfield N.Y.
Valise contains my clothes, Tibetan seal, position paper on Narcotics pre-
pared for late Sen. R. Kennedy (including NY Times clips re police ac-
cused of criminal activity)—springboard binder of typed poems, several
large copybooks of original mss. handscript of poem I have been working
on "These States" since 1965, unique copy. Also front pages of last few
days Toronto and Montreal newspaper & complete file of Montreal *Logos*
newspaper in one of which I have a short text.

Wordy Birds on TV.

1969

Kerouac's white stocky body naked under bedsprings wounded dead warm—The shrouded stranger.

November 10, 1969   7:45 AM

Party—Introducing 3 editorials by Robert Lowell written re Conspiracy Trials in Boston.

3:40 PM

Mansfield Hotel, nap—seated at luncheonette counter with Naomi looking cute spit curled 1930's, we had a sweet conversation, I wake after telling her (remembered her soul), "pray for me momma."

November 11, 1969

At giant cocktail banquet in colonnaded foyer of St. Francis Hotel San Francisco city, party Republicans gathered and so I lean against a pillar observing & radiant, Shirley Temple nods approval at me, & Ronald Reagan smiles.

Nov [no date given] 1969

9:30 a.m.—Woke with pain in chest—cough, cold spread to lungs & raw dizziness, probably temperature—white fog out window, last nite Vice President attacked the image networks for casting negative shadows on his brain—

Dreamt I was in Philadelphia all dressed up to escape the army, and found this lady psychiatrist's name in my notebook, recommended by Herman Kahn?, and so after long conversation she wouldn't write a protective

1969

letter to draft board for me—I sat in Playboy Club luncheonette with her a half hour, explaining, she had on short green dress, listening, but wouldn't accept my plight—I needed a letter to get out of the army, or jury, or to go abroad. I *turned* and left, she wouldn't at first accept check for consultation (then I realized I'd canceled all checking accounts)—she did not want to charge for this meeting, I found on querying her. Gave her $10 cash—the general depression of spirit in the Nation as result of Spiro Agnew's National Speech, accusing News Media of creating Credibility Trust Gap hitherto blamed on the government.

4:05 a.m.   November 17, 1969

Flu End 3 Darvon sleep dreamt I was in strange city wandering downtown Skyscrapers Newark 1930's Chicago 1980's Vast ancient buildings rising to black sky arrived in old nightclub soul food political song hangout. Saw Leroi with his nose bashed in, broken healed boneless scarred in mid-face—he lifted his eyeball to show me butchered corpse-face the man the Mafia Police Society had done to his body last year—the war wound—the folk I was part of—had shown him Iron force, fist or heel— he pushed his nose aside with thumb and center of his face was flat except for scar tissue gleaming in Night Club light.

We were upstairs part of political gathering from some political Art History Convention connected more with Chicago Winter conspiracy than Panther fellowships of Blacks, as there were dumpy revolutionary girls and stylish white models with black persons lying on giant couch by the entrance door in party meeting room off a corridor which led from Waterfront bar neon jukebox and plastic den—booths overlooking refrigerators in the water down steps below in the basement tides coming in and out gently.

Leroi lying across from me talking a little haughty & intense but close, showing me the damage done his face and warning of the magic he'd

1969

learned as real, the powers he now commanded that were specific miracles of God—

Pray to Kerouac's young soul to transcribe this dream aright—

I had helped him carry some clothes into the next room after we'd lain there talking awhile—I wondered if it was safe here or if the police would raid suddenly fire-bombing upstairs all hell loose & me in middle with others trapped as pair bullets crashed into beds—but there were white persons whitey there so there must be some connection to the Justice Department spies, liberals, or lawyers protecting us from police chaos lying there in the big party bed—

I had dropped one of Leroi's red hip boots into the water below while carrying his clothes to the next room, I negligently pushed the other boot after it and said that's awright—we'd been dozing together finally in the community room pushed close his brown-toed stocking up near my soft crotch on the nod—& then with a lady svelte hostess arranged his works & gathered his possessions and then I noticed, literally as he promised, performed sexual magic, reciting an African Summons Prayer, as the boots lifted themselves humanly out of the water and drifted above the bar-pianos up in the air till they slowly settled into his hands. The hostess noted it as I did, she clutching at Leroi and I marveled at his adeptness, certainly miracles of material power I had no say over and knew nothing about. If he could do that, then he must be right be right in every way. Still, was that magic OK to play, was it right and worthwhile to move boots, & make them fly slowly like that? [. . .]

4:43 am

Had this evening read Leroi Jones' article in Theatre Section Sunday Times & recovering from flu gone to last night's sleep with medicines brooding over his lost love, Kerouac's recent heavy death, drunk hearted, he'd denounced me for politics a month before & I'd written him a week

1969

before a cheerful reply defending Dellinger from his meanish caricature, so thinking on Jack's phrase, "Leroi, soft," slept, lost, much genius soul friends estranged or dead.

5:35 am

. . . leading to the sewers of history where asshole gas disrupts the vomit of the day.

& if I'm enfeebling the Honkie, why doesn't he encourage me for it instead of putting me down like that? Asserting his manhood romantically over mine or [?]? Anyway, Carmichael told me in London "pacify all whites," which I'm doing.

NYC

6 Billionaires that control America
the "Chief insists of Eternity" in
                this present degenerate age
Blake and Kerouac laughing at me
                in the clouds!

G. S. Reading Poesy at Princeton[41]

Gold beard combed down like Chinese fire
hair shining gold over th'oar, braided at skull nape—
gold turning silver soon—worn face young
forehead wrinkled over deep-glanced smile,

41. First draft of "G. S. Reading Poesy at Princeton," *Collected Poems*, 545.

1969

tiny azure earring, turquoise finger stone, Paramita beads centered by
    ivory skull-nut—
On Doer Mountain, in ship's iron belly, sat crosslegged on Princeton
    couch,
body voice rumbling bear sutra to younger selves—her long hair rug, dun-
    gareed legs lotus-postured;
or that half-indian boy his face so serious woe'd by tree suffering
more compassionate to boar, skunk, deer, coyote, hemlock, whale
than to his own now sprung cock. O Lizard Dharma
what doth breath, that Aums thru elm bough & rock canyon loud as thru
    his mammal skull hummed,
hymn to bone-chaliced minds now multiplied over planet colleges
so many, with such cheek hollow gaze-eye tenderness, Fitzgerald himself'd
    weep to see
those celestial faces, students become longhaired angelic Beings on planet
    doomed to see thru too many human eyes—?
What heavenly machine we sit in, Woody Woo's and lounge carpeted cur-
    tained fibred synthetic—
Voice waves from Gary's breast to gentle bellies hardened for genera-
    tion—
Princeton in Eternity! Long years fall, December's woods in snow
alcohol trembling in immortal eyes, Fitzgerald & Kerouac weeping on
    earth once—
The voice moves thru time, old vows and prophecies remembered, moun-
    tain prayers repeated,
earth voice echoing hollow under round electric lamps.

Dec 4, 1969

1969

The specter of the violence during the 1968 Democratic National Convention refused to go away. In late 1969, a group of eight men, indicted for conspiracy to cross state lines to incite a riot, was placed on trial in what has to be one of the biggest judicial farces in American history. Bobby Seale, one of the eight men and a leader of the Black Panthers (who had little to do with the events in Chicago), was gagged and chained to his seat. Seale was tried separately, leaving the Chicago Seven, as the defendants were called, to stand trial.

Allen Ginsberg was one of those called by the defense to describe the events of that week. Before his testimony on December 10–11, he recorded some of his thoughts in his journal.[42]

December 9, 1969

Flying back to Chicago conspiracy trial—read letters from Marquette Jail Cell Revolution from John Sinclair, & Abbie Hoffman's *Woodstock Nation* Reply [. . .]

Now the oval's reversed
Lake Michigan on Bottom Blue
Soft Reflection of Baby Heaven Light
Above, White Clouds streak thick High Roof.

Notes on trial testimony Chicago Dec. 11, 1969

Around Abbie Hoffman
March 17—press conference

42. A transcript of Ginsberg's testimony, *Chicago Trial Testimony*, was published by City Lights Books in 1975.

Foss   Americana Hotel
Collins
Phil Ochs
Al Kooper
Sanders
USA Band
Festival of Life

Meeting on Apt. with Abbie

June—50 letters a day inquiring hassling around permits
Grant Park permit changed to permit for Lincoln Park—they accepted
that.

Report on Abbie called me August 9—report on meeting with David Stahl
(unproductive) urged me to come in—
August 12?—

  Colin Pearson's house meet with Abbie—dinner and told of meet
with David Stahl & Carl Busch; then went to see Gregory—asked about
room—Abbie said Lincoln Hotel—then phone call to farm, no progress.

Meet eat Nite in Free Theatre—August 14—

  Urging people to leave park—also Abbie reported on unsuccessful
meeting with police chief Linsky—& led people out OMing—

Mon Morn 11 a.m. August 26
  Press conference
  Gas began—cannisters
Tuesday morn 6 a.m. beach prayer meeting

1969

Tuesday nite at Colosseum after dinner 8 p.m.
    I went down several seats
    & sat with Abbie—tear gas
    also in front of Lincoln Park—Cross priests—after colosseum—
    after gassing of clergymen
    Abbie in disguise been threatened
    Abbie was arrested Wed.—we met again in Grass on Thursday—

    God's in trouble
  going about as a
      great black cloud
talking out of a thousand
       mouths
worrying if he
can keep peace
as the planet sticks
  its knife in the
    moon's face.

Dream AM December 12, 1969 Chicago

    A little mouse running round the table, falls on the floor, a little
white pus spot flowers on its back, then as it runs more the white flower
opens & it winds still on its back split open white foetus-like inside—body
pulp burst open, dead.

State Street aglitter w/ vibrations, Lights—Chicago

1969

Hope opens the door to Hell

NYC   7 p.m.   Dec 14, 1969

----

each telephone call burns a
                flower
books eat trees.

Om Sri Krishna Kali Ya Mamah

December 21, 1969—Miami Dream—drifting along into a snowbank con-
versation with Bill Graham, I'm shy, explaining paranoia to him, envious
that he respects me—Who began the distrust, he asks about the Mother-
fuckers,[43] and I say, enlarging the debt, "Hitler,"
  And add as the enormity sinks in both of our consciousness "and Stalin
. . . both began the invasion of police agents into human brainwaves"—we
go on down along grove side in snowbanks—he grabs me by seat of pants
to keep me from stumbling—"you still reading?" I say, "yes, a thousand
times, all over nation" embarrassed that he invites me to read at Fillmore
Auditorium and I become in his eyes a money act, so I shy away from the
unspoken invitations he gave years back . . .
  Back lying in bed ashamed to dream revealing my reactionary & chau-
vinism with moneyed entrepreneur since tomorrow I read for Daily
Planet in Miami, paid by them $1200 to C.O.P., & they'll lose money, I
fear.
  I never read the whole, never wrote the whole tale of Haledon Avenue
sex bondage magic spellchickencoop Earl trauma [?] 7-9-10. Dr. Spock
today denounced sex magic books——

  43. Radical activist group in the late sixties.

1969

What effect will *Please Master* poem have on kid minds? on John Snow's boys?

Had lain in bed praying for deliverance from Earth tonite before sleep—I pray more & more, eloquently to my mind now the last few days, unloosed tonite all prayers at once for rendering bonds. Reading *Valentinian Speculation* cosmos theories of pleasure & aeons in Hans M. Jonas book (the Gnostic Religion, Beacon Press).

Dream at Castel Haiti Hotel—

December 26 . . . Silver worm train glittering in sky, shivering cells of the train wavering in heaven above Port au Prince or Miami.

December 27.

Peter or Neal entering a tunnel under ocean with track cross country— they stop to change pillows, stack pills, steal chance or steal perhaps pillows? I'm left behind when they cross Haitian border, see guards delay nervously, & leave me behind holding several plastic vials of drugstore amphetamines, sleeping pills, & psychedelics—

In Petionville, Haiti

Sunday, Dec. 28, 1969—"moulted professionally"

Dream 8 a.m. Hotel Petionville, Haiti

In back of taxi cab with Weston La Barre,[44] discussing the peyote psychedelic cult & my essay on public solitude. I see a paper he's written

44. Weston La Barre (1911–1996) was an American anthropologist and writer *(The Human Animal, The Peyote Cult, The Ghost Dance)*.

1969

that has blue ditto photo style xerox reproduction of an old letter I wrote, describing early peyote trip & recommending it to youths. I say, "Well, I've had further thoughts, questions, reconsiderations . . ." He continues, "all the psychologists who've been in the field, all the anthropologists & psychometric priests have had a professional position, have moulted professionally as a consequence of this experience."

Wake after several days depression, last night creole architect asked me wasn't it a shame the degeneration of Beat Generation he'd read about in *Temps Moderne*[45] into the Hippie style fad: we were standing in front of Hotel Choceroune nightclub door lights where half a hundred cars—limousines & rattletraps—were waiting while music poured out, carry meringue drums from organic baritone, from bowels of the nightclub.

I'd come from "voodoo" ceremony with Louis & Edith, theatrical possessions danced by Katherine Dunham Night Club Artistes—at end they passed out [?] from the mixing bowl & by mistake I tasted a corn kernel, fishy codliver goat pill amanstion all over mouth-roof.

45. *Les Temps modernes* was a magazine published by Jean-Paul Sartre.

1969

1970

Allen Ginsberg's Family, a mural by Richard Avedon photographed
on May 3, 1970, at the Alexander Hamilton Hotel in Paterson,
New Jersey. Photograph copyright The Richard Avedon Foundation.

The frequency and volume of Ginsberg's auto poesy decreased at the beginning of the new decade. He had not grown tired of the form, but his attention was demanded closer to home, particularly at the Cherry Valley farm, which still needed a lot of work. He cut short his spring reading and lecture tour and spent much of the spring and summer at the farm.

The war in Vietnam continued to occupy his mind. Richard Nixon seemed clueless about how to end the violence and destruction. Ginsberg remained one of the war's most visible critics. He brooded obsessively about the fates of Timothy Leary and John Sinclair, both countercultural figures who, in Ginsberg's mind, were being punished with prison sentences for their leadership in radical causes. There appeared to be a conservative backlash to the events of the late sixties, a fight brought into sharp focus on May 4, when the National Guard opened fire on unarmed antiwar demonstrators at Kent State University in Ohio. Four young people lost their lives.

Dream Cherry Valley 21 Jan. 1970

A pipe full of hash at midnight like down in attic "God is the intersection point of all dimensions of being and non-being" ... arrived as definition ... then slept, headache & depression, first time bethought me after reading "Golden lads & girls all must chimney sweepers come to dust" and "Brightness falls from the air Queens have died young and fair/Beauty is far and flower which wrinkles will devour" Garden in his bedroom of the old age of my desire, Lucien asleep in bed in my root quiet & I alone upstairs for the night.

... dreamt in Rome come thru the tunnel in automobile onto marble corridor floors, I got out to see, went thru door & got lost on rainy city street carrying a record album & a bag full of provisions—went looking for my room, lost still arrived at the downtown stadium—last row up our streets whilst the stage far below was visible—folk crowded I all filled up the bowl—I asked a family lady what was playing & she shrank away silent, it was sylphides opening or some WQXR Damrosch popular orchestral favorite—

Anyway, I knew my hotel was several blocks north of the stadium & felt better.

Woke, took Darvon for headache, and aludrox pill for upset stomach, my left eyelid still tearing from temporary paralysis last year,[1] my right skull hemisphere a little sensitive because of teeth nerves subtle erosion exposed at root of upper eyeteeth.

I am sick I must die,

Timor Mortis Conturbat Me.

Jan. 23, 1970

With scientist friend (who?) our visit to suburb side street to Bob Dylan's house—arrive at dusk, I see there's a piano in living room so I can play new song to the musician who, I'm relieved, opened the door and invited us in. But I have to eat first, so I go round the corner (B-way near Columbia 103rd St) to the local Eat shoppe Deli and try to sit down—mothers are moving from shoppe to shoppe, lunch cart to dinette, over orange-shoed argument about the aesthetic of bringing up children—I wonder why I'm wasting my time here on the public street instead of visiting talking singing with Dylan.

---

1. Ginsberg contracted a case of Bell's palsy.

1970

Jan. 25, 1970   Watching Ray Charles

Television always cutting off ecstasy—Bland images—wildness, jazzy genius, poetry, actuality, disease, nakedness, death of anima, ecstasy of animal all zapped off the screen & substituted with predigested ideologic brainwork plastic image of man.

Jan 28, 1970

Riding round in long car from Interview to trial to interview, I notice it's a hearse, curtains tacky but strong. I'd been in court & local poet lawyers had got me out of that scrape after some violently abusive language by prosecuter—"this monster of obscenity & paranoia stalking the classrooms of the effete snobs of the Nation"—arriving back at friend's house's (as in Lowell Jack Kerouac's brother in law) driveway, couple finally lawyers or chemists come out & say I got three phonecalls—newspapers & magazines & radio stations to interview—but I have to go away in hearse to plane or party.

Feb 1, 1970 (7 a.m.) Dream:

Space is a perpetuity Habit
Space Students are Heroes.

Had dreamt I'd gone to funeral with Kennedy's (as I'd been to Olson's pallbearing with poets) and there was a matter of $1,000.00 check I owed or that I owed—to return to the Chancy Estate?—I was sitting at the Funeral table (at Academy poets) wondering who to give it to, and should I give it back—

This re: Harvey Brown's sudden transmit of thousands of $ to COP Inc.

Woke and slept again, dreaming that I explore the foundations of an

1970

issue of *Life* Magazine in a furniture warehouse, & I notice painted on to the end of a 2x4, as if stenciled on each copy of the mag—"space is a perpetuity Habit"

so I think, ah, Burroughs: has been understood by their movie editor?— and a Learyesque influence in "space students are heroes."

Karma+cause/effect relations Ecology.

Dream Feb 2, 1970—

We're in Cuba/Haiti i.e. a military country, walking around, long wide streets perhaps it's a South American palermo because in old low suburb there are a few Grocery stores standing in white light by a school playground—What that?—a young policeman arguing with an older blue suited bureaucrat, looks like the bureaucrat's winning that kinda policestate's that—further down the street two policemen arguing with each other!—

I'm due at the Cathedral. Peter & Gordon accompany me to the services I'm supposed to give—Down a side street I see the last bulk of Rose windowed Cathedral side—& look at our watch when we near the Cathedral steps, I keep insisting on knowing the right time—8:15—we got quarter hour—because I have to go back to the hotel to get prajnaparamita text & Harmonium—wake. They were annoyed at my sudden imperiousness.

White cloud cover, black woods, slushy snow, the coldest weather's past, I still have a month to stay.

Peaceful lamplit pinboard wall,
Top hat battered on a nail,
   Fire rope & afric beads hung
      windowside, gas heater hum\
         inhalation, lamp hiss &

1970

                    Gold Brightness above
A picture of blue oceaned globe, clouds over
            Latinamerica brown andes & green
                Amazon heights rondured
                    mist veiled vast in
                        empty blackvast
photo over Ganges roadstone bath shat
        white robed bathers, Brahmins
        under umbrellas, Vishnuinath's small spires
        rising to shiva near the burning ground
& manikarnika next
                        Rimbaud in oval frame
Tacked up staring thru clear eyes tiny pupils
One direct back to XX century, one turn'd
        Aside photographer's assistant powerflare
                Eternal Time.
Blue Buddha'd Tibetan canvas sewn at edge,
        blue green orange red halo,
            black jewel of world held
One hand on his crosslegged lap,
        Right hand beckoning approval
                bestowing Palm forward
                    at his kneerobe—
Conch shell filled with incense sound
                waves—
Diamond Mexican blanket woolthick woven
        Bedcover, conspiracy capers
        50c class war [?]
Clock ticks, blue plastic stomach
        Ache medicine by bronze match tray
Poems by dead Kerouac booked on
        "Adventures in Poetry" mimeo mag

                    1970

New York Towle Padgett Brainard
    Waldman Saroyan Berrigan
O'Hara Ashbury sat in chairs
    somewhere Mind—overhead Whitman
tacked with push pins in soft pine pillow-wall
    old white beard even-eyed
        grey wrinkle browed sentinel
    open collarflapshirt, grey vest
        thick on his body—
Not long ago Olson had old hair to neck
    & laughed at his own giant tender corpse—
Mouth set serious thin in cancer heart stroke body
        hands folded in coffin-suit
    Ceramic string tie clasp azure at his neck
        seen in Eternal Time,
            "Glorious Charlie!"
Earth given to us this way!
    We who live can only try
        auroras, personae, Maximus,
            Blake Thomas Taylor at bedside—
Books with statues heads Haitian woodcarved,
    brass hash waterpipe, papers
        U.S. Narcotics Bureaucracy Police
        Activity decades back
Boxes of old letters answered, vanity drawers
    filled with xerox mss. essay prose
Against the wall round mirror lifesized Allen
Bearded bald, eyeglasses gleaming gaslight,
Black haired effigy sprightly
    observant in silver glass
under Baron Samedi, his blackface

1970

tophat tails & snaky love,
　　pants creased shiny, holding up
　　creased balance-scales of judgment
　　　　skull nailed, swastika signed
　　　　　　by rumbottle Bible shine
Bank calendar on door, it's Feb 12, 1970
　　Twelve-0-1-A M, exact by tiny
　　　　　　clockticks—
Clothes rack with cloth bathrobe,
　　green parka I climbed Glacier peak
That boy with Chinese beard left guitar
　　leaning against rockingchair—
And the bookshelves of Kabbalah
Milton Dore engraving Zohar
　　Ages grub the Buddhists Tantra
　　　　Guide to stars & planets.
And old small office desk, portable dinette
　　from 2nd hand store, stamp books
　　& pencils, flashlight & Tibetan Mani Seal
Dorje on the Shelf, is that the Baron's top
　　Hat hung on the wall nail
over the kerosene lamp—& the
window glazed opaque water cold
　　snow.

Copy from drafts
　　　　Vingaretti in Heaven
Wrinkled eyes
　　old fawn's mottled ears
White hair whisp'ring round his skull

1970

in heaven business suit,
shrunk body flying over earth
    across seas, thru bedrooms
—crooked-mouth'd cackling laughter
    Echoes from Brazil to Oklahoma.

Pray release the pioneer psychologist Dr. Timothy on normal bond till sentencing. He is considered by many good people to hold honorable if controversial opinions and it is not useful to deny bond and abruptly jail so famous & theorist for his unpopular views—such an imprisonment is proper neither to science nor jurisprudence.

                    Allen Ginsberg
        Guggenheim Fellow Poet/National Arts Letter Grantee

                      Feb. 25, 1969

Telegram re: Leary to Judge

March 2, 1970

Children of Futurity look down
    on America thru cloud time
Weep for the wounds of woe nailed
    into planet hand foot & heart

ITT Data Systems
    (Soulless blue neon)
Paramus, NJ, soulless Paramus

1970

March 3

Get yr guitar
take off your pants
& sing me the blues

March 5

Eclipse

On football field
Old Dominion University
Norfolk—the family
The Sun's white diamond
Ringed by black moon.

Virginia Beach, N.C.

Fags vs. the Pigs in Chicago

Meat fags, gasoline fags, electric fags,
fags Presidential, National fags, vice-
Presidential fags, Abbie Hoffman fags, Judge J.
Hoffman fags, D A fags stool pigeon junky
fags, Mafia fags & Southern Senator Military
Committee Tobacco whiskey Napalm fag
racists, black fag, Arab Jewish
war fags, Chicago Mayor violence fag
Daley addict of real estate Caesar w/ guard.

1970

March 25,

Albuquerque

Nanao—Chanting, free style

"Give me a Koan?"
"—" "Give me a koan!"
"O.K. Where is Ryoanji Garden?"
"I don't know."
"It's a very good answer."
Turning around to make his bed.

Clap Clap Clap Clap! "Which hand making sound?"
"I don't know which."
"Your ears making sound."

Conversation with ?

   There's too much rhetoric & violence,
   Kesey afraid to go out with guns.
   World square & job oriented
      Inflation—lack of jobs
   Go back to non-violent roots
     "Z" movie re Greece

March 26

   Dream near Taos—Young kid on motorcycle comes to pick me up, &
takes me to centertown San Francisco reading—we zoom thru heavy

1970

metal traffic up viaduct under bridge to above Broadway North Beach & stop to get time, see if it is getting late—I have reading that night. I ask him if he's free, he says yes that night's free—I wonder if I should give him $10.00 money keep him happy.

April 2

LA → San Diego by Air

A definite layer of gas, mist gas, haze blanketing the flats of L.A. from plane window seen, the brown fog thickest several thousand feet up grey— opaque, pressed down by the blue ocean of clean air so that above the flat surface of smog, snowpeaks of Mount Whitney tipped through.

Long Beach, Huntington, La Guna, La Jolla—the smog extends along the coastline, rising like grey thick cotton overland behind the thin beach sand border between earth and the ocean set smooth against the continent's flat edge.

Looking back to L.A., the haze profoundly thick, impenetrable, shrouds the entire city in all particulars. And it stretches overland, thinner but still obviously grey—shroudy over the hills as we pass south—A fearful vision, visible to any airplanes voyaging executive manager capitalist decisionmaker.

April 19

Over cloud's bright wooly blanket covering Midwest—plane L.A. jetting to Chicago.

Kerouac dead
I lay in the bathtub looking at plaster cracks in

1970

> the ceiling—
out of this glorious abyss,
What this dirty wall of old matter that closes
> round my mind?

Continuation "These States"

> To New Haven[2]

Spring green buildings, white blossom
> -ing trees, sparse evergreen
> grass on broken brown rocks
by blue sky-mist open asphalt
> car lanes
woodsprig breathing upward
> branch'd to sun in Midheaven
Noon journey under iron braced
> car viaducts over fields
> to red barns under steep
> woodbrown hills—
Ironrusted flat auto streetcars boxed
> on truck & jeep passing
> thru green cut—
"Namu Samanda Motonan," thrice
> New Haven's Mayday picnic
> O Maypole King ah
> Krishnaic springtime
Oh holy Yale Panther Pacifist
> conscious populace awake

2. First draft of "May King's Prophecy," *Wait Till I'm Dead*, 99–100.

1970

alert sensitive—under
children's bodies—and a
 ring of quiet Armies
 round the town—
angelic students cooking brown
  rice for scared multitudes
Oh souls all springtime
 prays you
Quietly pass mantric peace
 Fest grass freedom
 thru our nation thru
 your holy voices' prayers
Your bodies here so tender
 & so wounded with
 Fear
Metal Gas fear, the same fear
 Whales tremble
  war consciousness
Smog City—Riot Court Paranoia
 —Judges, tremble
 Armies weep your fear—
O President guard thy sanity
Attorneys General and Courts
 obey the law
and end your violent
 War Assemblage
Unconstitutionally forc'd
 on us the Populace
O Legislators pass your
 creeds of order
& end by proper law
 illegal War!

1970

Now man sits in acme
        consciousness over his
        machine covered planet—
Springtime's on, for
        all your sacred &
        Satanic Magic!
Ponds gleam heaven
        Black voices sing their
        ecstasy on car radio
Oh who has heard the scream
        of death in Jail?
Who has heard the quiet
        Om under wheel whine
        and drum beat by
railyards outside the
        wire towers outroads
        from New Haven?

Paterson, May 6

Went in Washington to War College Park, into the open building, went upstairs to the Main Automatic Boxer, looking down on center stage (football-field-size) where Ali Akbar Khan school of music was putting on a musicale—everybody in upper row seats dressed white and lacy & powdered—one couple left their seats so I sat down, legs dangling over void, huge drop hundreds of feet to the floor of the stadium below me. Panoramic—I moved a few seats & went around to look closer—

Onstage crowded together an amazing chorus of beggars & as I looked closely fairies & yogis all mass-voiced harmonizing in chorale rising (as one powdered queen kisses t' other on the neck near me onstage) with tablas & tambouras centerstage—a small stage where I'm standing now—

1970

some kind of circus in front—I walk around the building & open a door—
it's the meat icebox, Jerry Rubin or some old friend from WW II is still
the procurement chef—

"Still stealing steaks" I ask as he picks up a couple red eye steaks from
the ice tray—(are we watched by CIA?)—I go to front gypsy-camp doorway
façade—which is probably rear of Arlington Monumental opera house—
& open stride, see the Chinese opera star with long hair singing on the
glass porch, as in a Fortune Telling Machine, I go in interrupting him to
ask where's that Main chorus show I'd been observing before; he halts his
aria to talk points thru a narrow ship's corridor (as Jerry Newman-Ru-
bin's been in ship's iceboxes) & then studies his music paper to see where
he'd left off operatic Canto.

—9:30 AM dream

May 9
White sunshine on sweating skulls . . .

I have no home, no place to die.

Ashbury Reading

Cuffs rolled, Galois in right hand, Double Dress
   on Podium
Watch gleam by microphone, monotone of
   office & blue-striped shirt—
Tie & jacket on a chair, "refreshed & somehow
    younger"
Shaved chin in neon glow, voice in a Coffin of days,
   that average springtime

1970

syntax talking thru war, river food, "mountains
        shaking" but the voice talks
as mind talks, undisturbed & loquacious,
        as cigarette smoke leaves the mouth,
thin shapes of thought trembling in air, forming
        satanic eyebrows & noses,
blue clouds moving thru neon, rivers rolling
        over themselves, brain cauliflowers.

                           May 14, 1970
                           Barnard College Gym

All the elm trees blighted so
      Cut down trunks thick-white
      sawed, but ends of giants greenleafed
          lain on the lawn, on Elm Street
          in Richfield Spring.

May 23   Dreams—7:50 AM

    Bird chirp electric beep out window—

    Louis, Peeter & I upstairs building visiting hermit-spinster's house—
sitting on porch lookin' at moon, there's a blink reflection of Bombs or
flying saucers or Martian flares intermittent as bird chirps—clouds pass
by and I go inside to get away from possible radiation—
    Louis comes inside and walks gingerly on sideboard windowseats—
climbs thru hole-door to kitchen while I cry "Don't make a move" afraid
he'll fall out. Edith says, "He knows where he is, he can see." Pleasing!

1970

May 24

Home a week at farm—peas planted, asparagus beds set by Peter,
strawberries entered in soil, wrote over weekend 53 letters 32 postcards
reply to accumulated mail.

Barnswallows twitter electric
    on telephone wire, redbreast
hops on brown earth, tomato vines, potatoleaves
    shaggy green rows lay low under blue clouds
Horse wags his tail against July fly swarms
The empty hay truck wheezes away from the red barn—
    huge black tyres cracking rocks on the housepath—
Spotted dog settles scratching ears by new mown
    lawn & runs to follow garbagepail to Compost—
farmer stands in yellow sunlight & examines
        carrots—
Trees, transparent cornleaf, yarrow see
    gleam translucent in sundusk—
Mites buzz & waver over my golden haystack—
Car rests burnished, diamonds gleaming bumpers—
windless, maples stand at rest, balanced
    immobile branchtops in silence—
pierced by whistles, chirps, antennae quackles
    sweet cries & pierced earwarbles of the
    Bird Nation—
anonymous city ears don't know—overalls &
    red hat he trudges by the sawdust mulchpile
    already 2 years old in the green grass—
with his idiot brother in yellow gloves—
Peter Orlovsky in Quietude by

1970

gardenside takes off
his shirt
Farmer Bremser's[3] gathered a quart of
strawberries
while the windmill rests.

  "Dear Liszt—in distant cities
where pianos sing your glory—I salute you
in Immortality"—

If one person reads, it's literal Immortality
If no one reads, it makes no difference,
            no one knows the vain gaffes
I'm sitting on a haystack reading
            and writing.

He killed my heart as he always
did, always has, always will

What does he want, what treasure
            dipped in ocean salt
        rubber suited divers haul from Carib
            Galleons sunk with Spanish Gold
        or iridescent dust retrieved from the moon
            & spread on museum shelves,
That boy who follows me from city to city
        accosts me in dark nights, in bare

  3. Poet Ray Bremser was a guest at the farm.

1970

or under suburb streetlamps, holds
my hands, looks in my eye, takes me to a bed
in the slums, & lies with me naked, touching
        my breast and milk skinned hard on,
making love to me all night, wherever I go?

        —May 25, 1970

Dream:

Walking in Paterson up hill and over to the gulch where in ancient times we came to a tender valley at the far end of which rose stone peaks covered with a scraggly briar & elm forest where from our ancestors emigrated from old farms, I remember climbing up the savage hill to desert plateaus—Not a vast mountain range, but half century ago a familiar one, to get there you had to go thru schoolyard fence holes—

Returning to the site—perhaps in the belly of a leviathan ship—& crossing thru a motel

(as on Garret mountain I crossed thru highway construction equipment, great yellow Mafia caterpillar tractors manned by beefy yellow-hat workers)

And down street thru library & rental office of housing project, I came to the Great Divide of Northern Jersey and looked down into the canyon to see the pathways & rivercourses paved with buildings, modern smoothness of clean fresh asphalt and striped concrete—further down on valley floor, apartment complexes, industrial towers & gridworks, smoking chimneys—I can't find the old stone mountain peaks—all the traprock's been covered over to the very top!

I look at people in the Cafeteria-office & realize they all work there, their very presence is summoned by the asphalt, glass, paint, roadways &

buildings—they are all janitors of the robot construction that's destroyed the wilderness—

I begin talking, explaining anguished & incredulous, "You mean *this* is the Passaic Mountains? It's unbelievable! It's too big!! I was here just a few years ago! Who ordered this monstrosity! They *covered* the holy hills! Those hills were sacred here! It was the highest quietest purest recording area between New York and Mexican Sierras! It was rare silence place! This was the only place for meditation & silent recording! It *can't* be dispensed with! It'll all have to be torn down! It means the Death of America! When the hill goes, the Nation Dies! The nation becomes Robot! How dare they create this machine on the living Hill?"

—May 27, 1970

(June 11, 1970)
transcribed from
Sony tape[4]

Dusk in Buffalo, cow meditating head up on the knoll
in the silky sunlit dusk hour
green, with blossoming elm, fat grass, alfalfa
roughening the hills round Richfield Springs—
"Go East, Go West!" The madmen in the city scream—
Madmen in the country jack off in their silky cream.
Myron ploughs for us, sometimes we help 'em do the haying—
That Woodland museum is owned by Drummond's family
down there on Lake Ontario where Natty Bumpo
                                        in his leatherstocking
got the Injuns at the meeting Place,

4. Unpublished auto poesy.

1970

& Cooper built his Giant stone House
      & the Dutch sold all the land—
Mapped out in Amsterdam for money
            Exchanged in Amsterdam
Now Babe Ruth's #3 shirt & bat, and silver crown
            as the King of Swat
Best in Baseball's Hall of Fame—
baseball autographed & greying behind glass
      of the cancerous man who "loved kids"
Petrified creatures, just ahead—Rock Shop—
over the hill past the tiny reservoir—stars and stripes waving
        over the tombstone Mohawk Cemetery—
     fresh flowers scattered
            flag day approaching.

"Bingo Every Thursday" underneath the Spiked Widow's Walk
And on our left the towers of Ilion,
        and on our right a Northern Cloud
Wow! Glories coming down from black Heavens
     Hills ranged transparent—
Signs standing in the field hundreds of feet from the
    superhighway,
   beyond cows, beyond the tombstones on the hill, GULF
        Richmond Utica Services

standing like Spiders on high legs—
     daddy legal legs'
        far enuf away from the legal limit
so you can't bust the sign if you're a conservationist
     or the Governor of the bank.
Airplane flyin over th' American flag at

1970

Schuyler Service Exit, two
Cop cars
    resting like
       Cockroaches at State Police Driveway
and
  God, there's these Creatures tryin get in yr mind
    Banned, Reprehensible, Commercial
      mind-snatchers Banished, doomed
  to wait poised on their long pier feet
    several hundred yards from the Asphalt strip
where the Volkswagen Chevrolets speed by toward
    University destiny.
Two legged powertension electric wires walk up the
          valley
led by the orange sunball behind clouds
and a single spoke of a smokestack,
finger to the sky behind the suburb hurricane fence
protesting from the babies the highway—
one old Barn sags by the city Motel
    brown wood sunk to the ground—
  Stein said "There's no there there"—
  Houses living w/all the anonymity of a Golf Course—
      by the side of the Superhighway—

Green trees under grey sky standing in Animal yoga
  with damp ground
    doing wavy asanas in the wind,
  branches bending west.

1970

June 17, 1970

"Catastrophe"

Thru Path on the Rainbow—Indian songs—
Thru Berkeley Tribe—Jerry Rubin meets Charlie Manson—
Thru Clarel to Jerusalem—Herman Melville meets Hawthorne
    on a beach in England
Thru magazines, mimeo chapbooks, underground newspaper,
Thru letters, thru Diamond Sutra, thru the Zohar,
Thru soap boxes, xeroxes, newspaper clippings,
     plaster labels, theater tickets,
All day I read my *Karma,* I studied cardboard pages and Indian signs—
Till I fell asleep and dreamed of myself & my nation
    in catastrophe,
my home deserted my person in jail my state
     trapped in electric traffic court
all my loves ended, Peter abandoned, Gregory rejected,
    Jack in the Grave,
Earth & planet love in Heaven, man drifting away
    in a ship
falling asleep dying.

----

5 PM Fix Acetate record plant
Phone Gregory, Ticket for Yevtushenko?
O my house of mental cares collapse

I ain't wept enough, not heard the clink of iron—
Meant to bring peace, talked to by Swami,
  But was angry TV at Imaginary Female
  "I'm telling her right now"

1970

Shameful hypocrite self—
Displayed Wrong and Stupid Ego to Nation,
    Had Naomi Babbler
Oh what a big mistake!

Then go to Madison Garden Felt Forum no ticket
    Near Yevtushenko poetize
And back to Kaddish repeated, tears round the family table again—

Forgive me, goodnight God, be with me
    "Our Father . . ."

June 18, 1970—Dream

Walking down Broadway Paterson, carrying manila envelopes—for the phone company Capitalist who lives in an apartment near the library—near the old drug store/luncheonette a block from school #6—The hurricane comes downstreet, trees waving under grey wind-colored sky in purple light, roar of ocean trees agitated dancing—all my packages will get wet—I go in the Boss's apartment to separate out the seals—he shows me how, sticking gum on each envelope that needs closing—"You can stay here, & you'll be paid overtime while the hurricane lasts"—I feel better, safer, but (why'd I yell at Revolutionary Susan Sherman at the COSMEP[5] Conference?) (am I a fink cop out?) (sucking off capitalism?)—(Hurricane=Revolution trouble)—Naomi licked envelopes for Workman's Circle—I typed Gene's exploitative summons all shall be answered—meanwhile I'm safe in the hurricane—It's passing over & we have all our manila packaged prepared.

---

5. Committee of Small Magazine Editors/Publishers.

1970

June 20, 1970—Ill farm dysentery, slept & idled all day.

June 21, 1970

Paul Berkowitz arrived morn, then afternoon Bill Berkson, Jim Carroll, & we looked at Map of America for Southwest mountains & deserts they'd cross on way to Bay area California—and listened to new Dylan Self Portrait album—all differing emotions & moods from corny blue moon nostalgia hokum to hysteric-voiced wight-Isle honk—went to bed finished reading Fiedler's[6] *Being Busted*

and dreamt—I was in Village & as an old family house Hidden Terrace Newark (as I'd also heard from Kerouac—no, Leroi Jones today "Send white students June 16th Election quarters Newark"—Signed menu Amiri Baraka)—

found Dylan's house in Village & invited inside sat talking music, went to illustrate new songs, asked for piano or organ, maybe New Orleans fiddler was there & he have a chord, I aside for a C & Dylan bent his head to laugh with amusement, amazement, that I'd actually learned that smidgen of technical jargon & practical musicianship—he bent his head over to listen & laugh, hiding his head in his arms, I thought—& was going to sing him Blake's spring—when he began to vomit on the floor, thru his bent arms held round his head as in unconsciousness & sleep—so began to try and clean him up—the vomit almost mucous slimy intestinal as if end of a long disease—long sickness—he out cold as if half dead—I rushed to find towel to wipe up floor & in bedroom found his wife half naked pink flesh'd voluptuous nipple bust round bellied lying by cradle with children beside her, she warned off, this was common occasion?—She wouldn't

6. Leslie Fiedler (1917–2003), critic and essayist.

1970

move to help now—I could take care of it myself—(like w/Lucien years later)—so I wiped up floor, then went outside to the sidewalk & lowslung sportscars where I thought I'd left my shoulderbag, but couldn't find it—Dylan's disappeared, taken inside to sleep so we never did get to sing together—

I found Leary's lady friend from N.Y. Alan Watts' friends?—who kissed me & explained she'd rented her house to Dylan family, & in return she's rented for herself this whole Hotel/Motel spanning street with an old wood-Spanish style roofed bridge—and would I stop to look there before passing on to seek out Dylan's house—Did she have the old Number phone—I asked—as she led me past roomful of smoked lox platter—I did myself snatch some red sliced delicacy she held in her hand it turned out in my dreamguilt to be rare roast beefs not belly lox of Fish Saloon—

So we went downstairs thru Max Kansas City Motel Lounge where whitehaired bearded friends gathered old bohemian gossip around cocktail troup—

Dream broke 3 AM & I woke sore stomached & still uneasy—flu'd or dysenteried to pee.

June 28, 12:45 AM

Now I'll never read Zohar Hebrew
Never again go to Santiago de Chile or the
      Island of Chiloé,
Now I'll never lay my body naked on grass
      fingers tracing the Tree of Life on
      my belly
Now I'll never come again into Peter's or
      Neal's corpse mouth,
Now I'll never come crying giving my heart

1970

to strange boys off city streets,
And I'll never lay back bare ass before
        a strong cowboy & feel his veined prick
        push in throbbing steely red—
tender thumbs round my ears—
Now I'll never
        read the history of WWI, or
        Civil War,
Nor aloud mark page after page of Paradise
        Lost—
Nor read Genet's plays, or popular
        novels by Dickens & Balzac—
I'll never dream ice skating, gardening,
        dream gathering technology
Nor any techne for art work or money, now
        I'll never
learn skiing, water polo, daguerreotype
        photography, plumbing & electrical
        contracting, even English curricular
        for practice teaching at Montclair—
Now I'll never live forever, or live long
        enuf to learn Chinese
Much less edit all my mss—Nor
        ever paint great big pictures again
or live in a top floor skylight studio with
        blond singers from La Boheme
& go to museum and concerts together &
        just hold hands & stare at the sky
        clouds all afternoon a block from
        the zoo—
nor wander months in Europe's cathedrals,

1970

> or get married in Vatican—
Now I'll never read thru Saintsbury's
>   3 vols. Prosody
Now I'll never study yoga, nor
>   stay up reading all nite w/out
>   Heavy eyelids—
Now I'll never finish this poem, but
>   Only say
>   Goodnight to all.

I shd keep summer police state Journal—
—looking for night life, food, love, Soho—
nostalgia—I ended calling for Maitreya—

Wake, remembered sad conversation with Peter, he'd secretly spent all his bank money on great stores of Amphetamine, plastic packages later burnt in guilt in trashcan—no now no money more in hiding, tho his checkbook said full.

June 29, 1970

Dream—Moscow Nite—Yevtushenko autobiography renouncing some early escapades which left his friends drunk all night in a hotel—"Nosdrovszner"—"Nozdrovazzer"?—some word for Moscovites

----

July 1, 1970   7 AM

Waking, last night fireflies & rain, anger at Peter & Ray Bremser for drinking, lethargic despair day after day at farm dawdling, letters from Leary in jail & jailed John Sinclair unanswered. Black Panther Court ms. on my desk I need to type eyewitness intro transcripts of conversations

1970

with Aldrich & Bhaktivedanta hanging on bookshelves waiting attention
... birds squealing & chattering in summer fog on mountain field—"I
dreamed I saw Joe Hill last night" song on my mind as I lay in bed kidney
pee pain growing as mind went back over dream ... Jerry Rubin in Jail:
60 days went gossip from Radio ... see today's N.Y. Times?—How long
will I be out ... am I trapped in a Revolution ... Stay home and hide? ...
Mafia controls Chicago courts, Mayor Daley works out of Mafia machine
... read *Captive City* ... Pentagon is a Mafia branch... in irradicable ...
write a letter to the Times, Pentagon is Newspaper Cover ... Caldwell in
Stud Bar Frisco lone Black reporter under Judicial attack ... Gay lib gets
violently mad ... Gordon[7] up early emptying garbage, can hear cans rattle
under bird Chattery maple trees in white mist ... my heart bare in left
breast ... body heavy in bed, sneeze burp into red brakie's kerchief, Ker-
ouac dead ... belly un-yoga'd a bit fat, Peter's bestial abdominal bulge on
porch last night, he yelled at Julius by the Chickenhouse ... my guilt I do
no work on farm, Bonnie[8] or Gordon emptying garbage feeding chickens
7 AM, they work for me, I capitalist provide the cash ... not exactly
lumpen proletariat as Cleaver[9] defines the street man of America ... go
escape to England? ... Help! ... mss. for art works then ... mind churn-
ing, publishers gossip, teeth dawn-sick, gums blood tasting in bed ...
Cuppa Coffee now, or heavyeyed sleep late?—Tweet tweet tweetle—Love
in Jail, love in jail—mice gnawing on cardboard panel between walls ...
jack off in bed alone after my birthdays? too much, should save it for an-
other boy ...

----

7. Gordon Ball, filmmaker, writer, and the farm's manager. Ball's book *East Hill
Farm* is a comprehensive look at life on Ginsberg's Cherry Valley farm.

8. Bonnie Bremser, poet and wife of Ray Bremser.

9. Eldridge Cleaver (1935–1998), early leader of the Black Panthers, wrote *Soul
on Ice*.

1970

July 4, 1970—Orson Welles is in Paris, I go to find him thru Turkish bath labyrinth Place des Vosges finally on Ile St. Louis in huge lobby (as where James Jones[10] lived), I ring buzzer.

The lobby's a huge ornate old marble room—reminds me of old dream recorded otherwhere, wandering thru rotted basements & discovering sex steambaths—

My father Louis always gets in the way here—all these old men that blew me in Seattle—basements representations of Paterson really unconscious?

But I'm on Politic mission to see Orson Welles his voice friendly thru lobby wall electric talkie he instructs me to come upstairs his secretary be there but as I have a cold, himself be retired for the day.

Arriving 10th floor, an elderly but charming grey-templed athletic secretary man cheerfully leads me to huge glassed-in living room—Paul Swan's studio at Carnegie Hall, nostalgias of old bohemian musicians—drapes, photos, ivory tusk, carvings, Viennese posters—Auden's in Bavaria, Virgil Thomson in the Chelsea—

birds chirping on farm, dream disintegrating at 7 AM's yellow sunlight, I'd wakened half an hour or more earlier & seen red dawn clouds reflecting thru trees massed above house out north window.

Had dreamt yesterday morn of black politician friend in Coffin—after reading book *Captive City* (Ovid Demaris) re Mafia total control of Chicago—Newark Mayor Gibson and Leroi Jones on mind this morn too.

Dream July 8, 1970

"You can't say how much there is on appeal, but you can say there is a problem." Waking 7:30 AM to that phrase in radiohead—I'm being inter-

10. Novelist James Jones (1921–1977) won the 1952 National Book Award for his World War II novel *From Here to Eternity*.

1970

viewed on the dream air by a Washington lady friend, we're talking about Police State Conditions in U.S.A. and I'm saying it's not generally known in the middle class but such police state does exist here now in America as it does to great extent in France as it does clearly to consciousness in Czechoslovakia, as per example the exiled author Skovorecky[11] ... "The police state's here for the Panthers, for longhairs in Atlanta, and at the border at Mexico, for sick junkies & healthy grass smokers, for drafted boys struggling thru basic training stockade gunbarrel up the ass, for underground newspapers busted for sale, for students trapped by secret agents, for Universities invaded by gas police, for whole cities paying off Mafia strongarm Corporation Counsels, for bureaucrats controlled by garbage gambling slotmachine Service syndicates, for commuters stuck in broken cars on the smogcovered bridge."

July 13, 1970

Dream I attended a Press Conference, Byron Dobell[12] nominated candidate for Governor—he looked varicose nose—sign of age and maturity that he slip thru the roomful of Political newsmen with his bat—

Gregory here, one day drinking by roadside with Ray—beer cans found in the pond & their smiling faces turned snarling & screaming each other at dusk—Peter drunk also screaming in the garage—second day all calm & a wave of happiness passed thru tranquil grassy yard—yesterday more vodka & screaming and threats of death.[13]

Reading Mafia books last weeks—dreamt "The last three writer essays

11. Josef Škvorecký (1924–2012), Czech writer whom Ginsberg met while in Czechoslovakia in 1965.

12. Byron Dobell (1927–2017) was an American magazine editor, known for his work for *New York, Esquire,* and *American Heritage.*

13. Ginsberg's hopes for a peaceful, pastoral farm setting, drug- and alcohol-free, were often dashed when guests sneaked the contraband into the farm.

1970

by Nixon indicate predilection for violence among National Presidents."
… Meanwhile in locker room we're undressing, he's watching me take off my shirt, I have another shirt underneath and I see he observes that by accident I have a second underwear top beneath my first, as I slip them off my head he's got a scissors knife wrapped in his T-shirt which he, Nixon, sticks out at me threateningly, in fact puts my big toe to earth with point of knife, then opens the giant scissors to sandwich my foot in steel … I resign myself and say "Oh come come now that's against the rules…" but then shut up when I see he isn't going to squeeze the scissors shut over my forearm or leg, tho he keeps his mock gestures slow and serious not cracking a smile. Wake at 7:15 AM, heavy rain, grey sky, sitting duck quacking under the rusty sled where she's nested last 3 weeks, ducklings emerged & died, now she has no eggs under her, but she sits in midsummer.

July 21, 1970—4:30 AM—Dreamt we were arriving across Cosmic ocean in Aeroflot Cabin, ready to exit, with Andrei Voznesensky—at Cabin door I realized the rest of the USA trip would be under surveillance & turned to Phil Whalen who bulked large on line to go thru door, & advised him "once you start out in Russian Poetry Company the CIA keeps us surrounded with passports all the way so watch out—You sure you can stand this Big Brother trip? Because anyone going along crosscountry can't stop & get off till it's over. Meanwhile we're held up at cabin door & Voznesensky looks at Phil & jokes "you sure you are laying off Gary?" meaning to joke in lightheaded way, because Phil's so fat & might have fattened himself up by devouring his friend poet for food—"you sure you're laying off Gary?"

Gregory here on farm, two weeks now, & Gordon Ball with a violet bruise under his left eye—

1970

screaming to the bottom, "Assholes," drink anguish with sour cream on unsuspected finger tucking in the cigarette holed shirt.

July[14]   6:25 AM

Bird tree in humid dawn gold stillness I'm awake suddenly after mournful legal dream—Judge Hoffman[15] or another, a huge area's gathered, folk & defendants listening as he addressed audience, it's long after the trial, I go upfront to grassy seat at edge of semicircle near his bench in open park—he sees me & stares I sit stolid observing—all silent—and someone in audience cries out of commits contempt of court & runs fast to elevator exit—Hoffman runs after him motioning to Court attendants to grab the middle-aged objector—the victim slips past marblecolumned corners & would slip away from Guard's grasp when a space warp in my eyeball tricks him into walking too slow & suddenly the guards catch him under Hoffman's direction. He's returning to the Judge Bench, & in witness stand meanwhile Rolling Stones, having testified day before, are returned in calico drag with breasts nearly bare, dress fronts undone showing a slash of abdomen, in frilly country hats—and filed down from jurybox they're ready to sing *Ruby Tuesday*.

Waking as every day for months to Country, the heavy fear of police state continuous body depression at dawn—today Maretta Greer arriving by bus, kicked out of Pakistan—weeping on telephone—or Gregory in

---

14. Ginsberg lumped the next few entries under this "July" heading without offering specific dates of composition. They were recorded sometime between July 30 and August 6, the next dated entry.

15. Judge Julius Hoffman presided over the Chicago conspiracy trial.

1970

Buffalo solitary & drinking to angry tears—Sinclair in jail, revolutionary underground Press rolling out pretty-paged bad poetics—

July 30—8 AM—I'd been traveling abroad with Louis—we'd set up a little love nest in Mombasa—at least he'd taken a little sentimental care to arrange the walls of his study, putting cork boards up, covering a few square feet of wall, on which he framed the few photo/painters we'd been given—his own silhouette painted red-green especially—I looked at it & regret there was no more clearly visible face featured, once he dies there'll be no more face to see. Woke sad.

Preface to Timothy Leary's Jail Notes[16]
  Exquisite Religious Covenant—Leary's jail xerox

Read Leary mss. all nite to 4:30 then slept thinking need he be Acid Messiah, there's the Drugs already, need no more, they're there uncrucifiable—sleeping wake at 11:30 AM dreaming of Jean Genet—
          must've been the Chapel at Yale or Gettysburg or Duke, I was waiting to go on as guest after long period wherein I was part of Adult Education Program as a student—I flashed that it was curious I'd been at my age & stature as poet enrollee in Adult Education Poetry Course under an old tired teacher teaching composition by remote surprise or rote wise it was an isolated place like a mountain top radar relay station—feeling of slipping by police surveillance—waiting for class transporting contraband—arriving early dawn ... old lady goes into ladies' room & I saunter across courtyard to slip into telephone-booth-sited fold-

16. Ginsberg wrote the Introduction to Timothy Leary's *Jail Notes* (New York: Douglas Books, 1970).

1970

ing Men's room door ... In class we're going to discuss Genet ... the teacher already's gossiping, yes he says he's a complete case of thick cock Satyrhood—rimmed so badly his ass rim's red—can't use it perpetual in-flammation—They say between waking and appearing for breakfast he has to come at least 5 times to get his nerves steady ... I object saying it's obviously a lot of silly polite gossip or schoolcriticesque twaddle ... we wind up the lecture class laughing ... I still wake with the sensation I'm being followed.

What Ran Thru my Head on the Haystack

at sundusk weedrows
    standing in a corner of the garden
clang of pail in meadow "Bessie"
                    called from the Woods
horse neigh, and birdwhistle continues
    changing in back of the hills' brain—
cheep twitter cheep cheep twitter grill chirp
    Peter whistling to the pig, guitar
        plunks, strangers
arrived needing wood refuge, sent away
       with $20, couple on the road
The Dakini on farm dreams of Ladakh
      would leave in a day
Leary's spirit abroad, the velvet brown
      mushroom Teoanacatl god image
worshipped with the Three Jewels—
      Not read Sinclair's mail some
weeks, yet every morn first
      troubled thought for his
      Suffrance—

1970

and I am observer—to the Farm
   vegetables leafy headed row—
Green zucchini leafs flopeared
   together the spotted dog pads by
Ducks quack against twitter peawit—
   toot T'whistle
Radha & Godly dogs up gruff
   eyed smellnose
at Marijuana Fed-car cruising the
   dirt road behind the woods—
No, neighbor at sunset in Jail
   iron boxes, metal lacing
   Concrete houses—
Nature's serpent-eyes glittering—garter
   snakes curled into hay bundle
   tunnels—
an observer, weather music,
   or Notal moment languaged.
   or Teoanacatl worshipper
   too rare where priests suffer—
not got hi 1967–1970 till a mushroom
   button yesterday divided the jewel ferns
—Black Stone gang in the Times & Mafia?—
Mind too divided—Farm Silence
   or India escapeless snowy Karkoram North
—to answering mail poorly, & not
writing Sinclair. a torment
   of mind babble person
figuring taxes, call my
   brother, my lawyer, my
   agent, my publisher,

1970

    my friend in jail's lawyer,
Ugh! The desk littered with phone
    numbers and undecided paper
    business—whole comic strip
    books suppressed by Police
         —Zap!
Mind elsewhere on the haystack, my
    Kundalini, impossible arched
    potbellied uncomfortable in
haystack too bored to move—
    eyes closed dreaming of
        Huey Newton,[17]
should we let the pig off his collar
    in the weeds near the
    garden, or down by the cows tree?
Stars & crickets, last time I
    listened to the tiny rings
    grass floor firefly games—
& stars assembled in the wheel
    ring, hourglass & Pythagoras' jeweled
Constellations rolled across night's Clear Space
Sun down orange, glow
    between pines on the ridge—
one pea-wing on the telephone wire,
    and a redbreast hopping the
    greensward by
        the carwheels—
go to India with Maretta? Go lecture
    in Australia? Go stay
    my old Father.

17. Huey Newton (1942–1989) cofounded the Black Panther Party.

1970

> Go get an Agent—

Go in at farm bell ring eat vegetable
> supper.

> 8:10   6 Aug 1970

Raw moon
> diamond white
my own skull empty
> 'll be peace

7:30 AM Aug. 8, 1970

Leaving house with landlady & Ray Bremser after having paid week's rent in advance—it came to 9 francs or pesos or Czechoslovakian banknotes—the small ones—It must've been downtown Hungary—the old lady had a big two-family house left over from the war—so instead of paying daily I paid a full week, to settle matters—Ray in lobby down on his knees collapsed as I passed, just as she was following us down steps, he kissing my thigh in gratitude—I was embarrassed & avoided him—afraid she'd see—So we set up house in police state, like [?].

August 9, 1970   6:50 AM

Panic—I lost my harmonium, it was Peter's & I'm in a big theater at Yale invited to read, it's time to get into the Auditorium, maybe it's Australia, I can't find my way back to the Professor's office, I'm lost, I panic and begin calling "Help! . . . Someone please help me!" so the ladies lined up as ticket-taker-elderly usherettes move anxiously, & one greyhaired matron steps out to take me in hand—meanwhile I've got my shoulderbag, but a whole carton of cigarettes sticks out, red Pall Malls, & I get afraid Peter'll see me in the corridor smoking.

1970

August 13, 1970

"Then blind Salinas spoke" . . . fragment from dream . . . no remember.

waking

8 AM after headache rise 4:30 AM—Pete been ill, says work himself to sickness so he won't think of Speed. I wanna get rid of cows horse pig rest & simplify farm so's there's less work right now hydraulic ram needs daily adjustment dry august water level so low the ram drains the ceramic ground well-shaft of its minutely gallon & half flow, & stops. Need to dig and pipe supplementary well.

Barn needs roof-slats tacked, tin to stop rain from wetting winter [?] store, pig lady needs concrete floored pole sided pen, meadow needs barbed wire fencing, basement needs earth built up outside foundation wall to protect from winter wind the new built door & wall made of cinderblock we put in last year. If we don't get that wall heaped with earth or insulation as good as 4 feet below first line, all the vegetables we're canning'll freeze crack & spoil & the dry punkins & zucchini'll crystallize in October to rot and a rabbit hutch need be built. Porch needs fixing. Papers accumulating got to be taken off the lawn to Richfield Springs used paper, bottles sorted stored for re-use or dragged off to the dump one Saturday. Send for new propeller for the wind charger. Build bookshelves for the overflow, find a place for storage of historic underground press—

Prune the useful apple trees, & fence the new planted orchard & strawberry & asparagus patch. Get a tractor to plough up some open fields before they get too filled with willow bushes & chokeberry so we can plant timothy & clover & hay for the milk bearing beasts. Dig up the old tombstone from the path in the tiny cemetery of the Millson's under the apple tree. Build a few hermit's huts here & there in woods or meadows by trees—

1970

on farm house porch, thru maple boughs, full white moon
on shale car path by the cabbage row
        crickets, grasshoppers, unknown insects' music's
           electric zither rasping over field grass
      covering ground with tuneful chirps
          under moon's broad light flood
             platinum over shale shadow
         trees blotting blue sky
            stars sharp and few
Later I wore black hat over my brow, playing organ
      Chords in kerosene light
    A minor midnight gleaming
        stroboscope mid brain glimpsed

Aug. 18, 1970

Dreamt other night, of Huey Newton, the supple chested Panther, and also that I'd brought a pack of cigarettes to smoke.

        Nadir of disorganization, no flashlight at bed table, clock off time, three lights out in row, as thump of police dogs sniffing grass on attic's rough board crack, fire truck pulls past dream lawn, I bump head eye'd shudder heart's blood the weakling . . . nadir of fear, waking the police arrived at night, that time come then grave's shadow stretches over my thought, halfway—cough woke, red lit firetruck pulling in lawn for grass raid, high blood pressure fear shakes body up out of sleep—open eyes, no flashlight, nor ashtray, art provisions lapsed, grey fear and heavy eyes, no clock set for point clarity—mouth soured by a week's cigarettes—irritation yesterday not smoking I went back to bed depressed all morning—money lapsing, letters unanswered, Leary in jail, Sinclair in jail, war roaring silently on TV news, electric battery windmill too weak to depend on for day's work recording with new glittering xerox machine, days here long, I lost at organ keyboard fingering awkward "Can I see Another's Woe" ah Leary and "Sweet Sleep a Shell"—would I could sleep peaceful and not wake repeatedly in dark night uneasy, disturbed, unprepared, heartsick, heavy eyes ... body attacked, breakdown of physical tissues, heart [?] high blood pressure, wakeness, difficulty, no flash, demoralization of material shadow of the grave moving thru dream & wakened thought, eyes closed, effort wakened—grass in cracks of attic floor or near land or planted on me by State Pink-Firetruck's spotlights begin the weary money law trial—take out ads in pennysaver & convince the neighbors it's hopeless persecution & police state—costs too much to hide in this no-refuge anxious utopia, eating cake.

Dawn Light—
"Glory of Moral Order & energy shining round Dante's face"—he had strength & order to create scaled composition—my own affairs stupid chaos of unanswered letters from Leary to Poet's youth letters piling up round me—Huey Newton has a clearer path? At least can get up & speak from direct experience of prison guards' brutality & state folly & viciousness ... remote & cowardly away from city I rot tied to my own karmic feebleness, caretaking Julius half resentfully ... loving no one ...

Not even the hydraulic local electric wind charger system's working— and have made half a dozen folk dependent on myself for food, & laid down sobriety's dead rules for fear of police & neighbors ... all I need's more bedbugs, my cheek's bit Roo Coo Cooo Coo Coo chickenhouse dawnlight, wrongset clocktick sunrise, the animals awake wait us lazy guards of their prison, goats tied up in red barn I fitful sleep, I keep hearing call of chickens till quarter of seven is it?—I better get up, can't sleep for these thoughts. Didn't smoke all day yesterday—

* * * * * * * * * *

Consciousness expansion 10:30 p.m., August 22, 1970 Saturday evening, drowsy, reading prose poems on back in bed, eyes closed & few minutes later woke in gas light, a slight ache above left heart.

1970

* * * * * * * * * *

John Sinclair's still in jail 10 years/1 joint to agent impersonating dish-wash hippie family helper for art's sake. John wrote me half a year ago vi-olence & arms alas only way out this "white panther" path for him & [?] Pandemon—& thus I neurotically never wrote him back & he haunts my night musings—is now rain at 3 AM.

How's Skoversky the English [?] and his ex-actress refugee, sleeping in tent in the rain? So dark—are they ok?—Should I go to find out?

John Sinclair my cowardice, I wake up nightly haunted by his con-science.

September 1, 1970 Dream 6:40 AM

On way to Hong Kong hop, piloted in small plane by Japanese-Amer-ican friend now film director at Museum of Modern Art—

Searched by doctor who has to examine & pass us for Typhus—he finds hashish smuggled in our boots?—or in the Pilot's lavender underwear or small possessions—We're sitting at his desk, we were ready to get on ship delivering goods & arms & beds to War Zone Capital South Indochina—caught in that larger action, yet he's tripped the pilot up particularly with possession—We have confab—so "What're you gonna do with us?" He says he has to make preliminary police report simultaneous with medical re-port on our bodies for ship working—"What kind of rap or sentence is that?" He says he's not sure, but has to go thru with it, it may be only a formality given the vast war scene we're trapped in.

Brooding over weeks—in newspaper, a black group shot together with judge they kidnapped in mid-court trial—reading between newspaper lines saw the black man had won a hung jury previously on charge of as-saulting a San Quentin guard—San Quentin Neal'd been in for 2 ½ years set up by police for 2 sticks of grass in exchange for a ride downtown to

1970

S.P. terminal in his Brakeman's uniform—that he'd announced to jury before leaving "I had been unjustly accused"—that a huge fat District Attorney started the violent shoot out—that the court—break was obviously from scant date unrelated together in NY Times in any one day, valorous break-thru in net of Circumstance weaved by jail court police in S.Q. guards to murder or cripple the prisoner—Christmas?

Same week Tupamaros kidnapped an "American diplomat" in Uruguay to exchange for 150 political Prisoners—and shot him on Government refusal to deal—& U.S. newspapers particularly Times denounced breaking rules & disturbing diplomats—and several days later quoted [?] police chief to say that Diplomat Mitrione working for AID a U.S. paramilitary police agency, had been training secret antiguerrilla police & had "used torture" in his work.

The disturbance in both above newspaper public shockers is that liberal "media" i.e. N.Y. Times had violent editorials in both cases denouncing assault of law & order & neglecting the fact that in one case the Prisoner was being framed & assaulted by police bureaucracy & threatened with endless jail for *supposedly* & probably not actually assaulting his captor, and Mitrione the Diplomat in Uruguay father of children was a eyeglassed straight-lipped secret police specialist, in an occupying bureaucratic army, in a foreign country, who specialized in police state style torture.

Day after day such atrocities fill the newspaper while war goes on in Indochina larger—larger—U.S. now bombing Laos, Vietnam, & Cambodia from Thailand.

Sept. 2, 1970 4 AM

In rural hamlet, butchering a pig—the pig is set up ass down head to ceiling & hung there & puffed up with air tube. I saw the prune-like asshole distended as the body ballooned out—

1970

Our farmhouse pig don't Bite Me with Pink Satanic skin ears sleeping in the barn under crystal stars of chill fall night.

I see the distended body's that of human—it looks athletic-corpsed, still twitching headless, Peter in overalls sprawled on knees shoulders pitched to ground—or Neal's body in position helpless brainless legs spread buttocks up to be fucked, or football Jack's his legs flapping unstrung down on the floor—Was the head really gone?—the arm raised up as if to wipe nose, Neal's gesture, but missed a neckless trunk-hole!

The chicken I saw age 7 flapping around barnyard in New Jersey, blood spouting hysteric noises out of chopped erect neck; the lamb I saw in Birbhum sacrificed to Vishnu's name, flapped on the floor, bouncing between Brahmin's legs.

—I twitched in sleep, rousing to wake my body moved eyeless in bed—suddenly eyes opened, a headless body opened its eyes and saw it had been a twitching unconscious corpse.

Went out on grass to pee—Pleiades assembled over Maple tree bulk, Milky Way thick banded over Heaven.

Sept. 4, 1970

"Bland Rhadamanthus beckons him; salt blood blocks his eyes"—Laurel & Hardy?

Went to bed on the couch exhausted & drunk—they'd spent the last hour of their reunion sitting up, fat Oliver Hardy at the end of the couch sunk down by the round arm rest waiting to win his bet that the spit curl rising above his ear would stay down for at least an hour if he wet it with his finger dipped in boilermaker whiskey beer & smoothed it in place—during which our Stan Laurel'd sit next to him on couch back crosslegged like a faun getting drunk observing the hair-look & reminiscing exactly an hour about old times. They get groggier and groggier till Laurel lays his head against Hardy's shoulder bulk and murmuring sweet nothings like "Fill me your old time oomph" falls asleep halfway & then, uncomfortably

1970

poised, climbs down on the floor, just like I did in slavish worship thinks the dreamer, and curls up in his pants head pillowed on his two hands to die into devoted sleep at his old friend's side, beneath his gaze—& I waked forgetting Laurel & Hardy but remembering "Bland Rhadamanthus" after mind ran over the hour & all last night's sad letters to an Attorney General claiming the CIA might transport junk[18] for MEO tribesmen via Air America in S.E. Asia, & that, of 85% world's illegal junk supply made in S.E. Asia, much finds market in U.S. on account of Narco Bureau salesmanship of junk & the junk problem.

Ecologue[19]

In a thousand years, if there's History
America will be remembered as a nasty little
                              Country
full of Pricks, a thorny hothouse rose
                              bright & rotten swift
Cultivated by the Yellow Gardeners,
"Chairman Mao" for all his politics, head of a Billion folk,
              folk, important because old & huge
       Nixon a dude, specialized on his industrial
                       Island, a clean paranoiac Mechanic—
              An impertinence, irrelevant tribe, a side issue
Earth rolling round, spies on archaic tongues
                       fishermen telling island tales—
all autos rusted away,
                       trees everywhere.

18. Ginsberg's research led him to believe that the CIA was heavily involved in dope trafficking in Southeast Asia. His song "CIA Dope Calypso" (*Collected Poems,* 1,000) details the evidence he had gathered.

19. First draft of "Ecologue," *Collected Poems,* 550–60.

1970

At East Hill Farm. Back row: Peter Orlovsky, Denise
Mercedes, Julius Orlovsky, Gordon Ball. Front row:
Allen Ginsberg, Bonnie Bremser (Frazier), Ray Bremser,
Gregory Corso. Photograph by Allen de Loach.

Reading Whalen Falling asleep—
     Going nowhere
          on highway 17 north
   I got time to cure a foot,
        plant a tree for 10 years later,
           & eat the year's plums
              & Apples.
    Rough wind roar, maple tops mass
       shaking in window,
         a panic Cry from the garden
   Bessie Cow's loose near the Corn!

The little dakini playing her bells
    & listening to late baritone Dylan
  dancing in the living room's forgot almost
      th'electric supply's vanishing
        from the batteries in the pasture.

Chairs shifting downstairs, kitchen voices
    Smell of apples & tomatoes bubbling on the stove.
Behind the chicken house, dirt flies from the shovel
    hour after hour, tomorrow they'll be a big hole.

The editor sleeps in his bed, morning Chores are done,
    Clock hands move onward, the pig roots by flagstone
      pathways, papers & letters lie quiet
         on many desks.

   Books everywhere, Kaballa, Gnostic Fragments, Mahanirvana &
Hevajra Tantras, Boehme Blake & Zohar, Gita & Soma Veda, somebody

1970

reads—one cooks, another digs a pighouse foundation, one chases a Cow
from the vegetable garden, one dances and sings, one writes in a note-
book, one plays with the ducks, one never speaks, one picks his guitar, one
moves huge rocks.

> The wind charger's propeller
> > whirrs & trees rise windy
> one maple at woods edge's turned red.

Chickens bathe in dust at house wall,
> rabbit at fence wriggles his nose
> > bends to a handful of Cornsilk,
> dogs lie on wet ground
> > fly lights on windowside.

At the end of a long chain, Billy makes a Circle in grass
> by the fence, I approach
> > he stands still with long red stick
> > > stretched throbbing between hind legs

Spurts water a minute, turns his head down
> to look & lick pee squirt—
That's why he smells goat like.

Brahms & Shiva's beards & knee fur are
> > Matted with thistles, they baa in the field
> > > & stand still as I pass, watching—

The horse by barbed wire licking salt
> lifts his long head and neighs
> as I go down by willow thicket
> > to find the 3 day old heifer.

1970

At bed in long grass a hundred flies
        sit on her wet brown fur
her mother stands, nose covered with flies.
        Her big sister Cow moves close
           To be scratched behind small horns.

The gas tank truck rolls down the gravel drive—
        A hole's been dug for the copper pipe—
           Dogs rush forward barking.

The well's filled up—
        the Cast iron ram
          that pushes water uphill
            by hydraulic pressure
              flowed from gravity
      Can be set to motion soon,
           & water flow in kitchen sink tap.

Some nights in sleeping bag
        Cricket singing networks dewy meadows,
      white stars sparkle across black sky,
falling asleep I listen & watch
      till eyes close, and wake silent—
        at 4 AM the whole sky's moved,
a Crescent moon lamps up the woods.

& last week one Chill night
          summer disappeared—
    little apples in old trees red,
      tomatoes red & green on vines,
    green squash huge under leafspread,

1970

               corn thick in light green husks,
sleepingbag wet with dawn dews
          & that one tree red at woods' edge!

Louder wind! they'll be electric to play the Beatles!

At summer's end the white pig got so fat
         it weighed more than Georgia
             Ray Bremser's 3 year old baby.
     Scratch her named Don't Bite Me under the hind leg
         and she flops over on her side sweetly grunting,
             nosing in grass tuft roots, soft belly warm.

Eldridge Cleaver exiled w/ bodyguards in Algiers
Leary sleeping in an iron cell,
         John Sinclair a year jailed in Marquette
Each day's paper more violent
          War outright shameless bombs
               Indochina to Minneapolis—
a knot in my belly to read between lines,
          the lies, beatings in jail
language replacing broken noses—
               Short breath on the couch—
Declaration at dawn in bed—
         wash dishes in the sink, drink tea,
               boil an egg—
brood over Cities' suffering millions two hundred
             miles away
           down the oilslicked, germ-Chemicaled
             Hudson river.

1970

Ed[20] comes down hill
        breaks off a maple branch
                & offers fresh green leaves to the pink eyed rabbit.

Come out of the kitchen door with a handful of cabbage leaf
            the white rabbit runs to the chickenwire
                  & stands waiting, alert.

Under Birch, yellow mushroom
           sprout between grassblades & ragweed—
      Eat 'em & you die or get high & see God—
                  Waiting for the exquisite mycologist's visit.

Winter's coming, build a rough wood crib
        & fill it with horse dung, hot horse dung,
            all round the house sides.

Bucolics & Ecologues!
        Hesiod the beginning of the World,
                Virgil the end of the World—
& Catullus sucked cock in the country
        far from the Emperor's police.

Empire got too big, cities too crazy, garbage-filled Rome
            Full of drunken soldiers, fat politicians,
                movie businessmen—
      Safer, healthier life on a farm, make yr own wine
            In Italy, smoke yr own grass in America.

20. Ed the Hermit, one of Ginsberg's neighbors.

1970

Did Don Winslow the mason come look at the basement
      So we can insulate a snug root cellar
              for potatoes, beets, carrots, radishes, parsnips,
         glass jars or corn & beans
Did the mortician come & look us over for next Winter?

Black flies walking up and down the metal screen,
             fly's leg tickling my forehead—
        "I'll play a fly's bone flute
        & beat an anti's egg drum"
                    sang the Gulch Quechua Injun
                    high on Huilca snuff in Peru
                    Mediaeval DMT.

Phil Whalen in Japan
        stirring rice, eyes in the garden,
             fine pen nib lain by notebook.

Jack in Lowell farming worms, master of his
            miniscule deep sore.

Neal's ashes sitting under a table piled with
        books, in an oak drawer,
            sunlight thru suburb windows.

O wind! spin the generator wheel, make Power Juice
To run the New Exquisite Noise Recorder, & I'll sing
          praise of your tree music.

Pond's down two feet from drainpipe's rusty top
       Timothy turned brown, covered with new spread manure

1970

sweet smell in strong breeze,

it'll be covered in snow couple months.

& Timothy covered in snow in San Luis Obispo?

His mind snowflakes falling over the States.

Squash leaves wave & ragweed lean, black tarpaulin

plastic flutters over the bass-wood lumber pile

Hamilton Fish's Congressional letter

reports "Stiffer laws against peddling smut"

flapping in dusty spiderwebs by the windowscreen.

What's the Ammeter read by Windmill? Will we

be able to record *Highest Perfect Wisdom* all day tomorrow,

or Blake's *Schoolboy* uninterrupted next week?

—out in the garden

rain falls over the grass, leaves, roofs,

rain on the Laundry

Fine rain-slant showering the grey porch

Returnable Ginger Ale Bottles

on the wood rail, white paint flaked

off into orange flowered

blossoms

Out by the garden haystack,

No gardensnakes today, too damp

To sun on a ledge of dried grass.

*   *   *

Night winds hiss thru maple black masses

Cassiopeia zigzag

Milky Way thru cloud

1970

Grey light shine from
            farmhouse window upstairs
       empty kitchen wind
            cloud wet grass

                           September 4, 1970

The baby pig screamed and screamed
           four feet rigid on grass
         screamed and screamed
              Oh No! Oh No!
       jaw dripping blood
             broken by the horse's hoof.

Slept in straw all afternoon, eyes closed,
          snout at rest between paws—
     ate hog mash liquid—two weeks
             and his skull be healed
     said the Vet in overalls.

That bedraggled duck's sat under the door
        June to Labor Day, three hatched
            yellow chicks dry fur bones found
              by the garage side—
    two no-good eggs left, nights chillier—
          Next week, move her next
             to the noisy chickenhouse.

We buried lady dog by the apple tree—
        This mama's two spotted puppy litters
     All except one Radha daughter
         sniffed her bloated corpse, flies

1970

whisping round eyeball & dry nostril,

sweet rot-smell, stiff legs, anus puffed out,

Sad Eyes chased the milk truck & got killed.

How many black corpses Andrew they found in the river

Looking for Goodman, Cheney, Schwerner?[21]

Man and wife, they weep in the attic

after bitter voices,

low voices threatening.

Broken Legs in Vietnam!

Eyes staring at heaven,

Eyes weeping at earth.

Millions of bodies in pain!

Who can live with this Consciousness

And not wake frightened at sunrise?

The farm's a lie!

Madmen growing giant organic zucchini

mulching asparagus, boiling tomatoes for winter,

drying beans, picking\ cucumbers

sweet & garlicked, salting cabbage for sourkraut,

canning fresh corn and tossing Bessie husks—

Marie Antoinette had milkmaid costumes ready,

Robespierre's eyeball hung on his cheek

in the cart to the tumbril—

Black Panther's teeth knocked out in Paterson,

red blood clotted on black hairy skin—

Millions of bodies in pain!

21. Andrew Goodman, James Chaney, and Michael Schwerner, three civil rights activists, were murdered in Mississippi in June 1964.

1970

One by one picked yellow striped soft potato bugs off withered brown
leaves

      dropped them curl'd up in kerosene,
          or smeared them on ground with small stones—
Moon rocket earth photo, peacock colored,
             tacked on the wood wall,
     globe in black sky
        living eyeball bathed in cloud swirls—
            Is Earth herself frightened?
              Does she know?
Oh No! Oh No! the continuous scream
        of the pig
             Don't Bite Me in the backyard,
             bloody jaw askew.

Uphill on pine forest floor
     Indian peace pipes curl'd up thru dry needles,
     half translucent fringes, half metal blossom

Small dam's logs & twigs silted
     hold up small pond water
           trees gnawed down, fallen across creek bank,
     fish gathering minnow rippling surface
     frog sat half out on mud shallow
          & stared at Universe—
So many fish frog, insect ephemera & old Hemlock
        thick rooted on a mossy bank
          hung over swamp fern
     —so many Ezekiel wheeled Dragonflies
          hovering over creek marsh grasses
They won't even know when humans go

1970

Waking 2 AM clock tick
                    What was I dreaming
          my body alert
                         Nanuya princes at heart, breath heavy?
     Justice Dogs sniffing field for Grass Seeds?
        Would they find a little brown mushroom button
                              tossed out my window?
                    FBI read this haiku?

Four in the morning
                    rib thrill eyes open—
                              Deep hum thru the house—
          Windmill Whir? Radar Blockhouse?
                    Valley traffic 5 miles downtown
When'll Policecar Machinery assemble
                              outside State Pine Woods?
               Refrigerator jet, gas water heater
                              air vent?
          Head out window—bright Orion star line,
               Pleiades and Dipper shining silent—

Bathrobe flashlight, uproad Milky Way
          Moved round the house this month
—remember Taurus' Horn up there last fall?

White rabbit on goat meadow, got over the chickenwire circle?
          Hop away from flash light?: Wait till Golly
                              Wakes up!
Come back! He'll bite you! Here's a green beet leaf!
                    Pwzsxt! Pwzsxt! Pwzsxt!

Tiny lights in dark sky
          Chirps singing tall grass

1970

Stars & Crickets everywhere
Electric whistle-blinks
tweedle-twinks
Squeak-peeks
planet
zephyr sizzle
Squinks

Grasshoppers in cold dewy fall grass
Singing lovesongs as they die.

* * *

Morning, the white rabbit stiff, eyes closed,
lain belly up in grass, tooth nosed,
beside the manure pile—dig a hole
—Shoulda introduced him to dogs in daylight—

Cripple Jack drove up
to judge the ducks—
All eggs sterile,
smashed on rock, wet guts
& rotten-throat smell—
Bedraggled duck mother,
dragged off straw nests
& pecking skin at my wrist,
All afternoon walked up and down quacking
Thru chickenwire fence

Pig on her side woke up,
slurped beet juice, rooted at porch wood
ignorant of broken head bones—

1970

Green corn, big cabbage, oversized squash, peak tomatoes
                   & dry onions
        Sent to neighbors up hill—

Attic window lit between trees,
        Clouds drift past the sickle moon
       Morning dew, papery leafs & sharp blossoms
               of sunflower ripped off battered stalks,
         Who'd do that! Too late
           To fix the barbedwire fence,
              Intelligent Bessie Cow strays in moonlight.
Leary's climbed the Chainlink fence & two strands of
                  barbed wire too[22]
             This weekend, "Armed & Dangerous,
               Signed with Weathermen!"
           Has Revolution begun? "World War III?"
May no Evil Eye peek thru window, keyhole or
            Sunlight at his white haired face!

Now's halfmoon over America,
       leaves tinged fall red blush scattered overhill,
       down pasture singular trees orange foreheads think
            Autumn time in pines—
The maple at woods' edge fire-red's brighter
Australian Aborigines' Eternal Dream time's come true—
Usta be bears on East Hill; fox under the old Hemlock,
Usta be otter—even woolly mammoths in Eternal dream time—
Leary's out in the woods of the world—cockroaches immune

22. Leary executed a daring prison escape and fled to Algeria, where he stayed
with Eldridge Cleaver and other Black Panthers living in exile.

1970

                                    to radiation?

Richard Nixon has means to end human Worlds,

                   Man has machines for Suicide,

Pray for Timothy Leary in the planet's Woods!

                           Om Mani Padme Hum

                              & Hare Krishna!

"As we forgive those who trespass against us,

                   Thy Will be done

                            on Earth as in Heaven"

          Oh Bessie you ate my unborn sunflowers!

"God never repeats himself" Harry Smith telephoned tonite.

We may not come back, Richard Nixon.

                 We may not come back, dear hidden Tim.

Will Peter fix the sink's hand pump? the basement freeze?

             If we go to Australia to enter Eternal Dream time

                    one winter in Arnhem land

                Can we drain the tank & pipes?

Backyard Grasses Stink, if kitchen's drained

                  in septic tank, will Bacteria die

                       of soap, Ammonia & Kerosene?

       Get rid of that old tractor or fix it!

                 Cardboard boxes rotten in Garageside rain!

Old broken City desks under the appletree! Cleanum

                 up for firewood!

Where can we keep all summer's bottles? No deposit

No return! Gas pumps, broken mandolins, old tires

                      not enough room

in the rotten shed. Ugly backyard—Shelf the garage!

1970

Where stack lumber to see? A pighouse to build? O Gas!
           Money for Electric Generator? Where keep mops
                        in Wintertime?

Leary fugitive, Sinclair jailed next decade—
        Police killed 4 blacks in New Orleans
                CIA deals opium
      83% of World's illegal opium's fixed
        In Central Intelligence Agency's Indochinese Brain!
J. E. Hoover's a sexual blackmailer.
Pentagon Public Relations boodles 190 million plus 1969.
Fed State Local Narcs peddle junk—
Nixon got a hard hat from Mafia,
          Times pities "idealistic students"
Fascism in America:—
         i.e. Police control Cities, not Mayors nor
                  philosophers—
          Police, & Police alone, cause most crime.
Preventative Detention now law in D.C.
        Mexico and Senegal close borders to Adam
                  Longhair.

So many apples in abandoned orchards,
        & such fresh sweet Cider, supper tonite—
        red cooked tomatoes & parsley
             Onions & cabbage fried on iron
Plenty water, last night's rain filled earth,
        groundwells overflow, hydraulic ram
             works ready again,

Ecologues! the town laundry's detergent phosphate
     glut's foul'd clear Snyder's Creek

1970

     down town in the valley
   & have a beautiful boy in the house,
    Learn keyboard notation, chords & improvise
       Freely on Blake's mantras at midnite.
Hesiod annaled Beginnings
      Annal ends for no man.

Hail to the Gods, who are given Consciousness.
Hail to Men Conscious of the Gods!

     Leary jumped over the moon!

Noon after noon Billy goat Baas at the end of his chain
          in the grass—

3 AM
   owl hoots' four notes call
      from pine woods downhill?
     What do dogs hear?

   Leaves tinging big maples,
     entire hillsides turned wet gold,
   one night lightning,
      Leaf death's begun, universal September
      emerges in dream—colors & electric tempest—
Goats bells near the house, not much in the
       garden they can eat now anyway,
    & cow got best tops and mangles
       already—

Birds squeak & chatter as Rooster call
   echoes round house wall

1970

locust whistles all night—
Grey sky waiting rain, or dry chill.
Hundreds of black spotted tomatoes
        waiting near the kitchen wood stove
apple cider for morning drink
        in the leaky icebox.

Civilization's breaking down! Freezer tray's
        lukewarm, who knows why?
The year old Toilet's leaking at the heel—Wind
        Charger's so feeble batteries are almost down—
"Useless! Useless! The heavy rain driving into the sea!"
Kerouac, Cassady, Olson ash & earth, Leary the Irish
        couch on the lawn,
Black Magicians are screaming in anger Newark to Algiers,
How many bottles & cans piled up in our garbagepail?

2:30 AM Sept. 6, 1970

    At piano in apartment in anonymous city—a museum floor?—in company, I notice this fellow in worn dirty grey tweed coat & cap skulking near the piano—I say (others watching) "I say, are you in any kind of trouble or something?" and he looks at me—I look closer recognize him, who? Peter Du Peru[23] but no he looks more ragged—shudders against piano, silent as JULIUS. I regret opening my mouth—to ask him—he *is* in trouble & I was just making conversation to look good in front of friends in the room—now I realize I can't help, I'm scared, I don't want to help anymore. Woke, thinking there was a doorknock.

----

23. San Francisco friend of Ginsberg.

1970

Sept. 6   Dream 7:17   AM

"And wish to lead others when they should be led?"

trying to sing that in dream, Charlie Mingus[24] in background helping deepvoiced owl sound behind me as I mistake notes.

Sept. 8   6:30 AM

Living in White House, mascot or advisor—conversation with Nixon very quiet, I get up from leather sofa seeing he's working at desk in summary room—glance in his eye, nod, & leave by French-door down spacious corridor toward my own room, certainly able to give sharper-pointed advice than by threatening him—Yet I don't in dream discuss the war, this time I don't bring up controversy.

Sept. 22—Pollution

". . . the oceans, where life has diminished by 40% in 20 years. Fish disappear. Flora too." J. T. Cousteau, *Time,* September 28, 1970

Sept. 23   Dream—

In house in Boston, settling down for night after driving round Gloucester a bit—missed the old train out—"Eternal dream-time" summer resort?—I'm lost, where to stay? Where's the hero?—I go inside, big mansion—Who lives here? Driving that car before, thru Amsterdam Leidseplein or thru ocean Grove esplanade & bridges near Bradley Beach or abutting on Asbury Park? Miami in a parking lot?

Around the back of the house (as downstairs in the battleship-grey basement and door of the Gloucester Funeral Home) there's big porch,

24. Charles Mingus (1922–1979), influential jazz bassist and band leader.

we're going out for the night—I don't know what to do with myself—Need a father—Lookee there's Charles Olson in the back room, all bathed and hugely cherubic pink laughing and putting on his shirt

"Where you going?"

"Out to the North Shore Bar."

"Can I come?"

"Of course you can," he tells me.

Sept. 24, 1970—on Ferryboat house, walking across river thru Ferryboat Corridor—Many ferryboats lined up side by side, some mothballed inactive some still detached & active—one section's been turned into lofts and houses, living quarters—long corridor goes all the way thru to other side river, I walk thru that with Gordon Ball who photographs the receding boxed space after wide-windowed corridor—The biggest neatest size of cathedral or old Turkish bath dream-building-basement, is up for sale as an apartment—(I go home to die says mind—If I ever get back into that building in waking consciousness)—out the window I see the stairway to the Captain's Pilot Cabin's in good shape so the boat (land) is worth buying. This future Boy's Club or gay place bar or artists studio space.

Sept. 24, 1970—6 AM

Luncheonette counter Leroi Jones sitting friendly, talking relations changed he at ease myself much more insecure—"Let the blacks have the power, what a mess we whites have made!"—but we're having a talk after years of silence—Jack was a redneck, proudly?—Leroi gives me advice, where to go, what to do, what to read. He's now more relaxed—The revolution's on—I wander off to balcony, stairway downstairs to Co-op lunch cafeteria—They sell packages of crudely packed coffee. I notice the brown stuff's wrapped in wood box held together with paper—like in Cuba, home made crudeness to Amenities—saves plastic—

Don't remember more.

1970

* * * * *

If "Moloch whose fate is a cloud of sexless Hydrogen" is prophecy, what have I prophesied, & what will become of me? Every day this degenerate demoralization of self at dawn, a huge depression & dour stink rising from my too soft farmhouse bed.

If I get so disturbed about politics what'll happen to my soul if I get cancer or when I get Ulcer heart? I have no god.

If Death is what we are after we will have it fast.

If Life is what we are after we will not have it Forever.

"The System" is responsible for the prisonment of John Sinclair &
        Timothy Leary—

These were not exceptions to the rules of Justice.

       These men are too famous—

The conscience of the entire nation is implicated—the entire system,

Local, State, and Federal Courts, Local state and Federal Police

Local State and Federal Newspapers & Television, Radio the Fourth state

New York Times and the Motor Industry

Harvard psychology Department and Treasury department and Health education

     & Welfare Cabinet men.

Dream   Oct. 2, 1970

Rural city, in a field walking & talking with Bob Dylan about . . . coming out of maybe San Jose concert hall—(his first song "You expect much")—crossing asphalt street to his truck, puts his hand thru my grin shyly—"But where do you want to settle now?" I ask, "inside or outside the country?" because I'd heard gossip from managers he was restless & wanted to move, and play in public.

1970

GURU OM[25]

Car wheels roar over freeway concrete
Night falls on Dallas, two buildings shine under sickle moon
Many boys and girls in jail for their bodies poems and bitter thoughts
My belly's hollow breath sighs up thru my heart
Guru Om Guru Om enlarges in the vast space of the breast
The Guru has a man's brown belly and cock
long hair white beard short hair orange hat
The bliss alone no business for my body but to make Guru Om dwell
    near my breast
shall I telephone New York and tell my fellows where I am silent
shall I ring up my own head & order my own voice to be silent
how giant, silent and feather-soft is in the cave of my body eyes closed
to enter the body is difficult, the belly is full of bad smelling wind
the body is digesting last weekend's meat and thinking of cigarettes,
    thinking of—the bright eyes of boys
What acid sight hours equals eight hours' Guru Om continuous
    attention—
the Guru is equal to the Om of the Seeker
Guru Guru Guru Guru Guru Guru Guru Omkar Das Thakur thin
    voic'd recommended "Give up desire for children"
Dehorahava Baba sat on the Ganges and described eat & drinking
    pranayam
Nityananda floated thru his giant body
Babaji's hand the hand of a dead man in my dead man's fingers
out the plane window brown gas rises to heaven's blue sea—
how end the poetry movie in the mind?
How tell Kabir and Blake & Ginsberg shut their ears?

25. First draft of "Guru Om," *Collected Poems*, 561–62. Ginsberg would work on this poem over the next two days.

1970

Folded in silence the invisible Guru waits to fill his body with Emptiness
I am leaving the world, I will close my eyes & rest my tongue and hand.

                                                                October
4, 1970

    Over Tennessee? to Dallas

Harbinger—
    Basses "Can I see another's woe?" Flute & Violas "And not be in sorrow too?"

The Fashion Promoter on Dallas Airplane—
    "Oh you can't tell if the smog out the window's really bad ... at least the factory's producing, better than people on welfare ... after all, people make a living advertising ... I read an article on how organic agriculture also poisoned the land ... putting in all those organic fertilizers, nitrates & ammonia ... these pages of fashion, they're horrible ... but there's always someone who wants ... What good does the bald eagle do? I'm just as patriotic as the next person but I don't see why we need the Bald Eagle ... If people are poor and dirty it's their own fault, they don't teach their children to leave garbage alone ... The middle class, no wonder the middle class wants to Crack down ...
    "You see the difference between the sky's blue & the air down on the ground, it's brown human waste products?"

"Fasten your seat belts."

    "Actually I don't like birds, I think they're dirty."

1970

Sun glories thru cloud
    gold lightness threaded thru smog
    grey shafts over smokestack
       Rays out thru cumulus mouths
Fallen solid on Dallas.

Hard metal whirring
    eyes closed, brain whistle
    airplane roar, trembling body—
    Oh! For the softness of No atoms

Dream wandering up Palisades Heights overlooking New York Apartments and Turkish bath basements, some brother goes in to score for junk or other grass in men's room ... I follow hours or dreams later and fish out of the water tank a tiny orange-fringed transparent bodied shrimp-like creature which playfully jumped out of water and now flops on tile floor desperate to get back in the toilet tank, I cup him in my palm—see his shrimp eyes like tibetan eyeballs, horrified of the intelligent life—and rush to find his water tank—I can't! It's disappeared? Where? Where? put the squirming delicate soul? I wake terrified, the transparent shrimp straining itself to death exhaustion in my hands, and I can't find the water bowl ...

Dallas asleep in predawn darkness horizon dim, solitary car roar out of city.

October 5, 1970

To look in the City without hatred[26]
the orange noon edge sunk into blue Cloud

26. See "Guru Om," *Collected Poems*, 563.

1970

a second night autos roar to an afro Downtown towers' horizons
airplane moving between moon and white-lit bank towers
lightning in haze over twinkling-bulbed city flats
it is mind-City risen particularly solid.
What elder age grew such cities visioned from these far towers' windows
Seraph armchaired in Babylonic Déjà vu from Hilton Inn?

Guru Om "Sea pumps dead as Lake Erie and century ... 40% fish from
oceans disappeared gone last 20 years."

October 6, 1970

Dallas buildings' heaped rock tangled steel electric lit under night's quar-
ter moon[27]
Cars crash at dusk at Mockingbird Lane, Drugstore Supermarket signs
revolve with dumb beckoning persistence over North Central Freeway
Leary leaped over the wall with a sword, Errol Flynn in the grave, flags
& bombs fly over Dallas' stock exchange
oil flows thru the Hilton faucets, gasoline fumes smother Neem trees in
Ganeshpuri—
Maya revolves on rubber wheels, Samsara's glass buildings light up with
neon, Illusion's doors open on aluminum hinges—
my mother should've done asanas & Kundalini not straightjackets &
Electroshock in the birthdays of Roosevelt's FBI—
Where in the body's the white thumbsize subtle corpus, in the neck they
say
where's the half-thumbjoint black causal body, down in the heart hidden?
where's the lentil-sized Cosmic Corpse, a tiny blue speck in the navel?

27. See "Guru Om," *Collected Poems,* 562.

1970

All beings at war in the Gross body, armored Cars & Napalm, rifles &
   grass huts burning, Mace on Wall Street, tear gas flooding the fallen
   stockmarket.
Look in halls of the head, the "nervous leg halls," the universe inside the
   Chest dark baby kingdom in the skull

October 7, 1970

Dream: in commune on hill side, I go to bed with no sheets, young girl
at my side and long thick lingam of boy in next bed lain aside my thigh,
so I hold lingam-head in my hand. Boy like Poet Thurber, girl lays breast
weight on me. Rub lingam, warmth, I have hard on too, where's every-
body? They sleep that way or another when more people come. What eat
all winter? See this big can of Preludin? from welfare, and powdered
milk.

Dream Oct. 11, 1970

Up main street with Denise, main St. Buffalo or Niagara Falls
into second floor front apartment—Julius is there with the new Mafia rel-
atives—he's sat in closet between rooms in the dark, I look with horror
it's like old times, images from morons of River Street Paterson, opium
den Calcutta—He sits stolid in the dark—Her brother's come from New
Orleans or L.A., supposed to be tough—I'd just won a funny drab painted
Volkswagen at an auction, examining it looks oh—Whazzat, the back
door's all beat up crumpled hardly closes!—I coulda replaced the paint and
made it shiny but not the outside door—Her brother comes back and I put
my hand between his arm and body to go elbow to elbow—"Don't touch
me I'm black"—"you are not you're yellow and orange" because he does
have light mulatto red hair almost orange skin—I go downstairs to make
a phone call.

1970

Friendship Airport Baltimore

October 13, 1970

Capitol's pearl domed
   Behind black Factory Smog,
     Airport skyline.
(Pearl-like behind smoke.)

October 13, 1970 D.C.

11,000 feet high—
   "Look at the way it riffles . . . like
   downy mattress . . . you know if
   you fell into it you'd never hit bottom—

   "Somehow you feel that you gotta
   save humanity just so everybody can
   feel like you do when you're feeling good?"

Oct. 16 St. Kitts
   St. Kitts by air—tropic Holland—green fields & roads, medieval tower cones, plane down over Basseterre—center mountain range surrounded by sugarcane squaresacres.
   Antigua—no downtown but Postoffice & Coca Cola bottling Co—small market, courteous ladies with bandanas, one sold me a "golden apple" skin sliced off like a tough sweet young mango—"Taxi?" "No I'm here already."

1970

Oct. 26, 1970

Black gas over Boston
    settled in blue sky,
        grey cloudhaze hung
            over Harvard's red blocks
Some thick smoke layered
    under sky above Hartford's
        fuming smokestacks
rust gold October tree masses
    sitting silent, breathing
        thin blackness.

Halloween Oct. 31, 1970

Lay down mid afternoon drowse reading Soham Japa by Muktananda Paramahamsa Swami & fell asleep restfully drifting into a closed room, concrete blockhouse or jail, wherein apparitions trans-shifting, of guards and wars and armed police moving down iron corridors, and in that horror meditating, my atman dissolved out of my body transcending my head skull, so I began intoning Om A Hum Vajra Guru Padma Siddhi Hum, then realizing it was not my exact mantra practiced, opened my eyes from meditating, uncanny feeling of presence in the room, heard a thousand twangling instruments in midheaven gloom above my head, as if seeing another brown Rimbaudian world, as I began deep toned utterance of Guru Om, Muktananda Paramahamsa appeared and was heard singing anciently old hajan of permanent place of Bliss. Woke from dream within dream still intoning Guru Om.

Nov. 7, 1970

Greyhound back to farm from N.Y. where saw Charles Reznikoff read old poetry about Manhattan 1920 walking in park—young Puerto Rican girl in wool dress sitting leaned against old apartment door just reading comic book, lonely, seeking a commercial cigarette.

I sit every morning about an hour, breathing slowly thru whole body repeating "Guru Om" mantra in heart area, back straight, body slowly relaxed and meat heavy, mind moving over impossibly multitudinous mass of letters on my desk unanswered, proofs, mss. to correct, my own springboard binder of last 5 years poems lost on airplane between Virgin Islands Antigua and Bermuda so I have to recollect all the published scraps & works from magazines and tapes; letters from N Y Times editors requesting short essays on Fall of the World & underground Newspaper censorship mimeo poetry books to read, readings to give & teaching next week in Buffalo and Rochester, essays on CIA peddling opium to write from huge files accumulated, history of the politics of Junk Bureaucracy also accumulated in documents to render public visible from newspaper clips in filefolders and old medical Academy bulletins letter to Tim Leary in Algiers, letters to Snyder to write & Whalen, my brother's son to relocate in Cherry Valley, room to rearrange, buy file cabinet & put them in place of awkward mirrored dressing table I've been using couple years, sitting to do daily, poesy rewritten my desk piled with messages, recordings of Blake to arrange & company to produce them to be negotiated, financial accountings to keep for C.O.P., Inc. tax battle with war government to pursue, books on yoga and Boehme & Blake to examine, Neal's mss. to correct, all more than I can complete but only dabble into, my own last week's dreams at night faded unwrit, entire farm to supervise, the Fall day and red autumnal woods bluesky to dwell in (while I sit and work in upstairs room addicted to paper careers)—and I should really go to India & contemplate my nervous system.

Go down to bathe.

Nov. 11, 1970

Dressed up, went out of hotel apartment I was sharing in the City with friends who that day had other business, perhaps Dallas or some Banking

Center in Texas—I walked downstairs as suggested, the Underpass thru Main Street called (Tyler St.?) one of three commercial center Boulevard main drags. I'm dressed up in expensive vested sharktooth business suit, buttoned in center, and as I pass down the subway staircase, a couple of men trudging up pass me one with hippie walrus mustache who reaches out hand and pats my stomach in passing—a gesture I intuit he must've learned from me some bygone poetry reading travel year—I call back, "Delightful, well done ... do it again ... see you," still in tones of over-dressed securities executive, encourage his future.

Misty moonlight midnight
        Piss on grass
black cat steps near from barn.

I stoop and stroke soft fur,
        He cries and purrs
on the wet flagstone, waiting

Kitchen door opened, I snarl
        No no, setting kitty
aside from the doorsill, shutting door

Nov. 17, 1970   University Motel Buffalo

Woke after; long dream ending in bed with Burroughs, Joan Burroughs watching us from couch nearby on the twinkling floor of 5 and 10 cents store. Bill and entwined, and with a sudden movement (his legs wrapped round my waist) I push he pushes sharply and my cock enters his ass, then we rest long time he in slight pain so I slowly slide in to the base and almost begin to come—a long pleasant hold in the wet warmth and embrace face to face, and Joan's presence next to us.

1970

Woke, Maretta in next bed, after last nite's friendly conversation with Gregory about the End of the World, in huge grey Victorian house attic room with student fairies.

"Have You Seen This Movie?"[28]

November brown truck branches stretched rare-leaved
    field rows, pond woods under hill green green
    old maple hairytrunks leaned-rooted
    up to highway asphalt grass marge
Farmhouse roofs crost fields concrete [?]
    hornvoice "Raindrops"
    lightleaved [?] cornstalks dry brown
Great woodlegged wiretowers threads stretched
    above highway, white sun fallen West
Radio "the sight of Bobby Seale bound and gagged at Trial"
    denied lawyer presumed innocent The Radio Bible Hour
M D A Love Drug Cure Junk Habit? Highway franchise
    gas station discourage credit cards ask address document
Rochester exit one mile blue sky fring'd with clouds'
    whale ghost-blue schools north drift
    above metal double row's arms pull wires droop'd
    along thruway's village houseflats against basewoods—
    Stonepiles' indigo chess & millstone yard lawn
    flashing out Volkswagen window—
High, high Manson signed on Trial, how many folks in jail
    for grass Ask Congressman?
Highway crash! Politics! Police! Dope! armed robbery
    Customary E. 10th Street, no insurance possible

28. First draft of "Have You Seen This Movie?" *Collected Poems,* 563–64.

1970

Brown deer tied meat footed dead eye dead eye horned across blue car
    trunk, old folks front seat, they're gonna eat it!
Help! Hurrah! What's Going on here? Samsara? Illusion?
    Reality?
What'll all these trailers row'd up hillside, more people?
        towers, stones in brown hollow,
How can Lyca sleep? Cows on Canandaigua fields lactate into
      rubber & stainless steel pails
                milkhouse machinery vats ashine
Revolutionary suicide! Driving on Persian gasoline?
Kill Whale and ocean? oh one American myself
      Shits 1000 times more Chemical Waste into freshwater
        & seas than any single Chinaman!
America Suicide Cure World Cancer! Myself included
      dependent on Chemicals, wheels, dollars, metal
      Coke cans Liquid propane batteries marijuana
      lettuce avocados cigarettes plastic pens &
      milkbottles—electric
in N.Y.C. heavy habit, cut airconditioners isolation from
      street nightmare smog heat study decentralized
      Power sources 10 years not Atomic thermopollutive
      monolith.
Om. How many species biocided from Earth realm?
      O bald Eagle & Blue Whale with giant piteous
                  Cat squeak & wail
Oh Wailing Whale ululating under ocean's sonic roar
    of despair!
Sing thy Kingdom to Language deaf America! Scream
      thy black Cry thru Radio electric Aether—
Scream in Death America! or did Captain Ahab not scream
      Curses as he hurled harpoon
into the body of the Mother, great White Whale Nature
    Herself,

1970

thrashing in intelligent agony innocent vast in the oil Can
      sick waters?
All Northvietnam bomb-Cratered ruined topsoil more bombs
      than many WW II's
1270 swamp lethacid by Monsanto & Pentagon &
      [?] Academy Death-brains?
What wisdom teaching this? What Mafia runs N.J.? What
      Mafia knows J. Edgar FBI?
What Schenley's whiskey Fleischman's Hoover Institute?
What opium's passed thru CIA agents' airplane's
      luggage in Saigon, Bangkok, Athens, Washington?
What narcotic agent's not dependent on Shit for a living?
What loudmouth law & order politician's not hip deep in
      Mafia blood & smog money?
What Bank's money created ex nihilo serves orphan, widow,
      monk, philosopher?
or What Bank's money serves real Estate destruction Asphalt over widow's
      garden? Serves old Nick in the Pentagon?
[?] Mickey Mouse talk blind words in White House Mirrors!
old Indian prophecies believe Ghost Dance peace will Come
      restore prairie Buffalo or Great White Father Honkie
or be trampled to death in his dreams by the returning herds'
      thundering reincarnation!
Oh awful Man! What have we made the world! oh Man
      Capitalist exploiter of Mother planet!
Oh mother hating motherfuckers of tenderest Passaic & Hudson,
      self-polluters of Mafia and Fensine Chemistry oh
      vain insect sized men with metal slaves by Great Lake
      Erie, poisoned by dollars.
Lackawanna criminality in school board [?] Theft!
Buffalo Evening News "Bid Tampering Probed in Lackawanna" headline
      folded on rubber floor, car vibrating smooth to sun ruddy [?] clean
      fruit—

1970

Radio hissing enough words dashboard noisemusic—Any minute
        Apocalypse rock—
Brown of pelican eggs softened by DDT, Seals' livers poisoned
        to Northman. Oceans Dead 2000 AD.
Television citizen 6% Earths Americans ingest 45%
        planet's raw matter alchemized by Syracuse
          General Electric Power Brown robot palace near
          8 lane Thruway's exit before Ramada Inn
Trucks sleeping on brokenhearted embankment past
        Iron-strutted passages,
fields aglitter with damp metallic garbage under
        th' electricwire trestles—
And woods survived it another Thanksgiving's brown
        sacred silence—
Lights on cars frost western Lane grey twilit pales
        on rolling robotland.

Nov. 21, 1970

N. Y. Times ads for Dope Prohibition: quarter page 11 Park and
        Tilford Blended Scotch Whiskey
Quarter page 13 next to quarter page Mylai Massacre Military
        Trails J. B. Whiskey pours more pleasure
Quarter page Manson opposite p. 19's Smirnoff "leaves you breath-
        less, the Czars were happy to get it"
White Horse's 8th page discreetly stacked next to Agnew's praise
        of Achieved Goal Media—p. 17!—
Bombay Gin pours 5 in Naked Martinis in Space two pages later
Movies and Insurance past the Editorial Page, at Sports p. 37
        Old Forester Bottles occupy on 8th page under Today's
        Game Card Nov. 21, 1970

1970

Sportsman Drinker's old Pipe played 8 inches overpage, facing Am-
    bassador Scotch's Mild Sensation below Aqueduct and Fox
    Horse news—
And Clan MacGregor—Oh dusk my eyes grow dim!—bottle stands beside
    the Times Encyclopedia Almanac!—p. 40.
Bell's the Scot's Scotch inset next leaf by Used Cars—
Financiers need no encouragement, a last reminder for Bardinet's
    Brandy accompanies TV schedules.
"Waves of Tet Pound S. Vietnam" again again again today. Bowers
    In Vietnam, decades pass, Bring the War Home!
MFU Las Vegas Kirkorian promised 30 grand to Frank Costello's
    Mafia undersecretary Tramonti in Senate Hearingroom!

Dec. 25, 1970

    Dream two mornings ago 9 AM after finishing Tea Ceremony adapta-
tion for Sonam Kazi—a woman's hand chopped off, she rolled her shin
and touched it in the bone hole the raw meat hand not bleeding but dark
red and soft she tried to stitch back to the dry stump . . . telephone rang.

Xmas Day 1970

A pigeon faces icy sidewalk outside Greyhound's
scratchy money order sign'd glass door—Ludwig II Bavaria's mad
Castles save later centuries' economy with tourist Lira—
Flags may be desecrated, always been, Supreme Court sd—
Dancing Kings vanish in white snow on Albany's
street curbs—intervals between thoughts' movie
frames be void, did'ja ever see thought stop?—
Sit down and watch the N.Y. Times vanish, Vietnam

1970

war screens dumb, American—Body in the Brain,
Speech in throat, mind in heart, Diamond teacher's
Lotus power's blissful sentence

Milarepa Haiku[29]

Sound   Hiss, Gaslamp
                                  Night wind shakes the leaves.

Smell   Hemp smoke in the wood hall,
                                  Kerosene leaking from the lamp base
                                    knocked off the desk.

Sight   Yellow light on knotted wall,
                                  Alladin Chimney brass,
                                   wick cutter, pencil bottle
                                     plaster passport, staple shine.

Taste   Who am I? Saliva,
                                   vegetable soup,
                                    empty mouth?

Touch   Hot roach, breath smoke
                                   suck in, hold, exhale—
                                    light as ashes.

Intuition   Eyes lid-heavy, dreamed yesterday dawn
                                kissing the two eyed horse,
                                  reading books, bodies close, talking.

29. First draft of "Six Senses," *Wait Till I'm Dead*, 102–3.

1970

East Hill Farm in winter. Photograph by Gordon Ball.

WELDED ENDS

Poetry

Music

University
Note Book

VERNON
VR
ROYAL

NAME *Helen Hurley*

SUBJECT *November 14 - 17, 1971*

Nessme Road region n88.

S-1115 (05-4100)   10 IN. x 8 IN.   100 SHEETS   WIDE RULED & MARGIN

S. E. & M. VERNON CO., ELIZABETH, N. J. 07208 • A DIV. OF THE MEAD CORPORATION

WELDED ENDS

1971

Ginsberg intended to spend a portion of 1971 in Australia with Lawrence Ferlinghetti, but he faced too many pressing social, political, and literary obligations to allow the travel. He remained committed to an album featuring the best of his live recordings of his poetry. He also began compiling an ambitious new volume of work that combined his auto poesy and journal poems: The Fall of America, *as he was calling this book, would be his largest single volume of poetry to date. He dedicated more effort to his study of Buddhism, and his social and political activism extended beyond his continuing protests against the Vietnam War. Ginsberg's drug files, now recognized as one of the most extensive compiled by a private citizen, had grown to include evidence that the CIA was drug trafficking in Southeast Asia. His spring series of university appearances included detailed lectures on these and other nonliterary topics; a book of featured lectures and informal meetings with students was recorded, edited, and assembled by Gordon Ball, his old farm manager, into the book* Allen Verbatim. *As his journal entries indicated, he seemed to be everywhere he felt his voice was needed.*

Dream January 1, 1971—Noon

Passing Canal Street "Artists" Workshop Commune Building after wandering avenues downtown with Don Cherry.[1] I lost him coming out of loft Hotel where I had my own studio—Mills Hotel on Chelsea or Fonkey Block over a decade ago—arrived at Artist Workshop Gate-Door, traffic in streets, his white baby handed to me outside the door. I crooned high

1. Jazz musician friend of Ginsberg.

plaintive harmonies to the music echoing in the building, holding little boy in my arms—then entering, walked to center of huge ground floor recording loft—on elevated platforms, like zoo isolation or Guru's high seats many, human creatures each tied chained or bandaged to his throne ... lepers, speed freaks with raw bone hanging trussed from knobby knees, skeletal musicians all living there and tended by sound machines, ever ready, and a huge black healthy organist nurse set high up in the center of the room, waiting for the right moment to signal engineers to record the extreme death-geniuses—like legendary Indian torture/mutilation warriors at dawn singing the sunrise on planet horizon.

January 8, 1971 4:30 AM Dream Story

"That's all I can see out the window of the senses."

Woke in Hotel Room where I'd taken new monthly lodgings alone, looked out window and saw long-legged naked man, young ballet actor, lying in bed 1 room below mine opposite, covers over him, eyes closed. That's all I can see out the window, and he opens his eyes and is staring directly up at me—I withdraw into shade and peek out down at him, he's risen naked and gone out his roofgarden (place like Jim Thurber's years ago on upper Polk St. S.F. where we visited—I'd slept with Jim as kid student—years later met didn't recognize him now poet later he turned on speed later years to Christ commune renounced poetry, renounced drugs, a father of newborn child over phone when I'd called to return a bundle of his early MSS I'd re'd anonymously in mail once he was busted in Laredo—Peter too on amphetamine and off years later much changed with new [?] of work and yelling purity)—The dream neighbor out on roofgarden in roominghouse 14th street east of 8th Avenue with boy and girl friend was enacting some orgy scene from a play for my eyes I guessed as I spied lights turned out, safe from his returning glance, behind my new room's window many floors above the fearful street.

1971

I went back to my old room at the Chelsea, found Charles Henri Ford with Company of several young Manson-esque acid heads, International Satanist Actors, who cajoled me to stay awhile, relax and company them, free rent there where I'd always lived and owed new week's rent if I were to stay overnight—I thought well I'll stay awhile, till they too went into an odd personal act which required my financial help or moral participation to raise money to put on show—some sinister ballet dumbshow, a long legged mountebank in two-tone ballet tights taking a strained position against the wall with young girl, I felt oppressed in their presence, finally went to closet to collect my few clothes and possessions gather them and announced my resolve to move my room—stay here and that's all I can see as out the window here in the room same oppressive dumbshow—Harry Smith there drinking too?—I woke, thinking to blame C. H. Ford but no, it was me, my dream not his real self I represented—that spare room waiting for me as in old dreams years ago of a room I shared at Columbia U. 114th St. with my brother, an unused apartment belonging to us that I'd always had—an old dream from the late 40's written down somewhere. Woke peed downstairs shook down coalstove and added shovels of noisy coal to the red ember bed wondering interlocking dream life's meanings— windows of senses? old dumbshow of life with Peter on farm and secret refuge cheap apartment in Lower E. Side's East 10th St. 4th floor still available? Repeated demands for money from Harry, Gregory as last nite by phone, Chelsea Hotel room last month where I'd recorded with Miles, tape of new blues songs in company I felt mildly uncomfortable joining to use their large room for any convenience, C. H. Ford I saw at Yoko Ono/John "Legs" film show? Ford wanting me to go out after to bar but I declined despite his long lost friendliness and gossip of Greek CIA? Shadow of Mafia over dream? Repetition of Samsara left thru window of senses, as I'd jacked off before sleep dreaming of screwing Joe Army again after 25 years? Worship Guru Om or Om a Hum Vajra Guru Palma Siddhi Hum, Hindu Gury Kriya Kundalini personalist yoga or Tibetan Dzogchen No Mind meditation? Still smoking again? in mid morning darkness—

1971

have to get up in an hour and feed fitten' ration to cows, water them and goats and dogs and chickens and pig and horse, give animal hay and cats arguing with pig and cleaning dung from stalls with Julius and Maretta.

Jan. 8, 1971 Continued.

8 AM—Woke late, dreamt I'd wandered to meadow and riverbank in India, same soft green light thru bushes, bulrushes and trees as seen in [?] movie with Swami Satchitananda—went on knees to edge of water and peeked thru the green high grass, saw a tiny Island (as under Howrah bridge, but in rural anonymity far from Cities) on which two robust grey bearded old holymen were performing morning Surya devotions, making mudras, offering prasad, arranging on altar of leaf-cups, rearing fragment of each large leaf and adding it onto the bottom of the leaf-cup with each ritual mantra and mudra down in the water, standing at waterside in dhoti cloth wrapped around midriff—nostalgia for the few hours I'd spent in Antigua—and had come from some chaotic scene with trolleys and cows in Calcutta or New York,

Woke, went downstairs, Mirabelle black and white spotted Dalmatian with puppies in box under elevated wooden bed in Peter's room had shat all over the rug—I'd fed her extra last mostly corn having to get on hands and knees, scrub carpet with soap and chlorox and bathe Mirabelle in bathtub after she's abandoned all rational hope and curled up alone in the hay, nose buried in brown stained short fur, trembling.

Every day's chores—feed fitten' ration to goats, cows, horses and pig, bucket of water for each, l arge and small leafs of hay-bale for each except pig who steals loose hay from goats—help Julius, clean cowflop and horse turds from stalls and pile it in wooden cribs around the house, wheelbarrowing hay-dung thru the snow from barn floor to house-side. Then empty water buckets, feed dogs mixing coffee-cans full of store-food with hot wa-

1971

ter brought from house, clean out chicken coop water through and fill that with fresh water, give chickens and ducks (who among all 30 lay only one egg a day now dark wintering in coop) scratchfeed mostly corn, and laying mash I wooden cup the length of the sidewalk. Call horse back from snowy pasture and cajole him back to stall, bar it with lumber-plank since he's kicked out the stall door-hinge. Play with grunting pig who butts my knee with his nose and runs squealing after I kick him in the act of stealing goat hay—he fights with the dogs over their food, they snap and bark and drive him back inside farm from their hay-strewn lean-to.

Two nights ago closed trapdoor in chicken house in snow at the closed door, outside, I'd not seen her leave and she returned after I went in the house, chores done and thought at dusk. Cremated the hen with trash paper in burning barrel.

Cow moos softly undertone waiting her feed bucket while horse paws and knocks his wooden door pig squeals and grunts and noses into water buckets upsetting them, Junior goat snuffles and snorts and waves his brass-tipped horns—two lady goats pregnant, no milking to do, one brown stray dog pregnant by Godly the black father, one stumpy legged runt girl goat the sweetest nature in the barn, ears frostbit at birth and hoofs half clubbed, last winter's deathly freeze as she was born, Peter and Gordon Ball saved her and gave her five sisters and brothers away.

Jan. 13, 1971

Sitting in SW terminal with Jerry Malanga,[2] there's been a dangerous fire outside in airfield near tanks and pipes, now under control—we're in bed inside the heavy glass door so hard to push open—of the waiting room,

2. Gerard Malanga (born 1943), poet, photographer, filmmaker, and actor, most well known for his association with Andy Warhol during the 1960s.

1971

Caribbean plane station, waiting together—conversing, there's a large whoosh! and a fireball, a meteorite from Heaven, flared down vertically outside the terminal by the chain link fence, and phloomp! arrows bright down right into the maze of gas pipes and tanks—we lie there as liquid begins sprinkling by the fence, incredible omen of luck he says, we notice the gas burning, oh oh, let's go out and check it—we go thru the door on way down aisle to other doors—my God are they even open, yes, people rushing back into building, the fire grows heated, I start walking fast to get to the building away from the draw of the heat and the terrible explosion that'll come any minute, Gerry's already run forward inside, I'm trying to push open a door but the heat's sucking me backward and I wake.

The omen: one meteor can set the world afire.

The omen: Willard Maas and Marie Menken both poets dead, are signal'd meteoric from the sky.

Jan. 12, 1971

Kerouac MSS presently at Sterling Lord's[3] office:
Variant mss *Desolation Angels*
Pomes All Sizes
Other odd poems loose (other than *Blues*[4]) (which are strictly Disciplined to one Notebook size)
Play: *Beat Generation*
Visions of Cody
"And the Hippos were Boiled in their Tanks" 1945 (W. Burroughs)
Pic
Jan. 24, 1971

3. Kerouac's literary agent.
4. *Mexico City Blues.*

1971

The Ballad of Tommy the Traveler

Tommy the traveler come to town
Geneva and other Colleges near
Tommy I hate to put anyone down,
But doublecrossing creates Fear.

Tommy the Traveler, did you not talk
Of violence, bombs and Hashand fire?
Tell me dear Tom, which students would balk
And leave your double presence higher?

Did you turn on, did you sell legal drugs,
With license and lie for the F.B.I.?
Did you make hot bombs, did the Sheriffs there
Pay you to teach students how to die?

Did you pass your ass as SDS[5]
From Rochester to Hashand's radical girls.
Did you ask for love, and propose B.S.
Revolution at Auburn, flash your pearls

in movie theater war, Camp like Weathermen
Scream in Dupont Circle "Kill the Pigs" at Hobart
Preach Violent Bombs and beating other men?
Fink and teach Freshmen Black Power Pop Art?

Tommy O Tommy, did you hate ROTC
So much you'd bribe to get the Key?

5. Students for a Democratic Society.

1971

Breaking windows you said was hotey totey
At the sit in, outside agitator, see?

Tommy have you no grief for suffering man
That you mock like a soldier at Christ?
Didn't you teach a Fiery Plan
Like Satan, like Manson, like Nixon—you enticed

boys to arson for Mayday Morn,
and strike Martinez a godly soul,
With threat to kill and violent scorn—
The Assistant Dean saw you lose control!

Then to come back and bust the Dorms
with Police Cars and Sheriff Morrow's Squads
You who sold hash and queered all human Norms
is to call down the wrathful brains of the gods?

Tommy thy Father the CIA
often sells dope like you do
your Government Father makes wars every day
and pays you unemployment too.

Tommy Repent, Students Unite, wise minds
Collect a quarter millionbucks,
Teach Rockefeller through his Low Blinds
Man, and bluffs the state, his power sucks!

A land thus beats and spies on youths,
Bombs schools and pays for Asian War
Pollutes itself in very truth
Like Babylon that died of yore—

1971

Tommy take your bible back,

J. E. Hoover pray,

Police Chief McLaughlin, arrest yourself,

And suffer Judge [?] Delay,

Congressman Morton, wash off your filth.

Feb. 12, 1971

Returned to Cherry Valley yesterday—had spent weeks in N.Y. at Chelsea Hotel with Miles, auditing tapes 1954–1970 of poetry readings,[6] mostly flawed by drunk, scratched by overload, Muffled by rooms decade old—selected best readings/clearest recordings including fragments of tapes made in Neal's house San Jose '54, Albert Hall, Kalamazoo and Cortland Colleges, Ann Arbor, old San Francisco halls—working afternoons to 2 AM most nites, mornings up hour meditation almost every day and telephone busyness thru brunch haste.

My attention spread between researching CIA-Nationalist Chinese—Shan and Mao Tribe—Indochinese armed politics opium smuggling—now over half a year's correspondence and phone calls and ransacking files, Time-Life and my own. Also half year's pro-underground newspapers and psychopolitical dissidents—and foot thick dossiers court records, letters, clippings, complete search of Liberation News Service back issues to 1958—huge files on Leary, John Sinclair, late D. A. Levy[7]—ending with mass of material on opium, and on political repression—and myself too hurried and overworked to reduce it to essay prose white paper manifesto.

Also traveling to Detroit for John Sinclair last month and this month

6. Barry Miles, an English writer, met Ginsberg in 1965 and spent years taping Ginsberg's recordings of William Blake's poetry and organizing Ginsberg's tapings of readings.

7. D. A. Levy (1942–1968) was a Cleveland-based poet and publisher.

1971

several days Cornell-Hobart-Geneva, N.Y. raising money for Tommy the Traveler's victims—so wrote precise poem ballad.

Mobilization against war requests services organizing nonviolent civil disobedience this spring 1971—Where? How? When? May Day Washington sit down strike of a million people till war end?

Committee on Poetry Inc, now under investigation by Internal Revenue examiners so that may takes months of paperwork in addition to monthly hassles balancing checkbooks, compiling yearly trustees meeting notes, handing out money, resolving Cherry Valley Park White Elephant Woes—and lawyers to protest foundation will cost $3,000.00—will give land in California[8] to Phil Whalen and Lew Welch,[9] perhaps diminish use of farm and bid animals adieu.

Slowly composing rest of Blake's Innocence and Experience tunes, learning keyboard chords, now able to write for 2–3 chords, Dylan in car to Barbara's wedding said the combo is C F and G, and G C and D practical variations on these this morning.

Lost springboard binder of completed typed poems last few years, now must reconstruct from magazines where published, from tapes and notebooks.

Many dozen pages of recent poems, including Ecologue,[10] untyped.

Mail accumulating, prefaces to write for Kerouac's poems and Cassady's memorabilia, unfinished Yevtushenko translation—and not much love life.

I want to read mystic texts, Jewish, Gnostic, Kundalini, Hindu, and Tibetan Tantric to accord with my daily singin but no time left after letters, phonecalls, tapes.

8. Ginsberg had purchased land in the Sierras, near Gary Snyder's land, with the hope of building a retreat.

9. Lew Welch (1926–1971) was a poet and teacher, a close associate with many Beat Generation writers.

10. See *The Fall of America*, 147–61.

1971

Asked agent to arrange disposal/publication of poetry tapes, next Blake album, and set of Mantra records.

Overseeing Marietta and Bremser's woes travels homes—Orlovsky and Co., Miles, and Gordon dependent on my activity—

Calls from Gay Liberation, poetry mimeographs, starved mad communes and poets for help—going to Boston for JUCKE Cooperative next month, recommended by Denise Levertov.[11]

Must record in San Francisco this May, after zigzag U.S. tour to raise COP Inc. monies—more Blake, all to be organized—

Then split to Australia for reading tour with Ferlinghetti—and then China Hanoi Tibet Vietnam? India?

Buddhadeva Bose needs help in Calcutta—obscenity trials, stonings. My father wants to see me, my nephew Allen wants company and instruction, I'm too busy—

Study of Blake interrupted, the sound track of Blake poems for TV Film is done—

Decade journals typed sitting in N.Y.C. unread unedited several years now. When time for that?

Must edit giant prose book, Xeroxes piled up unread.

Must compile tapeworn texts of *Fall of America—These States*.

Must collect and edit all poems 1946–1970 for completed cycle hard cover book to send to Russia.

Must re-arrange German and Italian censored translations of texts messed up by Limes Verlag and Mondadori and must write lawyer letters.

Must pick up threads of War Tax resistance, as I haven't paid taxes in 3 years in War Protest but neglected to follow up with poems and propaganda essays, thus when I be challenged by Government I won't have time to resist, a blessing to go to jail?

Must arrange Dope Files in coherent order. Must collect personal papers 1971 tax and checking account record of my business.

11. Award-winning poet Denise Levertov (1923–1997).

1971

Must arrange publicitization of Sinclair's PEN protest letter. Must someday see Leary in Algiers. And spend a month with Burroughs in London. Must go see Swami Muktananda and Swami Satchidananda and Dudjom Rinpoche. Must visit Tibet and return to Benares.

Must answer Ansen's letter from Athens.

Must write poetry instead of doing all the unhappy Karma yoga inventoried here, some thigs forgot.

Thus 3 dreams today—slept all day. Couldn't face farm and world, exhausted, trying not to smoke nicotine—

My father fell down stairs, toy there lies pelvis parts press bulged at crotch, unhurt, I assisted and questioned him on floor, he was silent but no bones broke I dream.

Then I woke and slept again, Paul Blackburn[12] on floor was fucking me in ass as I sat on his cock from above—woke with spasms in sphincter fading echoed from dream.

Late afternoon dream, I lost my double barreled eyeglasses in watery hot dashboard tank of a car, glasses fell apart, melting the right stem—I fished around and couldn't reconstruct—or finally even find—the missing right frame and the lens ...

The barn full of newborn puppies and goats, the pigs more huge and nosey, horse quiet at the hay.

9 AM Feb. 13, 1971 Saturday from Gordon's bed—

Climbed up the top of the Celestial Empire State Bldg. with group of friends—"Mi Parland" remains on lips Movie Marie "The Body"? J.C. Holmes' favorite lady pianist? Marion UC Pastland? Eugene's Mineralogist Paterson girlfriend—

McPartland? since both Gordon's and my stomach rumbled?

12. Poet Paul Blackburn (1926–1971) was part of the Black Mountain group of poets.

1971

She was the name of the lady amid Scientific Revolutionary Company that gathered in tower room of the lunar Skyscraper to examine, having ascended for the first time as high as that control room outlook, the view of outer space blue visible, and the light of the bright sun shining thru the shuttered rooftop, and the universe distances groundward—distance so huge to moon floor and earth disc that the atmosphere swayed the eyeball's extended image as the in hot wind.

I adjusted the roof louvers, like grid-slats, to contain the sunlight to visible dimension, and noticed that each turn of the huge electronic knob changed the face of the sun light source—transforming it from one dim visible sun face into another human face look—finely adjusting the controls it finally narrowed and focused the sun's face into an image of my own—"The face of God is your own" I claimed, remarked, shouted, observed to my companions, as I revealed my own face in the shuttered fine gridwork on the roof thru which sun played images as thru more patterns.

And woke with the phrase, "The face of God is your own," thinking of Leary and Cleaver arguing over "reality" in Algiers.

Feb. 13, 1971

Bathrobe, Saturday Snow Fog out window's raindrops. Sitting at desk, smoking a cigarette, will I do yoga later today?—A mug of tea, letters piled urgent from jail, German publisher's bowdlerized *Howl*, Italian house lawyer's letter says cut reference to Pope and Cardinal Spellman and President from decade old TV medication text, high school girl's crayoned Salutation, Ansen's epistle from Athens to answer, Bose complaining of courts and beatings in Calcutta, vast foot thick files of underground media beatings and bombings and grass busts, on police paddling heroin everywhere, Central Intelligence Agency peddling opium decades from Burma and Laos, today's newspaper headlining Armies marched into dead Ho Chi Minh's mountains, weeks' hours of taxforms to scribe last Internal Revenue bust this farm and Committee on Poetry Inc, And what reply to

1971

Leary and Cleaver arguing in Algiers. Contending twist armed Revolution and Mystic Mind Change altering earth's eyeballs? I should write poems not letters to the N.Y. Times, I should write poems on Saturday morn.

Good Morning: 2/28/71

Woke early, dream Imamu Amari Baraka on street Algiers/Paterson NJ. I was out looking for Leary's refugee house, saw him in the African city Park early in the day dressed in Rosemary's[13] Baboushka burnous wrapped round his head in disguise, so's they could not get out to see movie & walk around town anonymous, we met in Park and walk talk ... shifts to entrance to Black meeting outside I see Baraka he's whispering some Shiite mantra to Allah sibilant under his breath I see he's really serious into his devotional practice & ask him what's his daily mantra he begins to answer but his teacher a political leader/spirit strongman tells him shut up now we got in line, and so I ask is there any prayer a white man can say? that I can be told? he said yes later get in line—huge line of black men around theater walls to below stage for inoculation or blessing or communion in some ancient adapted ritual, I get on end of line, waiting, Leroi had begun to answer but was silenced ... realized after waking shower that this month the UN banned LSD & gave it over to governments ...

11:30 AM Mar. 2, 1971
        "Oh, Corso's Elegiac Feelings American[14] Immortal Laurelled"
Hum! Hum! Hum![15]

13. Timothy Leary's wife.

14. Ginsberg considered Gregory Corso's volume of poems, *Elegiac Feelings American* (1970), a major work and strongly felt that it deserved more attention than it received.

15. Untitled poem, published in *Wait Till I'm Dead*, 105.

1971

Gregory Corso's genius Despised
    Muses bored,
Mediocrity is prized—
Bullshit the Award.
Hum! Hum! Hum!

                    (copied from scrap of paper—writ
                                    Meeting)

March 18, 1971

    Dream Wash., D.C.—Busted in front of hotel with Rennie Davis,[16] "because that without marriage you're going to live together in sin like a man."

April 2, 1971
                  Tallahassee Democrat
    By Nixon order
        "house arrest"
        Allowed Calley[17]
            His release is cleared
    by presidential order
murder of 22[18] Vietnamese civilians in the My Lai Massacre.

16. Antiwar activist Rennie Davis (born 1941) was one of the defendants in the Chicago Seven trial.

17. Lieutenant William Calley Jr. led the attack on unarmed South Vietnamese villagers in My Lai on March 16, 1968.

18. This figure is far below the number of Vietnamese killed in the slaughter. Ginsberg was probably repeating an early estimation.

W. M. Gates—Chairman local draft board "It has made murderers out of all of us"

"If anybody was having hanky-panky I don't know anything about it"

April 7, 1971

Robert Duncan[19] adds: For Kent State: 4 Sections carrying effegies in Procession, ceremony over Names, enters massed crowd pronouncing dead Names. Act out Shootings with effegies of the
Guard/Angels becomes a Passion Play, troupes of Kids, pageant pilgrimage and w/May Pole Dance and fucking strangers in Bushes—Demon Masks, Bread and puppets.
one hour open pray/chant/body sound formless utterance to be formed by the mass-arriving at end of evening, unison voiced one slogan.
Gospel Singing tambourine.
Jazz Band for Blacks New Orleans funeral Blues March
Chanting dead names different rhythms
Nixon prayer meeting
Circle singing all Guitarists and Flute players on campuses
a music hour
Gary Snyder: May Day: Walpurgisnacht night before, up in hills side lite fires fuck and dance, come down from hills at dawn bearing flowers which they leave at doorsteps of the townsfolk.

San Francisco. April 26, 1971

3:45 A.M. Went to sleep after midnight hours with Jimmy C., who described scoring from Mafia in N.Y. waterfront—short movie in upstairs

19. San Francisco poet and teacher Robert Duncan (1919–1988) accompanied Ginsberg on a portion of his 1971 lecture and reading tour.

1971

rickety house Marseilles. I'm passing from my room to dining room, wooden stairways—downstairs a couple of toughs, heavies, fellows are waiting in mortician doorway—they come upstairs and ask me my business—I'm sitting at table they crowd round like members of Bread and Puppets, one with half a Hitler mustache—I suddenly panic, realizing they're going to do me in I wonder why—I say, retreating from table, "well get it over with now quit or kill, I'm bored with all your stupid Karma." So they panic and get up to leave. "Let's see you throw some knives at us," one taunts me. I grab a handful of silver and throw it in his direction—clattering—they go back downstairs, waiting for me, I peek down thru stairwell, they're there, I worry.

Dream
> "... so that your joy in your era be relief
> instead of your intended wallpaper, grief."

HUM BOM[20]

Whom bomb?
We bomb them!
Whom bomb?
We bomb them!
Whom bomb?
Whom bomb?
We bomb them!

What do we do?
Who do we bomb?
What do we do?

20. First draft of "Hum Bom," *Collected Poems*, 576–78.

1971

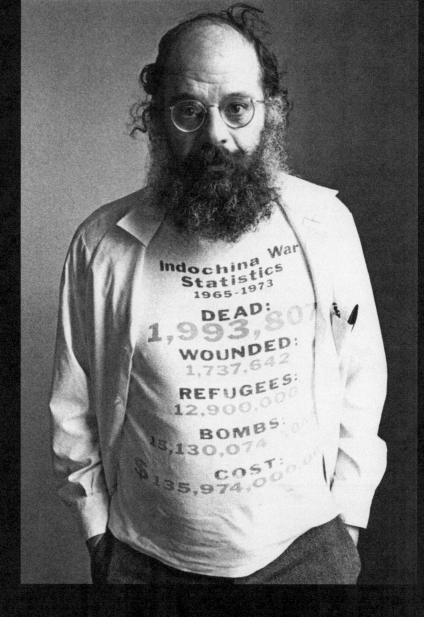

Ginsberg in Chicago, 1975. Photograph copyright Marc PoKempner.

Who do we bomb?
What do we do?
Who do we bomb?
What do we do?
U bomb! Who do we bomb?

Whom bomb?
We bomb you!
Whom bomb?
We bomb you!
Whom bomb?
We bomb you!
Whom bomb?
We bomb you!

What do you do?
You bomb! You bomb them!
What do you do?
You bomb! You bomb them!
What do you do?
You bomb! You bomb them!
What do you do?
You bomb! You bomb them!

Whom bomb?
We bomb you
Whom bomb?
We bomb you
Whom bomb?
We bomb you!
Whom bomb?
We bomb you!

1971

U.S. Shiva Mantra
Bixby Canyon
Allen Ginsberg   May '71

May 17, 1971

            Bixby Canyon
at dawn, on path to the ocean
        poison oak guards morning glory.

Year after year I come up this path,
        cross the brook—Ah,
    blue ocean under the bridge.

So many flowers—I don't know their names,
        blue, yellow, white, orange
    fringed soft petals

Sands shifted by the stream, rocks tumbled
        down the cliff—
    only the ocean's the same.

June 19. 1971—Dream
        At nightclub w/microphone, improvising about CIA.
                "I'm going to get personal now
                So I might as well float up to the ceiling
                I'm going to get personal now
                And sing to you about politics . . ."
        As I find myself floating up over nightclub tables toward
Chandelier, facing the band in the corner blowing along in my rhythm,

1971

> So if the band will keep up playing
> Melan-cho-ly

as I wake up.

Bixby Canyon. May 21

Dream—on train stopping over in Newark, Maretta Greer and I not sure where to get off—I walk to rear car and step down to platform, see conductor up ahead and ask, he says, get off when you want, this is Newark: I ask how long we'll be here—will I have time?—yes, get off now—

So I walk back and ask Maretta if she's ready she says yes but I see that we left the Vajra and Bell up at the end of the car—

Hundred got off already before Newark, I remember, and worry that we'll gather our possessions and get off in time.

Dream June 1, 1971

Sitting with Gary at Woolsey St. table "so that was the ancient measure of man—how far across the barn floor he could come. He who could spurt halfway across the barn floor was a complete man.

Gary sits there depressed—my attempt at basic conversation is so lame, as is my moral mind—

He's a woman film maker and dancer—"of course it's not that I don't love the Prince . . . I believed always in my own sex," she says in the household coffee booth!

> 8 A.M.
> Wrist in cast
> 1801 Woolsey St.
> Berkeley

1971

Demonstration Ritual
Hatha Yoga Asanas
Mantra
Sensitivity Session

June 30, 1971 4–4:45 AM

Set Blakes *Tyger*[21] to rhythmic tune—it is a heartbeat, divided 'twixt A major and A minor.

Recorded and completed sketch of all *Songs of Innocence and of Experience* this night.

Earth's Answer
Clod and Pebble
Holy Thursday
Chimney Sweepers
The Angel
Pretty Rose Tree
Little Vagabond
The Lily
A Divine Image
The Tyger

Thanks for this gift, Wm. Blake,
     my debt is paid,
  now I am free of thee and thy visions:
    it ends in thy heart beat.

----

21. At this point, Ginsberg was still attempting to set all of William Blake's *Songs of Experience* and *Songs of Innocence* to music.

1971

Dream—I was awake in a giant city bed—side by side everyone was asleep as the magic show went on, all of us on a building shelf above the street— I had come thru subway—

I woke in the subway, there was a girl on my left and a giant on my right—Ellsworth Bunker (Ambassador to South Vietnam)—

What does he like? I had some funky cheese. She said Ellsworth likes cheese. Ellsworth woke, like Ferlinghetti's dog Homer. I crumbled some cheese at the edge of the shelf for him to gobble. He began, he woke, he gobbled, then turned—turned up, and reached for a cigarette. Ellsworth! Ellsworth!

The phone rang in Berkeley on Woolsey Street. I woke in sunshiny morn.

July 1, 1971

Up in giant Texas building—really New York's Pierre Hotel, carpeted halls and elevators, visiting Trungpa Tulku—I sleep there and restlessly all night next to him (married to Saide Kaye) touch his prick as we lie side by side, he has small hard on and I persist—waking he asks what is it for? And we talk more—

After I leave I go buy cigarettes and change my mind and decide to go up elevator again and see him—when I get back I discover the 3 Boulder disciples sleeping out front of the door by the balcony rail on stretcher carts, then all nite not knowing he's up woken yet. I knock and open door: they're meditating in the dark. I want to come in and be his disciple and take instruction. I take out cigarette pack, he gets mad and says "what's that for? You're still stuck with that poison?"—I throw away packs "Is it some sort of test?" In the room after angry hesitation he'd sd, come back at 7, and asked if I knew how to make boiled beef. I said yes, so he said, come back at 4. We went down together, down elevator—suddenly

1971

continuing his sympathetic Boddhisatva sadhana he leans up against a drunk in the corner, presses mouth to the derelict's breast and cries, "Oh, oh, oh!" and then kisses him on the mouth, large open mouth kiss, making believe drunk cicilo! And repeats o! o! all the way down elevator.

... Love whispers in emptiness.

The last of many a thought, restless night falling asleep after quit smoking 2 days ago's irritability hangover, and chasing see all over Telegraph Avenue North Beach and stud and Capri bars, and ate turkey tonite with greasy stomach pain prolonged into wee morn hours, slept and woke again sighing happy in lower abdomen at thought 25 years old of Lucien's ass and eyes and lips—back to some kiss of 1950 and I woke breathing free and light hearted—then what to say to BBC? but the truth, what am I about?

July 28, 1971. Noon—

The 3 piece Zen Folk Trio in Nightclub, the 3rd white kid like musician Terry Riley singing "Shiki Shiki So Ku Ku"—in high, little fairy voice as part of ballad "... and at the Zen merchant/at the edge of town ..." which ends abruptly so the pianist leader says aside, as Gary Snyder bends over in nightclub darkness in a chair by cocktail table under roof of the cave-corner.

Dream Aug. 1, 1971

Woke after laborious happy long dream which ended chanting Om Ah Hum Vajra Guru Padma Siddhi Hum over and over.

1971

Aug. 19, 1971—2 AM–2:30 AM

Poems Assembled Vocalized

What themes run thru silver decades?
Childhood hidden hairy longings, mother's madness,
Love of lovers, and art Neal most bethought and Jack betongued
Friends of youth and politic years, The War and Fall of America,
C.I.A. and junk and grass, L.S.D, ecstasies and police state
Academies betraying genius scholarship suborned by Party Hack,
Sexual revolution and grass uprooted over a continent,
Airplanes and Soldiers flying home from Armageddon, trains and cars
through America, the body of Nation vocalized New York
to San Francisco, Change of Consciousness on Fresh Planet
or groans in Hadig Alley, Kali Yugas saving Voice
The Hari Krishna and Vajra Guru body chants,
Mass melas and the Human Be-in the Universe,
fellow poets of cosmic perception Corso and Burroughs,
labor alone, farm years and loves of Orlovsky,
Paris in green, Arctic ice floes, Mexican valentines,
Whitman walking the streets of Berkeley, a bearded radical
Studios and Television prophecies, Blake the Master
tuned and vocalized for children of centuries, London
lambent singing Eros Choruses, iron curtain police
and longhaired pale boys from Prague to Havana, lovers again.
India's beggars, lepers and saints' kind eyes, Kansas
Police fat by painted cars with Antennae terrific,
Black screams radio-jail fearful, old holy
light remembered in Manhattan's sky and Puget Sound's
glittery waters, definite bellies and mouths kissed
for decades, night strangers' tenderness, women
feared and enjoyed in bed and evening restaurants,

1971

orgies and promise of orgies 21st century, planet death
and the stinking Passaic, Erie Mafia haunting junked streets
and Copo peddling strychnine by the Hudson, Times Square
glittering in the forties, Almeda verdant with Shoeshine boys,
North Beach sunlit blue, Red Square and Wenceslas Place in
deep fluffy snow, Trafalgar at Dawn and Pere Lachese
at red dusk, white Parthenon and Bodh Gaya's brilliant hot neons,
Paterson's Falls in icy marijuana glory, my father's
wrinkled tender eyes, farm years with Bessie the cow
and the marsh willows, television gone to the moon, newspapers
blaring inferno gossip, headlined inky black Nerves,
Leary Martin Buber Celine Genet Satchidananda and Richard Helms,
The Saint of Dasaswamedh Ghat who said "I am saint no Ruled,"
bodies burning at Ganges side, corpse on Brindaban's RR tracks,
Glacier Peak's rocky summit-chair, cascade snowpeaks
ranged to world's end horrific in quiet sky—knapsacks
 and greybeards growing over continents, boats moaning
off African shore slum city beaches. Death and Death's
Dear Corpse dolls revealed, Kerouac in Coffin and Olson
beaknosed on white satin with a cross, Neal's velvet ashes,
cigarette smoke drifting thru noisy apartments, mad
telephone for busted bail, taxi money, uptown aluminum
offices in tear gas haze, the growth of Divine Love Trees
all over the metal world, Pounds whisper and Williams'
appealing thin voiced living room sofa talk, Aunt Rose
long dead, too long for her dear heart, suicides' sad
jabber at apartments' locked doors, my uncle Max
with his grand moustache and account books musing over Chaplin
and Rosa Ponselle's bell sweet sorrow old phonograph
old Eli Eli's in Newark and Jerusalem, Voznesensky's
guttural nose lifted in London summer night, my body
always thin or sway bellied like my mother, car crash

1971

fear, adrenalin paining fingertip and scalp at Void roar
surge of metal into abdomen and slippery rocks cracking kmnucke,
hospital stitch-pain and the aether in laboratories
floating over the moon, return to old cities, nostalgic
Déjà vu in Delhi, Paterson, Bronx, San Francisco's street
Perspectives under Bay Bridge, Pacific silence under red-
wood grove shade, methedrine maniacs chopping cedar down,
legs spread the pain bliss of fuckery, mouth swallow
heated white cocks, and hundred bodies more to kiss at breast,
endless vines in Chiapas thatch roofed log tomtoms, endless
trees and music, forests of particular trucks, lakes of saliva
over lung stew on gas stoves, oceans of elegant
ladies department stores—where turn, no place to go
but more—or the mind shining empty hanging in
the sky like the golden ruin.

Aug. 17, 1971

Went out walking looking for cigarettes, and stopped by counter of big country city store in Mexico England and saw Dylan again at counter—since he got job there "I've been able to come in every day," he leans over counter "and no one bothers me." I take one of his cigarettes, I lean gossiping—"Need six rooms." Long conversation about housing problems—just couldn't find apartment large enough so had to move out of city—to London where we were talking—"but I go in every day now to the store here and tend counter and no one disturbs me no it's a relief activity and I get something useful to me, musing "Why not palms?" Fred has a flat here. Fred Jordan? No, just Fred. Odd thing the friends here—work going down the road—call me La Baron. Sounds nice, and leave me alone"—La Baron.

1971

The world's an illusion[22]
Everybody dies the day after they graduate high school

August 30, 1971

September 2, 1971

Visited Salt Lake Refugee Camp, N. Calcutta—25,000 refugees since June 19. Only those living in camps are counted.

Kalamandir "Lila" Hatha yoga variety Vaudeville Show—then Chinese Restaurant talked Indian with Sally Grossman[23] then to Nimtala ghat sat with Citaram old bum sadhu who lay down on his thin towel on the brick floor of the burning ground and smoked some of our hash.

September 3 Friday—

Woke & cab to American Express changed $10 at regular money rates then to Handloom Industries Khadi I bought shirts longtime on line in hot overcrowded floor with only one hand made cashier writing several receipts for each purchase—then looking for Chowringhee, took rickshaw & walked toward hotel, hungry ate puris & lentil & 2 glasses of lhassi in shop under balconies near Chowringhee Hotel (no vacancies Calcutta crowded)—After to Hotel, took Harmonium case out to New Market changed $10 and went to Dwarkin & Sons Harmonium & Music Instrument builders—picked up so-so harmonium small 30 keys but not long-lived bellows—then, with case and harmonium under awnings of New

22. Untitled poem, published in *Wait Till I'm Dead*, 106.
23. Sally Grossman was married to record producer and agent Albert Grossman.

1971

Market, looking for fiber board case to fit the instrument—followed one grizzly dhoti-clad messenger from shop to shop, no such size could be bought, or found, left (irritated earlier boys following me with baskets to carry burdens) (I stept aside & bumped into Rickshaw)—Then home to Grand Hotel, rested briefly (I'd sat half an hour on pillows on floor waking) & walked down past Museum on Park, reached Park Street thought of Gregory's old "Revolution is the Solution" uttering Sura who once lived at YMCA with her businessmen boyfriend virgins visiting—to theater, met young poet who phoned Sunil Ganguly now working at Ananda Patrika Bazaar newspaper—so that nite Sandeepan with sweet laconic mouth asmoe & Sunil Chubby no older—and into lobby also Shakti Chatterji walked, fatter cheek'd a little chubbier jowled and tipsy—off to see Jyoti Datta now drinkless smokeless solitary with wife no respects Cora, walks barefoot—at his house on roof song Padmasambhava Mantra, rode to Sunil's house ate rice and Lentils & tea, Shakti chattering & Yowping drunk now on rum, enters his system he makes noise. Up till midnite—talking about older days, nostalgia for College Street Coffeehouse, could I remember places we went like the Transvestite's Bar—Chinatown closed down changed, goondas & Naslite types, legend or myth, 80 murdered near Sandeepan's house—Is hot chile peppers fried good or not—too sharp said Jyoti it attracts stomach to feed when there's no hunger. Car back alone with Shakti—"I loved you very much" he kissed my hand & touched my foot "Second rate your changing . . . Come see my wife & baby family" home in Sunil's car with driver Viswanath leaving drunk Shakti at his alley house.

September 4, 1971

Woke 7 AM & sat a few minutes, walked out after packing bags full of Harmonium books taperecorder Sony, suit & new nine rupees Khadi skirts, no store sells batteries on Chowringhee that early, Sidi & Beetle

1971

sellers preparing their green leafs for symmetric business—Black man white haired gaunt sat on sidewalk, girl with box of papers.

Later walking out with valise to a Ramakrishna Mission met Sunil played him Blake new tapes & Purna Das downstairs brought machine to porch whereat he sat with his aunts & friends.

Dance Concert, Incarnations of Vishnu—Uday Shankar next row remember him 1944 did he not do Indra all body ripple muscle suppleness from extended fingertip to extended fingers, decades ago down to the revolving buttocks—now 76 years old, two heart attacks, not dance but teach—

Thusti Camp Salt Lake again, conversation after hospital Rheumatic fever, newborn malnutrition, dysentery, gastroenteritis, nephritis one man, Blood poisoning one boy, many diarrhea tiny monkey sized wee old naked babes waiting silent, with mother or father in bed. Doctor says there's shortage of:
Chlorastrep Suspension
Enterostrep Suspension
Chlorastrep Capsule
Enterostrep Capsule

Guanamycin Porte Suspension
Terramycin-Multidose Vial

Up and down alleys of huts thru markets with wood & long bulb leaf vegetable greenstalks—

"Free Sheik Rahman & we'll go back" . . . 1 lackh people 2 lackhs—1000
Send army home

US should stop giving arms and money aid to West Pakistan, at least—
U.S. Can Control Yahya the Priest of the Politic West, snuffy nose I the Dungeon Inn slate-cobbled doorstep—

The bread line, mostly jolly babes friend as said in bus, 800 children 800 adults in raw mob round a semi-circle, the Police in brown army color shirts & jobs, they straightened the line—a few children strayed in the

1971

magic breadgiving semi-circle chased them out with fresh sweet French whistle—children play with lathi-armed guards, crowd laughs at each comic opera effort to keep them and impeccable smokeless-sweat falling on page, desk, all day—

"And send money"

Here one meal a day

rice dahl & some subji

Ran out of bread! the crowd cheered and broke ranks, some running to other line bread distribution center—60,000 folk, to free bread to only 25 men in thatch hut worked by this time—ran out of bread, announcement the crowd yelled cheer!

Back missing bus, by Red Cross which with Caritas organization & need working drumstick.

Fatigue closing eyes I forgetting ganja syntax

Visit Sept. 9 1973—Bogra

Road Conversation: 18 US Cobra Gun Ships

Helicopters delivers to W. Pakistan mid August

Enquire-

Crowded road thru (Habra) Charminar and Tabla shop, loudspeaker Indic voiced lovesong, taxi home bike [?], army truck lumbering empty Sikh soldiers with sufi turbans looking, our cab. A giant banyan before town by riverside, crowded with guests? Byacih carts with burlap bags & bricks on Jessore road.

Ramakrishna mission small camp rows of huts with saffron plastic spread over [?] old banyan trees rooted arched over roadside, trunks plastered with cow flop patties for fire fuel. To Mana Rhagina Mama "Uncles and Nephew" Camp, tearful of dead babes during cholera weeks ago, 12

1971

days walking, dehydration, ripe for cholera. Now straw huts between Banyan trunk bordering road, above flooded brown canals, many bicycles & walkers between villages, many Ramakrishna Mission encampments 10 km before Bongaon, "These people are not scared of flood, because Bangla Desh is full of water." They adaptable, these straw huts worried by roadside. "How people adapt, are trapped in Maya"—Salahuddin "The way we think of Maya, because Maya means Sympathy & Pity," Tantric Maya-Prajnaparamita Compassion? If pleasure, pain, Entering Bangaon. Entering Bangaon—

Things to do in Benares

Get airticket Benares Calcutta—[?] house
Find Naganana & Trilochin Sastri
Brass hookah
Lungi for Peter
Stock of towels
Shiva Trident & Fire Stick—Chisti
Find Radhabinod Pal
File
Harmonium—Veruni & Sons
Change money
Malas

Sipping tea from monk Cup
    Crow hopping bamboo pole (rafter)
                    14 Sept 71

1971

Doumil, Benares
    Poem Srikakulam   "The gun not in hands of people"
           J. P. Narag

Tr. Nagaland Muktinath

Man cuts decapitates other man's throat
as mechanic hits bolt to shift nut
you say—this is murder
I say, mechanism's broke down—
Don't turn yr face & shrug shoulder that way
I know you witnessed
bleeding
and blood's colored red—
But that's not enuf—
the real question's to know
What wet blood means—
This is not murder
But the iron has a new name.
Witness, if you really want to see,
Come w/ me I'll show you
The protected mansions of poetry in a language jungle,
where cowardice
let loose its strength & courage
like a few grey hairs
have disappeared in the dark.

Sept. 19, 1971

Cab born streaks the mind
gutters flooded, brilliant rain
splashing pavements lightning blue

1971

last time this city everyone was alive
Rickshawcycle sputtering, bus churning puddles
farting mighty, how many walk lonesome
wet where? Thin pants, silk blouse clinging
shoulder skin silent in street machine roar,
Millions at home in rain, laughing couple dry,
solitary youth with Asiatic nose, intelligent woman
grasped elbow "home with me?"—Mosquito
home universe too, arm itch, raindrop few,
Straight back, Guru OM! Boys love
maybe on Patchen Place or Patpong
till Brahma does or sleeps. Flood over Jessore Rd,
lightning over Toyota show window. Niagara
no bigger than a raindrop in Boukok. Straight
back, breathe deep, empty mind, who cares?

Sept. 28, 1971

"Airplane Utterances"

Rolling on the Highway under the moon
   freeway reflectors glaring the curve
      Red trucks blinking yellow tail-lights
         Towering on the road
           Under pass, half moon
  Coughing on the road past
    Alcohol advertisements Whiskey Scotch
      Bombs, Lake Tahoe advertised in
Giant Signs glaring against the sky into the driver's eyeball—
    4 taillights on great ranging moving carpaths night-glittering hills
        south past Army Street

1971

Potero Hill, green and elements
        lamped above the gastank
California Limited Rentals
     More Scotch Whiskey than CIGARETTES!
Advertising cigarettes, Who own the hiway lites???
Advertising Automobiles
     Advertising giant-tail
       (tail) jet travel,
          roaring in the wind
Leaving Pacific, past Candlestick Park
          exit sign under concrete viaduct
          lifted by concrete pillars
            above the lamp—
Bayshore, Marlboro Nicotine
        Volkswagen, "Black and White
      Scotch for People who know the difference" Enco
for Gasoline, Bayside Hotel
United Crusade, and Old Crow made by good Kentucky hands with
   ice glittering brown whiskey pictured
Who are they advertising? Coffee *and* cigarettes?
   Who was advertising that?
         "Kent! and Coffee"—
Costa Brava Restaurant, Bayside Motel,
And now, Neal's Space,
     as Neal rode swiftly down the grade—
     High Mountain under the moon?
South San Francisco Hills—the Armies of Electricity
   now crawled up the hill blue glittering,
         in clear night—
O it's so scary all those cars god,
   Everytime I get high and I go out on the road
       I get scared.

1971

Greyhound Aluminum rolling by,
　　　　w/ symmetric lights in top and Bumper
　　　　　　shining red thru the windshield.
Cry at a helicopter, all lit up, and goin' slow, over the Bay?
　　　　　　blue night shine,
　　　　　　　　Oakland's blue needle glitter—
　　　　　　　　on distant shore
What's lights down there? San Bruno San Mateo, grew
　　　　　　　　over that whole hill—
There's a taxi goin out to the Airport—
"American's Seven Forty Seven Luxury-liners to New York, Chicago,
　　　　　　　　　　　　　　and Dallas"—

　　Trains and great big long
　　　　　　　　shelter building for What?
　　　　American Bridge—
　　　　　　　　U.S. Steel—looks a third a mile long
　　　　Nobody workin' there now.
Bennets, by white Furniture, Blue Neon, grand opening.
　　　Rebuked by the walking wiretowers' aluminum—
　　　　　　　　"Transmission Towers!" Om!
Men switch to Jim Beam—
　　　　　　　　Generation Gap, we never heard of it—
　　　　　and a bottle of Jim Beam gleaming leaning against the city
　　　"World's finest Bourbon since 1795"—They had a Franchise!
And the rest of the Franchise,
　　　　　　　Holiday Inn, Shell, Phillips
　　Fly Northwest Orient only 747 to Hawaii
　　　　　　　Imperial Hotel Railway Hotel—
Airways Rent a Car Free Airport pick up.
　　　　　　　Pack and Fly.
　　Buffalo cigarettes,
　　　　Restaurant International,

1971

Wells Fargo
Advertising Bank Loans
On to Marlboro Country, a giant cowboy
sitting against the wall
as big as a Transmission Tower,
Some faint symphonic music issuing from the car dashboard

Neal jogged over smooth 4 lane roads
There are signs, Airport shops, airport itself, Airport Exit 1 mile,
Western Airlines lites its red sign

Powerful bus, passenger sleeping dark windowed.
White lights streaming above invisible car past
American Airlines Freight System Terminal
lit up w. its warehouse doors
yellow Light down Caution Lane, Turn off—
arched lamps,
The great span of lights, United Airlines
at the end of a lane of symmetric lightshine Poles
lifted above neon snowy ceiling
Standard Station
S.F. Intnl. Airport Altar Throne
Electric Moloch
sitting spreading its wings of Fluorescent Concrete.

American Airlines? around the Air Terminal—
China Airlines, T.W.A.!
SFO Helicopter American—California,
Dadah Dadah—Da da Dum!
Pilgrimage to San Diego—Listen to
Every word Spoken inside Convention,
want to hear every word spoken

1971

flowing access
to all the words swiftly felt and spoken
inside the Convention Arena—
They have the right to know.
Otherwise
That's what it turns out
to be,
selected delegates who buy
their way in.

Oct. 1, 1971   St. Pete., Fla. Chez Stella
At Sterling Lord's
Compleat *Visions of Cody*
And the Hippos were Boiled in Their Tanks
Pomes All Sizes
Doctor Sax screen Treatment
Note O.K. 7-10-69
Keith Tennison's copy On Road original MSS letter to Sterling Lord Dec. 16, '68 from F. B. Adams Morgan Lib.

"I transmit to you herewith the org, MSS of Jack Kerouac's *On the Road* just as it came to us from Mr. Keith Tennison. It is my understanding that you will hold this for ultimate disposition by Mr. Kerouac ..."

Note from Sterling's pen—"It's in my safe at last, and seems very brittle."

Sterling.

Recordings:
Jack K., Steve Allen Poetry for the Beat Generation
Hanover Records HML 5000   Dot Records Dot #3154
Jack Kerouac Blues and Haikus

1971

Hanover Records HM 5006   (exc. Dot Series and Al Cohn Tenor)
Readings by J. K. on the Beat Generation
Verve Rec. MGVI 5005-Norman Granz Producer

Oct. 3, 1971

Photo'd by Avedon,[24] Peter in braids self w/ shell Rosary from Kyoto—
"Here we are again back in eternity."

Oct. 4

Western Gnostic is the same as Eastern Mystic.

Oct. 5

"The facts are *always* very interesting. If you can get people to tell
them ..." C. Reznikoff, in conversation in Bryant Park this afternoon.

Oct. 6, 1971
                New Orleans at W. S. Merwin[25] reading

My face? familiar handsome
W. S. Merwin, gaunt cheeked man
hawk eyed glance and straight nose

24. Photographer Richard Avedon (1923–2004).
25. W. S. Merwin (1927–2019) was a prolific poet known for his antiwar stance
during the Vietnam War.

1971

early laurelled hair, eyebrows
fine raised above eyeholes,
straight lines below cheekbone,
drawn from tearduct to mustache
and a voice begun in solar
plexus, firm speech rising
issued from my skull thru

        straight lips.

October 9, 1971   In Yoko, Lennon's Room Syracuse Hotel

    Brought Vajra, Vajraghanti, incense, finger cymbals, harmonium and
began singing Vajra Guru Mantra—Lennon on Guitar and Spector[26] Har-
monizing; then to Om Namah Shivaya—later a local Nurses' Song too
slow which picked up at end—and ended Om Mani Padma Hum—when
I began Ja Padma Sambhava mantra—Jonas Mekas there recording—
Lennon jumped up said "Let me go get my guitar"—gave Ringo finger-
cymbals and Klaus Voorman later got guitar—student from Syracuse too
blood guitaring in room—they sang Irene, I sang for him and die verse
they left out—Spector "The Life and Death of the Party" screaming at
Paul Krassner earlier (when I read U.S. Politics Wash Poem) (for K's es-
say Bruce is Dead Satire) and Spector drunk almost crashed roof of plas-
tic and glass labyrinth leading to Toilet Center shimmering clean.

        September on Jessore Road[27]

Millions of babies watching the skies
bellies swollen, with big round eyes

    26. Record producer Phil Spector, who produced, among many artists, the Beat-
les, George Harrison, and John Lennon.
    27. First draft of "September on Jessore Road," *Collected Poems*, 579–86.

1971

On Jessore Road—long bamboo huts
Noplace to shit but sand channel ruts

Millions of babies in pain
Millions of mothers in rain
Millions of brothers in woe
Millions of children nowhere to go

Millions of aunts dying for bread
Millions of uncles lamenting the dead
Grandfather millions homeless & sad
Grandmother millions silent & mad

Millions of daughters walk in the mud
Millions of children wash in the flood
A million girls vomit & groan
Millions of families hopeless & lone

Millions of Souls 1971
homeless on Jessore road under grey sun
A million are dead, the millions who can
Walk toward Calcutta from East Pakistan

Taxi September along Jessore Road
Oxcart skeletons drag charcoal load
Past watery fields thru rain flood ruts
Dung cakes on treetrunks, plastic-roof huts

Wet processions   Families   walk
Stunted boys   big heads dont talk
Look bony skulls   & silent round eyes
Starving black angels in human disguise

1971

Mother squats weeping & points to her sons
Standing thin legged   like elderly nuns
small bodied   hands to their mouths in prayer
Five months small food   since they settled there

on one floor mat   with a small empty pot
Father lifts up his hands at their lot
Rice ration, lentils   one time a week
Milk powder   for war weary babies meek

Two children together   in palmroof shade
Stare at me   no word is said
Tears come   to their mother's eye
Pain makes mother   Maya cry

No vegetable money   work for the man
Rice lasts four days   eat while they can
Then children starve   three days in a row
and vomit next food   unless they eat slow.

On Jessore road   Mother wept at my knees
Bengali tongue   cried mister Please
Baby at play I was washing the flood
Now they won't give us   any more food

The pieces are here in my celluloid purse
Innocent baby play   our death curse
Identity card   torn up on the floor
Husband still waits   at camp office door

Two policemen are surrounded   by thousands of boys
Crowded waiting   their daily bread joys

1971

Carry big whistles   & long bamboo sticks
to whack them in line   & keep them from tricks

Breaking the line   and jumping in front
Into the circle/sneaks   one skinny runt
Two brothers dance forward   on the dirt stage
The guards blow their whistles & chase them in rage

Why are these infants   massed in this place
Laughing in place   & pushing for space
Why do they wait here to cheerful   & dread
Why this is the house where they ration the bread

The man in the bread door   Cries & comes out
Thousands of boys & girls   take up his shout
Is it joy? is it prayer? "No more bread today"
Thousands of Children/at once   scream Hooray!

Malnutrition skulls thousands for months
Dysentery   drains bowels all at once
Nurse shows disease card   Enterostrep
Suspension is wanting   or else chlorostrep

Refugee camps   in hospital shacks
Newborn lay naked   in mother's thin laps
Monkeysized week-old   rheumatic babe eye
Gastroenteritis   makes thousands die

September Jessore   Road Rickshaw
50,000 souls   in one camp I saw
Rows of bamboo   huts in the flood
Open drains,   & wet families/waiting for food

1971

Border trucks flooded, food cant get past,
American Angel machine please come fast!
Where is Ambassador Bunker today?
Are his Helios machinegunning children at play?

Where are the helicopters of U.S. AID?
Smuggling dope in Bangkok's green shade!
Where is America's air Force of Light?
Bombing North Laos all day and all night?

Where are the President's Armies of Gold?
Billionaire Navies merciful Bold?
Bringing us medicine food and relief?
Napalming Viet Nam and causing more grief?

Where are the tears that   weep for this pain?
Where can these families go in the rain?
Jessore Road's children close their big eyes
Where will we sleep when Our Father dies?

Who shall we   pray to for rice and for care,
Who can bring bread to this shit flood foul'd lair?
Millions of children alone in the rain!
Millions of children weeping in pain!

Ring O ye tongues of the world for their woe
Ring out ye voices for Love we don't know
Ring out ye bells of electrical pain
Ring in the conscious American brain

How many children are we who are lost
Whose are these daughters we see turn to ghost?

1971

What are our souls that we have lost care
Ring out ye musics and weep if you dare—

Where is our knowledge of tears of the soul?
Where are the loved that make the world whole?
Where is the bread that born we must eat?
What babe life is this that on Jessore's great street

Cries in the mud of the thatch'd house sand drain
Sleeps in huge pipes in the wet shit-field ruin
Waits by the pump well, Woe to the world!
whose children still starve in their mother's arms curled.

Is this what I did to myself in the past?
What shall I do Sunil Poet I asked?
Move on and leave them without any coins?
What should I care for the love of my loins?

What should we care for our cities and cars?
What shall we buy with our Food Stamps on Mars?
How many millions sit down in New York
& sup this night's table on bone & roast pork?

How many millions of beer cans are tossed
in Oceans of Mother? How much does She cost?
How much work, cigarette dynamite waste
Aluminum garbage, plastic whiskey unchaste

Cigar gasolines and asphalt car dreams
Stinking the world and dimming star beams
How many Americans sit through the night
Watching meat flags wave War News fright?

1971

How many millions of children die more
before our Good Mothers perceive the Great Lord?
How many good fathers pay tax to rebuild
Armed forces that boast of the children they've killed?

O you who can hear us we cry in the rain
Pity us all   we feel all of your pain
Finish the war in your breast   with a sigh
Come taste the tears in your own human eye

Send us your medicines   food if you can
Stop sending tear gas   to West Pakistan
Pity us millions   of phantoms you see
Starved in Samsara   on planet TV

How many souls   walk through Maya in pain
How many babes   in illusory rain?
How many families   hollow eyes lost?
How many grandmothers   turning to ghost?

How many loves who never got bread?
How many Aunts with holes in their head?
How many sisters skulls on the ground?
How many grandfathers make no more sound?

How many fathers in woe
How many sons   nowhere to go?
How many daughters   nothing to eat
How many uncles   with swollen sick feet

Millions of babies in pain
Millions of mothers in rain

1971

Millions of brothers in woe
Millions of children   nowhere to go

Nov 14–16 1971

Ginsberg hoped that one day he would be able to set some of his poetry to music. He'd been hearing blues forms since the days of his youth, when he passed by a Baptist church and listened to Gospel singing wafting out of the building. He had loved the recordings of Bessie Smith, Ma Rainey, and Billie Holiday enough to see the lyrics of their songs as poetry and enter them in his early notebooks. He was envious that a long poem by Bob Dylan, set to music, would be memorized by people who were incapable of committing a single stanza of written poetry to memory.

Ginsberg had been flitting about the edges of recording music for years, accompanying his chanting or singing mantras on his harmonium, setting Blake's Songs of Innocence *and* Songs of Experience *to music, and, more recently, after being challenged by Chogyam Trungpa Rinpoche, his Buddhist teacher, to improvise his poetry onstage, occasionally in song. One evening in early November, Ginsberg was improvising onstage when Bob Dylan and musician David Amram[28] slipped into the reading. Afterward, Dylan asked Ginsberg if he could improvise like this willingly, and he encouraged Allen to record songs. He offered to accompany Ginsberg at a recording session. Ginsberg needed no further prodding.*

Ginsberg entered the Record Plant in New York and, with Dylan, Amram, and others playing behind him, recorded "Vomit Express," a semi-improvised (Ginsberg had ideas of the song's lyrics scribbled on papers) song about an upcoming reading trip to Puerto Rico. It turned out well. Subsequent sessions produced successes and songs that were scrapped because they didn't work. At best, Ginsberg's voice was average, his prowess on harmonium passable and limited to a few chords, but he was happy to be recording.

28. David Amram (born 1930) was a composer, musician, and arranger friend of many of the Beat figures.

1971

Spuatu hall

I'm going down't Pacih kiw

I'm loing down on the midnite plane

I'm going down on the vomit express

I'm going down with my suitcase fuew —

1 gonna take an owneu vacation
~~I'm going down with my oldest lip~~
(2) I'm over ~~Florida~~ ~~and~~ blue ~~hu~~
3 Rise up ~~get out~~ of ~~the~~ madhouse nation
See ~~what~~ the America's

(4) I'm going down with my older freud   tender

                                      peter NG
                                  refraen

we know eachother 20 year
Seen murders + we wept tears
Now were going to take ourselvs free time
Wandring round Soutsin Poverty Cleane

                                  refraen
                                  peter NG

1 Start ~~plyin~~ wile poor old ladies
3 Blazin ~~to townite doe~~ ~~in~~ wobley   air
4 all night long cheapest fare
2 Everybody crowded drunk + Crazy

                                  refraen
                                  pete —

Vomit Express[29]

I'm going down to Puerto Rico
I'm going down on the midnite plane
I'm going down on the Vomit Express
I'm going down with my suitcase pain

You can take an ancient vacation
Fly over Florida's blue end
Rise up out of this madhouse nation
I'm going down with my oldest tender friend
       I'm going down, etc.

We know each other now 20 years
Seen murders and we wept tears
Now we're gonna take ourselves a little bit of Free Time
Wandering round southern Poverty Clime

Start flyin with those poor old sick ladies
Everybody in plane crowded & drunk & they're crazy
Flying home to die in the wobbly air
All night long they wanted the cheapest fare

Land there dawn on the airfield I never been there
Except once walking round on the airfield in the great wet heat

29. First draft of song "Vomit Express," *First Blues* (New York: Full Court Press, 1975), 1–2.

1971

Walk out & smell that old mother lode of shit from the tropics
Stomach growl Love O friends beware—

Me & my friend no we won't even drink
& I won't eat meat I won't fuck around
Gonna walk the streets alone cars all blink & wink
Taxi buses & U.S. gas all around

Start with poetry at the University meet kids
Look at their breasts touch their hands kiss their heads
Sing from the heart maybe the Four Buddhist Noble Truths
Existence is suffering, it ends when you're dead

Go over & walk on the mountain see the green rain
Imagine that forest vines got lost
Sit crosslegged meditate on old love pain
Watch every old love turn to ghost

See raindrops in the jungle Rainbows ants & men
Brown legs walk around on mud roads
Far from U.S. Smog war again
Sit down Empty Mind   vomit my holy load

Come back to earth, walk streets in shock
Smoke some grass & eat some cock
Kiss the mouth of the sweetest boy I can see
Who shows me his white teeth & brown skin joy

Go find my old friend we'll go to the museum
Talk about politics with the cats and ask for revolution
Get back on the plane & chant high in the sky
Back to Earth to New York Garbage streets fly

1971

I'm gonna come back with Frightens in the heart
At New York's electric eternity here
Pull the airconditioner plug from the wall
Sit down with my straight spine and Pray!

I'm going down to Puerto Rico
I'm going down on the midnight plane
I'm going down on the Vomit Express
I'm going down with my suitcase pain.

Nov. 17, '71

GOING TO SAN DIEGO[30]

Come to San Diego   whole world gonna swing
I'm going to San Diego   Let them brass balls sing
O Mister San Diego,   find out what my Future bring

Gonna San Diego,   walk out on that street
Gonna San Diego,   hello who Ever I meet
Goin there happy   Gonna take my lonely feet

Gonna San Diego   Salute your body soul
Salute San Diego   Shake your jelly roll
Republican Convention there be a great big fruit bowl

Gonna San Diego—Announce the end of the War
Gonna San Diego—ain't gonna murder no more
Tell them politicians stop acting like a whore

30. First draft of song "Going to San Diego," *First Blues*, 3.

1971

Gonna San Diego—raise a holy cry
Gonna San Diego—Sing like I could die
O Lord let there be Tears in every eye

Gonne to San Diego Gonne to San Diego
Gonne to San Diego Gonne to San Diego
Gonne to San Diego Gonne to San Diego
Gonne to San Diego Gonne to San Diego

Gonne to San Diego   gonna take my blues along
Gonne to San Diego—sing a peaceful Song
Oh San Diego, I won't do no wrong

Come to San Diego   Show you're a peaceful man
Old Mr. Nixon better   bow down to Uncle Sam
All them Caucus best   elect the lamb

Nov. 17, 1971

JIMMY BERMAN RAG[31]

Whozat Jimmie Berman
I heard you drop his name
Whadd'ze got to say
what papers is he sellin?
I dont know if he's the guy
I met or aint the same—
Well that Jimmie Berman was
a boy that is worth tellin':

31. First draft of "Jimmy Berman Rag," *First Blues*, 4.

1971

Jimmie Berman on the corner
Sold the New York Times
Jimmie Berman in New York
He had a long long Climb—

Started as a shoeshine boy
Ended on Times Square—
Jimmie Berman whatzat rose
You got settin' in your hair?

Jimmie Berman what's your sex
Why ya hang round here all day?
Jimmie Berman What Love Next
O What (God) do you pray?

Who you wanna sleep with tonite Jimmie Boy
Would ya like—Come with me?
Jimmy Berman—O my love,
Oh what misery—

Jimmy Berman do you feel
the same as what I do
Jimmy Berman won't you come home
And make love with me too?

Jimmie Berman I'll take my clothes off
Lay me down in bed
Jimmy Berman drop your pants
I'll give you some good head

Eighteen year old Jimmie!
The boy is my delight!

1971

Eighteen year old Jimmy
I'll love him day and night!

Now I know I'm getting kinda old
To chase poor Jimmy's tail
But I wont tell your other lovers—
It be too long a tale.

Jimmy Berman please love me
I'll throw myself at your feet—
Jimmy Berman I'll give you money O
Wont that be neat!

Jimmie Berman just give me
your heart and yeah your soul
Jimmy Berman please come home
With me I would be whole

Jimmie Berman on the street
Waitin for his god!
Jimmy Berman as I pass
Gives me a holy nod.

Jimmy Berman he has watched
And seen the Strangers pass—
Jimmy Berman he gave up
He wants no more of ass.

Jimmy Berman does yoga
He smokes a little grass,
Jimmie Berman's back is straight,
He knows what to bypass—

1971

Jimmy Berman dont take Junk
He dont shoot speed neither
Jimmie Berman's got a healthy mind
And Jimmy Berman is Ours—

Jimmy Berman, Jimmy Berman
I will say Goodbye
Jimmy Berman, Jimmy Berman
Love you till I die—

Jimmy Berman, Jimmy Berman
Wave to me as well—
Jimmy Berman, Jimmy Berman
We've abolished Hell!

Allen Ginsberg
Poetry Music Notebook
November 1971

Nov. 28—Indexing my tape library anew, after Miles' effort—
    recruiting new scholars with money & promise of
    contact with Dylan. Drawing red circle in pencil
    around face mask of a moon visaged kid.

Nov. 29, 1971—7:20 AM   Bouqueron P.R.

Great Red Tough Kundalini Swami & fat big aide in a room, inquire
after my wealth, I complain of trouble in left knee and left shoulder—he
takes me over & feels in every part—(in a room like Krishnamurti's)—
puts me over his knee turns me upside down feels my joints, cups my balls

1971

& Cock—I have no hard on, or slight sexual swelling but no stiffness I no-
tice—and while holding genitals down he feels every inch of my stomach
muscle which is tense, as ever, in dream—Then he puts me down and goes
to his bag of tricks & pulls out a read red-thread toy, a singlestring wax
catgut ball which when open emits plucked notes, twang twang, I laugh
as he hands it to me, Music therapy, some strange yogic chords in mind
for me to learn.

"We didn't have time to relax & explore, this will do for now."

"All time later, OK," I say.

I pick up the Twang Ball.

There's a little of my old chewing gum on it, and I notice his red headed
snake—the snake and Shiva serpent all painted up natural color, Copper-
red body & scarlet almost lipstick'd skull top diamond back.

"Is it poisonous?" I ask, handing the snake over to him—He takes it by
the head between his fingers—apparently not, but he does handle it first
by getting the head in hand.

8:30 AM

Kerouac and Stella send message, he wants to spend Christmas in
wood clearing at farm—off country road the wooden square I wonder? oh
the nostalgia! But it's not like Cherry Valley. It's like Camp Nichtge-
deiget[32]—In my body lying in bed in this motel at the Southwest Corner
of Puerto Rico, old fumes of Nostalgia, Lucien[33] sick in next bed—I lay
there in dawn light, eyes closed, thinking I'll be back on the farm in time
to keep Jack & his wife company—then I realize he's dead—the nostalgia
still flooding my body, breast & temple.

Light glitter on window shade off the Calm ocean surface.

32. A communist camp where the Ginsberg family vacationed when Allen was a boy.
33. Lucien Carr.

1971

November 30, 1971

Burger King & McDonalds in Arecibo.

Dec. 2, 1971

Whiskey Willie
acts so silly
Getting on the plane
Aristotle
on the throttle
Gave his ass a pain
Willie purser
Got much worser
fixen up the Scotch
Millie Stewart
Really blew it
Spilled it in her Crotch,

Joe the Cracker
red hijacker
Sidled up on board
Willie drinking
got so stinken
Didn't see his hord
Mollie's panties
in the pantry
Lay there getten dry
While Cracker Joe
Got up to go
Get the Pilot high.

1971

In the Cabin,
Ari Crappen
Round the pilot's stick—
pulled the bummer
of the summer,
asshole full of prick.
Door was open
No word spoken
Cracker stole inside
With a pipe from
Nowhere, pipe bomb—
O that pilot cried!

"Off to Cuba
Me & you boy
& 60 passengers
Land that plane there
Bring my pain there
These my final words."
Willie's liquor
'd made him sicker
Than a Moscow dog
As for Mollie
Gee by golly/alcoholic fog.

Here's the story
without glory
that's the final fact
Willie Millie
Aristotle
all fell in the act—
Not one policeman

1971

Kept the place man
Waved his blue bandana—
All their laughter
Ever after
Rose from old Havana.

My name is Lucien
And eye flee
to find a
place to be;
But what eye found
was only so
And that's what eye'll
always find
          Lucien

L: I stink, I sweat
    and I am a man too
    I sometimes think the
    end will come
    But then I think of you.

A: I love, I laugh
    I am an angel boy
    or if I am not
    Earthy jew
    you are my golden goy.

L. If all is gone
    you know eye's here

1971

and what better have you to do
than laugh & love
with a lonely friend
the whole mother fucking
thing through.

A: Why I could cry
and give my soul to god
For lovely friends get so dam drunk
They crap out on the nod.

L. I love, I die and
I don't care
But my friends they die too
I care so much it breaks my heart
So my life is theirs too.

Lucien said that
Allen was quiet.

L: If I could ever get away from the idea
that any Ruination of me did not
destroy you too
then gladly would
I sell my soul and
my body too

A: We live, we age
the whole affair's a farce
there never was no guilty ruin,
just an older arse.

1971

L: (God)
What "they" cut out of me when Jack died
will never be replaced
The goodness gone must live along
or why?
Or else What the Fuck?

I met a little Jew boy
    He lived down the hall[34]
He didn't know Shit from
            Shinola
But many, many years befall
He came back to me
    Con mucho, mucho

A: O Pain   O day
    When love gets drunk with fear—
  I see the present pass away
    and past become more dear.
L: Don't Revise Your
        Original
            Mind
    Oh Jack
        it is
        because

34. Ginsberg and Carr had rooms near each other when both were attending Columbia University, and they met formally one evening when Ginsberg knocked on Carr's door and inquired about a classical music recording that Carr was listening to. They became close friends, and, through Carr, Ginsberg met Jack Kerouac and William S. Burroughs.

1971

You were that we
Are!!!

Love is a part of the
   meat of your
      Heart
As the loved person
   goes
So goes a
   Piece
     of
Your   Heart

And   as one does not die
      then one becomes as indelibly
      attached
      that there is no end.

A: Near Thought—
    Creatively.

O Love Sweet Face
Kissed with rare sober joy
I took you for your self sown grace
When you were a proud boy—

Body! Ghost Soul!
I want you manifest
Spirit in joyous body whole—
a nameless marriage blest,

1971

(Envoi by L.C.)
Because the timeless Master
treats us all the same
& for a pleasant Smile
Plays us this here game.

I want to P.S. for half moon week

O Boy What You don't know about Me

I know you think I'm some kinda fat old fool
Bald head behind, sweat dripping from my tool
but what you don't know is I live by loves golden rule—

If I see someone lovely, I go right up and say
Hey Mister Baby you look like the King of May
And if he don't sock me, he kisses me right away

I know you think I'm some kind of terrible queen,
But what you don't know is the love I felt & seen
If you could only guessed what I now like me you'd shout & scream

It's all in your mind, & it's in my mind too
And what's in my mind O Baby is that I still love you—
Now you can wave your hands & put me down it don't matter what you do

You got to see me honey, look me in the eye
See how helpless I am & take off your own disguise—
Then it doesn't matter who loves who, both of us be wise.

1971

Airplane, airplane, fly me way out West
Hey big engine carry me home to rest
If you can't take me then, walking be next best

Airplane airplane, get me out of here,
Hey sweet machine, sky is bright & clear,
Take me up there, nothing more to fear.

Airplane Airplane

Bodhisattva Karma Blues

Sitting on my butt listening to Rinpoche

Tellen all about Tantra
Tell me all about tantra hit me in the face
                                     with your shoe—

Dharmakaya Ballad

Hear me little children
         that harken to the blues
Me & my friends will now pronounce
         Some tender ancient news—

Here's the way you sit your body
         on the holy path
Here's instructions for yoga
         to conquer Mental Wrath

1971

Get a quiet room to hide in
   a thin mattress on the floor,
Bare walls but for Sacred Pictures
   Buddha on the door

Altar, incense smoke curls up
   clean Japanese pine smell
Photos of the Gurus, gaze in
   Silent heaven silent hell

Empty mouth when you wake up
   clean face hair combed neat bed
Touch yr heart & offer your image
   God food milk candy sacred head

Now sit down & cross your legs
   Sit up straight & relax,
Hang your spine from the ceiling
   Give your thoughts the axe—

Breathe deep slow & meditate
   Now silent air comes in
rests in place inside, flows out
   Nothin to lose or win—

watch your mind go climb the walls
   Let it go up and down
Every time thought comes back to you
   Catch it in Holy Sound

Chant a mantra silently
   at heart at belly or head

1971

Shalom or Soul or Guru Om
      or lords prayer can be said

Concentrate your mind one place
      Let it come & go
When it comes back to the heart
      Say Shalom loud & slow—

Sit an hour everyday
      Meditate in peace
Keep your back straight while you pray
      & breathe in empty ease.

What's the Gain? and what's the loss?
      Try it and find out—
Don't take anyone's word for Boss
      & Don't eat meat with sauerkraut—

Stop smoking, get in bed all day
      & kiss your lover's lips & play
Genital tender games till dusk.
      By then the anger goes away.

Find a Guru if you can
      Ask all teachers what they know\
Remember Death is never far—
      Go far out of your skull as can go.

One Prayer in all the Universes
The poet strangely sat in silence

1971

Recording Mix Notes
Dec. 2, 1971

Raghupati Take 1—loose
       take 2—OK-4
       take 3—no background vocal

Jimmie Berman—OK-4
Nurses Song—OK-10
Jessore Road—OK???-10
Hari Om Namo Shivaya—No

Goin Down to P.R.—OK-5
Goin to San Diego—OK-3

Greaser Jams
1.
2. Best with O's—OK-2 min.

Skip James Blues to G. W.

The first time I saw your eyes
   My heart jumped in my mouth
Angel look in black disguise
   My car was driving south
But God let me see you by surprise
   Next time you kissed me on the mouth.

Last thing I'm worried about
   boyfriend got jealous of yr face
Next last thing I worry 'bout

1971

Is it my money fame you chase
Because I love you so much Gary
   I wish I could put you in my place.

First it was your cheeks I wanted
   then it was your sweet talkin mouth,
then your songs got me haunted
   then your white belly down south
When you let me get down there Gary
   Like drinking water in a desert drouth—

 Hey lover I know you don't believe me
   I find you think it some old lie
I been talkin too much must sound creepy
   But I rather be dumb & look in your paradise eye—
O honey honey honey hold me
   & I'll stay with you tonite tomorrow goodbye

I know we can't be together forever
   But here we are hugging & kissing today
If I could keep you, God give me power,
   I'd get down on my knees & pray
The reason I act mental & talk sour
   Is I'm afraid God's going to take me away—

Sometimes I want to suck your cock
   Sometimes I got to get down on your ass,
my belly feels like a sweet soft rock
   I get on my knees in the grass
and kiss your body from foot to forelock
   When I get to your lips I just can't pass,

1971

Honey you know what I feel in my breast,
    It's like an empty summer wind
Sung in the middle of winter that's the best
    I wish I could show you my mind—
If you see how I loved you, if you guessed
    you'd turn me over on my behind—

You'd fuck me in the mouth & in the rear
    you'd sit up & make me go down,
You'd make me cry, you'd talk into my ear
    you'd make me grovel on the ground,
You'd take me any way you want no fear,
    maybe the sweetest hearts I ever found.

I know this sounds like an old song
    How could still feel that holy way?
But I'm not afraid, my heart is never wrong
    and what I feel I'm not afraid to say
More I feel it more I sing it long long long.
    Love is so old it might last all day.

Stomp yr Hat Jam

Stop Gasoline
Finish the Machine
Knock up all the Cars
Send them to Mars

      trouble seen   /   Robots too mean
      electric shit   /   Come never quit

1971

getten late   /   another Fate
don't wanna die /   Iron in eye

Always choose   /   happy News
Human lover lips /   then apocalypse

Suck my Cock   /   lick my rock
Fast pass   /   up the ass

slow down   /   mess around
go moon   /   on the ground

off that Jet   /   never get there yet
walk a little bit   /   take a shit

Don't pay a dime /   take your own time
Don't be a fool   /   heart school

Born skull   /   Bright full
pants full of lead /   stop when you're dead

God in my bed   /   stand on your head.

Down in Puerto Rico

Drove down thru La Perla
Shacks at the fortress bottom wall
Junkies & Muggers
Passed thru clouds on top of El Yunque
Smelt the roots of El Fanguito

1971

Sucked up the juice of coconut
ate the sweet white meat
Saw the beercan piles by the roadside
Slept with the poets by the beach
Atlantic waves crashing in my ear
Banana stands at Liuquillo Beach
Scientific Marxist yah on downers
Independents talk with the towners
and the horn fell off the Avis car
Blue light blink on Police Cars
Blue cobblestones on old San Juan Streets
& American Hertz advertises
                    "This is a motorist's island."
Operation Bootstrap Hotels & highways
& 129,000 Junkies in La Perla.
Bamboo on top of the mountain
That white turtle meat like
                    intelligent saliva
Penuelas got smog burning up the air
            no name on the factory
Windsill covered with vines

Goodbye Electricity this is my last stand
Goodbye lightbulbs, darkened over the land
Goodbye wires passed from hand to hand

Goodbye Robots, ain't gonna ride Cars no more
Goodbye airplanes, I get to keep the score
Goodbye autos, I'm going to walk so poor

1971

You & I lobster, entangled
together forever
                    swimming thru the worlds.

Dec. 3, 1971
  Take off yr pants and sit down and play me the blues.

Dec. 28, 1971

  Meditate Morning 10–11 AM—recurrent mind wrangle with Journalist
C. L. Sultzberger about his attitude, indifference to CIA opium peddling
accusations I keep making.
  And the rest of thought bulk, the incomplete recording of Jessore Road
w. Bob Dylan.
  A few minutes sunk into my own light body.

Dec. 29, 1971

  Meditation—hour [?] spined emptiness ended worrying about COP,
Inc.—debt to me, can I buy the farm with it? And what to do about offer
of California land near Gary Snyder's Kitkitdizzie now for sale when I've
no cash.

1971

Julian Beck, Phil Ochs, Peter Orlovsky, Wavy Gravy
(Hugh Romney), Judith Malina, Steven Ben Israel,
and Allen Ginsberg in Central Park, summer 1972.

POSTSCRIPT

DENVER TO MONTANA, 1972

Ginsberg had hoped to complete his auto poesy explorations of America with the end of the Vietnam War, but it did not happen. Vietnam dragged on with no end in sight, and Richard Nixon, running for reelection in 1972 and a shoo-in to win, talked about ending the war but clearly had no plan in mind. Ginsberg decided to conclude The Fall of America, *as he was calling his new volume of poetry, with "September on Jessore Road" from 1971.*

Although he was moving on, he didn't abandon his obsessions with America and the war. He intended the following to be the closing to The Fall of America, *but publishing deadlines prohibited his including it in the volume.*

Denver to Montana Beginning 27 May 72

West of Laramie, Elk Mt. snow covered top—Medicine Bow Mts. ranged black—that Road still ribbons past red sandstone buttes—"Looks like you shd be a yogi on each rock"—down the vast green valley floor

Like Utah, like America, mountain rookeries cliffed distant under cloud-fished transparent sky—the Blue Shield, that might be heaven over the Ferris Mountains' precipices (illustration) striped under snow dusty pine ridges.

Great Divide Basin up Rt. 287 grey mud lake at Muddy Gap—Rock wall leaned up from colossal ditch, smooth stone sheet cracked by brush upsprung—Rattlesnake Range rocks bunched up in mountain piles north blue sky'd—Dry wood snowfences snaked straight up hill south of the highway, wood slats x'd together.

Overhill, dinosaur snouts, blue rock brains—Sweetwater River meandering under split rock to oasis down below Rattlesnake Range—hunters, trappers, Indians—along the Oregon Trail, that gap on the mountaintop, "where Manjusri's Sword cleft the peak"—

& we'll be at Sakajawea's grave ere sundown, Buddhists—She took those White Folks doublecrost Northwest, & squealed on her own Folk Nature—Empty Montana abides—straight ahead the 2 lane road under the yellow sun, on full moon night, Buddha born—Snow pockets on wooded ridges South—

We're at the end of the poem America, these States a failure, spoilage of Earth—the war's still on, 7 years later no mantra did end it, no politics, no pity, no reason, no Peace march, no immolation—Vietnam afire with bombs all Karma exhausted—

Here it's sweet space enough, but Whitman Melville Crane & Kerouac're Dead—The Bitter Prophet at Jeffrey City's Grocery Store—America's first Uranium Mill—hundreds of trailers camped around the highway South of Gas Hills they say where they mine that radiant shite—

Green Mountains snowflecked—Clouds dwarfed in blue sky yellowed by dusk—& there's Wind River snow mountains rising diaphanous as Clouds over ice slough—The water's disappeared since the '49er's day. Old Denver Larimer Street's destroyed.

Abruptly, sliding past dirty snow, into sandcastle valley panoramic below, entering ever vast valley dry desert—car descending & descending & descending immensely—Imagine on bicycle or roller skates—down into butte bluffs' distance.

Into Wind River Reservation Flats, slept by Bull Lake, crows chattering at dawn, dreamt the busdriver from Tibet wouldn't stop for the old Puerto Rican lady—

Postscript

Compassion, I called her back on the bus, I asked the Man to halt & let her on,—into Wind River Canyon, icy rock peaks Big Horned far north, Teton ice slopes rising West—Striated bluffs above the hunting ground Valley, Crowheart Butte

in great space, Hollywood had French Horns announce these mountain panoramas—down to Wind River's brown bubbling bed, vast alpine meadows sloped to valley bottom, red worn cliff foreheads loom in sunlight, high snow shelves in wingèd space, black ravens over farmland pasture, cows in wet grass, horses cavorting, mounting each other at a distant fence.

What War? Corrals down to frothy river, wood houses, log barns—up over Togwotee Pass, Pinnacle mountains topped by a space shelter, and to Tetons ranged snowy along Horizon—

"Murmurs of Almora and Manali", we recalled Evans-Wentz' name, frogs grockling innumerable on pine hillside—far down there the cows graze on a valley roadside before ice crags risen big titted—

High on Rendezvous Mt. gazing cross Gros Ventre Valley Jackson Hole roads etched distant, Crag-rock'd snow skirts round Teton's grand stone-peaks, lodgepole pine fringed glaciers—To Moose, A Ah Sha Sa Ma Ha 3 Chords C F G—Change Gurumantra?—Silent openeyed half hour gazing cross green soft valleyfloor—silent clouds slowshifting thru blue dimnity—

Along Cowlands sweet, slept bright morning—a canoe under pines on String lake by the brown bridge, Grand Teton and sister-heavenpeaks reflected shimmering snowy-golden cold-flaming crest-light cold firedrops onto Jenny Lake's wavelet mirror surface —"Heart of Peace,"—my Bodhisattva Name—A Ah Sha Sa Ma Ha, in normal voice—

Renounce the constellations' Kundalini body-trip interior "buzz & flash"—high grass red Volkswagon moving round slow curb along lodgepole woods' asphalt lane in Yellowstone Park toward aisles pinecrested up narrow white line under bright bluewhite heaven zephyrclouded Gliding

Postscript

guided by Maharshi Valmiki dashboard photo'd sat haloed crosslegged, string'd violin in lap,

Karmapa heavy boy face Kagyu King right arm as if saluting, holding his Dakini wovenhaired black hat-crown on's head, wing'd & Doubledorje embroidered on front, Kalu Rinpoche seated forearms crossed, smiling with pursed long lips, eyes gazing downward—fists loosely closed & wrinkled.

A path thru the Great Divide—Anandamayi Ma, hair flowing down ageing eyelids eyes in open samadhi glance—moonfaced Trungpa Rinpoche smiling & immobile serious lipped—Campers & autos following the curved road down to Old Faithful—snow spotted over DeLacy's Creek bank mid tall pine's short-branched needled-fur round-stalktips—"Let It Be" on radio—

War Lingers in Deva Loka Memory, Laird orders Montana missile site work ended—N. Viets several days ago at An Loc—tanks from Moscow—China rail end & Hanoi raided, Haiphong harbor mined, air strikes on industrial plants, hospital bombed,

7 million bombcraters: 1/2 Vietnam Lethecided?—How many years restore green leaf to bombcrater? Denise said a million years for one inch of Fertile Soil—Bargain Destiny Kissinger Treaty Kosygin SALT—Jobs in Montana—

Lovely!—give the missile land to young settlers!—subsidize Old Faithful—Happy lads who play guitar & climb New Zealand's mountains & smoke grass—Mist steaming out of Paradise Earth flats—Yellowstone Walt Disneyed—sulphur gas? Pipes & Asphalt—

Earth crust thin, clear water bubbling in the limestone chalice sore— a few spurts of hot water, and the entire gush of underground rock-boilt steam and spout gargle rises mistcolumned—a tiny American flag fluttering from the brown wood Palace Lodge—

Farewell Grammar School—America love it or leave it—We came to our safety at a giant parking lot—The Camper ahead pulling toward Old Thumb—the white geyser rises in the lodgepole snow-scattered bowl

Postscript

hills—I was high, I only saw it stream up once, been waiting since grammar school for this photo.

Who Guru? "Yr own heart is your Guru"—pines, blue auto parked by three-foot snowbank'd roadside over Continental Divide—not many "colored folks" here—that couple cats Afro with truck—White snowlip down to the road—above, a brother mass of tall reddish brown straight tree trunkpoles—old feller w/ binoculars looking at the distant wooded mountain's snow temple-side—

No Conclusion War, 7 years after—Whose Patience?—Who died in the snow, in the mud? Who suffered bombs flagellating gas needle phosphor plastic pellets—What land lodgepole pine whose seeds open in the fire??—O look Mountains in the distant deep—

Riding auto'd thru the day—Sunlight flashing in windows, white jeep in front windshield rolling downhill, wind soughing car side—Absaroka Range, Crow People snowpeaks encircling the flat watershining panorama high horizoning Yellowstone Lake—

Spruce Forests line the shore, carpeting the flat uplands, snowy Rockies surrounding horizon—Headache, sweet watermelon, Is that breakfast steak—? Hare Krishna Guru Om What mantra remove my headache—or poor mortal-bellied painhead nauseous body.

Ah! Ice white in the blue lake, snow ranges cloud puffed, clouds floating in smooth water.

Heavy spout Old Faithful, satanic limestone hotwater beards, slept in tourist camp, singing Blake (Om Mani Padme Hum) Ah Ah Sha Sa Ma Ha—leaving Yellowstone, down stream sulphur heat flows thru a dragon mouth spout into bubbling brown cold river—Unreal vast spaces muraled against sky azure, vein-peaked mountain-misted "Be Here Now" Lama cliffs robed with Pine shoulder vest's granite snout lifted to cloud puff—Midheaven Sun enlightening the green rilled valley floor, road to Bozeman up from Mammoth Hot Springs thru the grassy hill-walls risen west under leviathan-bellied Cloud mass afloat lost in space—mist-bodied vast

Postscript

pigs over granite mountains—O snowfields melting in consciousless light blue heaven, clouds risen from snow ridges connected with long piney shoulders—Light in the vast air-blue'd sun glary valleyfloor grassed bushed housed & treed at foot of hills rolling with rich pine forests thousands of feet above a meadow fringe streamed down green beside the tiny auto road down to a brown farmhouse—as big as the Valley to Xauen—

Heaven heaven Heaven here, earth risen mellow granitic—cows in flats, wet with irrigation pipes above ground in great streaming wheels—sun browned valley heart ploughed with humans' tools, cowherd chasing ahead of the cowboy! An old feller on a horse with hornrim glasses, riding calm with his dogs—by the speckled highway, cross the irrigation ditch's squarewired fence, field clustered with yellow blossoms—

Thru narrow granite shoulder pass gate descending to brown & rotten detritus at mountain foot—stuck with telephone poles & pines—out thru vast spaces west on 90 double lane, sun still over sky's center, shining down on Yellowstone's peaks south behind us—

Farm area west, stockades & sidings, railroad crossing tracked on a neatly banked electric polecross'd hillside, stone mouths op'd from the ground—ah what luxury here, the peace of the valley floor—one stripe of snow cresting the hill meadow—all this water gushed out of earth & left cattle in fields grinding their white jaws with green juices—Slow autos moving by the War Field, sad generals typing messages to Washington—Over there, Over there, the bombs fall from air—Bombs on North Vietnam, rumor of the wounded damned—Hell fires, steel Barbs—napalm on the human hand—

Filling all space   Pain may displace yellow fields of grassy cloth, brown dry weedstalks kneeling in bog—Steel grey-painted truck-rear lifted gorilla ass square over hot road under hot electric wires—Asphalt over the green meadowpark, low hills capped with spruce, needle arms lifted

Cattle! Stomping in iron cages rattling & clanking truckloaded over

Postscript

Bozeman Pass—down thru a warm valley again—high snows on Jim Bridger Range floating North over treestanding hillsides soft humped—Dinosaur ridgemount of brown rock walled west, did Jim Bridger & Kerouac pass thru here?

Buddha tin barn, metal Buddha cars, Buddha hillsides scraped open for highway where the slow tractor rolls—That crest mounted with split-rock ear-haired pine fibrillations—another range of snowheads

Spanish peaks of Madison Range south, Bridger Range north, out of Bozeman thru long valley floor to Three Forks, dipped my hand in "the essential point of the northwest region of the continent," Missouri headwaters begin between rock hills where 3 rivers flow together clean brown-silted off the wall that hides Northwest, all flowing East.

Jefferson Gallatin Madison streams converge in a quiet spot, grass still growing to the rivers' marges—Lewis & Clark picnicked here with Sacagawea approaching her Shoshone family for horses to cross the Great Divide—sweet smell of Dogwood on the isle.

Slopes westward over the valley, up the great hill and down to new mountains—brown snowflecked walls over canyon deeps where the road winds visible miles distant to valley floors—and slow across the plain to Butte—See the huge Crater dug by Anaconda "One look at Butte make you shudder," sd Jack—No Wonder—

A hole in the ground big as the Moon, and a town perched on the hillslope overlook, dwarfed by the shelved open pit—Wobblies here, Joe Hill singing his Death in America?—Who's the Anaconda man that dug that wound of dust?—and whazzat oil derricks scatted midtown Butte—Wide Main Streets whizzing past lined with redbrick hotels—I'll get back to you O Butte—O W. C. Fields America this your bitter secret town—"An ecological disaster"—that I caused myself speeding by with my Copper Calliope Gas Buggy Throttles open farting monoxide myself—As the open pit loosens dust clouds covering roofs of Butte, chimnies & pumps & broken earth & oil spooled in the gravel field by the highway—half the ghetto overrun with refuse piles of giant earth—

Postscript

Dependent on destroying Mamma, digging a big noisesome hole in her Copper belly? Everybody lives here gotta be mean! Gotta drink thru dirty mustache bars & fight on Saturday Night because

All here like the butchers, dependent on murder of sentient nature, this town has no excuse to be but digging a hole in the World—

Out thru high hills down to valley again—What's that sitting on the plains under the Continental Divide under the big cloudy sky, a chemical factory Montana?—and West 'neath the next mountain's gate to Flint Creek Range, Anaconda town, stinking the earth around—"Remove that dark Satanic Mill" the largest smokestack in the world 1971 pouring out smoke, while sulphur smelter gas belches as if copper & money & plumbing were going out of style—Roadsign "Anaconda the largest smokestack" they're advertizin!—North on 90 thru Deer Lodge Valley where they couldn't spell 100 years ago

30 Myles to

Grass Hop Per

Digins

Gold Creek flowing west—

Little Satanic Truckmachine gushing black Diesel smoke wavering across highway shoulder white line, piled with Cedar Corpses—sheep in rainy meadows under green sloped Garnet Mountains—Open Sky grey lightning clouds southwest striking Sapphire Mountain snowpeaks—

Mountains horizon'd around us days now—Springtime air's rainy sweetness—brown wood barns in wet grass, stream's green marge sown with dogwood & dandelion—

But riding thru narrow valleys, under pleasing green mountains—see how strip logging cut roads thru piny hillside, the bulge of earth barely greenspotted now, streams of pebbled rubble flowed downhill, think a fire'd burnt it out—White glories shafted thru grey clouds on bareshouldered hilltops—eroded earth creeps down in wavelets, can't hang on to bedrock—& Giant Antennae mazes rise thru the pass, electric towers

Postscript

strung over Railway cut & old dirt road & 6 lane highway laid flat on valley floor with telephone poles dwarfed under cottonwood green Spring leafage—May May Maytime back, Man's Devastation written on Montana hills, mangy earthsides in rain—& rich pine forests impenetrable untouched above Turah, approaching Missoula.

"And all the hills echoèd," my Poems, Om Namah Shivaya, improvised Dharmachakra Blues, Om Ah Hum Vajra Guru Padma Siddhi Hüm, A Ah Sha Sa Ma Ha and ten minutes of silence in the Student Union ballroom.

Drove south with geologist: to Bull Creek Canyon, a rock crag overlooking warm green valley, Bitterroot River flooded, biggest in 50 years—chanting on the stone ledge Om Muni Muni Mahamuni Shakyamuni Svaha—snow peaks up canyon at our back, down below thousands of feet the forest usta carpet earth down to the river—Crow and Flathead gathered here together, went out the valley south to chase buffalo once a year—

Rest of time, Pacific Northwest winds balmed the winters—Indians winter'd there, & got horses late—pulpmill at head of Northern Valley hazed atmosphere round Missoula, & down between Sapphire Mts. & Bitterroot Range—

From Bob Curry—Aluminum industry uses 1/3 U.S. Power supply Pentagon/War/Defense/Military uses 40% of all U.S. Production & Energy. Have to cut American Consumption by 2/3 to survive.

North on 93 into Flathead Indian Reservation, Mission range snow peaks north—stop at the Cowboy Indian Bar with Gerry McGahan.—condor at Joko river bottom, Arlee P.O.—Overhill—there 'tis twenty-five solid peaks ranged snowy South to North the Mission Range, and another green valley floor, cottonwood & pine riverbottoms near St. Ignatius—Flathead Lake azure in the ozone pines—"dirty" snowmelt cleansed molten blue on valleybottom.

Postscript

Mosquitos piercing dusk with their Bodhisattva blood bellies tranquil—slept by the lake, bright stars crowding heaven with points of ancient space ship light—sentinel Mission Mountains guarding the valley, houses by lakeshore, young boys smooth breast skins, tiny sexiness—Who's the Ghost of the Road? Who white bearded after decades in the night cries Woe! or Wow! mantric Salutation to the Fall of America, soul emergent, nature not too grand to poison DDT beercan urine in the cleanest largest freshwater lake left in the country . . . a few green algae specimens already taken from the bottom—Cottageside craps or township run off, farmer's pesticides—

Up up past Flathead Lake's pure transparent blue chill morning—Wild hay in the fields, cut some next week—up thru Glacier's gated mountains slopes—for days surrounded by rotten craggy striated peaks, snow fielded, up McDonald Lake sides, mountains gleam white in mirrory snowmelt, cold fresh drink. Doubled peaks & passes green cedar'd, Twin Medicine Lake's triangular crags motionless in morning light, Blackfeet plains land rolling east to Browning's smelly vomit bars—

Babb Motel & Cabins firewood, quiet day to read Jack's *Visions of Cody*—antique prose on human love in tragical America—Chief Mountain's stupa like Sarnath's worn dome, drove over border Waterton's forests & fields running over downside mountain wall, ranges swarming North to bleak lone white Alaska vastnesses over Canadian wrinkled crag-range white fields hell-mooned & marooned subarctic overlapping planet top frigidity ice-skyscraper'd cityless horizons.

Four Noble Truths pronounced over & over in the shooting star magenta peppered green grass meadows of Chief Mountain—See Springtime plains roll East acold & emeralded with new June, Neal & Jack dead beneath the planet topsoil or ash'd to past—Who'll I tell the gory peak truth to Now, Oh Shimmering Kundalini, to what kind mind, whose soul light illumine my moony musings—Go fast on Chief Mountain alone & have another vision, peaceful ones—Where's all the dead Indians' Medicine bags buried, in my heart? Where's all the mighty Blackfeet heroes,

Postscript

covered with glacier lillies? Where's all the beat down drunken speedy hearted bards martyred in the War Age? Where's all the 60,000 poison heroes died in Vietnam?

Where's all the blue whales gone from ocean, bison murdered on the plains? Where is Four Corners when the Strip Mines devour Sacred Heartland, coming out the sockets of Hollywood car lot operators, toasting the Playboy Bunnies tear gas'd on their plastic penthouse sofa studios?

Up to the sun, dead heroes, up to the sun in search of America, Hoerner Waldorf's pulpmill gassing the air o'er Missoula, up to the sun ice mountains walled silent snowed manless all winter—climb up to the sun dead hero & prophecy this land its Dharma, the Law of Strong Nature, Noble Truth of Suffering's cause & end, Cessation of manufacture, 8 noble steps to STILL THE KARMA OF ODD FOSSIL CARS.

Right view of the scale of our eating the Ego Meat, burning out matter & wood of our selves to make house slaves in smog—Straight action restoring the slash cut fields of our love to Indian deer, fresh speech of the planet, conduct becoming owners of primordial property, Indian blood once spilt now flooding forests in Vietnam—

Excellent labor to keep our souls pure, fed with our hands or the hands of Shaman's sweet friends, don't wanna work for robots to gobble up mountains near Salt Lake & Butte & spew forth Brimstone vapors poison gas on your kids—endless exuberance washing the earth & the air—

Right & left mindfulness of freshwaters' taste, not fat of the milk carton stewing in rotten tomatoes at garbage dumps, Mekong swampside burnt out by our Assholes newspaper Klaxons—napalm that flowed out of White House basements, gas that poured tearful thru television's leaky colortubes—

By dusk down to Butte, past Anaconda's smoke stack lifted half as high as the poisoned mountainside, sulfurous mist suffusing the highway— Anonymous red-grey factories perched lone by grey stone rubble piles, red stonepeak hills lifted in prayer on plains rolling down into Hell City—

Postscript

Butte at last O Kerouac now test your vision'd America—brimstone pouring thru the sky, smelt in the tiny blue car—insect derricks below the red mine school, scholars gazing at a hole in the moon? Piles of sand by the hospital, hills of dirt-fill, wrecked autos in the ravines, Metal Bank surrounded by giant ash piles—old America red tarpaper housetops & wood sides, Matter-Junkie Town—

On top of the city Montana Avenue's rocks overlooking the pit, & the fiery lip of the garbage dump smoking, pronounce a mantra to purify—Om Dzogchen Guru Mahaka Ka Kaya Ka Ka Kaya—with the scarlet robed nun at dusk at the burning ground in America, tin cans & old poetry "Helios" magazines in flame—The wooden ruins of Butte dancing in the fire, old balconies and porch rails once leaned on by hopeful muscular lovers fresh from the dust mines of the World's Mountain—now with cracked bones & dry eyelids mummied under earth—into Shiva's flaming mouth—

Well let Shiva try swallow 100 years of toothpaste metal gunk, they made a lake a mile long, solid as grey jello—

Mucking machine after dynamite blast scooping up ore, Jackleg shakes the shit out of you, trucks in the Berkeley pit, them fuckers are big—one of these days all Butte be a big pit, Columbia Gardens a park always supposed to be there, founded by Clark the Copper King, for "Richest Hill on Earth," Anaconda now destroys—for copper, silver magnesium gold, It's a mining town—

There's about 100 of the mines all over the place—the Holey City of Butte—Kerouac watched old cardplayers here, W. C. Fields sat all night at a green card table—the miner with yellow hair sells snow

Trieste Butte's gay bar burned down couple years ago—Some trucks go over the edge into the great pit, took half an hour to cut the driver out of the cab 20 feet above ground.—Burlington RR, Anaconda & Montana Power Co. (secretly Anaconda) and Butte Water Co. (Also Anaconda)—controlled by Chase National Bank N.Y.—

Postscript

J B M place $26 million in red . . . own all Montana—smog from the Stauffer Chemical plant gets power from Bonneville meets smoke from Anaconda stacks & settles over Butte with dust from the pit—150 trucks can park in 3 minutes flat—for 25 or 30 dollars a day, the old timers gobble Speed—"War of Copper Kings"—Clark's trust fund for Columbia Gardens just a gimmick to get the land—

Mafia runs the bars & police chief, the Union's "taken care of", guys with shoulders a foot thick—Anaconda's lawyers buy cabins on Flathead Lake—"Lotta dust tonight" down in the hole, silicosis & emphysema (copper dust, sharp, in lungs)—Anaconda won't pay, takes all your wind away, sue them & you get blackballed

Police power a dedicated business with the guns protecting Anaconda, lots of payoff, police chief is the Mafia in Butte with Anaconda, "hand in hand," sd/the short darkhaired spiritual truck driver in the hole—who'd known Neal in Palo Alto: "Now see this young college student is high on LSD living in Redwood City" (as Cassady explained the situation to imaginary parents acting out all 6 levels & later 16 sides of every question, to the boy I met years later at Butte's Terminal Bar)—who thus quoting recollected Neal—

GM & GE's Unit Rigs, electrohaul diesels thousands horsepower, wheels brought in on a Great Northern train, the driver'd thought Neal a "wild man in his house" till he saw it was all entertainment—Neal traded pants with him—Jo Ricker's still in jail—so this was Hugh talking to me, an old Palo Alto student exiled to Butte, because busted in Bay Area—like Neal got 2 1/2 years for couple reefers—who knew Neal, "oh yeah! I'm a follower". And kissed me back, as I left walking down the street

past Skagg's Drug Store Jimi Hendrix psychedelic poster, guitar in flames in the great window—Now drunk to "M & M's" old man's bar for poker steak—Tong Wars were settled here, Fez Club built with Gothic roofcap slate, parquet floors for Mr. Clark's son's parties, opium, turn of the century in Chinatown—Miner's Union was dynamited, sent in Militia

Postscript

in flatcars brought in on ore train tracks in the 20's. "I dreamed I saw Joe Hill last night"—Snowy highlands lording over the flats—that's where the City'll move with Safeway when the pits eat downstairs mansard roofs—Charlie Judd's New Deal Bar, Charlie in front of Miller's Shoe repair at dawn—

Warehouse district folded, built for "Bigger Butte"—BAPRY, Butte Anaconda & Pacific RR get land rights all the way to that big smokestack 30 miles west—birds fly thru clouds of smoke, bellyup found dead. Canadian honkers migrating—Beryllium arsenic cyanide smoke—"I crave attractive women"—built 1916, Socialist Hall has cracks in the brick facade, mining subsidence, whole city underneath interlaced with tunnels, getting all they can out of the hill—

Driving in Giant Dynamo tyre trucks—Frank H. Little hung by company gunmen from the R.R. trestle, tookem' out of hotel room & drug him down here—all the politicians always employees of Anaconda—

Headwaters of Columbia River at Columbia Garden—Om Tare Tu Tare Turey Svaha Tare Tare Taré" and—Silver Bow Creek's iron sulphide brown waters Canalled flowing under old manganese plant smokestack—gallis frames like satanic teepees on top of Butte's rise at dawn—used to have gun turret on top for strikes—

Walkerville dump smoking, a fiery giant plateau, Om Namah Shivaya, Bom Bom Mahadev! Brass serpent atop red brick's Owsley Block—1892 Miner's Building now's Jeannie's Cathouse over Stockman's Bar

Anaconda killing the town, Butte was notorious for its cathouses—put all the Negroes on the roof & dynamited them—Curtis Music Hall 1892 now Gamer's fine food—"Overland Rye—Cures the Blues" Jan 8, 1972 2:30 pm leavin Butte.

The Unit Rigs GM made—"Too bad they don't build autos so solid"—200 ton Unit Rig works day & night, graveyard shift to dawn, to sunset red over brass replaceable parts' solidities' electric whine—never breaks down Rolls Royce perfect, when it does, change parts & it runs again in 5 minutes.

Postscript

Later, Ruby Valley in blue day haze south toward Virginia City—back to the pit at dawn—they make them to run forever, and the bigger the pit the more Unit Rigs & tunnels spread out—Columbia Gardens be ate up in 2 years—even the flats' suburbs blocks, cheaper to work them out than Butte downtown farther away—

cows lying down by the range fence roadside where the people are, in vast Ruby Valley—in Silver Bow County under Silver grey clouded sky over Tobacco Root Mountain snow spotted peak mass pyramids.

Jefferson or Ruby River bottom snaked out silver under silver heaven at Silver Star Montana, tufted acres, watery cottonwood tree floods—rain on windshield, summer odor over Jefferson Acre Lots for Sale—horses necks bent to green ground by the new Cottage on cinder blocks.

O Road, it is there justified by mind, the travels & lovers past, gas waste on the planet, transmission of flash universe—Who's left alive? The horny breasted keggers drunk virgins screaming graduated from school 200 yards from the Spring Source of River Columbia, top of the Continental Divide on the Metal Hill? Flashing eyed intelligent talking about Source of Consciousness, Who boasts angelic beauty now American boy?

American President, whom Chase Bank-Anaconda controls in this our present war, have you kissed the holy breast of the most beautiful mine-worker in America? Nixon go down on yr knees and adore the great pit filled with toothpaste metalslime! Anaconda's great green gyzym o'er spreading the Hell abyss floor.

Sarva Duhkha, Sarva Anicca; first noble truth of Butte 'et by its own Being the money pit—no need 40% war metal, what percent pennies & quarters money waste? Cut down 2/3 appetite changing grasping attachment to Anaconda matter & cut Chase Manhattan's growth octupus-tentacles, so reduce consumption to human measure—

& that copper sustains the electric world about us, from the pits of Butte & Salt Lake. The Electric Blinking Transistor Intelligence systems are Copper wired—Hollywood shines out of the pit at Butte & out of the coal of Four Corners. Blue lilac's sweet smell over Butte, & blossomed down Ruby Valley floor.

Postscript

Hundreds of cows stretched out at roadside by rail track's grassy shoulder at Laurin, 3 day trek to high mountain meadows for summer grazing, bring 'em back to green valleyfloor this fall, it's mellow juice, a raw Ankh branded crude on brown fur rumps, cowflopshit medicine spread on one festering mammy's buttock Om Ah Hum.

A valley more vast, Sphinx mountain conglomerate Lord ten thousand feet helmeted up from the plain, alluvial fan moistening green tree roots dark at stream bed side, sloped huge grass shelf'd plains overhanging the tufted rich Madison riverbottom barn'd & signposted. That snow water flows to Three Forks. And years ago my mother went to see the doctor with her headache & a hole in the heart.

Giant ravens come down to the Butte Pit at Dawn, from over the Hill— Rig operators throw food out the cab windows at 4 am—all work stopped for dawn lunch "Gaté Gaté Paragaté Parasamgaté Bodhí Svaha" vibrating in the metal cab on moon land—

Soft grassy slopes rising to pines over Madison's green river. Power & glory the flat roads' white line, that masters these distances we glide roaring acrost. Oh now I seen space, same as Columbia Gorge. Grey trees drownd in Crown Quake Lake.

Past Faithful Gyser spouting whitely, chill rain return to Teton, mist wrapt dusk tops snowy ranged above grey shining lake under Heaven June I'm 46 years here. Mountains meditating late afternoon, all night, all morn, fogs drifting past their heads like thoughts, dreams round our knees, white meditation, Zogchen Rinpoches, Precious Ones at rest, covered with rainbows, snout full of clouds, pink-snowed at sun set.

END
Of Fall of America

APPENDIX A

ALLEN GINSBERG'S DESCRIPTIVE NOTE ENDING *THE FALL OF AMERICA*

AFTER WORDS[1]

Beginning with "long poem of these States," *The Fall of America* continues *Planet News* chronicle taperecorded scribed by hand or sung condensed, the flux of car bus airplane dream consciousness Person during Automated Electronic War years, newspaper headline radio brain auto poesy & silent desk musings, headlights flashing on road through these States of consciousness. Texts here dedicated to Whitman Good Grey Poet complement otherwhere published *Wichita Vortex Sutra* and *Iron Horse*. The book enters Northwest border thence down California Coast Xmas 1965 and wanders East to include history epic in Kansas and Bayonne, mantra chanting in Cleveland smoke flats, Great Lakes hotel room midnight soliloquies, defeatist prophetics Nebraskan, sociable kissass in Houston, sexist gay rhapsodies, elegy for love friend poet heroes threaded through American silver years, pacifist-vowelled changes of self in robot city, wavecrash babbling & prayers air-

1. *The Fall of America*, 169.

bourne, reportage Presidential Chicago police state teargas eye, car crash body consciousness, ecologue inventory over Atlantic seaboard's iron Megalopolis & west desert's smog-tinged Vast. Back home, Mannahatta's garbage love survive, farm country without electricity falltime the harvest's the illegal Indochina bomb paranoia guilt. Guru Om meditation breaks through onto empty petrochemical wonderland, & so adieu to empty lov'd America. Book returns to Pacific flowered seashore with antibomb call, then across ocean great suffering starvation's visible, bony human *September on Jessore Road* ends as mantric lamentation rhymed for vocal chant to western chords F minor B flat E flat B flat.

Allen Ginsberg

October 7, 1972

Appendix A

APPENDIX B

ACCEPTANCE SPEECH FOR 1974 NATIONAL BOOK AWARD FOR *THE FALL OF AMERICA*[1]

Poem book *Fall of America* is time capsule of personal national consciousness during American war decay recorded 1965 to 1971. It includes one prophetic fragment, written on speakers platform of May 9, 1970, Washington DC Peace Protest Mobilization:

> White sunshine on sweating skulls
> Washington's Monument pyramided high granite clouds
> over a soul mass, children screaming in their brains on quiet Grass
> (black man strapped hanging in blue denims from an earth cross)—
> Soul brightness under blue sky
> Assembled before White House filled with mustached Germans
> and police batons, army telephones, CIA buzzers, FBI bugs
> Secret Service walkie-talkies, Intercom Squawkers to Narco
> Fizz and Florida Mafia Real Estate Speculators.
> One hundred thousand bodies naked before an Iron Robot
> Nixon's brain Presidential cranium case spying thru binoculars
> from the Paranoia Smog Factory's East Wing.

1. Allen Ginsberg, *Deliberate Prose,* edited by Bill Morgan (New York: HarperCollins, 2000), 19–20.

Book here honored with public prize, beat proclaim further prophetic foreboding that our United States is now the fabled "damned of nations" foretold by Walt Whitman a hundred years ago. The materialist brutality we have forced on ourselves and world is irrevocably visible to dictatorships our government has established thru South and Central America, including deliberate wreckage of Chilean democracy. From Greece to Persia we have established police states, and throughout Indochina wreaked criminal mass murder on millions, subsidized opium dealing, destroyed land itself, imposed military both openly and secretly in Cambodia, Vietnam and Thailand.

Our quote "defense of the free world" is an aggressive hypocrisy that has changed the very planet's chance of survival. Now we have spent thousands of billions on offensive war in decades, and half the world is starving for food. The reckoning has come now for America. $100 billion goes to the War Department this year out of $300 billion budget. Our militarization has become so top-heavy that there is no turning back from military tyranny. Police agencies have become so vast—National Security Agency alone the largest police bureaucracy yet its activities are almost unknown to all of us—that there is no turning back from computerized police state control of America,

Watergate is froth on the swamp: impeachment of a living president does not remove the hundred billion power of the military nor the secret billion power of the police state apparatus. Any president who would try to curb power of the military police would be ruined or murdered.

So I take this occasion of publicity to call out the fact: our military has practiced subversion of popular will abroad and do so here if challenged, create situations of chaos, take over the nation by military coup, and proclaim itself guardian over public order. And our vast police networks can, as they have in last decade, enforce that will on public and poet alike.

We all contributed to this debacle with our aggression and self-righteousness, including myself. There is no longer any hope for the salvation

Appendix B

of America proclaimed by Jack Kerouac and others of our Beat Genera-
tion, aware and howling, weeping and singing Kaddish for the nation
decades ago, "rejecting yet confessing out the soul." All we have to work
from now is the vast empty quiet space of our own consciousness. AH!
AH! AH!

Written April 17, 1974

Appendix B

SELECT BIBLIOGRAPHY BY AND ABOUT ALLEN GINSBERG

Ball, Gordon. *East Hill Farm*. Counterpoint, 2011.

Ginsberg, Allen. *Airplane Dreams*. Toronto and San Francisco: House of Anansi and City Lights Books, 1968.

——. *Allen Verbatim*. Edited by Gordon Ball. New York: McGraw-Hill, 1974.

——. *Collected Poems 1947–1997*. New York: HarperCollins, 2006.

——. *Composed on the Tongue*. Edited by Donald Allen. Bolinas, Calif.: Grey Fox Press, 1980.

——. *Deliberate Prose: Selected Essays 1952–1995*. Edited by Bill Morgan. New York: HarperCollins, 2000.

——. *The Fall of America: Poems of These States 1965–1971*. San Francisco: City Lights Books, 1972.

——. *First Blues: Rags, Ballads, and Harmonium Songs 1971–74*. New York: Full Court Press, 1975.

——. *Iron Curtain Journals*. Edited by Michael Schumacher. Minneapolis: University of Minnesota Press, 2018.

——. *Iron Horse*. San Francisco: City Lights Books, 1974.

——. *Planet News: 1961–1967*. San Francisco: City Lights Books, 1968.

——. *South American Journals*. Edited by Michael Schumacher. Minneapolis: University of Minnesota Press, 2019.

——. *Wait Till I'm Dead: Uncollected Poems*. Edited by Bill Morgan. New York: Grove Press, 2016.

Morgan, Bill. *I Celebrate Myself: The Somewhat Private Life of Allen Ginsberg*. New York: Viking Press, 2006.

Schumacher, Michael. *Dharma Lion: A Biography of Allen Ginsberg*. New York: St. Martin's Press, 1992; revised and updated edition, Minneapolis: University of Minnesota Press, 2018.

Schumacher, Michael, editor. *First Thought: Conversations with Allen Ginsberg*. Minneapolis: University of Minnesota Press, 2017.

Select Bibliography

INDEX

Index

Index

Index

Index

Index

Index

ALLEN GINSBERG

(1926–1997) was born in Newark, New Jersey. As a student at
Columbia College in the 1940s, he began close friendships with
William Burroughs, Neal Cassady, and Jack Kerouac, and he
later became associated with the Beat movement and the San
Francisco Renaissance in the 1950s. After jobs as a laborer,
sailor, and market researcher, he published his first volume
of poetry, *Howl and Other Poems,* in 1956. "Howl" defeated
censorship trials to become one of the most widely read poems
of the century. His poetry collection *The Fall of America*
received the National Book Award for poetry in 1974.

MICHAEL SCHUMACHER

is the author of *Dharma Lion,* the comprehensive biography of
Allen Ginsberg, and editor of *First Thought: Conversations with
Allen Ginsberg,* as well as Ginsberg's *Iron Curtain Journals:
January–May 1965* and *South American Journals: January–
July 1960,* all published by the University of Minnesota Press.